Certified Internet Webmaster (CIW) EXAMINATION OBJECTIVES
CERTIFICATION   Master CIW Enterprise Developer
EXAMINATION TITLE   Application Developer
EXAMINATION CODE   1D0-430

W9-BYN-057

CIW is administered by Prosoft Training. For more information on this certification program, please visit http://www.course.com/certification/ciw.

The CIW Program recommends that candidates review the following examination objectives to help prepare for the certification examination.

Exam Objective ID	Examination Objective Name	Chapter(s)
Section		
1.01	Explain Web-based form handling using the Common Gateway Interface (CGI) and HTTP.	Chapters 7-9
	For objectives 1.02 through 1.06, please refer to materials at http://www.ciwcertified.com	
1.02	Create a simple Perl script to handle common environment variables.	
1.03	Use Perl statements to create a hit counter.	
1.04	Demonstrate Perl file-handling and data output capabilities using a flat-file database.	
1.05	Integrate databases with Perl using ODBC and SQL.	
1.06	Discuss CGI security issues pertaining to Perl scripts.	
Section	**Dynamic Server Pages**	
	For objectives 2.01 through 2.04, please refer to materials at http://www.ciwcertified.com	
2.01	Install and configure PHP on Web servers.	
2.02	Create basic PHP scripts that demonstrate essential language features.	
2.03	Perform basic database functions using PHP, including file handling, querying, and data modification.	
2.04	Prepare a PHP application for deployment with debugging and error-handling techniques.	
2.05	Install and configure ASP on Web servers.	Chapter 5
	For objectives 2.06 through 2.07, please refer to Web Warrior texts:	
	Active Server Pages, ISBN 0-619-01525-X, and Internet Programming, ISBN 0-619-01523-3	
2.06	Create basic ASP scripts that demonstrate essential language features.	
2.07	Discuss the object-oriented nature of ASP.	
2.08	Perform basic database functions using ASP, including file handling, querying, and data modification.	Chapter 8
2.09	Prepare an ASP application for deployment.	Chapter 8
	For objectives 2.10 through 2.11, please refer to materials at http://www.ciwcertified.com	
2.10	Discuss database security issues.	
2.11	Discuss the role of project management in application development.	

BRIEF CONTENTS

TABLE OF CONTENTS

Preface

Database-Driven Web Sites will familiarize you with different approaches for creating Web pages that interact with a database. The number of Web sites being used to support electronic commerce applications and other applications where the user interface is presented as a series of Web pages is growing astronomically. Since many of these applications are data-intensive, system architectures consisting of Web sites coupled with databases will be the logical choice for future system applications. In this book, you will learn how to create Web pages that interact with a Microsoft Access database by means of the following technologies: client-side scripts, using VBScript; server-side scripts, using Active Server Pages; and compiled server programs, using the CGI protocol in Visual Basic programs, and using HTML dynamic-link libraries written in Visual Basic. Although this text provides examples using the Access database and Microsoft programming languages, other popular languages are discussed, and the concepts presented can be used to create programs using other database and programming platforms.

THE INTENDED AUDIENCE

Database-Driven Web Sites is intended for the individual who wants to create dynamic Web pages that interact with a database. A review of Visual Basic programming concepts is provided, but users should have previously taken an introductory Visual Basic programming course. Background chapters are provided on using the Access database environment, creating SQL queries, and using HTML at the code level. No prior knowledge of database concepts or HTML is required. Additionally, you should be familiar with the Windows operating system and with using Internet Explorer to view Web pages.

THE APPROACH

As you progress through this book, you will practice the development techniques by studying code samples, looking at sample Web pages, and creating a series of Web pages that illustrate techniques to create dynamic Web pages. Data about two fictitious organizations, Clearwater Traders and Northwoods University, are used throughout the book to illustrate the concepts and develop the techniques discussed. Each chapter concludes with a summary and review questions that highlight and reinforce the major concepts of each chapter. Several Hands-on Projects are included at the end of each chapter to let you practice and reinforce the techniques presented in the chapter. Additionally, three ongoing Case Projects are included with each chapter to let you create database–driven Web pages based entirely on your own design. To complete the Case Projects, you should complete each chapter in sequence.

OVERVIEW OF THIS BOOK

The examples, tutorials, Hands–On Projects, and Case Projects in this book will help you achieve the following objectives:

♦ Understand different approaches for creating dynamic Web pages that interact with a database

♦ Learn how Web servers interact with database servers and browsers to create dynamic Web pages

♦ Become familiar with relational database concepts and learn how to create queries using SQL

♦ Create Web pages using HTML code

♦ Create dynamic Web applications that interact with a database using client-side scripts, server-side scripts, and compiled server programs

♦ Understand when different dynamic Web application development techniques should be used in Web applications

In **Chapter 1,** you will learn about the architecture of the World Wide Web, review the differences between static and dynamic Web pages, and become familiar with the different techniques used to create dynamic Web pages that interact with a database. **Chapter 2** reviews relational database concepts and terms, introduces the sample databases that will be used in the tutorials and hands-on projects throughout the book, and allows you to become familiar with the Microsoft Access database environment. You will create database tables in Access, and learn how to insert, update, and delete data records in Access. In **Chapter 3,** you will learn how to create SQL queries to view and search for data, and to insert, update, and delete data. You will use SQL queries in later chapters when you create dynamic Web pages. **Chapter 4** provides an introduction to creating Web pages using HTML code. **Chapter 5** explains how Web servers work, and introduces Personal Web Server, which is a desktop Web server that you will use to process and display the dynamic Web pages you create. **Chapter 6** provides a rapid overview of Visual Basic programming, and allows you to create Visual Basic applications that interact with a database using the ADO data control. Chapter 6 also describes how to create ActiveX documents, which are Visual Basic programs that can be downloaded from a Web server and displayed using Internet Explorer. **Chapter 7** explains how to create HTML forms, and describes how to create client-side scripts using VBScript to validate form inputs and create cookies to store data values. **Chapter 8** describes how to create server-side scripts that process user inputs and display database data using Active Server Pages. Finally, in **Chapter 9,** you will learn how to create compiled server programs to create dynamic Web pages that process user inputs and display database data using the CGI protocol and using ActiveX dynamic-link libraries.

FEATURES

♦ **Chapter Objectives:** Each chapter in this book begins with a list of the important concepts to be mastered within the chapter. This list provides you with a quick reference to the contents of the chapter as well as a useful study aid.

♦ **Step-By-Step Methodology:** As new concepts are introduced in each chapter, ongoing tutorials provide step-by-step instructions that allow you to actively apply the concepts you are learning. As you proceed through the tutorials, less detailed instructions are provided for familiar tasks, and more detailed instructions are provided for tasks that illustrate new concepts.

♦ **Data Disks:** Data disks provide files for the sample databases used in each chapter and files needed to complete the tutorials.

♦ **Figures and Tables:** Figures help you visualize Web architecture components and relationships, and also provide code samples. Tables list examples of code components and their variations in a visual and readable format.

♦ **Tips:** Tips provide you with practical advice and proven strategies related to the concept being discussed. Tips also provide suggestions for resolving problems you might encounter while proceeding through the chapter steps.

♦ **Chapter Summaries:** Each chapter's text is followed by a summary of chapter concepts. These summaries provide a helpful way to recap and revisit the ideas covered in each chapter.

♦ **Review Questions:** End-of-chapter assessment begins with a set of approximately 20 review questions that reinforce the main ideas introduced in each chapter. These questions ensure that you have mastered the concepts and understand the information you have learned.

♦ **Hands-on Projects:** Along with conceptual explanations and step-by-step tutorials, each chapter provides Hands-on Projects related to each major topic aimed at providing you with practical experience. Some of these involve enhancing or extending the exercises in the chapter tutorials, and some involve creating new applications. Some of the Hands-on Projects provide detailed instructions, while others provide less detailed instructions that require you to apply the materials presented in the current chapter and previous chapters with less guidance. As a result, the Hands-on Projects provide you with practice implementing database-driven Web site development skills in real-world situations.

♦ **Case Projects:** Three Case Projects that run throughout the book are presented at the end of each chapter. These Case Projects are designed to help you apply what you have learned in each chapter to real-world situations. They give you the opportunity to independently synthesize and evaluate information, examine potential solutions, and make recommendations, much as you would in an actual business situation. The content of each chapter is cumulatively applied to the Case Projects, allowing you to create programs that build upon the knowledge you gain throughout the book.

TEACHING TOOLS

The following teaching tools are available when this book is used in a classroom setting. All of the teaching tools available with this book are provided to the instructor on a single CD-ROM.

Electronic Instructor's Manual. The Instructor's Manual that accompanies this textbook includes:

- Additional instructional material to assist in class preparation, including suggestions for lecture topics.
- Solutions to all end-of-chapter materials, including the Review Questions, and when applicable, Hands-on Projects and Case Projects.

Course Test Manager 1.2. Accompanying this book is a powerful assessment tool known as the Course Test Manager. Designed by Course Technology, this cutting-edge Windows-based testing software helps instructors design and administer tests and pre-tests. In addition to being able to generate tests that can be printed and administered, this full-featured program also has an online testing component that allows students to take tests at the computer and have their exams graded automatically.

PowerPoint Presentations. This book comes with Microsoft PowerPoint slides for each chapter. These are included as a teaching aid for classroom presentation, to make available to students on the network for chapter review, or to be printed for classroom distribution. Instructors can add their own slides for additional topics they introduce to the class.

ACKNOWLEDGMENTS

Thanks to the team at Course Technology for their support and encouragement during the writing of this book. A special thanks to Amanda Brodkin, a superb editor who made working on this project a pleasure.

Thanks to the reviewers who provided plenty of comments and positive direction during the development of this book: Michael V. Ekedahl, University of Nevada, Las Vegas; Hermann Gruenwald, University of Oklahoma; Anne Nelson, High Point University; and Carol Schwab, Webster University.

Thanks to our colleagues in the MIS Department who continue to support and encourage our authoring efforts. Thanks to the people who allowed us to use their images as Northwoods University faculty members. Thanks to the student groups who provided the ideas for the case study databases, and thanks to all of the students in our courses at the University of Wisconsin, Eau Claire, who continue to teach us how to teach.

This book is dedicated to Kyle and Lauren, who will probably continue to ask "Are you writing ANOTHER book?" Thanks for your support, patience, and love.

Mike and Joline Morrison

READ THIS BEFORE YOU BEGIN

TO THE USER

Data Disks

To complete the tutorials and projects in this book, you will need Data Disks that contain source files that have been created for this book. You will be instructed to save on the Data Disks the solution files that you create while completing the chapter tutorials, Hands-on Projects, and Case Projects. Some of the source files and solution files are very large and take a long time to load and execute if they are stored on a floppy disk, so we recommend that you store the Data Disk source files and completed solution files on a hard disk that is either on your local workstation or on a network file server to which you can connect. If you cannot do this, then you must save your work on floppy disks. The following paragraphs describe how to set up your Data Disk files both for a hard disk and a floppy disk installation.

Hard Disk Installation

If you are going to copy the Data Disk source files from a file server, your instructor will tell you the drive letter and folder that contains the source files that you need. Source files for the Access database files you will need to use (which have an .mdb extension) have been provided for both the Office 97 and Office 2000 versions of Access. **Copy only the .mdb files for the version of Access that you will be using.** The Office 2000 Access files have regular filenames (for example, "northwoods.mdb"). The Office 97 Access files have "97" appended as the last two letters in the filename (for example, "northwoods97.mdb"). Your instructor will tell you which Access version you will use.

To create your Data Disk, start Windows Explorer, navigate to the Data Disk folder provided by your instructor, select all of the subfolders, and copy them to the folder on your hard drive where you want to store your Data Disk files. There are folders for Chapters 1 through 9 in the book. All of the folders contain files you will need to complete the tutorials and end-of-chapter Hands-on Projects, and some of the folders contain subfolders.

Many of the code examples in this book require you to enter a folder path to your Data Disk. Figures that accompany these instructions often reference a folder path that shows the Data Disk as being on drive A. Unless you are working from floppy disks, the folder path you will enter will be different than the one illustrated in the figure.

Floppy Disk Installation

If you are asked to make your own Data Disks using floppy disks, you will need 15 blank, formatted high-density disks. You will need to copy a set of folders from a file server or standalone computer onto your disks. Your instructor will specify the computer location, drive letter, and folders that contain the files you need. The following table shows you which folders to copy onto each of your disks, so that you will have enough disk space to complete all the tutorials, Hands-on Projects, and Case Projects. Some of the disks will be used to store solution files that you will create when you complete the chapter exercises, so you will create an empty folder on these disks.

Data Disk	Write this on the disk label	Create or copy these folders (and the files they contain) on the disk
1	Database-Driven Web Sites Chapter 2 (Source files; Tutorial and Hands-on Project solution files)	Copy the Chapter2 folder (copy only the .mdb files for the version of Access you will be using)
2	Database-Driven Web Sites Chapter 2 (Hands-on Project solution files)	Create a folder named Chapter2 (do not copy any files onto this disk)
3	Database-Driven Web Sites Chapter 2 (Case Project solution files)	Create a folder named Chapter2 (do not copy any files onto this disk)
4	Database-Driven Web Sites Chapter 3 (Source files; Tutorial and Hands-on Project solution files)	Copy the Chapter3 folder (copy only the .mdb files for the version of Access you will be using)
5	Database-Driven Web Sites Chapter 3 (Case Project solution files) Chapter 4 (All files)	Create a folder named Chapter3 (do not copy any files onto this disk) Copy the Chapter4 folder
6	Database-Driven Web Sites Chapter 5 (All files)	Copy the Chapter5 folder
7	Database-Driven Web Sites Chapter 6 (Source files; Tutorial and Hands-on Project solution files)	Copy the Chapter6 folder (copy only the .mdb files for the version of Access you will be using)
8	Database-Driven Web Sites Chapter 6 (Case Project solution files)	Create a folder named Chapter6 (do not copy any files onto this disk)
9	Database-Driven Web Sites Chapter 7 (All files)	Copy the Chapter7 folder
10	Database-Driven Web Sites Chapter 8 (Source files; Tutorial and Hands-on Project solution files)	Copy the Chapter8 folder (copy only the .mdb files for the version of Access you will be using)
11	Database-Driven Web Sites Chapter 8 (Case Projects 1, 2, and 3 solution files)	Create a folder named Chapter8 (do not copy any files onto this disk)
12	Database-Driven Web Sites Chapter 8 (Case Projects 4, 5, and 6 solution files)	Create a folder named Chapter8 (do not copy any files onto this disk)
13	Database-Driven Web Sites Chapter 9 (Source files; Tutorial and Hands-on Project solution files)	Copy the Chapter9 folder (copy only the .mdb files for the version of Access you will be using)
14	Database-Driven Web Sites (Case Projects 1, 2, 3 solution files)	Create a folder named Chapter9 (do not copy any files onto this disk)
15	Database-Driven Web Sites (Case Projects 4, 5, 6 solution files)	Create a folder named Chapter9 (do not copy any files onto this disk)

Throughout this book, you will be instructed to open files from or save files to your Data Disk (for example, "Open the clearwater.html file from the Chapter4 folder on your Data Disk.") Therefore, it is important to make sure that you are using the correct Data Disk when you begin working on each chapter.

Using Your Own Computer

You can use your own computer to complete the tutorials, Hands-on Projects, and Case Projects in this book. To use your own computer, you will need the following:

♦ **Microsoft Windows 95, Windows 98, Windows NT Workstation, or Windows 2000 Professional.** Your computer must also be configured so you can connect to the Internet. (You do not need to be connected to the Internet when you work the chapter exercises, but your computer must have the TCP/IP software loaded that allows you to connect to the Internet.) If you have Windows NT Server or Windows 2000 Server, you can work the tutorials, projects, and cases in the book, but your Web server interface and the steps you will use to configure your Web server will be different.

♦ **Microsoft Access 97 or Access 2000.**

♦ **Microsoft Visual Basic Version 6.0 Professional or Enterprise Edition.**

♦ **Microsoft Personal Web Server (PWS).** PWS is distributed with some versions of Windows 98 and Office 2000, and with Windows 2000 Professional. To determine if PWS is already installed on your computer, start Windows Explorer, and look to see if the PWS files are installed in a folder named Windows\System\Inetsrv. (The folder path for Windows NT Workstation and Windows 2000 Professional users will be Winnt\System32\Inetsrv.) PWS cannot be used on computers that are running Windows NT Server or Windows 2000 Server operating system. If your computer has either the Windows NT Server or Windows 2000 Server operating system, you can perform the book exercises using the Microsoft Internet Information Services (IIS) Web server, which is included with NT Server and Windows 2000 Server. IIS has a slightly different interface than PWS, and the steps to configure IIS are similar to but slightly different from the steps used to configure PWS.

If PWS is not already installed on your computer, Windows 95 and 98 users can download the software from Microsoft's Web site at no cost. To download the software, connect to **http://www.microsoft.com**, search for Personal Web Server, and then follow the links to the download pages.

Windows 2000 Professional users can install PWS directly from the Windows 2000 CD. After Windows 2000 is installed, place the Windows 2000 CD in your CD-ROM drive. If the Setup program does not start automatically, manually run setup.exe from the CD. Select Install Add-on Components, check the check box beside Internet Information Services (IIS), click Next, and then click Finish when installation is complete. The icon to start Personal Web Manager is located in the Administrative Tools folder in the Control Panel.

- ◆ **Microsoft Internet Explorer 4 or 5**. You can download a copy of Internet Explorer 4 or 5 from the Internet Explorer home page at no cost. Connect to **http://www.microsoft.com/windows/ie/**, and then click the Download link on the menu near the top of the Web page.

- ◆ **Data Disk**. You can get the Data Disk files from your instructor. You will not be able to complete the tutorials and projects in this book using your own computer unless you have the Data Disk files. See the Data Disk section for information on setting up your Data Disk files. The Data Disk files can also be obtained electronically from the Course Technology Web site by connecting to **http://www.course.com**, and then searching for this book title.

Visit Our World Wide Web Site

Additional materials designed especially for you might be available for your course on the World Wide Web. Go to **http://www.course.com**. Search for this book title periodically on the Course Technology Web site for more details.

TO THE INSTRUCTOR

To complete the chapters in this book, your users must use a set of user files, which are referred to throughout the book as Data Disk files. These files are included in the Instructor's Resource Kit. They may also be obtained electronically through the Course Technology Web site at **http://www.course.com**. Follow the instructions in the Help file to copy the user files to your server or standalone computer. You can view the Help file using a text editor such as WordPad or Notepad.

Once the files are copied, you can make Data Disks for the users yourself, or you can tell users where to find the files so they can make their own Data Disks. If your users store their data files on floppy disks, make sure the files are copied correctly onto the Data Disks by following the instructions in the Data Disks section, which will ensure that users have enough disk space to complete all the tutorials, Hands-on Projects and Case Projects in this book.

Course Technology Data Disk Files

You are granted a license to copy the Data Disk files to any computer or computer network used by individuals who have purchased this book.

1

INTRODUCTION TO WEB DATABASE PROCESSING

In this chapter, you will:

♦ Learn about the architecture of the World Wide Web

♦ Learn about Web addressing

♦ Review database concepts and understand the differences between personal and client/server databases

♦ Learn about the difference between static and dynamic Web pages

♦ Examine different technologies that can be used to create dynamic Web pages that interact with a database

---

The **World Wide Web** (**Web**) is an important component of the Internet. Commercial Web sites are riding high on Wall Street, and Web-generated sales are increasing dramatically. Along with getting information about a vendor's products and services, online customers need to be able to submit inquiries, select items for purchase, and submit payment information. Vendors need to be able to track customer inquiries and preferences and process customer orders. The demand for data-intensive Web sites is driving the merger between Web sites and database technologies. This chapter presents an introduction to Web concepts, a review of database concepts, and an overview of different approaches that are currently available for creating database-driven Web sites. We assume that you already have a basic understanding of computers, networks, and databases.

WEB BASICS

The Web consists of computers on the Internet that are connected to each other in a specific way, making those computers and their contents easily accessible to each other. The Web has a client/server architecture, which means that server-based applications communicate with client workstations over a network. Users at home or in offices work on client-side computers that are connected to the Internet, and use programs called **Web browsers**, or simply **browsers**. Two popular browsers are Netscape Navigator and Microsoft Internet Explorer. **Web servers** are computers on the server side, and are often at business locations. Web servers are connected to the Internet and run special Web server software. This software includes a component called a **listener**. The listener monitors for messages sent to it from client browsers.

A **Web page** is usually a file with an .htm or .html extension that contains **Hypertext Markup Language** (HTML) tags and text. **HTML** is a document-layout language with hypertext-specification capabilities. HTML is not a programming language, although it can contain embedded programming commands. The primary task of HTML is to define the structure and appearance of Web pages and to allow Web pages to embed hypertext links to other Web pages. When a Web server receives a message from a browser requesting a Web page, the Web server sends the requested HTML file (the Web page) back across the Internet to the user's browser. The Web page file is displayed by the user's browser as a Web page formatted according to the HTML tags it contains. The Web architecture is illustrated in Figure 1-1.

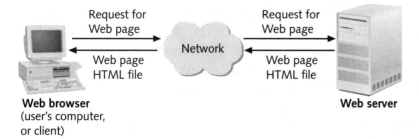

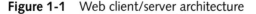

Figure 1-1   Web client/server architecture

Communication Protocols and Web Addresses

Communication protocols are agreements between a sender and a receiver regarding how data are sent and interpreted. The Internet is built on two network protocols: the Transmission Control Protocol and the Internet Protocol. Both protocols are required for any Internet activity to occur, and they usually are abbreviated and referred to as TCP/IP. When a computer is configured to connect to a TCP/IP network, TCP/IP networking software is installed and saved on its hard drive and in its internal configuration files. When the computer is booted, this software is loaded into its memory for processing TCP/IP network messages. The computer might be used to send e-mail, browse the Web, or act as a Web server. In all situations, the same TCP/IP processing software will be loaded into the computer's main memory when the computer is booted.

All data transported over the Internet (e-mail messages, files, Web pages, etc.) are broken into **packets**, or small chunks of data that can be routed independently through the Internet. TCP is responsible for breaking a long message into packets when the message is sent and reassembling the packets into complete messages at the receiving computer. IP specifies how messages are addressed.

Every computer that is connected to the Internet has a unique IP address that specifies the computer's network location. IP addresses are generally expressed as four numbers (ranging in value from 0 to 255) separated by periods (or decimal points). An example of an IP address is 137.28.224.5. Numbers of this type are difficult to remember, so an IP address can also be represented by a **domain name**, which is a name that has meaning to people and is easier to remember. Examples of domain names are www.microsoft.com, or www.amazon.com. **Domain name servers** are computers that maintain tables with domain names matched to their corresponding IP addresses. Domain name servers are maintained by **Internet service providers (ISPs)** that provide commercial Internet access for customers, and by organizations that have many users connected to the Internet.

Information on the World Wide Web is usually transferred using a communication protocol called the **Hypertext Transfer Protocol** (**HTTP**). Web browsers also support older Internet protocols such as the File Transfer Protocol (FTP). Whereas HTTP is used to send Web pages across the Internet, FTP is the primary protocol used for transferring data files such as word-processing documents and spreadsheets.

A user requests a Web page from a Web server by entering the Web page's Web address in his or her browser. A **Web address**, also called a **Uniform Resource Locator (URL)**, is a string of characters, numbers, and symbols that specify the communication protocol (such as HTTP or FTP), the domain name or IP address of a Web server, and optionally, the folder path where the Web page HTML file is located, and the name of the HTML Web page file. Figure 1-2 illustrates the components of a URL.

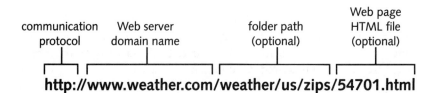

Figure 1-2   URL components

If the communication protocol is not specified in a URL, Web browsers by default assume the HTTP protocol. If the folder path is not specified, the Web server assumes that the default starting location is the Web server's **root document folder**. The Web administrator specifies the exact path to the Web server's root document folder when the Web server is configured. This folder can be any folder on the Web server's hard drive.

If the user only enters the Web server domain name in his or her browser, and does not specify the name of an HTML file, then the Web server sends its default home page to be displayed in the user's browser. Therefore, the Web administrator must also specify the Web server's default home page file name when he or she configures the Web server. Typical default home page names used by administrators are default.html, index.html, and home.html. Figure 1-3 shows an example of a URL (http://www.oracle.com/) that does not specify a folder path or HTML file, but displays the Web server's default home page.

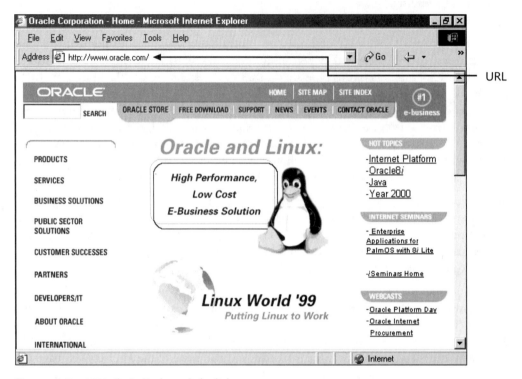

Figure 1-3   URL that displays default home page

When a user specifies a domain name as part of a Web address, the Web browser sends a message to its domain name server requesting the IP numeric address corresponding to the domain name. After receiving the IP address, the browser tries to contact the server listening on that address. If the user knows the desired IP address, he or she can save time by entering it directly, rather than using the domain name. However, domain names should be used if they exist. Although looking up an IP address from a domain name stored in a domain name server can slow response time, a Web administrator might change the IP address assigned to a server while retaining the same domain name.

URLs that specify a Web server address or domain name are called **Internet URLs**, because they specify a communication protocol, such as HTTP or FTP, as the first part of the URL. A URL can also be a **file URL**, which is an HTML file stored on the user's hard drive. A file URL is usually only used by programmers when they are developing new Web pages and want to see how the pages look when they are displayed in a browser. For example, to display a file named index.html that is stored on drive C in the \Webdocs folder of his or her computer, the programmer would enter the following file URL: file:///c:\Webdocs\index.html.

> 📍**TIP**   In a file URL, three slashes follow the file keyword.

Running Multiple Listener Processes on the Same Web Server

Most Web servers support both the HTTP and FTP protocols so that Web developers can send new HTML files to the Web server via FTP when old pages become outdated. Some Web servers run a second Web server listener to respond to and process administrator requests, which might be used to perform tasks such as starting or shutting down the Web server, adding new administrators, and installing new Web server programs. Running multiple listeners is managed through the concept of **ports**. A port is identified by a number that specifies which TCP/IP-based listener or server running on a computer, at a given IP address, is going to receive a message coming in from the network. Recall that TCP/IP software is loaded when a Web server is booted. When the TCP/IP software is loaded, a TCP/IP table that lists port numbers and associated server programs is also loaded. A message addressed to a specific IP address must always specify the port assigned to a specific server program listening at that address. Web servers are by default assigned to port 80, so browsers by default add port 80 to Web addresses. If the Web server administrator chooses to change, or reassign, the port to something other than 80, then the URL would have to indicate the assigned port. The following is a URL that indicates that the appropriate port is 81:

```
http://137.28.224.5:81/examples/example1.html
```

Other specific port numbers are reserved for common TCP/IP server processes. An FTP server usually listens on port 21. An Internet e-mail server usually runs two servers—one listening on port 25 for receiving and sending messages and one listening on port 110 for managing messages.

DATABASE BASICS

Databases store an organization's data in a central location, using a standardized format. For example, a database for a retail merchandise company might contain data on the organization's customers, products, suppliers, sales orders, purchase orders, and inventory on hand. The intent of a database is to store each data item only once to avoid redundant data, and to ensure that the data are consistent. For example, if the same customer's name and address are saved multiple times, variations in data values and formats can occur.

Different programs can be used to access and manage database data. The retail merchandising company's database might have programs for inserting, updating, or deleting customer data; adding or changing sales orders; updating product and supplier information; and updating inventory information. Each program interacts with the data in the database through the database management system (DBMS), which is a program that is used to manage database data and user access. The relationships among the database, the DBMS, and the programs are shown in Figure 1-4.

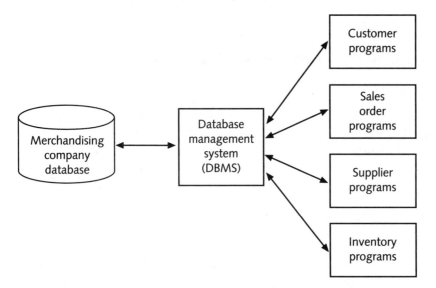

Figure 1-4   Relationships among database, DBMS, and programs

Personal and Client/Server Databases

The first databases were stored on large centralized mainframe computers that users accessed from terminals. As distributed computing and microcomputers became popular during the 1980s, two new kinds of databases emerged: **personal databases** and **client/server databases**. In this book, you will be using the Microsoft Access personal database system to provide data for your Web pages, because it is the easiest to install, use, and maintain in a classroom environment. However, all of the concepts, and many of the commands that are illustrated using Access, are equally applicable to client/server databases. It is important to understand the differences between personal and client/server databases, and when each type of database should be used.

Personal DBMSs such as Microsoft Access work well for single-user database applications that can be used from a desktop computer's hard drive. However, when a personal database is moved to a client/server environment and is used for multiuser applications, as shown in Figure 1-5, problems can occur.

The personal database software, data, and programs are stored on a file server. When a user makes a request to view, insert, update, or delete data, the request might require retrieving all of the database data, the DBMS software, and the programs for processing the data. When the user is finished updating the database, all of the database data must then be returned to the file server. This could involve transferring hundreds of megabytes of information across the network, when only a few bytes are actually needed. Newer personal databases use indexed files that enable the client to retrieve smaller subsets of the database, but regardless, personal DBMSs can put a heavy demand on client workstations and on the network.

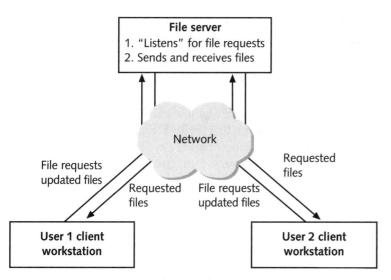

Figure 1-5   Using a personal database for a multiuser application

In contrast to personal databases, client/server databases such as Oracle and Microsoft NT SQL Server split the DBMS and the database programs. The DBMS is installed and runs on a server, while the database programs are installed and run on the client. The database programs running on the client send data requests across the network to the DBMS, as shown in Figure 1-6.

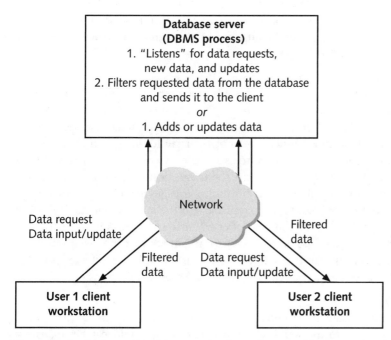

Figure 1-6   Using a client/server database for a multiuser application

When the client/server DBMS server receives a request, it retrieves the data from the database, performs the requested functions on the data (sorting, filtering, etc.), and sends only the final query result back across the network to the client. As a result, multiuser client/server databases often generate less network traffic than personal databases and are less likely to bog down because of an overloaded network.

Another important difference between client/server and personal databases used for multiuser applications is how they handle client failures. In a personal database system that is used for a multiuser application, when a client workstation fails as a result of a software malfunction or power failure, the database is likely to become damaged due to interrupted **action queries** (which are queries that change the data in the database by updating, inserting, or deleting data) that can negatively affect other users. A partially written record in a database file can sometimes make the entire file unreadable. In addition, update queries normally require locking the affected record or records during the update. If the client doing the update crashes before removing the lock, the records remain locked and unavailable to action queries by other users until an administrator runs a repair utility. Although the database might be repairable, all users must log off during the repair process, which can take hours. Action queries taking place at the time of the failure usually cannot be reconstructed. If repair is not possible, the database administrator can restore the last backed-up version of the database, but insert, update, and delete operations that occurred since the last backup are lost.

In contrast, a client/server database is less affected when a client workstation fails. The failed client's in-progress queries are lost, but the failure of a single client workstation does not affect other users. In the case of a server failure, a central synchronized transaction log contains a record of all current database changes. The transaction log enables in-progress queries from all users to be either fully completed, or rolled back. Most client/server DBMS servers have many additional features to minimize the chance of failure, and when they do fail, they have fast, powerful recovery mechanisms.

Client/server database systems also differ from personal database systems in the way that they handle competing user transactions. For example, when a user issues an action query, a client/server DBMS locks the associated records so that they are unavailable to other users for updating until the transaction is committed. In contrast, when a personal database such as Access is used for multiuser applications, it defaults to **optimistic locking**, which hopes that two competing transactions will not take place at the same time. Consider an airline seat ticketing system as an example. In a client/server system, the transaction to sell a ticket causes the database to read the table listing available seats and simultaneously lock all or part of it prior to updating it. Then the sold seat is marked as unavailable and the table is unlocked. Without the lock, a second sales agent could read the table after the first agent reads it but before the first agent updates a certain seat as sold. The second agent might see that the given seat still is available and inadvertently sell the same seat to a second customer. The ability to lock data records that are involved in action queries can be added to Access applications only through custom programming.

Personal and client/server database systems handle transaction processing in different ways. **Transaction processing** refers to grouping related database changes into batches that must either all succeed or all fail. For example, suppose a customer writes a check from a checking account and deposits it into a money market account. The bank must ensure that the checking account is debited for the correct amount and the money market account is credited for the same amount. If any part of the transaction fails, then neither account balance should change. Microsoft Access does provide procedures for grouping related changes, keeping a record of these changes in main memory on the client workstation, and rolling back the changes (reverting the database to its status prior to the last save) if the grouped transactions fail. However, if the client computer that is making the changes crashes in the middle of a group of transactions, the transaction log in main memory is lost. There is no file-based transaction log on which to base a rollback, and the partial changes cannot be reversed. Depending on the order of the transactions, a failed client could result in a depleted checking account and unchanged money market account, or an enlarged money market account and unchanged checking account.

Finally, client/server database systems have a built-in security model that can be used to limit the operations that users can perform on the database, and limit the data that a user can access. Personal databases have fewer security options, which are not as flexible to use and maintain as those offered by client/server database systems.

In summary, client/server databases are essential (1) for database applications where many users might be inserting, updating, or deleting data at the same time, (2) for mission-critical applications because of their failure handling, recovery mechanisms, and transaction management control, and (3) for systems requiring a robust security system to govern user data access. Production systems with many users will usually require a client/server DBMS. However, client/server databases are more expensive than personal databases, more complex to install and operate, and require more powerful client and server hardware. Personal databases are useful for Web installations where the only database operation is viewing data and no action queries are used, and where less robust recovery and security systems can be tolerated. In this book, you will be using the Microsoft Access personal database to create Web-based applications because it provides a convenient and satisfactory learning platform. A longstanding and still useful guideline is that when a personal database is used for multiuser applications, usage should be limited to no more than 10 concurrent users if action queries are allowed. If security or the ability to recover from client or server failures is important, use a client/server DBMS regardless of the number of concurrent users.

DYNAMIC WEB PAGES

Web pages can be either static or dynamic. As its name suggests, a dynamic Web page provides more immediate and specific information than a static page, and therefore dynamic Web pages play an important role in the creation of database-driven Web sites.

In a **static Web page**, the page content is established at the time the page is created. Whenever a user accesses a static page, it displays the same information. Static Web pages are useful for displaying information that doesn't change often, and for navigating between HTML Web page files. In a **dynamic Web page**, also called an **interactive Web page**, the page content varies according to user requests or inputs. One type of dynamic Web page queries the database and displays data, but does not change it. These user requests use a database-driven Web site with dynamic Web pages. Figure 1-7 illustrates the architecture of database-driven Web sites.

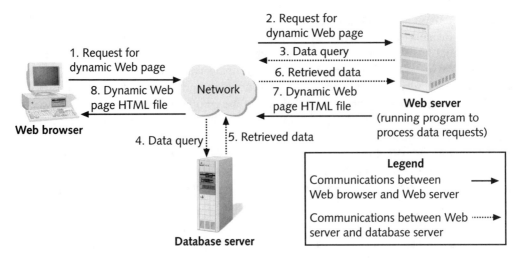

Figure 1-7   Database-driven Web site architecture

The user first makes a request for a dynamic Web page, and the user's browser forwards this request to the Web server. The Web server then starts a program to process the request. This program composes a database query, and sends it to the database. The database sends the requested data back to the program, where the data are formatted into an HTML Web page by the Web server. The Web server then sends the dynamic Web page back to the user's browser. Using the Web to access a database is often referred to as Web/database processing.

Dynamic Web pages can also be used to change the database's contents on the basis of user inputs. A form is presented to the user to allow him or her to enter data that will insert new data records, or modify or delete existing records. This input is translated into an action query by a program running on the Web server, as shown in Figure 1-8.

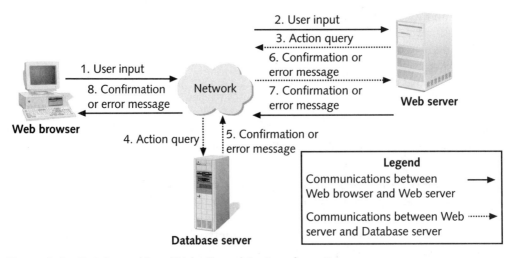

Figure 1-8   Database-driven Web site architecture for action query

This query is then forwarded to the database server, where it is processed. If the query is successful, a confirmation message is returned to the Web server, and then forwarded to the user's browser. If the query is not successful, an error message is returned to the Web server and forwarded to the user's browser.

Approaches for Creating Dynamic Web Pages

Dynamic Web pages can be created using server-side processing, or a combination of server-side processing and client-side processing. With **server-side processing**, the Web server receives the dynamic Web page request, performs all of the processing necessary to create the dynamic Web page, and sends the finished Web page to the client for display in the client's browser. With **client-side processing**, some processing is done on the client workstation, either to form the request for the dynamic Web page or to create or display the dynamic Web page. Technologies that will be used in this book for illustrating server-side and client-side Web/database processing are shown in Figure 1-9, and discussed in the following paragraphs.

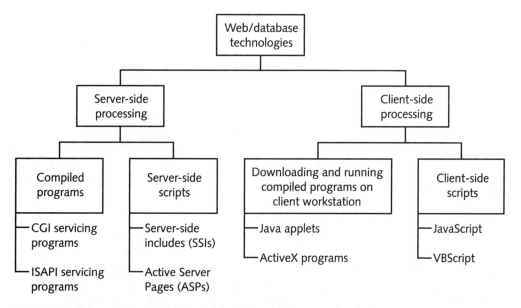

Figure 1-9   Server-side and client-side Web/database technologies

Client-side Processing

One approach to client-side processing involves downloading compiled executable programs stored on the Web server to the user's Web browser and then running them on the user's workstation. The user's browser and operating system must have the ability to run the executable program file. This program interacts with the user and, as needed, sends and retrieves data from a database server. An example of a technology that uses this approach is a Java applet.

Java is a programming language that is a simplified subset of C++. It is commonly used to create Web applications, called **Java applets,** that can be downloaded from a Web server to a user's browser and then run directly within the user's browser. Since the Java applet runs in a generic Java runtime environment supplied by the browser, the Java applet runs identically on any operating system and with any Web browser. For security reasons, Java applets can receive data from a Web server and send data to a Web server, but can't read data from or write data to any files on the user's workstation.

Another technology that sends a compiled executable program to the user's workstation is Microsoft's ActiveX. ActiveX programs can be created using many different programming languages and environments, as long as those languages support Microsoft's ActiveX protocols. The primary difference between an ActiveX Web program and a Java applet lies in the security model. Java applets have a strict security model to keep them from harming the client computer on which they run. A Java applet cannot access, update, or delete files on the client computer, and it cannot access client computer operating system functions. Conversely, ActiveX applications have complete access to the client computer's operating system and files. For this reason, ActiveX programs are generally used to create intranet applications, while Java applets are usually used to create Internet applications. (An **intranet** is a self-contained internal corporate network based on Internet protocols but separate from the Internet.) ActiveX programs can be distributed over the Internet. However, users who download and use ActiveX programs generally do so only if the source of the program is a certified source that is known to be trustworthy. Security mechanisms such as certificate authorities, which are used to ensure the safety and security of downloadable programs, are discussed in Chapter 6. For intranet applications, ActiveX programs are created by a company's information systems staff and distributed as Web programs on the company intranet, rather than as conventional client/server applications. In this book, you will create programs using Visual Basic, and then convert them to ActiveX programs that can be displayed using a Web browser.

Another client-side processing approach involves client-side scripts. This approach allows uncompiled code in languages such as JavaScript or VBScript to be typed into the HTML document along with the static HTML text. Tags indicate to the user's browser that this text is code. If the user's browser has the capability of recognizing and interpreting the code, the code is processed by the browser. (If the browser cannot recognize and interpret the code, then the script code is displayed as text in the user's browser.) More complex user interfaces are possible with this approach than with straight HTML, and it allows user inputs to be checked for correctness on the user's workstation rather than on the Web server, thus reducing network traffic and improving application performance.

Server-side Processing

The most common server-side dynamic Web page technology uses HTML **forms**, which are enhanced HTML documents designed, like paper forms, to collect user inputs and send them to the Web server. HTML forms allow users to input data using text boxes, option buttons, and lists. When the form is submitted to the Web server, a program running on the Web server processes the form inputs and dynamically composes a Web page reply. This program,

1

called the servicing program, can use a variety of approaches to process inputs and create dynamic Web page outputs. Form servicing programs can be compiled executable programs, or uncompiled programs (scripts) that are interpreted and processed when they are run.

Popular languages for creating compiled server programs are Java, Visual Basic, and C++. In this book, you will learn to create HTML form servicing programs using Visual Basic as the programming language, and the **Common Gateway Interface** (**CGI**) protocol as the method for communicating between the HTML form and the servicing program. A disadvantage of using CGI-based servicing programs is that each form submitted to a Web server starts its own copy of the servicing program. A busy Web server is likely to run out of memory when it services many forms simultaneously. As interactive Web sites have gained popularity, Web server vendors have developed proprietary technologies to process form inputs without starting a new copy of the servicing program for every form. Examples of technologies addressing this problem include Netscape's **Netscape Service Application Programming Interface (NSAPI)**, and the Microsoft **Internet Server Application Programming Interface (ISAPI)**.

Another approach for creating dynamic Web pages using server-side processing uses server-side scripts. A server-side script is uncompiled code that is included within an HTML Web page file to extend its capabilities; for example, enabling the HTML Web page file to perform database queries. When a user's browser requests a Web page that contains a server-side script, the script is interpreted and processed on the Web server, and the resulting data are displayed on the Web page that is returned to the user's browser. Examples of technologies using this approach include **Server-side includes (SSIs)**, and Microsoft **Active Server Pages (ASPs)**. HTML form inputs can also be processed by Active Server Pages.

SUMMARY

In this chapter, you learned that a Web server is a computer that is connected to the Internet and runs a software process called a listener that listens for requests for Web pages from users. Users request and display Web pages on their computers using programs called Web browsers. A Web page is a file, with an .htm or .html extension, that contains Hypertext Markup Language (HTML) tags and text. A user requests a Web page from a Web server by entering the Web page's Web address, or Uniform Resource Locator (URL). A URL is a string of characters, numbers, and symbols that specifies the communication protocol, the domain name or IP address of a Web server, the folder path where the Web page HTML is located, and the name of an HTML Web page file.

Databases store an organization's data in a single central location, using a standardized format. Personal database systems such as Microsoft Access are primarily for single-user database applications that are stored on a single user's desktop computer. Personal databases are desirable for Web installations where the only database operation is to view data, and robust recovery and security systems are not required. When personal database systems are used for multiuser applications, problems can occur. Client/server databases split the DBMS and programs accessing the DBMS into a process running on the server and the programs running on the client.

Web/database interfaces can be created using dynamic Web pages, where the HTML page varies on the basis of user requests. Several different technologies can be used to create Web/database interfaces using both server-side and client-side processing.

REVIEW QUESTIONS

1. What are the possible file extensions for a Web page file?

2. What is a protocol?

3. What does HTTP stand for, and how does it distinguish the Web from the rest of the Internet?

4. What is the name of the main Internet communications protocol?

5. How are domain names associated with IP addresses?

6. What is a URL? What are the possible components of a URL?

7. Why should you normally use a domain name rather than an IP address within a URL?

8. What is a dynamic Web page, and how does it differ from a static Web page?

9. Describe two approaches that use client-side processing to create dynamic Web pages.

10. Describe two approaches that use server-side processing to create dynamic Web pages.

CHAPTER 2

RELATIONAL DATABASE CONCEPTS AND INTRODUCTION TO MICROSOFT ACCESS

In this chapter, you will:

♦ Review relational database structures and terms

♦ Become familiar with the case study databases that will be used in this book

♦ Learn how to create database tables, and insert, update, and delete data using Microsoft Access

To create a database-driven Web site, you must create the Web pages that are displayed to the user, the database that stores the underlying data, and the linking mechanism between the Web pages and the database. You should always create the database first. In this chapter, you will review how a relational database is structured and review relational database terms. This chapter assumes that you are already familiar with relational database concepts and terms. You will be introduced to the case study databases that will be used in the tutorials and chapter exercises throughout the book. Then, you will create the database tables, insert data records, and create SQL queries using Microsoft Access.

OVERVIEW OF RELATIONAL DATABASES

Early databases used a **hierarchical** structure, in which all related data had a parent-to-child relationship: a "parent" data item (such as a customer) could have multiple "child" data items (such as customer orders). Relationships between related data were created using **pointers**, which are links to the physical locations where data are written on a disk. Figure 2-1 illustrates a hierarchical database structure, where the CUSTOMER data represent the parent records, and the CUST_ORDER data represent the child records.

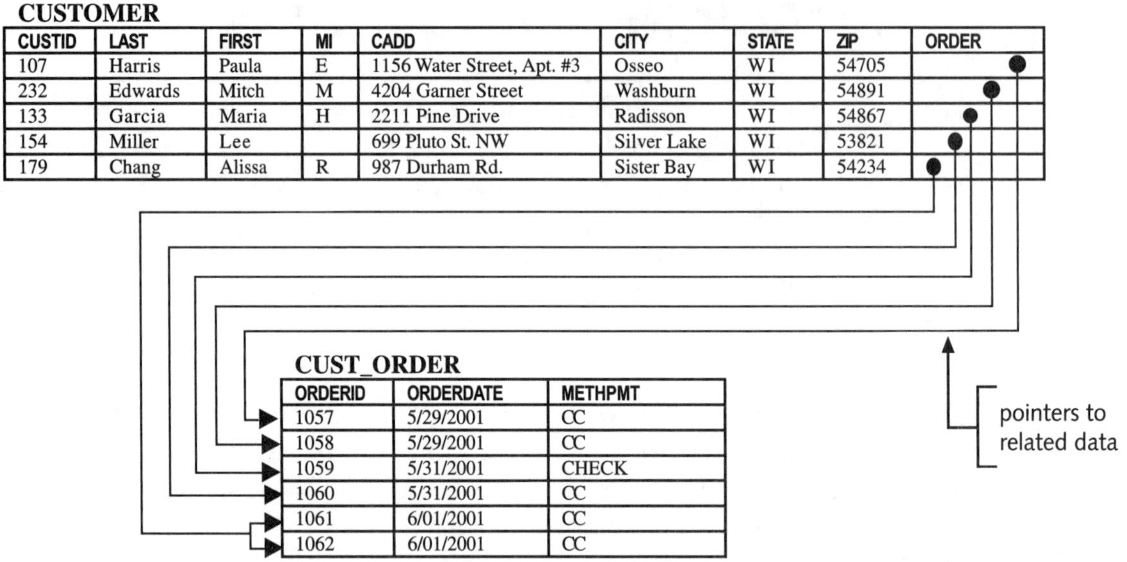

CUSTOMER

CUSTID	LAST	FIRST	MI	CADD	CITY	STATE	ZIP	ORDER
107	Harris	Paula	E	1156 Water Street, Apt. #3	Osseo	WI	54705	●
232	Edwards	Mitch	M	4204 Garner Street	Washburn	WI	54891	●
133	Garcia	Maria	H	2211 Pine Drive	Radisson	WI	54867	●
154	Miller	Lee		699 Pluto St. NW	Silver Lake	WI	53821	●
179	Chang	Alissa	R	987 Durham Rd.	Sister Bay	WI	54234	●

CUST_ORDER

ORDERID	ORDERDATE	METHPMT
1057	5/29/2001	CC
1058	5/29/2001	CC
1059	5/31/2001	CHECK
1060	5/31/2001	CC
1061	6/01/2001	CC
1062	6/01/2001	CC

pointers to related data

Figure 2-1   Hierarchical database

Customers are linked to their associated orders data by using pointers–Order ID 1057 is associated with customer 107 (Paula Harris), order 1058 is associated with customer 232 (Mitch Edwards), and so on. Orders 1061 and 1062 are both associated with customer Alissa Chang. The problem with a hierarchical database structure is that since relationships are maintained by pointers that use physical data addresses, the data are physically dependent on their location on the storage media. It is difficult to migrate a hierarchical database to a new storage medium when the current storage medium becomes full, or when new hardware is purchased. This problem led to the development of relational databases.

A **relational database** structures data in **tables**, or matrixes with columns and rows. **Columns** represent different data categories, and **rows** contain the actual data values. Columns also are called **fields**, and rows also are called **records**. Figure 2-2 shows the CUSTOMER and CUST_ORDER data from Figure 2-1 in a relational database.

CUSTOMER   fields

CUSTID	LAST	FIRST	MI	CADD	CITY	STATE	ZIP
107	Harris	Paula	E	1156 Water Street, Apt. #3	Osseo	WI	54705
232	Edwards	Mitch	M	4204 Garner Street	Washburn	WI	54891
133	Garcia	Maria	H	2211 Pine Drive	Radisson	WI	54867
154	Miller	Lee		699 Pluto St. NW	Silver Lake	WI	53821
179	Chang	Alissa	R	987 Durham Rd.	Sister Bay	WI	54234

records

primary keys

CUST_ORDER

ORDERID	ORDERDATE	METHPMT	CUSTID
1057	5/29/2001	CC	107
1058	5/29/2001	CC	232
1059	5/31/2001	CHECK	133
1060	5/31/2001	CC	154
1061	6/01/2001	CC	179
1062	6/01/2001	CC	179

foreign keys

Figure 2-2   Relational database tables

Each individual record in a relational database table is identified by a primary key. A **primary key** is a field whose value must be unique for each record. Every record must have a primary key, and the primary key cannot be **null**. (In a database, a null data value means the value is indeterminate or undefined.) In the CUSTOMER table shown in Figure 2-2, the CUSTID field is a good choice for the primary key because a unique value can be assigned for each customer. The CADD (customer address) field might be another choice for the primary key, but this option has two drawbacks. First, two or more customers might live at the same address. Second, the field is a text field and is therefore prone to typographical, spelling, and punctuation data entry errors. This is a problem because primary key values are used to create relationships with other database tables. When you are looking at a relational database table, you cannot tell which key is the primary key, but you can identify fields that could be used as the primary key. These fields are called **candidate keys**. Once you have selected the field that will be used as the primary key, you must specify this field as the primary key when you create the table. Other users can use special commands to identify the primary keys in existing database tables.

> **TIP**   In this book, table and field names are identified by typing them in all capital letters.

Relationships among database tables are created by matching key values. In the CUST_ORDER table in Figure 2-2, the CUSTID field shows the ID number for the customer associated with each order. A field in a table that is a primary key in another table and creates a relationship between the two tables is called a **foreign key**. CUSTID is a foreign key in the CUST_ORDER table. A foreign key value must exist in the table where it is a primary key. For example, suppose you create a new record for ORDERID 1063 that specifies that the value of CUSTID is 200. There is no record for CUSTID 200 in the CUSTOMER table, so the order record does not make sense. Foreign key values must match the value in the primary key table *exactly*. That is why it is not a good idea to use text fields—and risk typographical, punctuation, and spelling errors—in the primary key.

Sometimes you have to combine multiple fields to create a unique primary key. Figure 2-3 shows a relational database with a STUDENT table that contains student data, a COURSE_SECTION table that shows information about different course sections, and an ENROLLMENT table that shows the courses in which each student has enrolled, as well as the student's grade in each course. In the ENROLLMENT table, the student ID (SID) field does not uniquely identify each row, because a student would probably enroll in multiple courses; similarly, the course section ID (CSECID) field is not unique, because each course section will proba-bly have multiple associated students. However, the combination of the SID and CSECID values is unique, since each student will enroll in a specific course section only once. The combination of fields used to create a unique primary key is called a **composite primary key**, or a **composite key**. Sometimes when you are looking for a candidate key for a table, you find that you must use multiple fields to uniquely identify a record.

STUDENT

SID	SLName	SFName	SMI	SAdd	SCity	SState	SZip
100	Miller	Sarah	M	144 Windridge Blvd.	Eau Claire	WI	54703
101	Umato	Brian	D	454 St. John's Place	Eau Claire	WI	54702

COURSE_SECTION

CSECID	SECNUM	DAY	TIME	MAXENRL	CURRENRL
1000	1	MWF	10:00	140	135
1001	2	TTH	9:30	35	35
1002	3	MWF	8:00	35	32
1003	1	TTh	11:00	35	35
1004	2	TTh	2:00	35	35
1005	1	MWF	9:00	30	25

— primary keys

ENROLLMENT

SID	CSECID	GRADE
100	1000	A
100	1003	A
100	1005	B
101	1000	C
101	1004	B
101	1005	A

— composite key

Figure 2-3   Example of a composite primary key

Sometimes a database table does not have a field that would make a good primary key. For example, suppose in Figure 2-3 that the STUDENT table did not contain the SID field. The student last name (SLNAME) or first name (SFNAME) field, or even the combination of the two fields, is not a good candidate key, because people sometimes have the same name. Multiple people can share an address and phone number. Furthermore, people often change addresses and phone numbers, and if the address or phone number is updated in the table where it is the primary key, it also must be updated in every table where it is a foreign key; otherwise, relationships are lost. A good database development practice is to create a surrogate key field, such as the student ID (SID) field shown in Figure 2-3. A **surrogate key** is a unique numerical data field that usually is generated by the database, and provides no unique information about the record. Its sole purpose is to be the primary key identifier for a record. In Figure 2-3, SID and CSECID are examples of surrogate keys.

THE CASE STUDY DATABASES

In this book, you will encounter tutorials and end-of-chapter projects that illustrate Web-driven database concepts using databases developed for Clearwater Traders and Northwoods University, two fictional organizations for which you will develop Web-based database applications. Next, you will learn about these applications, and view the structure of the database tables with which you will be working throughout the book.

The Clearwater Traders Sales Order Database

Clearwater Traders currently markets a line of clothing and sporting goods via mail-order catalogs. To remain competitive, company managers want to create a Web site to allow Internet customers to browse the catalog online, place orders, and check on the status of individual orders. The system must track information about customers and customer orders. It must also track inventory information so customers can find out if an item is in stock. The system will also have intranet applications: Clearwater Traders personnel must be able to add, update, and delete inventory items; update inventory amounts when new shipments of incoming goods are received; and modify item prices.

Figure 2-4 shows sample data for the Clearwater Traders database. The CUSTOMER table contains five customer records. In the first record, CUSTID 1 is Paula Harris, who lives at 1156 Water Street, Apt. #3, Osseo, WI, and her ZIP code is 54705. Her daytime phone number is 715-555-8943, and her evening phone number is 715-555-9035. Each CUSTOMER record has a unique username/password combination that enables customers to securely log on to the Clearwater Traders order tracking system to order new merchandise and check on the status of existing orders. CUSTID has been designated as the CUSTOMER table's primary key.

CUSTOMER

CUSTID	LAST	FIRST	MI	CADD	CITY	STATE	ZIP	DPHONE	EPHONE	USERNAME	PASSWORD
1	Harris	Paula	E	1156 Water Street, Apt. #3	Osseo	WI	54705	(715) 555-8943	(715) 555-9035	harrispe	asdfjka
2	Edwards	Mitch	M	4204 Garner Street	Washburn	WI	54891	(715) 555-8243	(715) 555-6975	edwardsm	kk2k88
3	Garcia	Maria	H	2211 Pine Drive	Radisson	WI	54867	(715) 555-8332	(715) 555-8332	mhgarcia	yynnyd
4	Miller	Lee		699 Pluto St. NW	Silver Lake	WI	53821	(715) 555-4978	(715) 555-9002	miller	ytrxx
5	Chang	Alissa	R	987 Durham Rd.	Sister Bay	WI	54234	(715) 555-7651	(715) 555-0087	changar	poimner

CUST_ORDER

ORDERID	ORDERDATE	CUSTID
1	5/29/2001	1
2	5/29/2001	2
3	5/31/2001	3
4	5/31/2001	4
5	6/01/2001	5
6	6/01/2001	5

CARRIER

CARRIERID	CARRIERNAME	CARRIERABBREV
1	Federal Express	FEDEX
2	United Parcel Service	UPS
3	Airborne Express	AIR
4	United States Postal Service	USPS

CUSTOMER_SHIPMENT

CSHIPID	DATESHIPPED	CARRIERID	TRACKINGID
0			
1	5/29/2001	1	AA899
2	5/30/2001	1	AA10022
3	5/31/2001	2	790002
4	5/31/2001	1	AA9972

ITEM

ITEMID	ITEMDESC	ITEMIMAGE
1	Women's Hiking Shorts	shorts.jpg
2	Women's Fleece Pullover	fleece.jpg
3	Airstream Canvas Shoes	shoes.jpg
4	All-Weather Mountain Parka	parka.jpg
5	Goose Down Sleeping Bag	bags.jpg

Figure 2-4   Clearwater Traders database tables

INVENTORY

INVID	ITEMID	ITEMSIZE	COLOR	CURR_PRICE	QOH
1	5	Rectangular	Blue	259.99	16
2	5	Mummy	Blue	359.99	12
3	1	S	Khaki	29.95	150
4	1	M	Khaki	29.95	147
5	1	L	Khaki	29.95	0
6	1	S	Navy	29.95	139
7	1	M	Navy	29.95	137
8	1	L	Navy	29.95	115
9	2	S	Twilight	59.95	135
10	2	M	Twilight	59.95	0
11	2	L	Twilight	59.95	187
12	2	S	Hunter	59.95	133
13	2	M	Hunter	59.95	124
14	2	L	Hunter	59.95	112
15	2	S	Red	59.95	102
16	2	M	Red	59.95	83
17	2	L	Red	59.95	95
18	3	1	Navy	39.99	121
19	3	2	Navy	39.99	81
20	3	3	Navy	39.99	53
21	3	4	Navy	39.99	61
22	3	5	Navy	39.99	48
23	3	1	Black	39.99	107
24	3	2	Black	39.99	134
25	3	3	Black	39.99	123
26	3	4	Black	39.99	94
27	3	5	Black	39.99	35
28	4	S	Spruce	199.95	114
29	4	M	Spruce	199.95	17
30	4	L	Spruce	209.95	0
31	4	XL	Spruce	209.95	12
32	4	S	Black	199.95	101
33	4	M	Black	199.95	4
34	4	L	Black	209.95	2
35	4	XL	Black	209.95	75
36	4	S	Red	199.95	79
37	4	M	Red	199.95	5
38	4	L	Red	209.95	13
39	4	XL	Red	209.95	56

INVENTORY_SHIPPING

INVSHIPID	INVID	DATE_EXPECTED	QUANTITY_EXPECTED	DATE_RECEIVED	QUANTITY_RECEIVED
211	1	09/15/2001	100		
211	2	09/15/2001	50		
212	2	11/15/2001	50		
213	5	06/25/2001	200		
214	6	09/25/2001	200		
214	7	09/25/2001	200		
215	12	08/15/2001	50	08/17/2001	0
216	12	08/25/2001	50		
217	29	08/15/2001	100		
218	30	8/12/2001	50	8/15/2001	0
218	32	8/12/2001	100	8/15/2001	100
218	35	8/12/2001	100	8/15/2001	50
218	36	8/12/2001	50	8/15/2001	0

Figure 2-4   Clearwater Traders database tables (continued)

INVENTORY_BACKORDER

BACKORDERID	INVSHIPID	INVID	DATE_EXPECTED	QUANTITY_EXPECTED	DATE_RECEIVED	QUANTITY_RECEIVED
1	215	12	09/01/2001	100	08/31/2001	100
2	218	30	09/15/2001	50		
3	218	36	09/15/2001	50		
4	218	35	09/15/2001	50		

ORDERLINE

ORDERID	INVID	ORDER_PRICE	COMMENT	QUANTITY	CSHIPID
1	1	259.99		1	1
1	14	59.95		2	1
2	2	39.99		1	2
3	29	199.95		1	3
3	31	188.96	Price discounted 10% due to shipping delay	1	
4	12	59.95		2	4
5	7	29.95		1	0
5	8	29.95		1	0
6	13	59.95		1	0
6	24	39.99		1	0

Figure 2-4   Clearwater Traders database tables (continued)

The CUST_ORDER table shows six customer orders. The first is ORDERID 1, dated 5/29/2001, and ordered by customer 1, Paula Harris. ORDERID is the table's primary key, and CUSTID is a foreign key that creates a relationship to the CUSTOMER table.

The CARRIER table lists the shipping companies that Clearwater Traders uses to ship its merchandise to customers. The table's primary key is CARRIERID, and it currently contains records specifying the names and abbreviations used internally at Clearwater Traders for four shipping companies. The CUSTOMER_SHIPMENT table is used to track the status of customer order shipments. The primary key of this table is CSHIPID, and it specifies the date of the shipment. This table contains the CARRIERID field as a foreign key to specify the carrier associated with each shipment. The TRACKINGID field is the carrier's internal identifier for tracking the shipment.

The ITEM table specifies different products that are sold by Clearwater Traders. ITEMID is the primary key of the ITEM table. It currently contains five items: Women's Hiking Shorts, Women's Fleece Pullover, Airstream Canvas Shoes, All-Weather Mountain Parka, and Goose Down Sleeping Bag. The ITEMIMAGE field contains the name of the JPEG image file that displays a photograph of each item. This image will be displayed on a Web page describing the item.

> **TIP**   JPEG (Joint Photographic Experts Group) is a standardized graphic file format that is often used for photographic images that are displayed on Web pages. JPEG files typically have a .jpg or .jpeg extension.

The INVENTORY table contains specific inventory information for different item sizes and colors. For example, for item 1 (Women's Hiking Shorts), the INVENTORY table contains a record for each size (S, M, and L) and color (Navy and Khaki) combination. It also shows the current price and quantity on hand (QOH) for each item. Notice that some items have different prices for different sizes. INVID is the primary key of this table, and ITEMID is a foreign key that creates a relationship with the ITEM table.

The INVENTORY_SHIPPING table contains a schedule of expected incoming product shipments from Clearwater Traders' suppliers. This table includes the inventory ID number (INVID), the expected arrival date and quantity of items, and the date and quantity of items that have been delivered. As you can see in the table, a shipment can consist of more than one inventory item. The primary key of this table is a composite key made of the combination of INVSHIPID and INVID. Remember that composite keys are required when no single field in the table uniquely identifies each record in the table.

Why is INVSHIPID needed in this table? First, without INVSHIPID, the primary key could be composed of both INVID and DATE, because it would take both of these entries to uniquely identify a record in this table. But what if there are two separate shipments of the same item arriving on the same day? And what if both shipments have the same quantity? INVSHIPID provides a useful way to distinguish that there are *two* separate shipments for the same item on the same day.

The INVENTORY_BACKORDER table shows back orders corresponding to shipments. Look at the records in the INVENTORY_SHIPPING table for INVSHIPID 218. When the shipment arrived on 8/15/2001, none of the units for items 30 or 36 arrived, and only 50 of the 100 units ordered for item 35 arrived. Clearwater Traders was notified that the missing units were back-ordered and would be shipped for delivery on 9/15/2001. The INVENTORY_BACKORDER records show the associated shipment ID, inventory ID, expected date, and expected quantity for each back-ordered item. The primary key of the INVENTORY_BACKORDER table is BACKORDERID.

The ORDERLINE table represents the individual inventory items in a customer order. The first line of order 1 is for inventory ID 1 (a blue rectangular Goose Down Sleeping Bag). In this order, one sleeping bag was ordered at a price of $259.99, and was shipped on 5/29/2001 via carrier 1 (Federal Express). The second line of this order specifies two units of inventory ID 14 (Women's Fleece Pullover, size L, color Hunter), with a price of $59.95 each, and also shipped on 5/29/2001 via Federal Express. Sometimes in an order, the price of an item is different from the price specified in the INVENTORY table because of special discounts, promotions, and so on. The COMMENT field contains text to explain special pricing or order instructions. For example, for order ID 3 and inventory ID 31, the COMMENT field specifies that a 10 percent price discount was given on this item due to a shipping delay. Note that the primary key of this table is not ORDERID, because more than one record might have the same ORDERID. The primary key is a composite key made up of the combination of ORDERID and INVID. An order might have several different inventory items, but it will never have the same inventory item listed more than once. Along with being part of the primary key, INVID is also a foreign key in this table because it creates a relationship to the INVENTORY table. If the CSHIPID field for a record is null, it indicates that the item has not yet been shipped.

The Northwoods University Database

Northwoods University is a small private university. The administration has decided to replace the university's aging mainframe-based student registration system with a more modern database system that students, faculty, and staff can access via the Internet using a Web browser. Its Internet accessibility means that users can log on either from campus or from remote locations. Students will be able to retrieve course availability information, register for courses, and print grade reports and transcripts. Faculty members will be able to retrieve student course lists, drop students from courses, add students to courses, record course grades, and view records for the students they advise. The system will also have intranet applications: staff members must be able to enter and update student, faculty, and course records. Security is a prime concern, so student and course records must be protected by password access.

Figure 2-5 shows sample data for the Northwoods University database. The STUDENT table contains fields for student ID (SID), student last name, first name, and middle initial (SLNAME, SFNAME, SMI), and student address, city, state, ZIP code, phone number, and date of birth (SADD, SCITY, SSTATE, SZIP, SPHONE, SDOB). The SCLASS field indicates whether the student is a freshman, sophomore, junior, senior, or graduate student, using the abbreviations FR, SO, JR, SR, or GR. The SPIN field stores student personal identification numbers to control data access. Each student has a faculty advisor, so FID (faculty ID) is a foreign key that refers to the FID field in the FACULTY table to indicate the student's advisor. SID is the table's primary key.

STUDENT

SID	SLNAME	SFNAME	SMI	SADD	SCITY	SSTATE	SZIP	SPHONE	SDOB	SCLASS	SPIN	FID
1	Miller	Sarah	M	144 Windridge Blvd.	Eau Claire	WI	54703	(715) 555-9876	07/14/80	SR	8891	1
2	Umato	Brian	D	454 St. John s Place	Eau Claire	WI	54702	(715) 555-2345	08/19/80	SR	1230	1
3	Black	Daniel		8921 Circle Drive	Bloomer	WI	54715	(715) 555-3907	10/10/81	JR	1613	1
4	Mobley	Amanda	J	1716 Summit St.	Eau Claire	WI	54703	(715) 555-6902	9/24/82	SO	1841	2
5	Sanchez	Ruben	R	1780 Samantha Court	Eau Claire	WI	54701	(715) 555-8899	11/20/82	SO	4420	4
6	Connoly	Michael	S	1818 Silver Street	Elk Mound	WI	54712	(715) 555-4944	12/4/83	FR	9188	3

FACULTY

FID	FLNAME	FFNAME	FMI	LOCID	FPHONE	FRANK	FPIN	FACULTYIMAGE
1	Cox	Kim	J	9	7155551234	ASSO	I181	cox.jpg
2	Blanchard	John	R	10	7155559087	FULL	1075	blanchard.jpg
3	Williams	Jerry	F	12	7155555412	ASST	8531	williams.jpg
4	Sheng	Laura	M	11	7155556409	INST	1690	sheng.jpg
5	Brown	Phillip	E	13	7155556082	ASSO	9899	brown.jpg

Figure 2-5   Northwoods University database tables

2

FRANK

FRANK	FRANKDESC
ASST	Assistant
ASSO	Associate
FULL	Full
ADJ	Adjunct
INST	Instructor

LOCATION

LOCID	BLDG_CODE	ROOM	CAPACITY
1	CR	101	150
2	CR	202	40
3	CR	103	35
4	CR	105	35
5	BUS	105	42
6	BUS	404	35
7	BUS	421	35
8	BUS	211	55
9	BUS	424	1
10	BUS	402	1
11	BUS	433	1
12	LIB	217	2
13	LIB	222	1

TERM

TERMID	TDESC	STATUS
1	Fall 2001	CLOSED
2	Spring 2002	CLOSED
3	Summer 2002	CLOSED
4	Fall 2002	CLOSED
5	Spring 2003	CLOSED
6	Summer 2003	OPEN

COURSE

CID	CALLID	CNAME	CCREDIT
1	MIS 101	Intro. to Info. Systems	3
2	MIS 301	Systems Analysis	3
3	MIS 441	Database Management	3
4	CS 155	Programming in C++	3
5	MIS 451	Client/Server Systems	3

COURSE_SECTION

CSECID	CID	TERMID	SECNUM	FID	DAY	TIME	LOCID	MAXENRL	CURRENRL
1	1	4	1	2	MWF	10:00 AM	1	140	135
2	1	4	2	3	TTH	9:30 AM	7	35	35
3	1	4	3	3	M	6:00 PM	2	35	32
4	2	4	1	4	TTH	11:00 AM	6	35	35
5	2	5	2	4	TTH	2:00 PM	6	35	35
6	3	5	1	1	MWF	9:00 AM	5	30	25
7	3	5	2	1	MW	5:00 PM	5	30	28
8	4	5	1	5	TTH	8:00 AM	3	35	20
9	5	5	1	2	MWF	2:00 PM	5	35	32
10	5	5	2	2	TH	6:00 PM	5	35	35
11	1	6	1	1	M-F	8:00 AM	1	50	35
12	2	6	1		M-F	8:00 AM	6	35	35
13	3	6	1		M-F	9:00 AM	5	35	29

Figure 2-5   Northwoods University database tables (continued)

ENROLLMENT

SID	CSECID	GRADE
1	1	A
1	4	A
1	6	B
1	9	B
2	1	C
2	5	B
2	6	A
2	9	B
3	1	C
3	12	
3	13	
4	11	
4	12	
5	1	B
5	5	C
5	9	C
5	13	
6	11	
6	12	

Figure 2-5 Northwoods University database tables (continued)

The FACULTY table contains faculty member data, including faculty ID (FID), and the faculty member's last name, first name, and middle initial (FLNAME, FFNAME, FMI). LOCID (location ID) is a foreign key that references the LOCID field in the LOCATION table, which shows the faculty member's office location. Other FACULTY table fields include faculty phone number (FPHONE), faculty rank (FRANK), and faculty personal identification number (FPIN), for system access security. The FACULTYIMAGE field contains the name of the JPEG file that displays a photograph of the associated faculty member. FID is the table's primary key.

The FRANK table is a **lookup table**, which is a list of legal values for a field in another table. Notice the variety of faculty ranks shown in the FACULTY table (ASST, ASSO, FULL, ADJ, INST). If users are allowed to type in these faculty rank abbreviations each time a new faculty member is added to the FACULTY table, typing errors might occur. If this happened, it would be impossible to correctly sort the FACULTY records by rank. The FRANK table shows the FRANK abbreviation, as well as a description of each rank in the FRANKDESC field. The FRANK field is the primary key of the FRANK table.

The LOCATION table shows information about all Northwoods University buildings, rooms, and room capacities, which are stored in the BLDG_CODE (building code), ROOM (room number), and CAPACITY (maximum room capacity) fields. LOCID is the table's primary key.

The TERM table shows the term ID (TERMID), a textual description of each term (TDESC), and a STATUS field, which shows whether enrollment for the associated term is OPEN or CLOSED, meaning that students can or cannot enroll in courses for the particular term. TERMID is the primary key of the TERM table.

The COURSE table shows the course ID (CID), call ID (CALLID), course name (CNAME), and credits (CCREDIT) for each course offered at Northwoods University. Call ID is a textual field that describes the department that offers the course and the department's number code for the course. CID is the primary key of the COURSE table. Both CID and CALLID are unique values for each course, and are thus candidate keys, but CID is a numeric surrogate key that is a better primary key choice.

The COURSE_SECTION table shows the detailed course offerings for specific terms and includes foreign key fields for course ID (CID), term ID (TERMID), faculty ID (FID), and location ID (LOCID). The table also contains fields to specify the section number (SECNUM), and the course section's day, time, maximum allowable enrollment, and current enrollment (DAY, TIME, MAXENRL, CURRENRL). CSECID is the primary key of the COURSE_SECTION table. The first record shows that CSECID 1 is section 1 of MIS 101. It is offered in the Fall 2002 term and is taught by John Blanchard. The section meets on Mondays, Wednesdays, and Fridays at 10:00 AM in room CR 101. It has a maximum enrollment of 140 students, and 135 students are enrolled currently. The FID field is an example of a foreign key field that can have a null value. In the records for CSECID 12 and CSECID 13, no FID has been assigned yet, so no FID values appear.

The ENROLLMENT table shows students who are currently enrolled in each course section and their associated grade, if it has been assigned. The primary key for this table is a composite key of SID and CSECID.

USING ACCESS 2000 TO CREATE DATABASE TABLES AND INSERT DATA

In a Web-based database system, users view database data through Web pages. The system developer must create the database tables, insert the data records, and create the programs that query the database and compose the dynamic Web pages that are displayed to the user. Now you will learn how to use the Microsoft Access 2000 personal database system to create database tables, and to insert and update records.

Although the focus of this book is not on database design, there are a few general database design principles with which you should be familiar:

- Group related items together in a single table. For example, the CUSTOMER table groups data items describing individual customers.

- Avoid creating tables in which a particular nonforeign-key field value might be duplicated many times in different rows. For example, if customer Alissa Chang makes several orders, then the information for each order should be placed in a second table separate from the CUSTOMER table, such as the CUST_ORDER table. It is all right to insert Alissa Chang's primary key, CUSTID, as many times as needed into the CUST_ORDER table as a foreign key "link" from the CUST_ORDER table to the CUSTOMER table, as shown in Figure 2-2, but you should not duplicate all of Alissa's information, such as her address and phone numbers, for each CUST_ORDER record.

- Avoid creating tables that will have many null values.

Creating Database Tables

In Access, a database consists of a series of associated database tables, queries, and user application modules (such as forms and reports) that are all stored in a single file with an .mdb extension. In this tutorial, you will create some of the tables for the Clearwater Traders database. First you will start Access and create a new database that will be saved in the Chapter2\Tutorials folder on your Data Disk.

To start Access and create a new database:

1. Click **Start** on the Windows taskbar, point to **Programs**, and then click **Microsoft Access**. The Microsoft Access dialog box opens. This dialog box gives you options for creating a blank database; for creating a database using database wizards, pages, or projects; or for opening an existing database file. The database wizards, pages, or projects option allows you to create predefined database table structures for common personal database tasks such as contact management or expense tracking. Since the Clearwater Traders database has a customized database table structure, you will create a blank database and then create the individual tables yourself.

2. Click the **Blank Access database** option button, and then click **OK**. The File New Database dialog box opens.

3. Open the list beside Save in, navigate to the Chapter2\Tutorials folder on your Data Disk, change the File name to **clearwater.mdb**, and then click **Create**. The clearwater: Database window opens, as shown in Figure 2-6. Maximize the window.

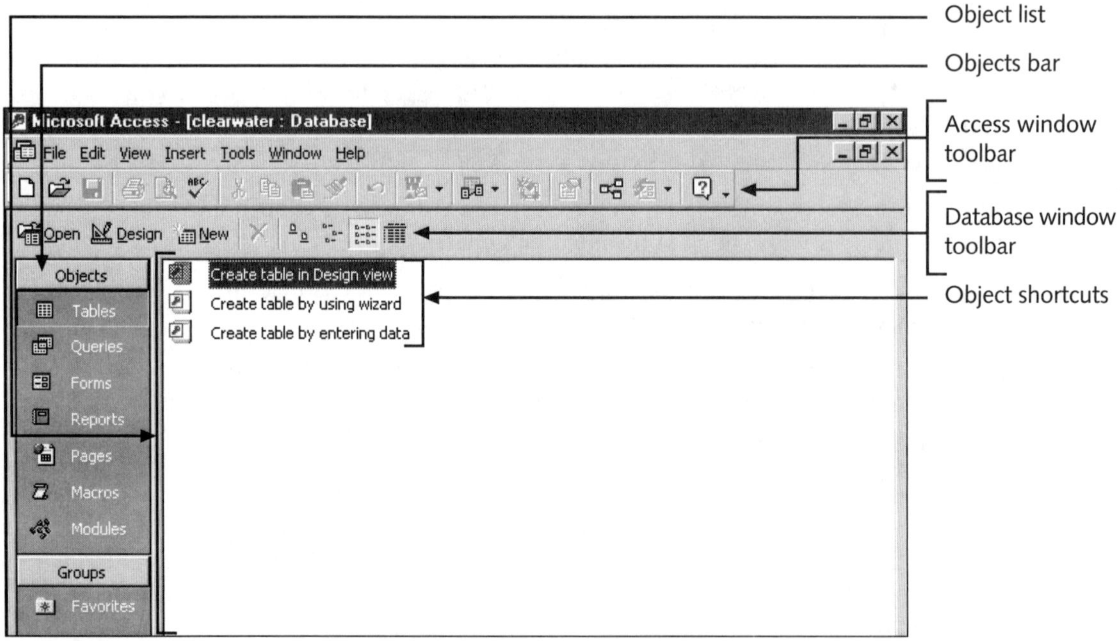

Figure 2-6 Database window

2

The Database window appears when you create or open a database. This is the control center for accessing all of the objects within a database. The upper toolbar is the Access window toolbar, which appears in every Access window and has buttons for common operations such as opening files, saving files, and copying and pasting objects. The lower toolbar is the Database window toolbar, which is displayed only in the Database window, and has buttons for managing the Database window objects. The Objects bar lists all of the possible object types in an Access database. You will be working with the Tables and Queries objects. The Object list shows all of the current database objects for the object type that is currently selected in the Objects bar.

At present, the Object list shows shortcuts for performing common tasks on the object type that is currently selected. Since these shortcut operations can be performed using other menu and toolbar selections, you will hide the shortcuts in the Object list.

To hide the shortcuts:

1. Click **Tools** on the menu bar, and then click **Options**. The Options dialog box opens.

 TIP If the Options menu selection is not visible, click ⯆ to display all of the Tools menu choices.

2. Click the **View** tab if necessary, click the **New object shortcuts** check box to clear it, and then click **OK**. The shortcuts are no longer displayed.

On the Database window toolbar, the Open button 🖼 is used to open the object that is currently selected in the Object list. For example, if you open an existing table, it is displayed in **Datasheet view**, which displays the table as a matrix, with each field displayed as a column and each record displayed as a different row. The Design button 📐 opens the selected object in Design view, where you can change its design properties. For a database table, you could add or delete fields, and modify field properties. The New button 🖃 creates a new object of the object type that is currently selected in the Object bar. The Delete button ✖ deletes the object that is currently selected in the Object list. The last four buttons on the Database window toolbar allow you to customize the Object list items by adjusting the icon size, whether the objects are displayed as a list, and how much detail is shown for each object.

Creating a New Database Table

Now you will create the CUSTOMER table in the Clearwater Traders database. Recall that all of the Clearwater Traders database tables are shown in Figure 2-4.

To create the CUSTOMER table:

1. Make sure that Tables is selected in the Objects bar, and then click the **New** button 🖃 on the Database window toolbar. The New Table dialog box opens.

   This dialog box allows you to define a table by directly entering data (Datasheet View), by explicitly specifying the table and field properties (Design View), by using a wizard to create the table based on table templates for commonly used table structures (Table Wizard), or by using a wizard to import or link data from another database or data source (Import Table or Link Table). You will create the CUSTOMER table using Design View.

2. Click **Design View** in the list box, and then click **OK**. The Table window opens in Design view. Maximize the Table window, if necessary, so that your screen looks like Figure 2-7.

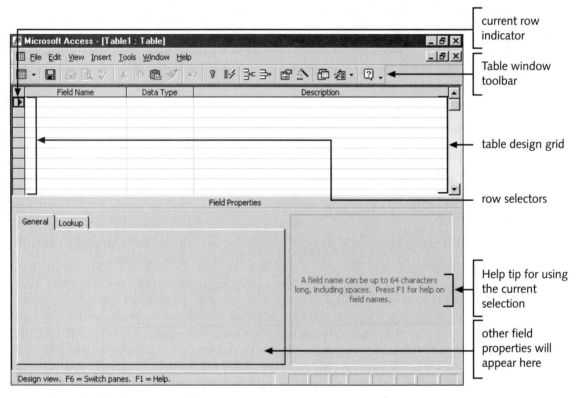

Figure 2-7   Table window

The Table window has a toolbar for creating or modifying the table structure and a table design grid for specifying the name, data type, and description of each data field. The buttons on the left side of the design grid are used to select a specific row. The row that is currently selected is indicated by the current row indicator.

A field name can be up to 64 characters long and can include any combination of letters, numbers, spaces, and special characters except the period (.), exclamation point (!), accent grave (`), square brackets ([ ]), or quotation mark ("). A field name cannot begin with a leading space. Although you can include blank spaces in a field name, this is not a good practice because it can produce errors within other applications. A field name must be unique within a table, but the same field name can be used in different tables.

The field data type specifies what kind of data will be stored in the field. Data types are used for two primary reasons. First, assigning a data type provides a means for error checking. For example, you cannot store the character data "Chicago" in a field assigned to hold numerical data. Data types also cause storage space to be used more efficiently by optimizing how specific types of data are stored. Table 2-1 summarizes the Access 2000 data types that you will use in this book.

Table 2-1   Access 2000 data types used in this book

Data Type	Description	Size or Value Range	Example of Data
Text	Character and number data that do not require calculations	1 to 255 characters	Paula
Memo	Long strings of text data	1 to 65,535 characters	Comment describing price adjustment on customer order
Number	Numerical data that can be used in calculations	Varies based on subtype	259.99
AutoNumber	Unique sequential number, incremented by 1, used whenever a new record is added to a table to generate a unique primary key	1 to slightly more than 2 billion	1
Currency	Special numeric data type for preventing rounding errors when manipulating currency values	-922×10^{-12} to 922×10^{12}	$259.99
Date/Time	Date and time values	1/1/100 through 12/31/9999	2001

The Number data type has a variety of data subtypes that can be used to specify how much storage space different Number data fields will occupy, based on the type of data that are stored in the field. These subtypes are summarized in Table 2-2.

Table 2-2   Number data type subtypes

Field Size	Maximum Number of Decimal Places	Range of Values	Bytes of Storage Space Occupied
Byte	None	0 to 255	1
Integer	None	$-32,768$ to $34,767$	2
Long Integer	None	$-2,147,483,648$ to $2,147,483,647$	4
Single	7	-3.4×10^{38} to 3.4×10^{38}	4
Double	15	-1.797×10^{308} to 1.797×10^{308}	8
Decimal	28	-10^{-28} to 10^{28}	12

The Date/Time data type has different formats that can be used to display date and time data in a variety of ways. These Date/Time formats are summarized in Table 2-3.

Table 2-3 Date/Time data formats

Date/Time Format	Example
General Date	5/29/01 10:10 AM
Short Date (default)	5/29/01
Long Date	Tuesday May 29, 2001
Medium Date	29-May-01
Medium Time	10:10 AM
Long Time	10:10:00 AM
mm/dd/yy	05/29/01

Now you will specify the properties of the CUSTID data field, which is the first field in the CUSTOMER data table.

To specify the properties of the CUSTID data field:

1. If necessary, click in the first Field Name space in the table design grid, and then type **CUSTID** to specify the first table field.

2. Press the **Tab** key to move to the Data Type column.

3. Click the **drop-down list arrow** to see the available data types, and select **AutoNumber**. You should always use the AutoNumber data type for primary key fields that must have unique values.

 You can also select the data type automatically by typing the first letter of the data type. For example, to select AutoNumber, you would type the letter a.

4. Press the **Tab** key to move to the Description column, and type **primary key** to indicate that CUSTID is the primary key of the CUSTOMER table. The purpose of the description field is to internally document that CUSTID is the primary key—you will actually specify CUSTID as the table's primary key later.

Notice that the field properties list on the General tab in the bottom-left corner of the screen now allows you to specify additional properties for the CUSTID field. Field properties in this tab will vary depending on the data type of the field. Since this book does not cover creating Access forms and reports, we will only define the field properties that are important for Web database programming. By default, the **Field Size** property for fields with the AutoNumber data type is the Long Integer subtype. Since you do not know the maximum number of customer ID values that will be stored in the database, you will accept this default. The default value for the **New Values** property is Increment, which means each successive value will be incremented by one. The **Indexed** property allows you to specify whether a field is indexed. An **index** provides a way of internally organizing data values so that a specific field can be located very quickly, much like an index in a book. Primary key fields are automatically indexed. Indexes should be used for fields that are frequently used for searching for a specific data value, or for foreign key values that are used to join two or more tables. Duplicate index values cannot be allowed for a field that is a primary key, since every primary key must be unique. For a field that is a foreign key, duplicate index values are usually allowed. Since CUSTID is the primary key of the CUSTOMER table, you will accept the default Indexed property value. You will leave some of the fields in the field properties list blank, because they are only applicable if you are creating Access forms and reports. The panel in the bottom-right corner of the screen provides hints about the fields specified in the General tab.

Specifying the Table's Primary Key

Next, you will specify that CUSTID is the primary key of the CUSTOMER table. To do this, you will use the Primary key button 🔑 on the Table window toolbar.

To specify that CUSTID is the primary key:

1. Click the current row indicator button to select the row containing CUSTID, and then click the **Primary key** button 🔑 on the Table window toolbar. The key symbol 🔑 appears beside the current row indicator, showing that CUSTID is the table's primary key.

TIP   Another way to designate a row as the primary key is to select the row, right-click, then click Primary Key.

Specifying the Rest of the Table Fields

Now you will specify the customer last name (LAST) data field in the CUSTOMER table. This field will have the Text data type.

To specify the customer last name data field:

1. Click the mouse pointer in the space directly below CUSTID in the table design grid, then type **LAST**.

2. Press the **Tab** key to move to the Data Type column, and then select **Text** from the list of available data types. The General tab in the bottom of the screen changes to allow you to specify additional properties for this text data field.

   Text data fields have some of the same properties as the AutoNumber data type you defined before. Again, many of these properties are specific to Access forms and reports and will be left blank. However, important field properties include the **Default Value** property. This specifies a default value for a field, which is a value that is automatically inserted whenever a new record is created. For example, the default value for the ORDERDATE field in the CUST_ORDER field might be the current date. Another important property is **Validation Rule**. This property specifies the conditions that field data must follow to ensure that correct data are entered. For example, you might specify that the value of the STATUS field in the CUSTOMER_SHIPMENT table must be either RECEIVED or INTRANSIT. The **Required** property specifies whether a field can be null or not. The **Allow Zero Length** property specifies whether the user or system can substitute a zero-length string ("") for a field value rather than leaving the field null, or undefined. The default for this property is No. The Allow Zero Length property should always be set to Yes for Text data fields, so that Web page database queries can be processed correctly. **Unicode compression** is a standard that governs character encoding and provides a 16-bit extensible international character coding system to support data processing in most major languages in the world. This property will be set to its default value, which is Yes.

3. Change the values for the Required and Allow Zero Length properties for the LAST field to Yes by clicking in the boxes next to the property names and selecting **Yes**. Your screen should look like Figure 2-8.

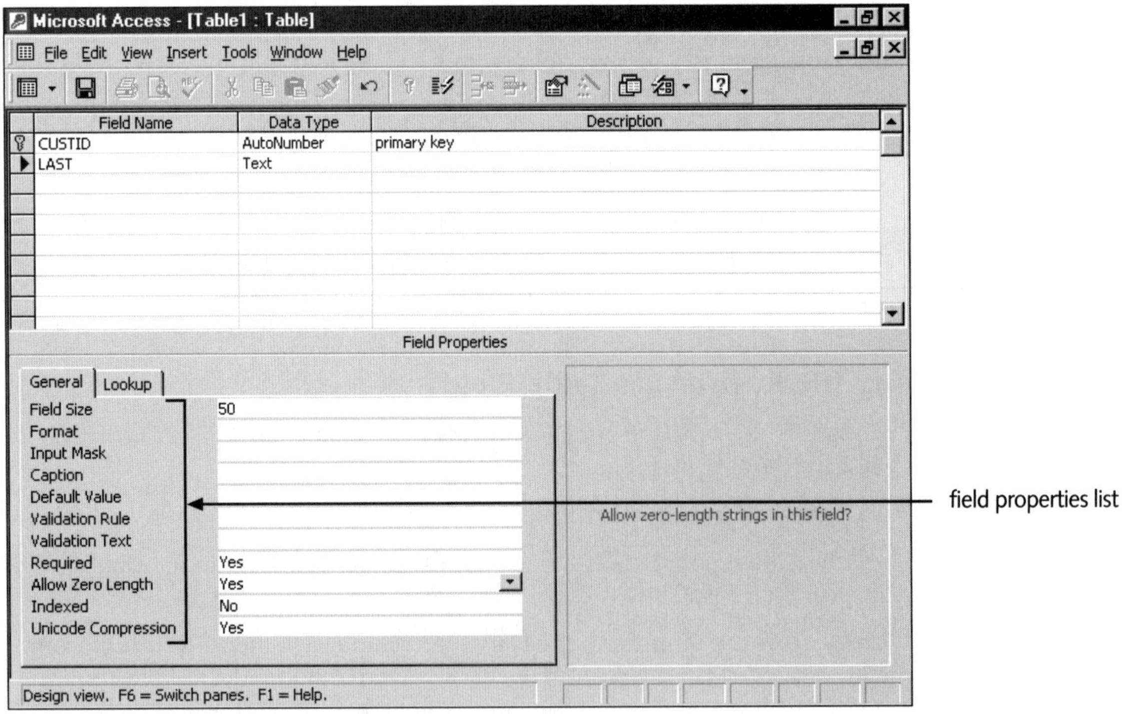

Figure 2-8   LAST field specification

Now you will specify the rest of the fields in the CUSTOMER table.

To finish specifying the field properties:

1. Type the field names and properties for the rest of the fields in the CUSTOMER table, using the following specifications:

Field Name	Data Type	Field Size	Default Value	Required	Allow Zero Length	Indexed
FIRST	Text	50		Yes	Yes	No
MI	Text	1		No	Yes	No
CADD	Text	50		No	Yes	No
CITY	Text	50		No	Yes	No
STATE	Text	2	WI	No	Yes	No
ZIP	Text	10		No	Yes	No
DPHONE	Text	15		No	Yes	No
EPHONE	Text	15		No	Yes	No
USERNAME	Text	8		Yes	Yes	Yes (No Duplicates)
PASSWORD	Text	8		Yes	Yes	Yes (Duplicates OK)

Saving Database Tables

When you click the **Save** button 🖫 on the Table window toolbar, only the active table is saved. There is no 🖫 on the Database window toolbar—you cannot save the entire database, only the current object. Access automatically saves the active database to disk both periodically and whenever you close the database. Whenever you are saving your database to a floppy disk in drive A, you should be careful to not remove the floppy disk from the disk drive while the database is open. If you remove the disk, Access will encounter problems when it tries to save the database.

When you save a table for the first time, you are prompted to enter the table name. Table names must conform to the same restrictions as field names: they can be up to 64 characters long, and they have the same restrictions on the use of special characters. Each table in a database must have a unique name. Now you will save the CUSTOMER database table to your Data Disk.

To save the CUSTOMER database table:

1. Click the **Save** button 🖫 on the Table window toolbar to save the table. The Save As dialog box is displayed.

2. Type **CUSTOMER** as the Table Name, and then click **OK**.

3. Click the **Close** button ✕ on the Table window to close the Table window. The CUSTOMER table is displayed in the Database window as an Object list item, as shown in Figure 2-9.

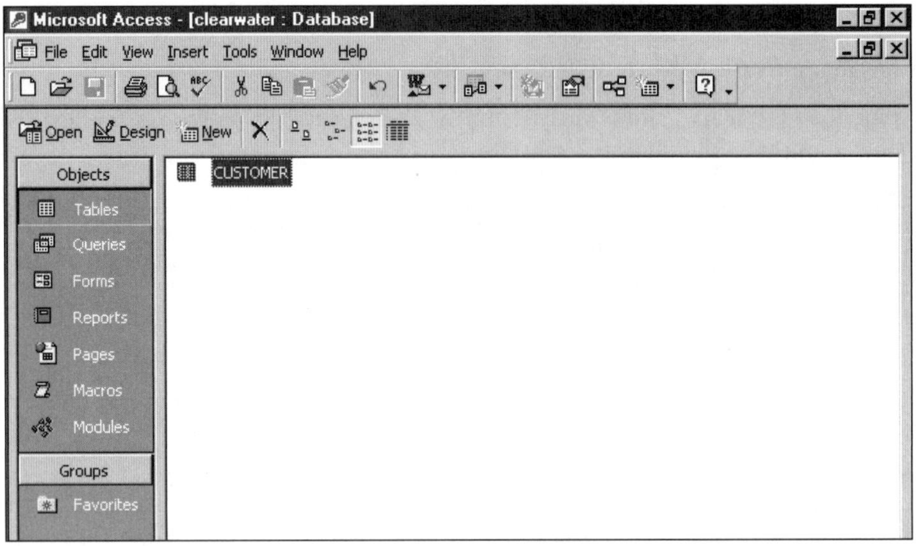

Figure 2-9 CUSTOMER table in Database window

Creating a Foreign Key Reference

Next, you will create the CUST_ORDER table in the Clearwater Traders database. This table has a foreign key field (CUSTID), so you will learn how to create a foreign key reference. Recall that the CUSTID field is the primary key in the CUSTOMER table and uses the AutoNumber data type. The associated CUSTID field in the CUST_ORDER table, where CUSTID is a foreign key reference, must use the Number data type. Recall that a value that is used as a foreign key must already exist in another table as a primary key value. Therefore, the CUSTID field in the CUST_ORDER table cannot use the AutoNumber data type, because the CUSTID field value has already been defined in the CUSTOMER table.

To create the CUST_ORDER table:

1. Click the **New** button [icon] on the Database window toolbar, and then create a new table in Design View.

2. Type the field names and properties for the fields in the CUST_ORDER table, using the following specifications:

Field Name	Data Type	Description	Format	Field Size	Required	Indexed
ORDERID	AutoNumber	Primary key		Long Integer		Yes (No Duplicates)
ORDERDATE	Date/Time		Short Date		Yes	No
CUSTID	Number	Foreign key		Long Integer	No	Yes (Duplicates OK)

3. Click the row selector beside ORDERID to make ORDERID the current row, and then click the **Primary Key** button 🔑 on the Table window toolbar to designate ORDERID as the table's primary key.

4. Click the **Save** button 💾 to save the table. Type **CUST_ORDER** as the table name, click **OK**, then close the Table window and confirm that the table is displayed in the Object list in the Database window.

Now you need to designate the CUSTID field in the CUST_ORDER table as a foreign key that is linked to the CUSTID field in the CUSTOMER table. The purpose of creating a foreign key relationship between two database tables is to enforce referential integrity. **Referential integrity** means that each foreign key value within a given table must have a matching value in the table where the value is a primary key. In the relationship between the CUSTOMER and CUST_ORDER tables, every CUSTID value in the CUST_ORDER table must have a matching value in the CUSTOMER table. To define a foreign key relationship in Access, you use the Relationships window, which displays the database tables graphically. First you will open the Relationships window and display the CUSTOMER and CUST_ORDER tables graphically.

To display the CUSTOMER and CUST_ORDER tables in the Relationships window:

1. Click the **Relationships** button 🔲 on the Database window toolbar. The Show Table dialog box appears, which allows you to specify the tables that will be displayed visually in the Relationships window.

TIP   Another way to open the Relationships window is to click Tools on the menu bar, and then click Relationships.

2. Make sure that the Tables tab is selected, and, if necessary, click **CUST_ORDER** in the table list. Click **Add**. CUST_ORDER appears in the Relationships window beside the Show Table dialog box.

3. Click **CUSTOMER** in the table list, click **Add**, and then click **Close**. The CUST_ORDER and CUSTOMER tables appear in the Relationships window. Resize and reposition the tables so that your Relationships window looks like Figure 2-10.

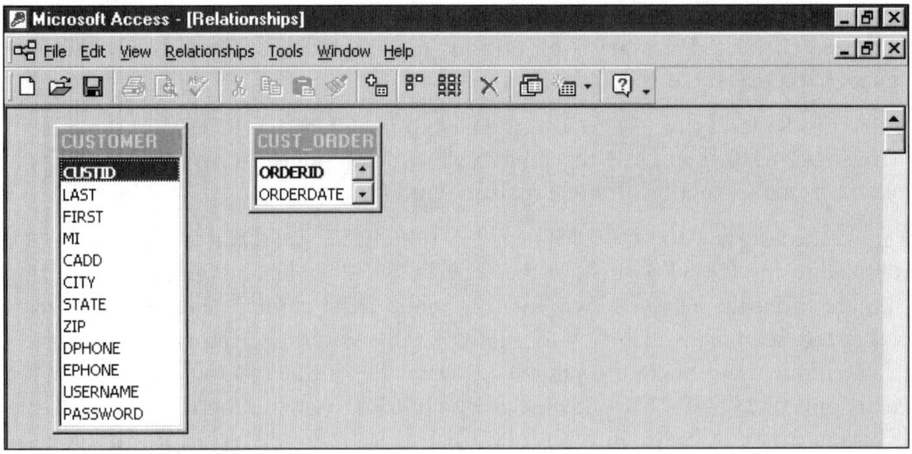

Microsoft Access - [Relationships]   _ 🗗 ✕
🖳 File   Edit   View   Relationships   Tools   Window   Help   _ 🗗 ✕

CUSTOMER
CUSTID
LAST
FIRST
MI
CADD
CITY
STATE
ZIP
DPHONE
EPHONE
USERNAME
PASSWORD

CUST_ORDER
ORDERID
ORDERDATE

Figure 2-10   CUSTOMER and CUST_ORDER tables in the Relationships window

> **TIP**   To move a table, click the table name and drag the table to the new location on the screen. To resize a table, place the mouse pointer on the table border, and drag the table border to the desired size.

Now you will create a relationship between the CUSTID field in the CUSTOMER and CUST_ORDER tables. To create a foreign key relationship, you "draw" a link between the related fields. You always start a foreign key link at the field that is the primary key and end the link at the field that is the foreign key. In this relationship, you will start the link at the CUSTID field in the CUSTOMER table (where CUSTID is the primary key) and draw the link to the CUSTID field in the CUST_ORDER table (where CUSTID is the foreign key). You will specify that the relationship will enforce referential integrity.

To create the foreign key relationship link between the CUSTOMER and CUST_ORDER tables:

1. Click **CUSTID** in the CUSTOMER table, leave the left mouse button pressed, and drag the mouse pointer to the CUSTID field in the CUST_ORDER table. The mouse pointer changes to  .

2. Release the left mouse button. The Edit Relationships dialog box opens.

3. Click the **Enforce Referential Integrity** check box. The check boxes for cascade updates and cascade deletes are now accessible.

 With a **cascade update**, every time a primary key value is updated, its corresponding foreign key record values are automatically updated. With a **cascade delete**, every time a primary key value is deleted, its corresponding foreign key records are deleted. In general, it is not a good practice to allow users to update (or change) primary key values, so you will not allow cascade updates. Similarly, it is usually dangerous to enable cascade deletes, because the system might automatically delete records that the user does not intend to delete.

4. Leave the Cascade Update Related Fields and Cascade Delete Related Records check boxes cleared, and then click **Create**. The completed relationship appears as shown in Figure 2-11.

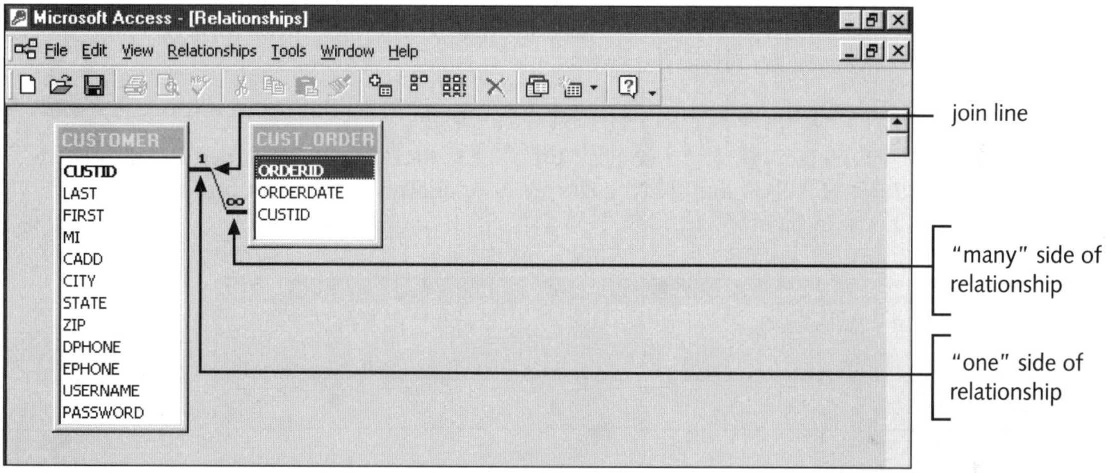

![Microsoft Access Relationships window showing CUSTOMER and CUST_ORDER tables with a join line. The CUSTOMER table lists CUSTID, LAST, FIRST, MI, CADD, CITY, STATE, ZIP, DPHONE, EPHONE, USERNAME, PASSWORD. The CUST_ORDER table lists ORDERID, ORDERDATE, CUSTID. The join line is labeled "join line", the "many" side of relationship (∞) and the "one" side of relationship (1).]

Figure 2-11   Foreign key relationship between CUSTOMER and CUST_ORDER tables

In Figure 2-11, a join line connects the CUSTID fields in the two tables. The join line is thick at both ends, which shows that the relationship enforces referential integrity. The relationship beside the CUSTOMER table has the digit 1 beside it, and the relationship beside the CUST_ORDER table displays the infinity symbol (∞). This indicates that for each CUSTID value in the CUSTOMER table, there can be many associated values in the CUST_ORDER table. Conversely, for each CUSTID value in the CUST_ORDER table, there is only one associated value in the CUSTOMER table. This is called a **one-to-many relationship**.

5. Click the **Save** button 🖫 on the Relationships window toolbar to save your changes, and then click the **Close** button ✖ to close the Relationships window. If you are asked if you want to save the changes to the layouts of the relationships in the Relationships window, click **Yes**. The Database window is displayed again.

Importing Tables from Another Database

So that you will not have to manually create the rest of the tables in the Clearwater Traders database, you will now learn how to import tables from another database. In the Chapter2\Tutorials folder on your Data Disk, there is a database file named Ch2tables.mdb that contains the CARRIER, CUSTOMER_SHIPMENT, INVENTORY, and ITEM tables for the Clearwater Traders database. Now you will import these tables into your Clearwater database.

To import the database tables:

1. In the Database window, click the **New** button on the Database window toolbar, click **Import Table** from the selection list, and then click **OK**. The Import dialog box is displayed.

2. Open the Look in list, and, if necessary, navigate to the Chapter2\Tutorials folder on your Data Disk. Select **Ch2tables.mdb**, and then click **Import**. The Import Objects dialog box is displayed.

3. Click **Options**, and confirm that the Import Relationships check box is checked.

4. Click **Select All**, and then click **OK**. The CARRIER, CUSTOMER_SHIPMENT, INVENTORY, and ITEM tables are now displayed in the Database window, as shown in Figure 2-12.

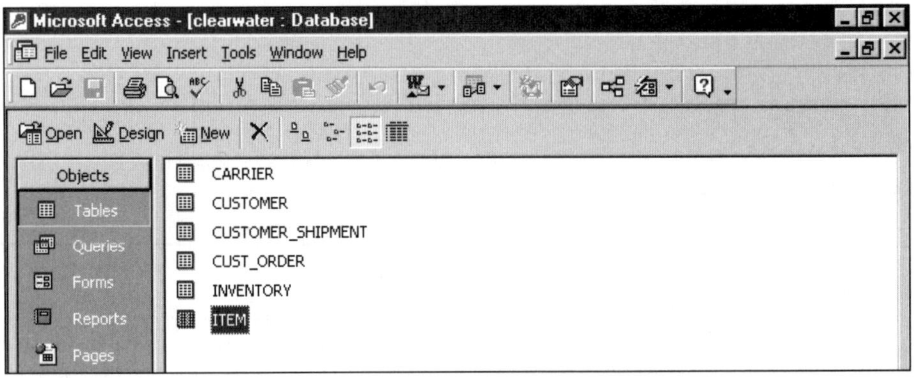

Figure 2-12   Clearwater Traders database with imported tables

5. Click the **Relationships** button on the Database window toolbar to display the Relationships window, right-click anywhere in the Relationships window, and click **Show All** to display all of the database tables in the Relationships window.

6. If necessary, rearrange the tables so that your Relationships window looks like Figure 2-13.

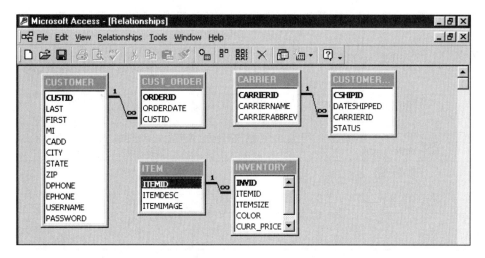

Figure 2-13   Relationships window with new tables displayed

7. Close the Relationships window, and click **Yes** to save the changes in the relationships layout.

Creating a Table with a Composite Primary Key

Review the INVENTORY_ SHIPPING table in Figure 2-4. This table contains records about incoming inventory shipments. Each shipment (identified by INVSHIPID) can contain multiple inventory items, and each inventory item (identified by INVID) can be in multiple shipments. Therefore, the primary key of this table is a composite key consisting of both INVSHIPID and INVID. When you create a table with a composite primary key, the individual fields that constitute the primary key cannot use the AutoNumber data type, because each field value does not have a unique key value. Sometimes a field that composes a composite primary key is linked to other tables as a foreign key reference. In the INVENTORY_SHIPPING table, the INVID field is linked as a foreign key reference to the INVENTORY table. As with any foreign key reference, this field must use the Number data type rather than the AutoNumber data type, since its values must first be defined in the INVENTORY table where it is the primary key. Now you will create the INVENTORY_SHIPPING table, and define its composite primary key.

To create the INVENTORY_SHIPPING table:

1. In the Database window, create a new database table in Design View.

2. Specify the database table fields as follows:

Field Name	Data Type	Description	Field Size	Decimal Places	Default Value	Required	Indexed
INVSHIPID	Number	Primary key & foreign key	Long Integer	0	deleted	Yes	Yes (Duplicates OK)
INVID	Number	Primary key & foreign key	Long Integer	0	deleted	Yes	Yes (Duplicates OK)
DATE_EXPECTED	Date/Time					No	No
QUANTITY _EXPECTED	Number		Integer	0	deleted	No	No
DATE_RECEIVED	Date/Time					No	No
QUANTITY _RECEIVED	Number		Integer	0	deleted	No	No

3. To specify the composite primary key, select the **INVSHIPID** row, press the **Shift** key, and then select the **INVID** row, while keeping the Shift key pressed. Release the Shift key. The current row indicator appears beside both the INVSHIPID and the INVID rows in the Table window.

4. Click the **Primary Key** button ⫐. The primary key symbol is displayed next to the row indicator beside both columns, designating them as a composite primary key, as shown in Figure 2-14.

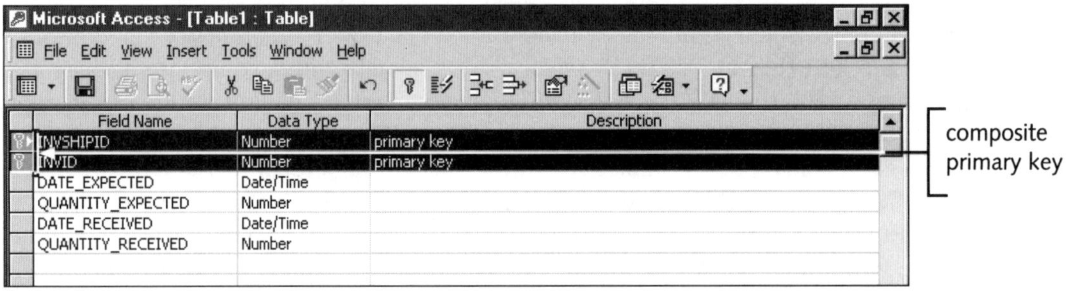

Figure 2-14   Table with composite primary key

5. Save the table as **INVENTORY_SHIPPING**, and then close the Table window.

To finish the INVENTORY_SHIPPING table, you must create the foreign key link between the INVENTORY_SHIPPING table and the INVENTORY table. You will do this next.

To create the foreign key link between INVENTORY_SHIPPING and INVENTORY:

1. Open the Relationships window, right-click, and then click **Show Table** to open the Show Table dialog box.

2. Select **INVENTORY_SHIPPING** from the table list, click **Add**, and then click **Close**. The INVENTORY_SHIPPING table is displayed in the Relationships window. Resize the table as necessary so that all of the fields are displayed.

3. Click **INVID** in the INVENTORY table, do not release the mouse pointer, drag the mouse pointer to INVID in the INVENTORY_SHIPPING table, and then release the mouse pointer so that the Edit Relationships dialog box is displayed.

4. Check the **Enforce Referential Integrity** check box, and then click **Create**. The new relationship is displayed as shown in Figure 2-15.

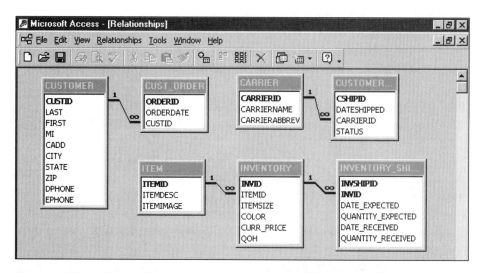

Figure 2-15   Relationship between INVENTORY and INVENTORY_SHIPPING tables

5. Close the Relationships window, and save your changes to the relationships layout.

Inserting Data

Now you are ready to begin inserting data records into the Clearwater Traders database tables. To insert data records into an Access database table, you open the database table's datasheet. Recall that a table's datasheet displays the table as a matrix, with each field displayed as a column and each record displayed as a different row. In a datasheet, you can insert data values much as you would insert data into a spreadsheet. To open a database table's datasheet, you select the database table in the Database window, and then click the Open button 📷; or, double-click the database table in the Database window.

In a datasheet, your changes are automatically saved every time you move the insertion point to a different field, and every time you close the datasheet. When you insert a record that has a field that is an AutoNumber data type, you skip inserting a value into the AutoNumber field. The next value in the AutoNumber sequence will automatically be inserted when you insert a value in another field in the record. When you insert a data value for a field that is a foreign key reference, you must be sure that you have inserted the data record where the foreign key reference is a primary key value first, or an error message will be displayed. Now you will insert the first two data records into the CUSTOMER and CUSTOMER_ORDER tables.

To insert the data records:

1. Double-click the **CUSTOMER** table in the Database window to open the CUSTOMER table's datasheet. The insertion point is currently in the CUSTID field, which has an AutoNumber data type. The word (AutoNumber) is displayed in the field to remind you that you do not need to enter a data value. Press the **Tab** key to move to the LAST data field.

2. Type **Harris**. Note that the number 1 is automatically inserted as the value for CUSTID. Press the **Tab** key to move to the FIRST data field.

3. Type the rest of the data values for customer Paula Harris, as shown in Figure 2-4, using the Tab key to move to the next field. When you finish the last field, press the **Tab** key. The insertion point moves to the CUSTID field for the next record.

4. Press the **Tab** key, type **Edwards** for the LAST field value for the second record, then press the **Tab** key again. Note that the number 2 is automatically inserted as the value for the next CUSTID.

5. Type the rest of the data values for customer Mitch Edwards, as shown in Figure 2-4. When you finish the last field, press the **Tab** key. Again, the insertion point moves to the CUSTID field for the next record.

6. Close the datasheet and display the Database window. Recall that your changes are saved automatically whenever you move the insertion point to a different field and whenever you close the datasheet.

7. Double-click **CUST_ORDER** in the table list to open the CUST_ORDER table datasheet.

8. Press the **Tab** key to move to the ORDERDATE field, type **5/29/2001** for the first ORDERDATE value, and then press the **Tab** key to move to the CUSTID field.

9. Type **1** for the value of CUSTID, and then press the **Tab** key to move to the next CUST_ORDER row.

> **TIP** After the insertion point is placed in the CUSTID field, an error message will be displayed stating that you have violated the referential integrity of the relationship if you move to another field without entering a value for CUSTID, or if you enter a value for CUSTID that does not correspond to a CUSTID value that is in the CUSTOMER table. If this error message is displayed, click OK, and then enter a CUSTID value that corresponds to a CUSTID in the CUSTOMER table.

10. Press the **Tab** key to move to the ORDERDATE field, and then enter the values for the ORDERDATE and CUSTID fields for ORDERID 2 in the CUST_ORDER table, as shown in Figure 2-4.

11. Close the CUST_ORDER datasheet.

2

Updating and Deleting Data

To update a data value, you open the database table's datasheet, edit the value you want to change, and then move the insertion point to a different record to save the change. To delete a record, you select the record in the datasheet, and then click the Delete Record button ⬚. Now you will update and delete a record in the CUST_ORDER table.

To update and delete a record:

1. Double-click the **CUST_ORDER** table in the Table list to open the CUST_ORDER datasheet.

2. Click the mouse pointer in the ORDERDATE field for ORDERID 2, change the order date to **5/31/01**, and then press the **Tab** key to move the insertion point to the next field. Note that the current row indicator changes to ⬚ to indicate that the row data have been changed.

3. Press the **Tab** key again to move the insertion point to the CUSTID field for the next data row and save the change.

4. Select the data row for ORDERID 2, click the **Delete Record** button ⬚ on the Datasheet toolbar to delete the record, and then click **Yes** to confirm the deletion.

5. Close the CUST_ORDER datasheet.

6. Close Access.

SUMMARY

❏ Early databases used a hierarchical structure, whereby data relationships between related items were created using pointers, which are links to the physical locations where data are written on a disk. Alternatively, relational databases maintain relationships using shared key fields, which are easier to manage and migrate to new storage media. Relational databases structure data in tables, where columns represent different data categories and rows contain records with the actual data values. Individual records are identified using primary keys, which are fields whose value must be unique for each record. Fields that could be used as primary keys are called candidate keys. A composite key is created when multiple fields are combined to create a primary key. A surrogate key is a field that is created solely for the purpose of serving as the primary key for a record. A link between two related records is created by copying the primary key value of one record into a field of the related record as a foreign key. When you design relational databases, you should group related items together into a single table.

❏ The Clearwater Traders database tracks information about customers, customer orders, the status of individual orders, and inventory information so that customers can find out if an item is in stock. The system also tracks incoming shipments and back orders from suppliers. The Northwoods University database tracks information about students, faculty, courses, course sections, campus locations, and student course enrollments. These databases will be used to illustrate Web-based Internet and intranet database applications throughout this book.

❑ In Access, a database consists of a series of associated database tables, queries, and user application modules (such as forms and reports) that are all stored in a single file with an .mdb extension in your computer's file system. In Access, the Database window contains an objects list that is used to get to all of the objects within a database, and the Relationships window is used to view the database tables graphically, and to create and view foreign key relationships. Tables can also be viewed in Design view, where their structure can be specified, or as datasheets, which can be used for inserting, updating, or deleting data. You can save individual tables in a database, and Access automatically saves the entire database whenever you exit the database. When you insert data using a datasheet, changes are automatically saved every time you move the mouse pointer to a new field or to a new record.

REVIEW QUESTIONS

1. When you create a database-driven Web site, should you create the Web pages first or should you create the database first?

2. How are relationships between data items created in a hierarchical database?

3. How are relationships between data items created in a relational database?

4. A _____ value cannot be null.
   a. primary key
   b. foreign key
   c. candidate key
   d. pointer

5. In a relational database, relationships among database tables are created using
   _____ .
   a. primary keys
   b. foreign keys
   c. candidate keys
   d. pointers

6. What is a surrogate key?

7. When should you create a surrogate key?

8. What is a composite key?

9. Describe how to save every table in an Access database.

10. In Access, the _____ data type is used for surrogate key fields.
    a. Number
    b. AutoNumber
    c. Text
    d. any data type can be used

11. Specify the primary key field(s), foreign key(s), and Access data type for the INVENTORY_BACKORDER database table in the Clearwater Traders database.

12. Specify the primary key field(s), foreign key(s), and Access data type for the ORDERLINE database table in the Clearwater Traders database.

13. Specify the primary key field(s), foreign key(s), and Access data type for the STUDENT table in the Northwoods University database.

14. Specify the primary key field(s), foreign key(s), and Access data type for the FACULTY table in the Northwoods University database.

15. Specify the primary key field(s), foreign key(s), and Access data type for the FRANK table in the Northwoods University database.

16. Specify the primary key field(s), foreign key(s), and Access data type for the LOCATION table in the Northwoods University database.

17. Specify the primary key field(s), foreign key(s), and Access data type for the TERM table in the Northwoods University database.

18. Specify the primary key field(s), foreign key(s), and Access data type for the COURSE table in the Northwoods University database.

19. Specify the primary key field(s), foreign key(s), and Access data type for the COURSE_SECTION table in the Northwoods University database.

20. Specify the primary key field(s), foreign key(s), and Access data type for the ENROLLMENT table in the Northwoods University database.

HANDS-ON PROJECTS

1. Start Windows Explorer, copy the clearwater.mdb database file you created in the tutorial from the Chapter2\Tutorials folder to the Chapter2\Projects folder on your Data Disk, and then rename the file Ch2Pr1.mdb.

   a. Create the INVENTORY_BACKORDER table according to the table specifications shown in Figure 2-4. Specify that BACKORDERID is a surrogate key that uses automatic numbering. Accept the default field specification properties, except as follows: Do not specify any default values for any of the fields, and label foreign keys by placing the text "foreign key" in the field description. Specify that all foreign key values are required.

   b. Specify the BACKORDERID field as the table's primary key.

   c. Create a foreign key link to the INVENTORY_SHIPPING table for the INVSHIPID and INVID fields, and enforce referential integrity. (*Hint*: Since the foreign key link is the combination of the INVSHIPID and INVID fields in the INVENTORY_SHIPPING table, you will need to create links to both fields in one operation by drawing the link, and then specifying the individual field associations by selecting the field names in the Edit Relationships dialog box.)

   d. Create the ORDERLINE table according to the table specifications shown in Figure 2-4. Accept the default field specification properties, except as follows: Do not specify any default values for any of the fields, and label primary keys and foreign keys by placing the appropriate text in the field description. If a field is both a primary key and a foreign key, use "primary key/foreign key" as the field description. Use the Currency data type for the ORDER_PRICE field. Use the Memo data type for the COMMENT field, and allow zero-length strings. Specify that all foreign key values are required.

e. Specify the ORDERID and INVID fields as a composite primary key for the ORDERLINE table.

f. Create a foreign key link from the ORDERLINE table to the CUST_ORDER table for the ORDERID field, and enforce referential integrity.

g. Create a foreign key link from the ORDERLINE table to the INVENTORY table for the INVID field, and enforce referential integrity.

h. Arrange the tables in the Relationships window so that all relationships are clearly visible.

i. Close the Ch2Pr1.mdb database.

2. If necessary, start Windows Explorer, select the Ch2Pr1.mdb database file from the Chapter2\Projects folder on your Data Disk, right-click, click Copy, right-click again, and click Paste to create a copy of Ch2Pr1.mdb. Rename the copied file Ch2Pr2.mdb. Open Ch2Pr2.mdb in Access, and insert the first two records into each database table according to the sample data displayed in Figure 2-4. (*Hint:* You will need to insert all records that are referenced as foreign keys first, so you might have to insert additional records into some tables. Do not worry if some of your surrogate key (AutoNumber) fields do not exactly match the values that are shown in Figure 2-4, but make sure that all of the foreign key references are correct.)

3. In this project, you will create the FRANK and LOCATION tables in the Northwoods University database according to the table structures shown in Figure 2-5. Create a new database named Ch2Pr3.mdb, and save it in the Chapter2\Projects folder on your Data Disk. Accept the default properties for all text fields, but change the Allow Zero Length property to Yes for all text fields, and do not specify a default data value for any fields. Label primary keys and foreign keys by placing the appropriate text in the field description. If a field is both a primary key and a foreign key, use "primary key/foreign key" as the field description.

a. Create the LOCATION table. Use the AutoNumber data type for the LOCID field, the Text data type for the BLDG_CODE and ROOM fields, and the Number data type for the CAPACITY field. Specify that LOCID is the table's primary key.

b. Create the FRANK table. Use the Text data type for the FRANK and FRANKDESC fields. Specify that FRANK is the table's primary key.

c. Create the FACULTY table. Use the AutoNumber data type for the FID field, and the Text data type for the other table fields except LOCID and FPIN, which will be assigned the Number data type. Specify that FID is the table's primary key, and create foreign key links to the LOCATION and FRANK tables.

d. Create the STUDENT table. Use the AutoNumber data type for the SID field, and the Text data type for the SLNAME, SFNAME, SMI, SADD, SCITY, SSTATE, SZIP, SPHONE, and SCLASS fields. Use the Date/Time data type for the SDOB field, and the Number data type for the SPIN and FID fields. Specify that SID is the table's primary key, and create a foreign key link to the FACULTY table.

e. Arrange the tables in the Relationships window so that all relationships are clearly visible.

2

4. In this project, you will add the TERM, COURSE, COURSE_SECTION, and ENROLLMENT tables to the Ch2Pr3.mdb database that you created in Hands-on Project 3. Use the table structures shown in Figure 2-5. Use Windows Explorer to copy the Ch2Pr3.mdb file to a new file in the Chapter2\Projects folder on your Data Disk, rename the new file Ch2Pr4.mdb, and then open Ch2Pr4.mdb in Access. Accept the default properties for all text fields, but change the Allow Zero Length property to Yes for all text fields, and do not specify a default data value for any field. Label primary keys and foreign keys by placing the appropriate text in the field description. If a field is both a primary key and a foreign key, use "primary key/foreign key" as the field description.

   a. Create the TERM table. Use the AutoNumber data type for the TERMID field, and the Text data type for the TDESC and STATUS fields. Specify that TERMID is the table's primary key.

   b. Create the COURSE table. Use the AutoNumber data type for the CID field, the Text data type for the CALLID and CNAME fields, and the Number data type for the CCREDIT field. Specify the CID field as the table's primary key.

   c. Create the COURSE_SECTION table. Use the AutoNumber data type for the CSECID field, and the Number data type for the CID, TERMID, SECNUM, FID, LOCID, MAXENRL, and CURRENRL fields. Use the Text data type for the DAY field, and the Date/Time data type for the TIME field. Specify that CSECID is the table's primary key, and create foreign key links to the COURSE, TERM, FACULTY, and LOCATION tables.

   d. Create the ENROLLMENT table. Use the Number data type for the SID and CSECID fields, and use the Text data type for the GRADE field. Specify that the table's primary key is a composite key consisting of CSECID and SID. Create foreign key links to the COURSE_SEC and STUDENT tables. Create a data validation rule that restricts the values of the GRADE field to A, B, C, D, or F.

   e. Arrange the tables in the Relationships window so that all relationships are clearly visible.

5. If necessary, start Windows Explorer, and copy the Ch2Pr3.mdb database file that you created in a previous project to a new file named Ch2Pr5.mdb. Open Ch2Pr5.mdb in Access, and insert the first two records into the STUDENT, FACULTY, FRANK, and LOCATION tables according to the sample data displayed in Figure 2-5. (*Hint:* You will need to insert all records that are referenced as foreign keys first, so you might have to insert additional records into some tables. Do not worry if some of your surrogate key (AutoNumber) fields do not exactly match the values that are shown in Figure 2-5, but make sure that all of the foreign key references are correct.)

6. If necessary, start Windows Explorer, and copy the Ch2Pr4.mdb database file you created in a previous project to a new file named Ch2Pr6.mdb. Then, insert the first two records into the TERM, COURSE, COURSE_SECTION, and ENROLLMENT tables according to the sample data displayed in Figure 2-5. (*Hint:* You will need to insert all records that are referenced as foreign keys first, so you might have to insert additional records into other tables. Do not worry if some of your surrogate key (AutoNumber) fields do not exactly match the values that are shown in Figure 2-5, but make sure that all of the foreign key references are correct.)

CASE PROJECTS

1. The Ashland Valley Soccer League would like to create a Web-based application to allow players and coaches to access information about game schedules online. Each game is identified by its date and start time, the two teams that are playing, the field ID, and the game status (pending, played, cancelled). Each team is identified by a team ID and team name (such as "The Force" or "Tornadoes"). Each field is identified by a field ID, description, and address.
   a. Design the relational database tables to represent this database.
   b. Create a subfolder named Ashland in the Chapter2 folder on your Data Disk.
   c. Create the database tables and foreign key relationships in Microsoft Access, and save the file as Ch2Case1.mdb in the Chapter2\Ashland folder on your Data Disk. Create a surrogate key for each table, using the AutoNumber data type.
   d. Insert five records into each database table.

2. Wayne's Auto World is a new car dealership that wants to create a Web-based system to allow customers to select, and configure, and price out vehicles. A car is identified by its make (such as "Chevrolet" and "Toyota") and model (such as "Camaro" or "Lumina"). Each model has an associated model year (such as "2002"). Each model has multiple trim lines (such as "Base" and "Z28"). The trim line determines the model's base price. Each trim line has associated options (such as "Power Package" or "All-Wheel Drive"), and each option has an associated cost that is added to the time line's base price to determine the cost of the vehicle.
   a. Design the relational database tables to represent this database.
   b. Create a subfolder named Waynes in the Chapter2 folder on your Data Disk.
   c. Create the database tables and foreign key relationships in Microsoft Access, and save the file as Ch2Case2.mdb in the Chapter2\Waynes folder on your Data Disk. Create a surrogate key for each table, using the AutoNumber data type.
   d. Insert five records into each database table.

3. Sun-Ray Video wants to create a Web-based system to allow customers to select video recordings or game cartridges online, check out items, and then specify whether they will pick up the item or have it delivered. The database needs to track each video in terms of its format (VCR, DVD, Playstation, etc.), and its associated rental cost. Each video has an associated Category (New Release, Action, Horror, Comedy, Sci-Fi, Children's, Games). When a customer selects a video, rental information must be recorded, including the date rented, date due, date returned, delivery status (delivered or pickup), rental cost, and late fee. (A $1 delivery charge is added for each item that is delivered. A late fee of $2 per day is charged for each late item.) The database also needs to track customer information, including customer last and first name, address, city, state, ZIP code, telephone number, user name, and password.
   a. Design the relational database tables to represent this database. Create lookup tables for the format and category information.
   b. Create a subfolder named Sunray in the Chapter2 folder on your Data Disk.
   c. Create the database tables and foreign key relationships in Microsoft Access, and save the file as Ch2Case3.mdb in the Chapter2\Sunray folder on your Data Disk. Create a surrogate key for each table, using the AutoNumber data type.
   d. Insert five records into each database table.

3

STRUCTURED QUERY LANGUAGE (SQL)

In this chapter, you will:

♦ Learn how to create SQL queries for viewing and searching for database records in a single table

♦ Practice performing arithmetic and group function operations on retrieved data

♦ Learn how to create SQL queries that join multiple tables

♦ Become familiar with creating a UNION query to combine the results of two unrelated queries

♦ Learn how to insert, update, and delete database records using SQL commands

---

Structured Query Language (SQL) is the standard query language of relational databases. When you create a database-driven Web site, it is desirable to use SQL as the query language to communicate between the Web pages and the database, because the queries that retrieve the database data will be the same regardless of whether you use Access, Oracle, SQL Server, or any other database platform. Using SQL will make it easier to migrate your Web page applications to other database platforms if you decide to change to a different platform later. The structure and syntax of SQL is the same across most database management systems, although different systems often recognize slightly different commands.

Microsoft Access can be separated into two major components: the Access application environment and the Jet database engine. The **Access application environment** is the user interface used to create tables, manage data, and create and manage database objects such as queries, forms, and reports created in Access. The **Jet database engine** is the underlying database management system that manages the Access database tables and processes the SQL commands for inserting, updating, deleting, and viewing data. These components can be used independently of one another: you could use the Access application environment to create queries, forms, and reports that insert, retrieve, and modify data in an Oracle or SQL Server DBMS; similarly, you can create applications in other environments that interact with the Jet database engine. To do this, you must use special software programs called **Open Database Connectivity (ODBC) drivers**. ODBC is a standard database communication protocol that enables a database application to interact with different DBMSs. Most DBMSs have an ODBC-compliant driver that allows database applications created in external environments to access the data in the database. Figure 3-1 shows how a database application can interact with a variety of different DBMSs through their associated ODBC drivers. The database application could be created in Access, or in an Oracle application development tool. The database application could also be created in a general application development language such as Visual Basic. It could also be a Web-based application.

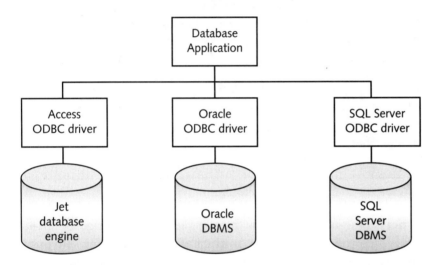

Figure 3-1   Relationships among a database application, ODBC drivers, and underlying DBMSs

In this chapter, you will use the Access application environment to create SQL queries for viewing, inserting, updating, and deleting database records. Beginning in Chapter 8, you will learn how to create database applications using Web pages that submit SQL commands directly to the Jet database engine.

USING SQL TO CREATE DATABASE QUERIES

A **query** is a question that can be answered by data stored in a database, such as "How old is student Sarah Miller?" or "How many rectangular Goose Down Sleeping Bags have been back-ordered?" Using SQL, you can retrieve data from a single database table, or you can use foreign key links to join multiple database tables to retrieve related data from multiple tables. You can specify search conditions to retrieve selected records and perform mathematical functions on retrieved data, such as calculating a person's age by finding the difference between his or her birth date and the current date. You can also group retrieved records and perform group functions such as finding the sum or average of a set of retrieved records.

Writing Queries to Retrieve All Data Rows from a Single Table

The basic format of a SQL query that retrieves all of the data rows from a single table is:

```
SELECT [column1, column2, ...]
FROM [tablename];
```

In this book, when the general format of a programming command is given, the data values that you must insert into the command are shown in square brackets ([ ]).

The SELECT clause lists the columns that you want to display in your query, with each column name separated from the next by a comma. The FROM clause lists the name of the database table involved in the query. The query is usually terminated with a semicolon (;). Now you will create a series of queries that retrieve data from the Northwoods University database. These queries will use a fully populated Northwoods University database file named northwoods.mdb that is stored in the Chapter3 folder on your Data Disk. Now you will start Access, and open northwoods.mdb.

To open the database:

1. Start Access, and open **northwoods.mdb** from the Chapter3 folder on your Data Disk. (Office 97 users will open **northwoods97.mdb**.) If necessary, click Tables on the Objects bar to display the Northwoods University database tables in the Objects list.

When you create a query in Access, you first create a new Query object in the Database window, and then work with the Query object in the Query window. In the Access application environment, queries are usually created using a technique called **query by example (QBE)**. The Access QBE query environment provides pull-down lists to allow the user to specify display fields and search conditions. After the QBE query is created, the Access application environment generates the associated SQL query, and submits it to the Jet database engine for processing. In this book, you will type the text of the SQL query directly in the Access application environment rather than specify the query using QBE, because the SQL syntax generated by QBE queries sometimes uses commands that are specific to the Jet database engine and are not compatible with other relational databases. Whenever possible, the SQL commands that you will learn in this book will be compatible with both the Jet database engine and with most other relational databases. Commands that are unique for the SQL syntax used by the Jet database engine, called **Jet SQL**, will be noted as such.

Now you will create a query to retrieve the first name, middle initial, and last name for every record in the STUDENT table of the Northwoods University database.

If you are using a floppy disk for your Data Disk files, you will need two floppy disks to store the tutorial exercises in this chapter. On the first floppy disk, create a folder named Chapter3\Clearwater and save all your Clearwater files in this folder. On the second disk, create a folder named Chapter3\Northwoods and save all your Northwoods files in this folder.

To create the query:

1. In the Database window, if necessary, click the **Queries** object on the Objects bar. Since the database does not contain any saved queries, the Objects list is blank.

2. Click the **New** button on the Database window toolbar, make sure that Design View is selected, and then click **OK**. The Show Table dialog box is displayed. The Show Table dialog box allows you to select the database tables that will be used in the query if you are creating the query using QBE. Since you will enter the SQL query directly, you will not select any tables, so click **Close**. The Query window is displayed in Design View.

3. Maximize the Query window.

The Query window has three views: Design View, which is used to create QBE queries; SQL View, which is used to view the SQL text associated with QBE queries and to enter SQL queries directly; and Datasheet View, which is used to view query results. QBE queries are always converted to SQL queries, and can be displayed in SQL View. When you create a new query, the Query window is automatically opened in Design View. Now you will display the Query window in SQL View, and enter the SQL query.

To display the window in SQL View and enter the SQL query:

1. Click the **SQL** button **SQL** on the Query window toolbar so that the Query window is displayed in SQL View. The term SELECT; is displayed. This serves as a template for a new SQL query.

> TIP   Another way to display SQL View in the Query window is to click View on the menu bar, and then click SQL View.

2. Click the mouse pointer after the T in SELECT, and then type the SQL query shown in Figure 3-2.

Microsoft Access - [Query1 : Select Query]

File Edit View Insert Query Tools Window Help

```
SELECT sfname, smi, slname
FROM student;
```
— type this query

Figure 3-2   SQL query to select all rows from the STUDENT table

> TIP   In this book, reserved words in SQL queries (such as SELECT and FROM) are always typed in uppercase letters, and other values are typed in lowercase letters to emphasize the reserved words and make the queries easier to understand and debug.

3. Click the **Run** button ⏴ on the Query window toolbar to submit the SQL query to the Jet database engine. The query result is displayed in Datasheet View, as shown in Figure 3-3. Note that the column names appear as column headings. Only the columns included in the SELECT statement are displayed, and the columns appear in the order in which they are listed in the SQL command.

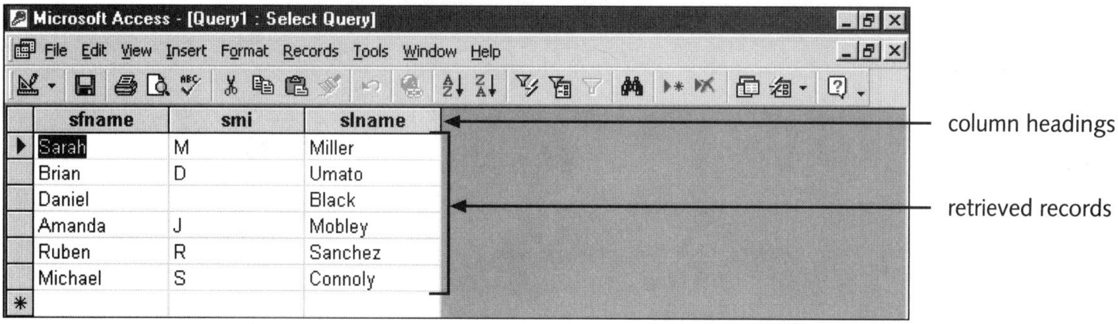

3

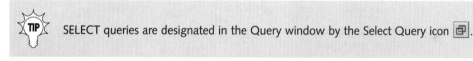

Figure 3-3 Query result in Datasheet View

4. Click the **Close** button ✖ to close the Query window, click **Yes** when you are asked if you want to save your query, type **StudentNames** for the query name, and then click **OK**. The StudentNames query is displayed in the objects list in the Database window.

💡 **TIP** SELECT queries are designated in the Query window by the Select Query icon 📧.

If you want to retrieve all of the columns in a table, you can use an asterisk (*) as a wildcard character in the SELECT statement, instead of typing every column name. Now you will create a query to retrieve all of the fields and all of the records from the LOCATION table.

To create a query to retrieve all of the fields and records from a table:

1. In the Database window, make sure that Queries is selected in the Objects bar, click the **New** button 📧 to create a new query in Design View, close the Show Table dialog box, and then display the Query window in SQL View.

2. Type the following query:

```
SELECT *
FROM location;
```

3. Click the **Run** button ⏴ to run the query and display the query result, as shown in Figure 3-4.

Microsoft Access - [Query1 : Select Query]

LOCID	BLDG_CODE	ROOM	CAPACITY
1	CR	101	150
2	CR	202	40
3	CR	103	35
4	CR	105	35
5	BUS	105	42
6	BUS	404	35
7	BUS	421	35
8	BUS	211	55
9	BUS	424	1
10	BUS	402	1
11	BUS	433	1
12	LIB	217	2
13	LIB	222	1
(AutoNumber)			

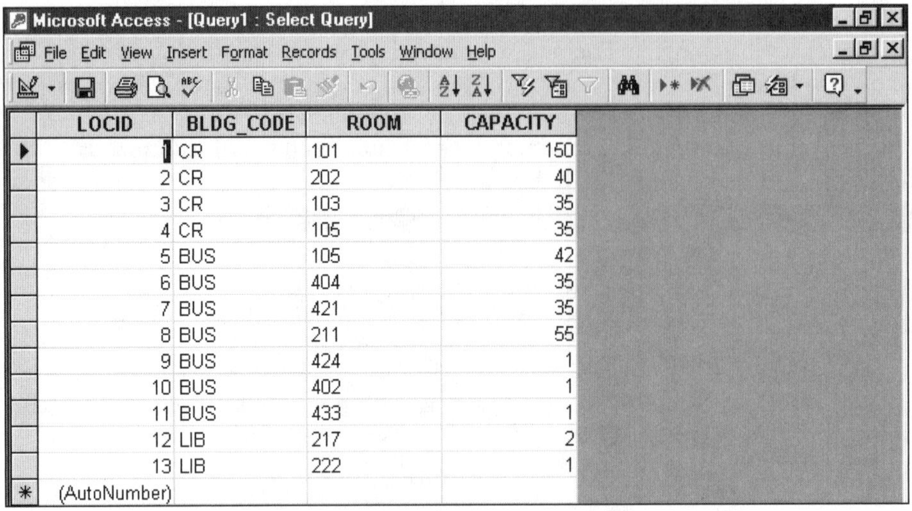

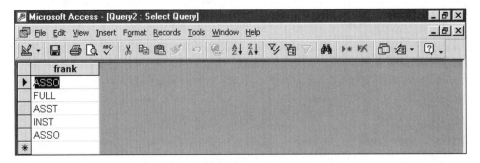

Figure 3-4 Query result showing all LOCATION fields and rows

4. Close the Query window, and save the query as **AllLocations**.

Sometimes a query will retrieve duplicate rows. For example, suppose you want to see the different ranks for faculty members.

To retrieve duplicate rows:

1. Create a new query using the following SQL command:

```
SELECT frank
FROM faculty;
```

2. Run the query. Your output should look like Figure 3-5, with the ASSO value displayed twice: once for faculty member Kim Cox, and a second time for faculty member Phillip Brown.

Microsoft Access - [Query2 : Select Query]

frank
ASSO
FULL
ASST
INST
ASSO

Figure 3-5 Query result with duplicate rows

To suppress duplicate values, you can use the DISTINCT qualifier in the SELECT clause immediately before the name of the field in which you want to suppress duplicates. This tells

SQL to display each value only once. Now you will switch back to SQL View, and edit the query so that it uses the DISTINCT qualifier.

To edit the query:

1. Click the drop-down list arrow beside the **View** button 🔲 on the Query window toolbar, and then click **SQL View** to display the SQL query text.

2. Edit the query as follows:

```
SELECT DISTINCT frank
FROM faculty;
```

3. Run the query. The query result should be displayed as shown in Figure 3-6, with the duplicate values suppressed.

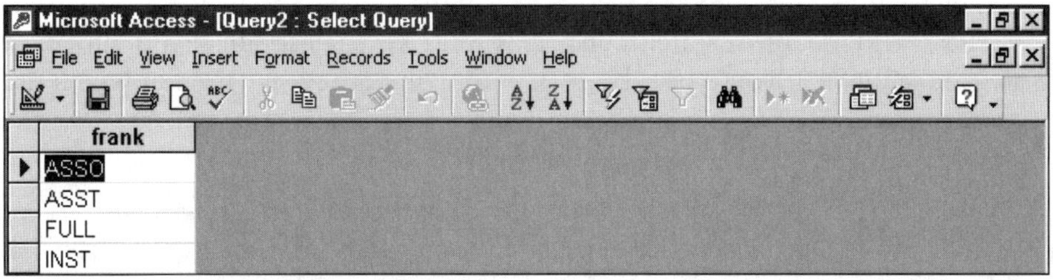

Figure 3-6   Query result with duplicate values suppressed

4. Close the Query window, and save the query as **FacultyRanks**.

Writing Queries That Retrieve Specific Records

Often you will need to create queries that retrieve specific data rows from a table. To do this, you must add a search condition to the query, using the following general format:

```
SELECT [column1, column2, …]
FROM [tablename]
WHERE [search condition];
```

The general format of a search condition is:

```
WHERE [expression] [comparison operator] [expression]
```

Every search condition must be able to be evaluated as either TRUE or FALSE. Expressions usually are field names (such as SCLASS) or constant data values (such as "SR"). Table 3-1 lists some common comparison operators that are used in SQL expressions.

Table 3-1   Common search condition comparison operators

Operator	Description
=	Equal to
>	Greater than
<	Less than
>=	Greater than or equal to
<=	Less than or equal to
<>	Not equal to

For example, the condition that finds all locations with a capacity greater than or equal to 50 is `capacity >= 50`. Comparison operators also can compare Text data type values. For example, the expression that finds student records where the SCLASS value is equal to SR is `sclass = 'SR'`. Text values in search conditions must be enclosed in single quotation marks and are case sensitive. If you type sclass = 'sr', you will not retrieve rows in which the sclass value is SR.

 TIP   In Jet SQL, text values in search conditions can be enclosed either in single or double quotation marks. The standard SQL notation for most databases uses single quotation marks, so in this book, single quotation marks will be used to enclose text strings.

Next, you will use a search condition to retrieve specific records in the FACULTY table. You will retrieve the first name, middle initial, last name, and rank for every faculty member who has the rank ASSO.

To use a search condition in a SQL command:

1. Create a new query using the following SQL command:

```
SELECT ffname, fmi, flname, frank
FROM faculty
WHERE frank = 'ASSO';
```

2. Run the query. The output for the selected rows is shown in Figure 3-7.

```
Microsoft Access - [Query1 : Select Query]                          _ 8 X
File  Edit  View  Insert  Format  Records  Tools  Window  Help        _ 8 X
```

ffname	fmi	flname	frank
Kim	J	Cox	ASSO
Phillip	E	Brown	ASSO

Figure 3-7   Result of query with search condition

3. Close the Query window, and save the query as **AssoFaculty**.

You can combine multiple search conditions using the AND and OR logical operators. When you use the **AND operator** to connect two search conditions, both conditions must be true for the row to appear in the query outputs. If no data rows exist that match both conditions, then no data are listed. When you use the **OR operator** to connect two search conditions, only one of the conditions must be true for the row to appear in the query outputs. Now you will create a query that returns all of the rooms in the BUS building that have a capacity greater than or equal to 40. The search conditions will be `bldg_code = 'BUS'` and `capacity >= 40`. To get the desired result, both search conditions must be true, so you will use the AND operator to join the two search conditions.

To use the AND operator in a search condition:

1. Create a new query using the following SQL command:

```
SELECT room
FROM location
WHERE bldg_code = 'BUS'
AND capacity >= 40;
```

2. Run the query. The output for the selected rows is shown in Figure 3-8.

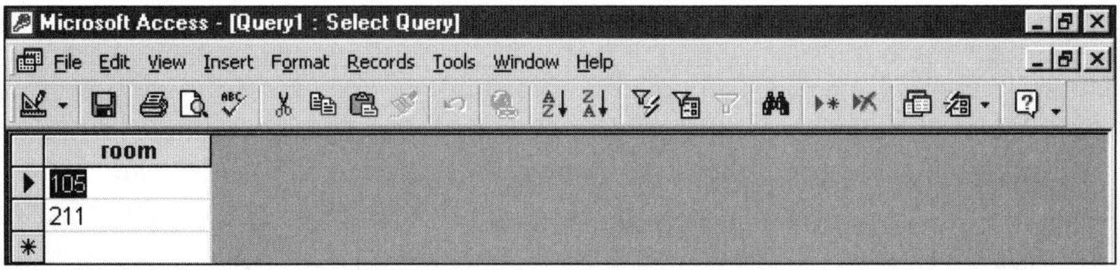

Figure 3-8   Output for query with multiple search conditions

3. Close the Query window, and save the query as **BusCapacity>=40**.

Now you will create a query using the OR operator that returns the first and last names of all students in the STUDENT table who are either seniors, or who were born before January 1, 1982. Recall that when the OR operator is used to connect two search conditions, a row is returned if *either* the first or second condition is true. If neither condition is true, no data are returned.

To use the OR operator in a search condition:

1. Create a new query using the following SQL command:

```
SELECT sfname, slname, sdob, sclass
FROM student
WHERE sclass = 'SR'
OR sdob < #1/1/1982#;
```

TIP To use a date value in a search condition in Jet SQL, you must enclose the date string in pound signs (#). For example, the date 11/20/2001 would be written #11/20/2001#.

2. Run the query. The query output, shown in Figure 3-9, returns the records for students Sarah Miller and Brian Umato, who are both seniors, as well as for Daniel Black, who is a junior, but was born before January 1, 1982.

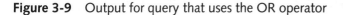

sfname	slname	sdob	sclass
Sarah	Miller	7/14/80	SR
Brian	Umato	8/12/80	SR
Daniel	Black	10/10/81	JR

Figure 3-9   Output for query that uses the OR operator

3. Close the Query window, and save the query as **OrQuery**.

You can combine the AND and OR operators in a single query. This is a very powerful operation, but it can be tricky to use. By default, SQL evaluates AND conditions first, and then SQL evaluates the result against the OR condition. You can force an OR condition to be evaluated before an AND condition by placing the OR expression in parentheses. To eliminate ordering problems, you should always place in parentheses the operation you want to have evaluated first. Now you will create a query that returns the building code, room number, and capacity of every room in either the BUS or CR building that has a capacity greater than 35. This query involves an OR operation (either BUS or CR) and an AND condition (AND capacity > 35). You will write the query with parentheses around the OR part of the search condition, so that the OR condition is evaluated first. This ensures that all rooms in either the BUS or CR buildings will be returned. The result will be evaluated against the AND condition, and only the rooms with capacity greater than 35 in either building will be returned in the final query result.

To combine the AND and OR operators in a single query:

1. Create a new query using the following SQL command:

```
SELECT bldg_code, room, capacity
FROM location
WHERE (bldg_code = 'BUS' OR bldg_code = 'CR')
AND capacity > 35;
```

2. Run the query. The query output, shown in Figure 3-10, shows the records for the rooms in either building that have a capacity greater than 35.

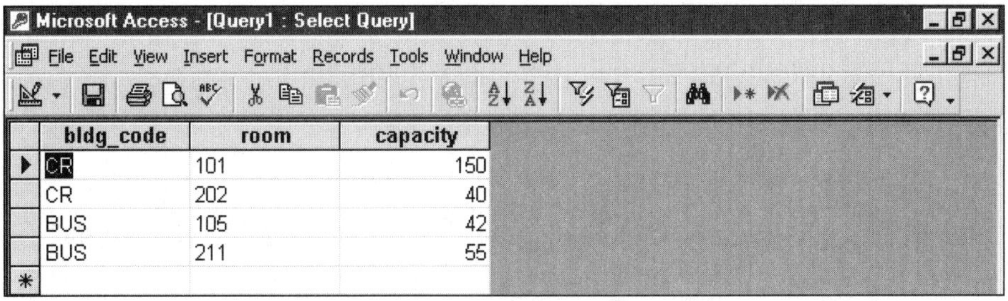

Figure 3-10 Output for query that combines the AND and OR operators

3. Close the Query window, and save the query as **AndOrQuery**.

Sometimes you need to create a query to return records where the value of a particular field is null. To do this, you use the following general format for the search condition: WHERE [field name] IS NULL. Similarly, to return records where the value of a particular field is not null, you use the format WHERE [field name] IS NOT NULL. Next, you will create a query to find all records in the ENROLLMENT table where the grade field has not been assigned and is currently null.

To create a query using the IS NULL search condition:

1. Create a new query using the following SQL command:

```
SELECT *
FROM enrollment
WHERE grade IS NULL;
```

2. Run the query. The query results are shown in Figure 3-11.

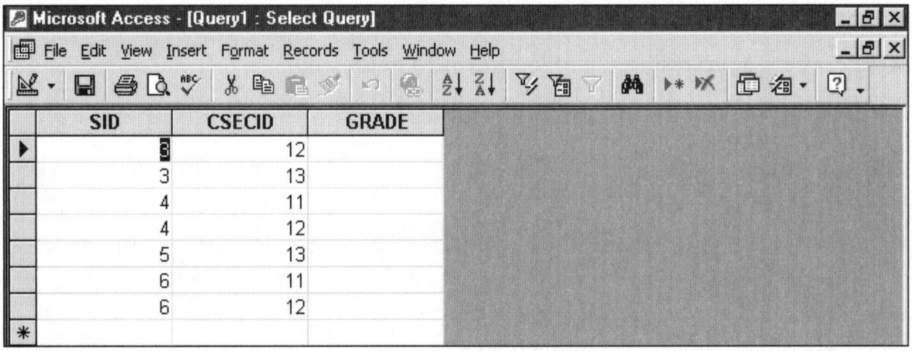

Figure 3-11 Output for query that searches for NULL values

3. Close the Query window, and save the query as **NullQuery**.

Next, you will create a query to find all records in the ENROLLMENT table where the grade field has been assigned.

To create a query using an IS NOT NULL search condition:

1. Create a new query using the following SQL command:

```
SELECT *
FROM enrollment
WHERE grade IS NOT NULL;
```

2. Run the query. The query results are displayed for all of the ENROLLMENT records where the GRADE field has a data value.

3. Close the Query window, and save the query as **NotNullQuery**.

Sorting Query Results

The query results you have seen so far have not displayed data in any particular order. You can sort query output by adding the ORDER BY clause to the end of the SELECT statement, and specifying the **sort key**, which is the column SQL will use as a basis for ordering the data. The general format for the ORDER BY clause is `ORDER BY [column name]`. By default, the data records are sorted in ascending order. If the sort key is a Number data field, records are sorted in numerical ascending order. If the sort key is a Text field, records are sorted in alphabetical order, and if the sort key is a Date/Time field, records are sorted chronologically from oldest to most recent. To explicitly specify that the records are to be sorted in ascending order, insert the ASC command at the end of the ORDER BY clause. To sort the numerical records in descending order, insert the DESC command at the end of the ORDER BY clause. Similarly, use the DESC command to sort Text records in reverse alphabetical order, and Date/Time fields from newest to oldest. Now you will create a query to retrieve all of the records from the LOCATION table where the room capacity is greater than or equal to 40, sorted in order of increasing capacity.

To use the ORDER BY clause to sort data:

1. Create a new query using the following SQL command:

```
SELECT bldg_code, room, capacity
FROM location
WHERE capacity >= 40
ORDER BY capacity;
```

2. Run the query. The query results are displayed, sorted by ascending room capacity, as shown in Figure 3-12.

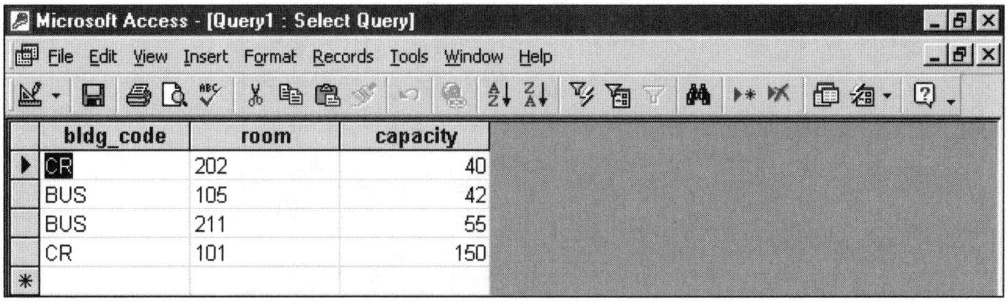

Microsoft Access - [Query1 : Select Query]

File   Edit   View   Insert   Format   Records   Tools   Window   Help

bldg_code	room	capacity
CR	202	40
BUS	105	42
BUS	211	55
CR	101	150

Figure 3-12   Output for query using the ORDER BY clause

3. Switch to SQL View in the Query window, and add the ASC command to the ORDER BY clause, using the following code:

```
ORDER BY capacity ASC;
```

4. Run the query. Note that the query results are the same as in Figure 3-12, since ASC (ascending) is the default sort order.

5. Switch to SQL View in the Query window, and change the ASC command to DESC in the ORDER BY clause, using the following code:

```
ORDER BY capacity DESC;
```

6. Run the query. The query results are now displayed sorted by descending room capacity.

7. Close the Query window, and save the query as **OrderQuery**.

You also can specify multiple sort keys to sort query outputs on the basis of multiple columns. You must specify which column gets sorted first, second, and so on. Now you will modify OrderQuery so that it lists all building codes, rooms, and capacities, sorted first by building code, and then by room number.

To modify the query to sort the data by multiple columns:

1. In the Database window, select **OrderQuery** in the Object list, if necessary, and then click the **Design** button to open the query in the Query window.

> TIP   Sometimes when you reopen an existing query in Microsoft Access, you will find that Access has inserted square brackets ([ ]) around the field names. These square brackets are not required unless field names contain blank spaces, so you can ignore them.

2. Modify the ORDER BY clause using the following code:

```
ORDER BY bldg_code, capacity;
```

3. Run the query. The query results are now displayed sorted first by building code, and then by room capacity, as shown in Figure 3-13.

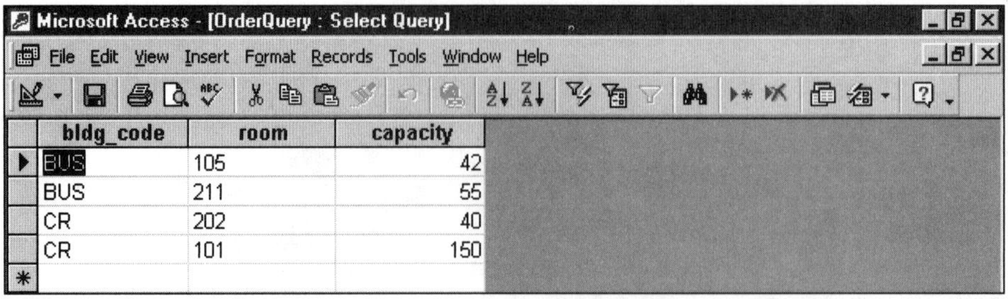

Figure 3-13 Query output sorted by multiple columns

    4. Close the Query window, and save the changes.

PERFORMING CALCULATIONS IN QUERIES

You can perform basic mathematical calculations on retrieved data. Table 3-2 lists the mathematical operations and their associated SQL operators.

Table 3-2 SQL mathematical operators

SQL Operator	Operation
+	Addition
-	Subtraction
*	Multiplication
/	Division

The general format for creating a calculated field is as follows: `[data field]` `[operator][data field] AS [alias]`. The `AS [alias]` part of the expression is optional. An **alias** is a name that serves as the column heading and is assigned to a calculated column to describe the column data. An alias must follow the same naming rules as other database columns: it must be 1 to 64 characters long, and be composed of characters, numbers, and some special characters. If you do not specify an alias for a calculated column, the DBMS will create a system-generated column name.

In the next query, you will display the course section ID, maximum enrollment, current enrollment, and the difference between the maximum enrollment and the current enrollment for each course section. First you will omit assigning the alias and view the system-generated column name. Then you will modify the query and assign an alias to the calculated column.

To create a query that calculates the difference between two data values:

    1. Create a new query using the following SQL command:

```
SELECT csecid, maxenrl, currenrl, maxenrl — currenrl
FROM course_section;
```

2. Run the query. The query results show the difference between maximum enroll-ment and current enrollment for each course section. Note the system-assigned column name, as shown in Figure 3-14. (The name of your column might be different from the one shown in the figure.)

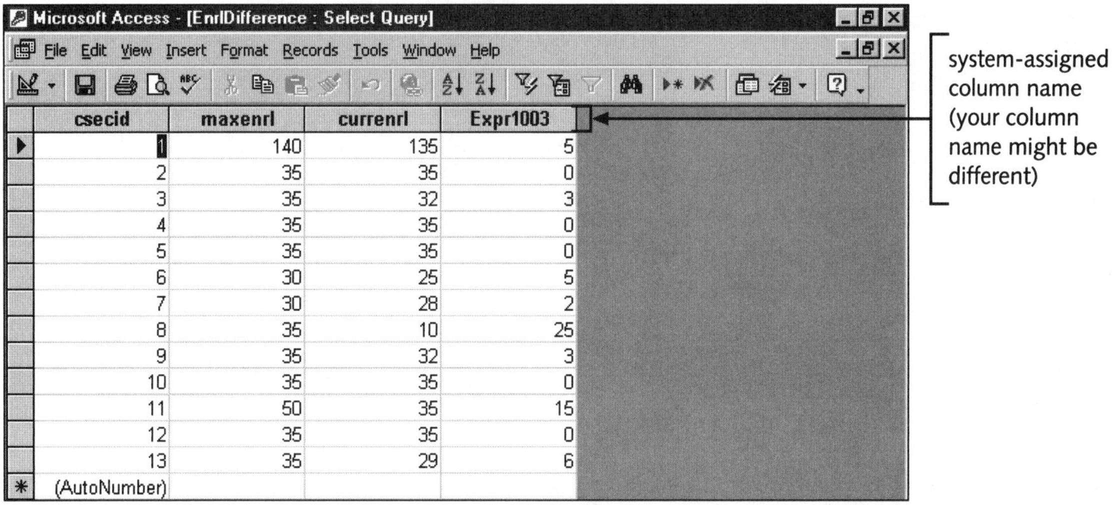

csecid	maxenrl	currenrl	Expr1003
1	140	135	5
2	35	35	0
3	35	32	3
4	35	35	0
5	35	35	0
6	30	25	5
7	30	28	2
8	35	10	25
9	35	32	3
10	35	35	0
11	50	35	15
12	35	35	0
13	35	29	6
(AutoNumber)			

system-assigned column name (your column name might be different)

Figure 3-14   Query output with calculated column values and system-assigned column name

3. Display the Query window in SQL View, and use the following AS command to modify the SELECT command to assign the column alias EmptySeats to the cal-culated column:

```
SELECT csecid, maxenrl, currenrl, maxenrl – currenrl AS
EmptySeats
FROM course_section;
```

4. Run the query. The column heading for the calculated column is now displayed as EmptySeats.

5. Close the Query window, and save the query as **EnrlDifference**.

Sometimes you need to combine multiple mathematical operations in a single query. For example, suppose you need to create a query that displays the first and last name of every stu-dent in the STUDENT table, along with the student's age. You can calculate the student's age by finding the difference between the current date and the student's date of birth. In Jet SQL, the **Date()** function returns the current system date. Now you will create a query that uses the Date() function to calculate ages based on birth dates.

To create a query to calculate student ages:

1. Create a new query using the following SQL command:

```
SELECT slname, sfname, Date() – sdob AS Age
FROM student;
```

2. Run the query. The query results are displayed as shown in Figure 3-15.

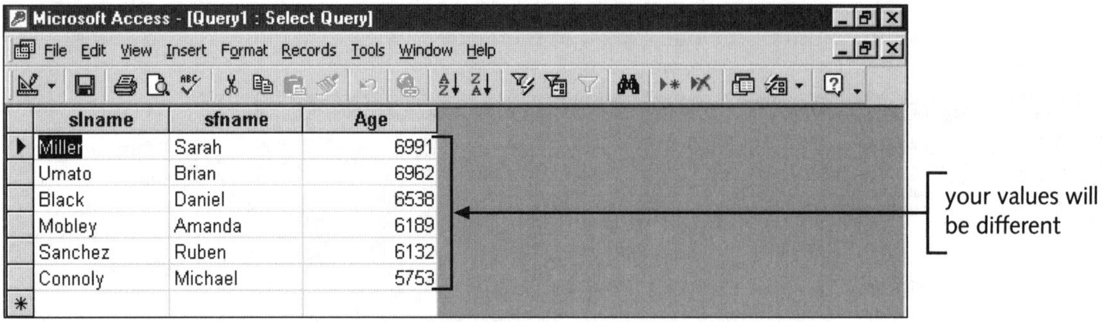

Figure showing Microsoft Access Query window:

slname	sfname	Age
Miller	Sarah	6991
Umato	Brian	6962
Black	Daniel	6538
Mobley	Amanda	6189
Sanchez	Ruben	6132
Connoly	Michael	5753

your values will be different

Figure 3-15   Output of query to calculate student ages

> **TIP**   Your query output might look different from Figure 3-15, depending on your current system date.

The query output doesn't look quite right, because it lists the calculated ages in days rather than in years. One solution to this problem is to divide this value by the number of days in a year, which is approximately 365.25 (including leap years). To display the query output in years, you will use the following expression: `Date() — sdob/365.25`. You can do this in SQL by combining multiple arithmetic operations in a single query.

SQL has the following **order of precedence**, which determines the order in which mathematical operators are evaluated within an expression: (1) denoting values as positive or negative (such as −3 or +16), (2) evaluating multiplication or division operations, and (3) evaluating addition and subtraction operations. To change the default order of precedence, you can place an expression within parentheses to force it to be evaluated first. By default, the expression in the previous query is evaluated as `Date()-(SDOB/365.25)` because the division operation is evaluated before the subtraction operation. However, your intent is to calculate the difference between the current date and the student's date of birth first, and then divide that result by 365.25. You can use parentheses to indicate that the subtraction operation should be evaluated first. Now you will modify your query to display the student age in years.

To modify the query to display the student age in years:

1. In the Query window, switch to SQL View, and then modify the SELECT command as follows:

```
SELECT slname, sfname, (Date()-sdob)/365.25 AS Age
FROM student;
```

2. Run the query. The query results (Figure 3-16) now show the student ages in years.

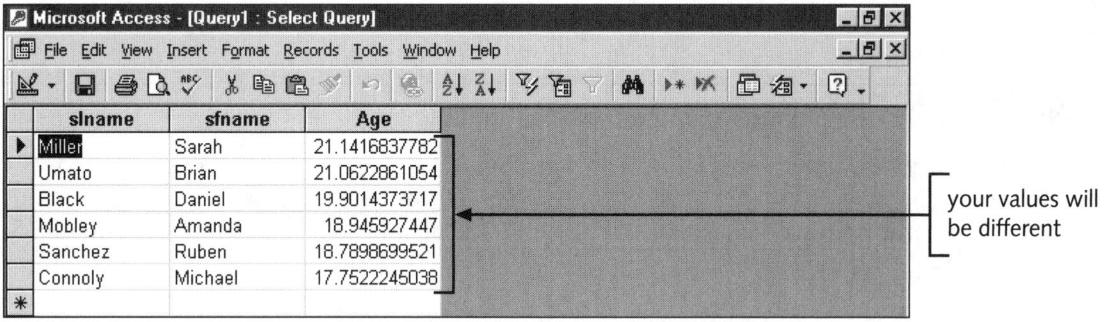

Figure 3-16   Student ages displayed in years

In Figure 3-16, each student's age is shown in years, with a fraction that represents the time since the student's last birthday. To remove this fraction, you will need to use the **Int** number function, which returns only the integer portion of a data value. A **number function** is used to manipulate a data value in a specific way, such as rounding it to a specific number of decimal places, or raising it to a specific power. The exact format and syntax of number functions are specific to the type of SQL supported by your database.

To use a SQL number function in a query, list the function name followed by the data values and other values required by the function (such as the number of digits to which the data value should be rounded, or the power to which the data value should be raised) in parentheses. Now you will modify your query to use the Int function to remove the fraction portion of the calculated student ages.

To modify the query using the Int function:

1. In the Query window, switch to SQL View, and modify the SELECT command as follows:

```
SELECT slname, sfname, Int((Date()-sdob)/365.25) AS Age
FROM student;
```

2. Run the query. The query results (Figure 3-17) now show the student ages in years, with the month fraction values removed.

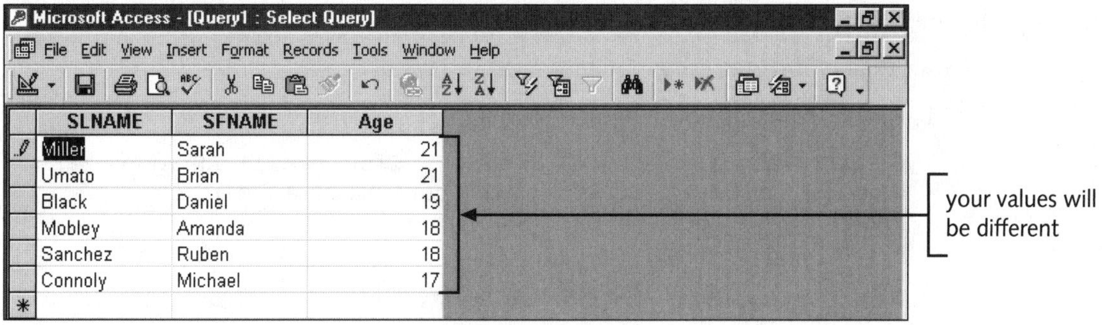

Figure 3-17   Student ages with month fractions removed

3. Close the Query window, and save the query as **StudentAges**.

USING GROUP FUNCTIONS IN QUERIES

A SQL **group function** performs an operation on a group of related rows specified in a query, and returns a single result, such as a column sum. You could use a group function to sum the total capacity of all rooms in the CR building. Table 3-3 describes five commonly used SQL group functions.

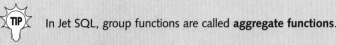 **TIP** In Jet SQL, group functions are called **aggregate functions**.

Table 3-3   SQL group functions

Function	Description	Example
AVG	Returns the average value of a numeric column's returned values	AVG(capacity)
COUNT	Returns an integer representing a count of the number of returned rows	COUNT(grade)
MAX	Returns the maximum value of a numeric column's returned values	MAX(currenrl)
MIN	Returns the minimum value of a numeric column's returned values	MIN(currenrl)
SUM	Sums a numeric column's returned values	SUM(ccredit)

To use a group function in a SQL query, you list the function name, followed by the column name, in parentheses, on which the calculation is performed, using the following general format: `[function name]([column name])`. Next, you will enter a query that performs group functions on the current enrollment fields for all courses in term ID 6. The query will specify the sum of all current enrollments, the average enrollment for each course section, the enrollment in the section with the highest (maximum) enrollment, and the enrollment in the section with the lowest (minimum) enrollment.

To create a query that uses group functions:

1. Create a new query using the following SQL command:

```
SELECT SUM(currenrl) AS Total, AVG(currenrl) AS Average,
MAX(currenrl) AS Maximum, MIN(currenrl) AS Minimum
FROM course_section
WHERE termid = 6;
```

2. Run the query. The query results are displayed as shown in Figure 3-18.

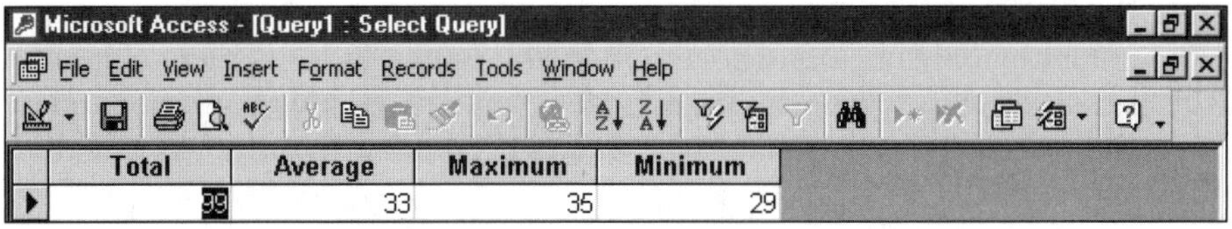

Figure 3-18   Query output with group functions

Sometimes you need to divide query output rows into groups that have matching values and then apply a group function to the grouped data. To do this, use the GROUP BY command. For example, suppose in the previous query, you would like to view the sum of all current enrollments, the average enrollment for each course section, the enrollment in the section with the highest (maximum) enrollment, and the enrollment in the section with the lowest (minimum) enrollment for all terms. You will modify the query so that it retrieves the current enrollment values for all terms, and then groups the data by term ID.

To modify the group function query using the GROUP BY command:

1. In the Query window, switch to SQL View, and modify the SQL command as follows:

```
SELECT termid, SUM(currenrl) AS Total, AVG(currenrl) AS
Average, MAX(currenrl) AS Maximum, MIN(currenrl) AS Minimum
FROM course_section
GROUP BY termid;
```

2. Run the query. The query result, shown in Figure 3-19, now shows the group function results for each term, grouped by term ID.

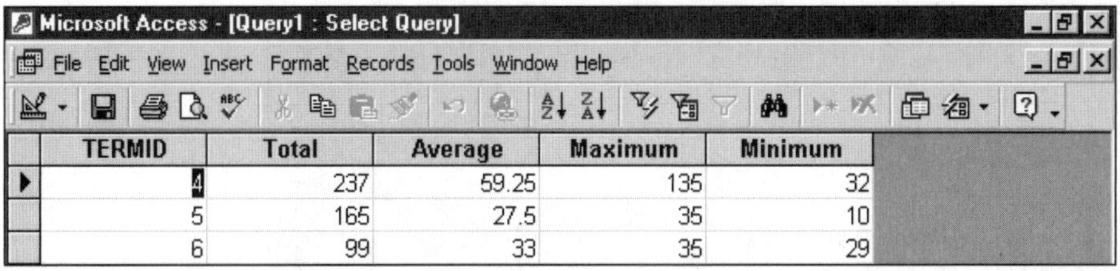

Figure 3-19   Query output using GROUP BY command

3. Click the **Save** button ![save] on the Query window toolbar, and save the query as **EnrlFunctions**.

If you create a query where one or more of the columns in the SELECT clause involves group functions and one or more columns do not, then the columns that are not in the group function *must* be included in GROUP BY clause, or the DBMS will issue an error message. In the previous query, the DBMS will retrieve a single value for the group functions: there can only be one value for the sum of the enrollments, one value for the average enrollment, and so on. However, an individual course section ID value cannot be associated with a single enrollment value, since the group function value is derived from multiple course section ID records. When you create a query with one or more group functions, you can group the output by only one other column, and you cannot list any other columns in the SELECT clause except the grouping column. Now you will modify the previous query to display an additional column value and course section ID, along with the term ID, and see what happens.

To modify the query to display an additional column value:

1. In the Query window, switch to SQL View, and modify the SELECT clause of the SQL command as follows:

```
SELECT termid, csecid, SUM(currenrl) AS Total, AVG(currenrl)
AS Average, MAX(currenrl) AS Maximum, MIN(currenrl) AS
Minimum
```

2. Run the query. A message box is displayed that states "You tried to execute a query that does not include the specified expression 'csecid' as part of an aggregate function." This means that you must include CSECID in the GROUP BY clause, since each group function value comprises multiple CSECID records.

3. Click **OK**, then modify the GROUP BY clause as follows:

```
GROUP BY termid, csecid;
```

4. Run the query. The data are displayed as shown in Figure 3-20. Note that the group function data are now calculated for each individual record, and each function returns the CURRENRL value for each individual CSECID record.

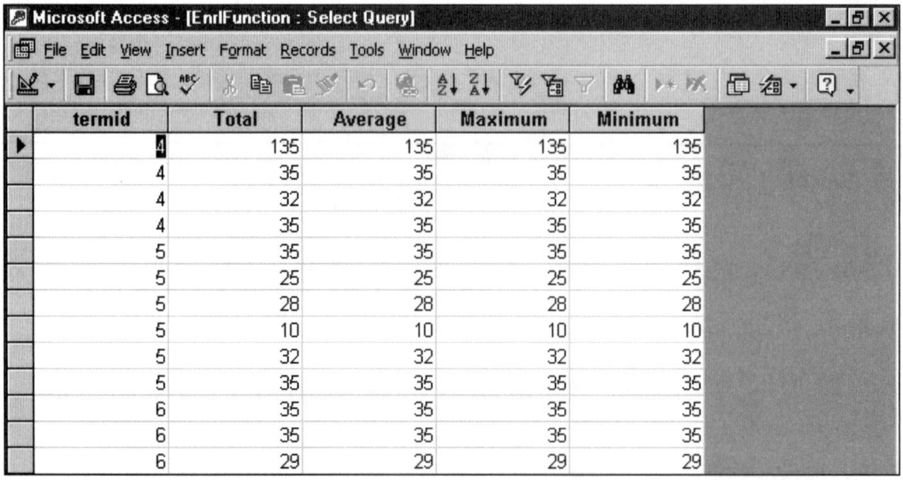

termid	Total	Average	Maximum	Minimum
4	135	135	135	135
4	35	35	35	35
4	32	32	32	32
4	35	35	35	35
5	35	35	35	35
5	25	25	25	25
5	28	28	28	28
5	10	10	10	10
5	32	32	32	32
5	35	35	35	35
6	35	35	35	35
6	35	35	35	35
6	29	29	29	29

Figure 3-20   Result of grouping query output by the CSECID field

5. Modify the GROUP BY clause so that it only groups the output by TERMID, then close the Query window, and save the changes to the query.

The COUNT group function returns an integer that represents the number of records that are returned by a given query. There are several variations of the COUNT group function that perform slightly different operations. The COUNT(*) version of this function calculates the total number of rows in a table that satisfy a given search condition. The COUNT([column name]) version calculates the number of rows in a table that satisfy a given search condition and also contain a non-null value for the given column. You will create a query that uses both versions of the COUNT function next. The query will use the COUNT(*) function to count the total number of courses in which student Daniel Black (SID 3) has enrolled, and the COUNT(grade) function to count the total number of courses for which he has received a grade.

To use the COUNT function:

1. Create a new query using the following SQL command:

```
SELECT COUNT(*) AS Enrolled, COUNT(grade) AS Completed
FROM enrollment
WHERE sid = 3;
```

2. Run the query. The query result, shown in Figure 3-21, shows that Daniel Black has enrolled in three courses and has completed one course.

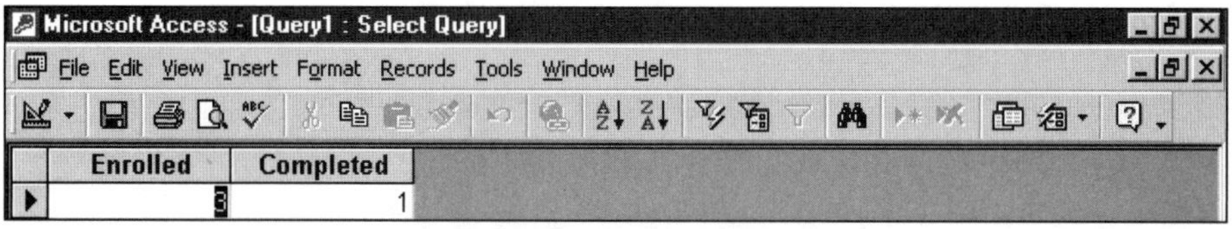

Figure 3-21   Query output using the COUNT group function

3. Close the Query window, and save the query as **CountFunction**.

CREATING SQL QUERIES TO JOIN DATA IN MULTIPLE TABLES

All of the queries you have created so far have retrieved data from a single table. However, one of the strengths of SQL is its ability to **join**, or combine, data from multiple database tables using foreign key references. The general format of a SELECT statement with a join operation is:

```
SELECT [column1, column2, ...]
FROM [table1, table2]
WHERE [table1.join column name = table2.join column name];
```

The SELECT clause contains the names of the columns to display in the query output. If you display a column that exists in more than one of the tables in the FROM clause, you must write the name of one of the tables that contains the column, followed by a period, and then write the column name with the name of one of the tables. Otherwise, the DBMS will issue an error message. This is called **qualifying the column**. You can qualify a column using any table name in the query that contains the column.

The FROM clause contains the name of each table involved in the join operation. The WHERE clause contains the **join condition**, which specifies the table and column names on which to join the tables. The join condition contains a reference to a foreign key in one table on one side of the equal sign (=) and the join condition contains a reference to a primary in the other table on the other side of the equal sign (=). Additional search conditions can be listed in the WHERE clause, using the AND and OR operators. Next, will you create a query to retrieve student last and first names along with each student's advisor's name. This requires retrieving data from both the STUDENT and FACULTY tables, and joining the tables on the FID, which is the primary key in the FACULTY table and a foreign key in the STUDENT table.

To create a query that joins two tables:

1. Create a new query using the following SQL command:

```
SELECT slname, sfname, flname
FROM student, faculty
WHERE student.fid = faculty.fid;
```

2. Run the query. The query result, shown in Figure 3-22, shows the names of the students as well as the last name of each student's advisor.

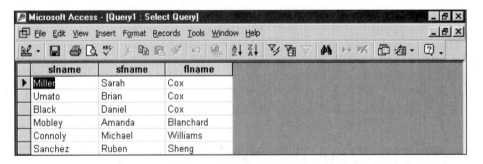

Figure 3-22 Query result from joining two tables

3. Close the Query window, and save the query as **StudentAdvisors**.

Now you will create a query that joins multiple tables and uses a search condition. You will create a query to list the location ID, building code, and room number for faculty member Laura Sheng. In the SELECT clause of this query, the LOCID field will be prefaced, or qualified, with a table name, because the LOCID field exists in both the FACULTY and LOCATION tables. You could preface LOCID with either LOCATION or FACULTY, since the value is the same in both tables for the joined records.

To create a join query with a search condition:

1. Create a new query using the following SQL command:

```
SELECT faculty.locid, bldg_code, room
FROM faculty, location
WHERE faculty.locid = location.locid
AND flname = 'Sheng'
AND ffname = 'Laura';
```

2. Run the query. The query result should show LOCID 11, BLDG_CODE BUS, and room 433.

3. Close the Query window, and save the query as **ShengLocation**.

In the previous examples, you joined two tables, but you can join any number of tables in a join query. When you join more than two tables, each table involved in the query must be listed in the FROM clause, and each table in the FROM clause must be listed in the WHERE clause in a join condition. Suppose that you want to create a query to display the call ID and grade for each of Sarah Miller's courses. This query requires you to join four tables: STUDENT (to search for SFNAME and SLNAME), ENROLLMENT (to display GRADE), COURSE (to display CALLID), and COURSE_SECTION (to join CALLID in COURSE to CSECID in ENROLLMENT). For complex queries like this, it is often helpful to draw a diagram like the one shown in Figure 3-23 to show the columns and associated tables that you need to display and search, as well as the required joining columns and their links.

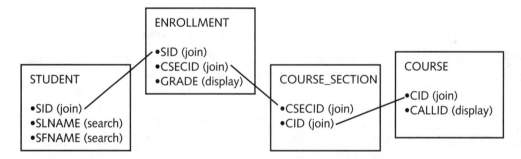

Figure 3-23   Join query design diagram

You can derive your query from the diagram by following these steps:

1. Place the display fields in the SELECT clause.

2. List all of the tables in the FROM clause.

3. Include the links in join conditions in the WHERE clause.

4. Include all of the search fields in the WHERE clause.

Note that you must always have one less join condition than the total number of tables joined in the query. In this query, you are joining four tables, so you must have three join conditions. Now you will create a SQL query to join four tables based on the design diagram shown in Figure 3-23.

To create a query to join four tables:

1. Create a new query using the following SQL command:

```
SELECT callid, grade
FROM student, enrollment, course_section, course
WHERE student.sid = enrollment.sid
AND enrollment.csecid = course_section.csecid
AND course_section.cid = course.cid
AND slname = 'Miller'
AND sfname = 'Sarah';
```

2. Run the query. The query result, shown in Figure 3-24, shows Sarah Miller's course call IDs and grades.

callid	grade
MIS 101	A
MIS 301	A
MIS 441	B
MIS 451	B

Figure 3-24   Query result from joining four tables

3. Close the Query window, and save the query as **MillerGrades**.

If you accidentally omit a join condition in a multiple-table query, the result is a **Cartesian product**, which is a situation in which every row in one table is joined with every row in the other table. Now you will open the StudentAdvisors query that you created earlier, where you show each student record along with each student's advisor, but you will edit the query by deleting the join condition. Every row in the STUDENT table (six rows) is joined with every row in the FACULTY table (five rows). The result is six * five rows, or 30 rows. Now you will create a Cartesian product by omitting a join condition.

To create a Cartesian product by omitting a join condition:

1. Open the StudentAdvisors query in SQL View, and delete the join condition so that the query looks like this:

```
SELECT slname, sfname, flname
FROM student, faculty;
```

2. Run the query. The query result in Figure 3-25 shows that each row in the STUDENT table is first joined with the first row in the FACULTY table (FLNAME "Cox"). Next, each row in the STUDENT table is joined with the second row in the FACULTY table (FLNAME "Blanchard"). This continues until each STUDENT row is joined with each FACULTY row, for a total of 30 rows returned.

3. Close the Query window, without saving the changes to the query.

When a multiple table query returns more records than you expect, look for missing join condition statements.

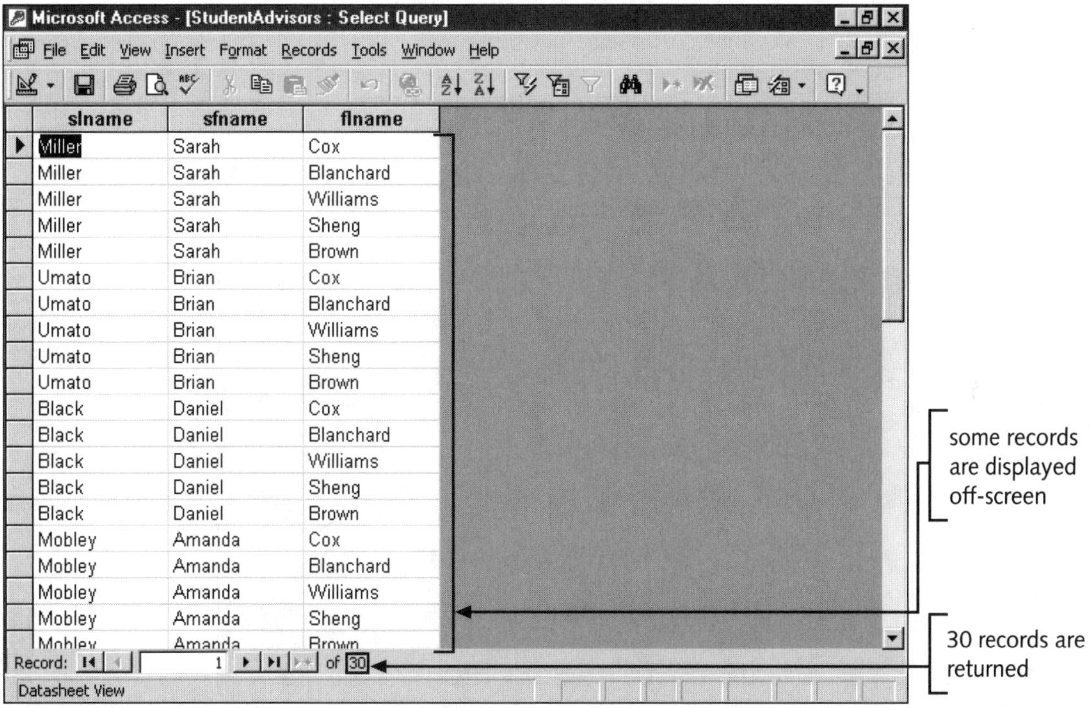

slname	sfname	flname
Miller	Sarah	Cox
Miller	Sarah	Blanchard
Miller	Sarah	Williams
Miller	Sarah	Sheng
Miller	Sarah	Brown
Umato	Brian	Cox
Umato	Brian	Blanchard
Umato	Brian	Williams
Umato	Brian	Sheng
Umato	Brian	Brown
Black	Daniel	Cox
Black	Daniel	Blanchard
Black	Daniel	Williams
Black	Daniel	Sheng
Black	Daniel	Brown
Mobley	Amanda	Cox
Mobley	Amanda	Blanchard
Mobley	Amanda	Williams
Mobley	Amanda	Sheng
Mobley	Amanda	Brown

some records are displayed off-screen

30 records are returned

Figure 3-25 Multiple-table query that displays Cartesian product

CREATING A UNION QUERY

A **UNION** query combines the outputs of two unrelated queries into a single output result. Suppose you need to create a query to list the last name, first name, and phone number of every student and faculty member in the Northwoods University database to create a phone directory. If you enter a query joining the two tables on the FID field, the listing will show the student information and the information for each student's associated advisor information, which is not what is needed. If you omit the join clause, the output will be a Cartesian product. A simple SELECT command cannot return data from two unrelated queries as a single output. You will need to create a query that uses the UNION set operation.

A UNION requires that both queries have the same number of display columns in the SELECT statement, and that each column in the first query must have the same data type as the corresponding column in the second query. Column headings in the output take the name of the column headings of the first query. The general format of the UNION query is [query 1] UNION [query 2].

Now you will create a UNION query to list the names, addresses, and telephone numbers for each student and each faculty member at Northwoods University.

To create a UNION query:

1. Create a new query using the following SQL command:

```
SELECT slname, sfname, sphone
FROM student
UNION SELECT flname, ffname, fphone
FROM faculty;
```

2. Run the query. The query result, shown in Figure 3-26, shows the student and faculty names and phone numbers.

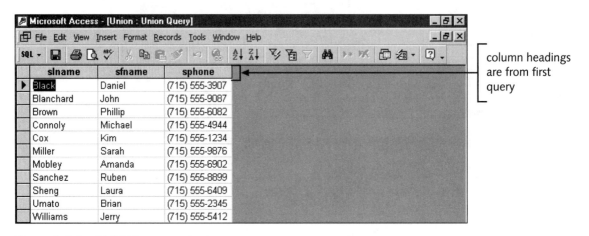

column headings are from first query

Figure 3-26   UNION query output

3. Close the Query window, and save the query as **Union**.

TIP   UNION queries are designated in the Query window by the Union Query icon ⌦.

4. Click **File** on the menu bar, and then click **Close** to close the northwoods.mdb database.

USING SQL TO INSERT, UPDATE, AND DELETE DATA

In the previous chapter, you learned how to insert, update, and delete data records in Access database tables using datasheets. Now you will learn how to perform these operations using the associated SQL commands. These commands create **action queries**, which are queries that change the data that are stored in the database. It is important to know how to manage data records using action queries. You will create programs in later chapters that use action queries to allow the Web server and database server to interact and modify the database contents.

Inserting Data Records

3

First, you will learn how to use the SQL INSERT command to insert new data records.

The SQL INSERT command can be used two ways: to insert all fields into a record at once or to insert a few selected fields. The basic format of the INSERT command for inserting all of the fields in a record is:

```
INSERT INTO [table]
VALUES ([column1 value, column2 value, …]);
```

You can only insert records into one table at a time using a single INSERT command. When you are inserting a value for all of the fields in a record, the VALUES clause of the INSERT command must contain a value for each column in the table, or the word NULL instead of a data value if the data value is currently unknown or undefined. Column values must be listed in the same order as the order in which the columns were defined when the table was created.

You can also structure the INSERT command so that it only inserts selected fields into a record. The basic format of the INSERT command for inserting selected table fields is:

```
INSERT INTO [table] ([column1, column2, …])
VALUES ([column1 value, column2 value, …]);
```

The column names can be listed in any order. The data values must be listed in the same order as their associated columns in the INSERT INTO clause, and the data values must be the correct data type. A NULL value will automatically be inserted for columns omitted from the INSERT INTO clause. When you are inserting data into a table that has a field that uses the AutoNumber data type to automatically generate surrogate key values, you omit inserting the AutoNumber data value, and the database will automatically insert the next value in the sequence.

Before you can insert a new data record, you must ensure that all of the foreign key records that the new record references have been inserted into the database. For example, in the first STUDENT record, the ID for Sarah Miller's faculty advisor is 1. This refers to FID 1 (Kim Cox) in the FACULTY table. The FACULTY record must be added before you can add the first STUDENT record, or a foreign key reference error will occur. Look at Kim Cox's FACULTY record in Figure 2-5, and notice that it has foreign key references to LOCID 9 and to FRANK ASSO. Therefore, these LOCATION and FRANK records must be added before you can add the FACULTY record. Thankfully, the records in the LOCATION and FRANK tables have no foreign key values to reference. Therefore, you can insert LOCID 9 in the LOCATION table, and FRANK ASSO in the FRANK table. Then you can insert the associated FACULTY record, and finally add Sarah Miller's STUDENT record.

The Chapter3 folder on your Data Disk contains a database file named emptynorthwoods.mdb, which contains the Northwoods University database tables with no data values inserted. Now you will open this file in Access, and insert the record for LOCID 9 in the LOCATION table. You will structure the command to insert all of the record fields.

To open the database and insert the LOCATION record:

1. In Access, click **File** on the menu bar, click **Open**, and open the **emptynorthwoods.mdb** database from the Chapter3 folder on your Data Disk. (Office 97 users will open **emptynorthwoods97.mdb**.) The Database window is displayed, showing the Northwoods University database tables.

2. Click **Queries** on the Object bar, and then create a new query using the following SQL command:

```
INSERT INTO location VALUES
(9, 'BUS', '424', 1);
```

Note that the LOCATION table has four columns: LOCID, BLDG_CODE, ROOM, and CAPACITY. The respective data types of these four columns are Number, Text, Text, and Number. The Number fields are entered as digits, while the Text fields are enclosed within single quotation marks ('). Data stored in Text fields must be enclosed in single quotation marks, and the text within the single quotation marks is case sensitive.

3. Run the query. When the message box stating that you are about to append 1 data row is displayed, click **Yes**.

4. Close the Query window, and save the query as **LocationInsert**.

 TIP INSERT queries are designated in the Query window by the Insert Query icon ⊕ **!**. The exclamation point (!) in the icon indicates that the query is an action query.

5. Click **Tables** in the Object bar, and then double-click the **LOCATION** table to open its datasheet. The datasheet is displayed with the new record inserted, as shown in Figure 3-27. Close the datasheet.

LOCID	BLDG_CODE	ROOM	CAPACITY
9	BUS	424	1
(AutoNumber)			

Figure 3-27   LOCATION table with new record inserted

The field values in the INSERT statement must be entered in the same order as the fields in the table, and a value must be included for every column in the table. When you insert a record into the LOCATION table, the DBMS expects a Number data value, then a Text data value, another Text data value, and then another Number data value. An error is displayed if you try to insert the values in the wrong order or if you omit a column value. If you cannot remember the order of the columns or their data types, open the table in Design View and verify the table's structure. Next, you will insert the ASSO faculty rank record in the FRANK table.

To insert the ASSO record into the FRANK table:

1. Click **Queries** on the Object bar, and create a new query using the following SQL command:

   ```
   INSERT INTO frank VALUES
   ('ASSO', 'Associate');
   ```

2. Run the query, click **Yes** to confirm appending the new row, then close the Query window and save the query as **FrankInsert**.

3. Click **Tables** in the Object bar, double-click the **FRANK** table to open its datasheet and confirm that the new record was inserted correctly, and then close the datasheet.

The next step is to insert Kim Cox's record into the FACULTY table. Since the FID field has the AutoNumber data type, and Kim's record is the first record in the table, you will use the INSERT command for inserting selected fields, and omit the FID field so that the DBMS will insert it automatically. You will only enter values for the FLNAME, FFNAME, FMI, LOCID, and FRANK columns, and omit the values for FID, FPHONE, FPIN, and FACULTYIMAGE column values.

To insert selected fields of a record:

1. Create a new Query object using the following SQL command:

   ```
   INSERT INTO faculty (flname, ffname, fmi, locid, frank)
   VALUES ('Cox', 'Kim', 'J', 9, 'ASSO');
   ```

2. Run the query, click **Yes** to confirm appending the record, and then close the Query window and save the query as **FacultyInsert**.

3. Open the FACULTY table datasheet, confirm that the record was inserted correctly, note the value of faculty member Kim Cox's FID, and then close the datasheet.

 If the FID for Kim Cox is a value other than 1, it means that you have inserted other records into this table previously. It is OK if the value is different, as long as each record in the FACULTY table has a unique FID value.

Now you will add the STUDENT record for Sarah Miller. You will enter values for SLNAME, SFNAME, SMI, SADD, SDOB, and FID, and omit the rest of the fields. The SID field has the AutoNumber data type, so its value will be inserted automatically. The SDOB field has a Date/Time data type. Access can store the year portion of the date using either a two-digit or four-digit format. You will configure the database so that years are stored in a four-digit format. (You will not be able to do this if you are using Access 97.)

To configure the database to store dates, using a four-digit year format (Access 2000 users only):

1. Click **Tools** on the menu bar, click **Options**, and select the **General** tab. The Options dialog box opens.

2. Under the Use four-digit year formatting selection, click the **All databases** check box, and then click **OK**.

To insert a date into an Access database, you must enclose the date string in pound signs (#). Sarah Miller's record will contain the foreign key value for the FID for faculty member Kim Cox, who is Sarah's advisor. For this value, you will use the FID value that you noted in Step 3 in the previous set of steps.

To add the STUDENT record:

1. Create a new query using the following SQL command:

```
INSERT INTO student (slname, sfname, smi, sadd, sdob, fid)
VALUES ('Miller', 'Sarah', 'M', '144 Windridge Blvd.',
#07/14/1980#, [value you noted for Kim Cox's FID in Step 3
in the previous set of steps]);
```

2. Run the query, click **Yes** to confirm appending the record, and then close the Query window and save the query as **StudentInsert1**.

3. Open the STUDENT table datasheet, confirm that the record was inserted correctly, and then close the datasheet.

Next, you will enter the record for student Brian Umato. Brian's address (454 St. John's Place) contains a single quotation mark. To enter a Text field that contains a single quotation mark, you must type the single quotation mark twice ("). Otherwise, the SQL interpreter assumes that the single quotation mark is the end of the text string.

To enter the record for student Brian Umato:

1. Create a new query using the following SQL command:

```
INSERT INTO student (slname, sfname, smi, sadd, sdob, fid)
VALUES ('Umato', 'Brian', 'D', '454 St. John''s Place',
#08/19/1980#, [value you noted for Kim Cox's FID]);
```

2. Run the query, click **Yes** to confirm appending the record, and then close the Query window and save the query as **StudentInsert2**.

3. Open the STUDENT table datasheet, confirm that the record was inserted correctly, and then close the datasheet.

Finally, you will enter the record for student Daniel Black. Daniel does not have a middle initial, so you must enter the word NULL instead of a value for the middle initial. Alternately, you could omit the SMI field in the VALUES clause, but you will include SMI in the

INSERT command and use the NULL keyword to learn how to use the NULL keyword in an INSERT command.

To enter the record for student Daniel Black:

1. Create a new query using the following SQL command:

```
INSERT INTO student (slname, sfname, smi, sadd, sdob, fid)
VALUES ('Black', 'Daniel', NULL, '8921 Circle Drive',
#10/10/1981#, [value you noted for Kim Cox's FID]);
```

2. Run the query, click **Yes** to confirm appending the record, and then close the Query window and save the query as **StudentInsert3**.

3. Open the STUDENT table datasheet, confirm that the record was inserted correctly, and then close the datasheet.

Updating Records

An important data maintenance operation is updating existing data records. Student addresses and phone numbers often change, and every year students (hopefully) move up to the next class. The general format of the UPDATE statement is:

```
UPDATE [table name]
SET [column1] = [new data value1], [column2] = [new data
value2], …
WHERE [search condition];
```

You can update records in only one table at a time using a single UPDATE command. You can update multiple columns in multiple records in the same table using a single UPDATE command when all of the records to be updated satisfy the search condition specified in the WHERE clause. Now you will create a new query to update student Daniel Black's SCLASS field to SR.

To create a query to update a record:

1. Create a new query using the following SQL command:

```
UPDATE student
SET sclass = 'SR'
WHERE sfname = 'Daniel'
AND slname = 'Black';
```

2. Run the query, click **Yes** to confirm the update, and then close the Query window and save the query as **StudentUpdate1**.

 TIP   UPDATE queries are designated in the Query window by the Update Query icon ⌁ !.

3. Open the STUDENT table datasheet, confirm that the record was updated correctly, and then close the datasheet.

Recall that you can update multiple records in a table using a single UPDATE command by specifying a search condition that matches multiple records. When you do this, the search condition often uses the greater than (>) or less than (<) mathematical operators, or the AND and OR operators. Now you will create a query that updates the SSTATE field for student IDs 1, 2, and 3 using a single command that instructs the DBMS to update SID values greater than or equal to 1 and less than 4 in the search condition.

To update multiple records, using a single UPDATE command:

1. Create a new query using the following SQL command:

```
UPDATE student
SET sstate = 'WI'
WHERE sid >= 1
AND sid < 4;
```

 TIP   If your STUDENT records have different ID numbers, you will need to modify the values for SID in the search condition to make your query work correctly.

2. Run the query, click **Yes** to confirm that you are about to update three rows, and then close the Query window and save the query as **StudentUpdate2**.

3. Open the STUDENT table datasheet, confirm that the records were updated correctly, and then close the datasheet.

To update all of the records in a table, you omit the search condition. Now you will update all of the records in the STUDENT table so that the SCLASS value is 'SR'.

To update the SCLASS value for every record in the STUDENT table:

1. Create a new query using the following SQL command:

```
UPDATE student
SET sclass = 'SR';
```

2. Run the query, click **Yes** to confirm that you are about to update three rows, and then close the Query window and save the query as **StudentUpdate3**.

3. Open the STUDENT table datasheet, confirm that the records were updated correctly, and then close the datasheet.

Deleting Records

Another important table maintenance operation is deleting records, which uses the SQL DELETE command. You can use a single DELETE command to delete one or more records from a single table. The general format of the DELETE command is:

```
DELETE FROM [table]
WHERE [search condition];
```

You should always include a search condition when deleting a record from a table to ensure that the correct record is deleted. If you omit the search condition, all table records will be deleted. Now you will delete the record for student Sarah Miller.

To delete a record:

1. Create a new query using the following SQL command:

```
DELETE FROM student
WHERE slname = 'Miller'
AND sfname = 'Sarah';
```

2. Run the query, click **Yes** to confirm that you are about to delete a row, and then close the Query window and save the query as **StudentDelete1**.

3. Open the STUDENT table datasheet, confirm that the record for SID 1 was deleted, and then close the datasheet.

 TIP   DELETE queries are designated in the Query window by the Delete Query icon ✗!.

When you delete a record, it cannot contain a field that is a foreign key reference to another record. For example, you cannot delete the record in the FACULTY table for faculty member Kim Cox, because FID is listed as a foreign key reference in the STUDENT table for student IDs 2 and 3. To delete Kim Cox's record, you must delete these associated STUDENT records first. Now you will delete all of the records in the STUDENT table by omitting the search condition. Then you will delete the record for Kim Cox.

To delete the STUDENT records and the FACULTY record for Kim Cox:

1. Create a new query using the following SQL command:

```
DELETE FROM student;
```

2. Run the query, click **Yes** to confirm that you are about to delete 2 rows, and then close the Query window and save the query as **StudentDelete2**.

3. Open the STUDENT table datasheet, confirm that all of the records were deleted, and then close the datasheet.

4. Create a new query using the following SQL command:

```
DELETE FROM faculty
WHERE ffname = 'Kim'
AND flname = 'Cox';
```

5. Run the query, click **Yes** to confirm that you are about to delete a row, and then close the Query window and save the query as **FacultyDelete1**.

6. Open the FACULTY table datasheet, confirm that the record was deleted, and then close the datasheet and the emptynorthwoods database.

7. Exit Access.

SUMMARY

❏ Structured Query Language (SQL) is the standard query language of relational databases. When you create database-driven Web pages, you use SQL as the query language. A query is a question that can be answered by data stored in a database. Using SQL, you can use various commands to retrieve data from a single database table, or you can use foreign key links to join multiple database tables to retrieve related data from multiple tables. You can specify search conditions to retrieve selected records, and perform mathematical functions on retrieved data. You can also group retrieved records and perform group functions, such as finding the sum or average of a set of retrieved records.

❏ To retrieve database data, you use the SQL SELECT command. In a SELECT command, the SELECT clause lists the columns that you want to display in your query, the FROM clause lists the name of each table involved in the query, and the WHERE clause specifies a search condition. To retrieve every row in a table, the data do not need to satisfy a search condition, so you omit the WHERE clause. If you want to retrieve all of the columns in a table, you can use an asterisk (*) as a wildcard character in the SELECT statement instead of typing every column name. The SELECT DISTINCT command is used to suppress duplicate records in the query output. Query outputs can be sorted using the ORDER BY clause. SQL has group functions for summing, averaging, finding the maximum or minimum value, or counting the number of records returned by a query. You can use the AS command to create an alias, which is an alternate column name that describes the output column data.

❏ To join any number of tables in a SELECT command, you must include every involved table in the FROM clause, and include a join condition for every link between tables in the WHERE clause. If you display a column in a multiple table query that exists in more than one of the tables, you must qualify the column name by writing the table name, followed by a period, and then the column name. If you accidentally omit a join condition in a multiple-table query, it results in a Cartesian product, which is a situation in which every row in one table is joined with every row in the other table. A UNION command combines the results of two queries that are not related through foreign key relationships.

❏ The INSERT command is used to insert new data records into a table. The INSERT command can be used to insert all of the data fields into a record, or to insert only specific fields. Before you can insert a new data record, you must ensure that all of the foreign key records that it references have been previously inserted. You can update database records using the UPDATE command. You can update multiple records in a table using a single UPDATE command by specifying a search condition that matches multiple records. You use the DELETE command to delete database records. Always include a WHERE clause when deleting a record from a table, because otherwise all table records will be deleted. You cannot delete a record if it is a foreign key reference to another record.

3

REVIEW QUESTIONS

1. Why is it necessary to use SQL queries in Web pages?
2. What is the Jet database engine?
3. When should you use the asterisk (*) character in a SELECT command?
4. When should you use the DISTINCT qualifier in a SELECT command?
5. To retrieve specific records, a query must contain a ―――――――――.
6. Write a SQL command that returns all of the rows in the STUDENT table where the value of SPHONE is NULL.
7. Write a SQL command that returns all of the rows in the STUDENT table where the value of SPHONE is not NULL.
8. True or False: you must always create a column alias for a column that contains a calculated value.
9. When do you need to use the GROUP BY function?
10. What is the purpose of the COUNT function? What is the effect of specifying the column within the COUNT function?
11. If you are creating a query that joins four tables, how many join conditions are required?
12. What error results in a query result that is a Cartesian product?
13. When is a UNION query required?
14. What is an action query? Give two examples of action queries.
15. How do you insert a record with a data field that has the AutoNumber data type?
16. True or False: when you use the INSERT command to insert all fields in a table record, you can list the field values in any order.
17. What data records must be inserted first before you can insert the record for CSECID 1 in the COURSE_SECTION table?
18. True or False: you can only update one table record at a time using a single UPDATE command.
19. How can you delete all of the records in the table, using a single DELETE command?
20. What data records must be deleted first before you can delete the first record in the ENROLLMENT table?

HANDS-ON PROJECTS

1. Save all of the following queries in the northwoods.mdb database in the Chapter3 folder on your Data Disk.
   a. Write a query named CourseQuery that returns the CALLID and CNAME for all rows in the COURSE table.
   b. Write a query named ClassQuery that returns the SCLASS field for all rows in the STUDENT table, and suppresses duplicate outputs.

c. Write a query named TermStatus that returns all fields in the TERM table where status = 'CLOSED'. Use the wildcard character to return all columns, and specify 'CLOSED' as the search condition in the query's WHERE clause.

d. Write a query named StudentMIQuery that returns the SFNAME, SLNAME, and SMI fields for every student who has a value for SMI.

e. Write a query named FacultyAdvisees that calculates the total number of students advised by faculty member Kim Cox. Use FFNAME and FLNAME in the search condition. Create a column alias named CoxAdvisees for the returned value.

f. Write a query named StudentGrades to list the course call ID, section number, term description, and grade for every course taken by student Ruben Sanchez for which a grade has been assigned. Sort the output so the Cs are listed first, followed by the Bs. (Hint: Use SLNAME and SFNAME in your search conditions, and search for records where GRADE is not NULL.)

g. Create a query named RoomUsage that lists the BLDG_CODE and ROOM of every room that is currently either in use as a faculty office, or in use as a classroom during the Summer 2003 term. (Hint: You will need to use a UNION. Use TDESC as a search condition.)

h. Create a query named StudentCredits to calculate the total number of student credits generated during the Spring 2003 term (student credits = CURRENRL ★ course credits). Use TDESC in your search condition. Create a column alias for the calculated column, and name the column Spring2003Credits.

2. Save all of the following queries in the clearwater.mdb database in the Chapter3 folder on your Data Disk.

a. Create a query named CustomerShipments that displays all fields from the CUSTOMER_SHIPMENT table where the carrier ID is 1.

b. Write a query named NavyInventory that displays the INVID, ITEMDESC, COLOR, and CURR_PRICE for all rows in the INVENTORY table where the color is navy. Use 'Navy' as the search condition in the query's WHERE clause. (Hint: You will need to create a query that joins the ITEM table and the INVENTORY table.)

c. Write a query named ColorQuery that displays the COLOR field from every row in the INVENTORY table, and suppresses duplicate outputs. Sort the output in reverse alphabetical order.

d. Write a query named BackOrderDays to calculate the number of days between the current system date and the DATE_EXPECTED for BACKORDERID 1 in the INVENTORY_BACKORDER table. Truncate the output to the nearest day, using the Int function, and display the output using a column alias named DifferenceInDays.

e. Modify the BackOrderDays query that you created in the previous project so that it calculates the number of months between the current system date and the DATE_EXPECTED for BACKORDERID 1 in the INVENTORY_BACKO-RDER table. Truncate the output to the nearest month, and display the output using a column alias named BackOrderMonths.

f. Write a query named OrderQuantity that displays the ORDERID and total quantity of each order in the ORDERLINE table. (Hint: You will need to use the GROUP BY function. Display the total quantity using a column alias named TotalItemsOrdered.)

    g. Write a query named UnreceivedShipments that displays the ITEMDESC, ITEM-SIZE, COLOR, DATE_EXPECTED, and QUANTITY_EXPECTED of every shipment in the INVENTORY_SHIPPING table that has not yet been received. (*Hint*: Use DATE_RECEIVED IS NULL as a search condition.)

    h. Write a query named UpdateQOH that updates the QOH for INVID 21 to 100 units.

    i. Write a query named PriceIncrease that increases the CURR_PRICE of every field in the INVENTORY table by 10 percent using a single query.

3. The following queries involve inserting and deleting data records. Refer to Figure 2-4 for the data values. (Fields with the AutoNumber data type might be assigned different values than the ones shown in Figure 2-4, depending on the next available AutoNumber value for the specific field.) Save the queries in the emptyclearwater.mdb database in the Chapter3 folder on your Data Disk.

    a. Write a query named InsertCustomer to insert the customer last name, first name, address, city, state, ZIP code, username, and password of customer Paula Harris.

    b. Write a query named InsertItem to insert all of the data values for item ID 1 in the ITEM table.

    c. Write the queries that are required to insert back order ID 1 in the INVEN-TORY_BACKORDER table. Name the first query Pr20Query1, the second query Pr20Query2, and so on. Name the queries to indicate the order in which they must be executed so that all necessary foreign key references are inserted in the correct order. Be sure to structure the INSERT command for the query that inserts the records into ITEM, INVENTORY, and INVENTORY_BACKORDER so that they take advantage of the AutoNumber data type of the data fields.

    d. Write the queries that are required to delete back order ID 1 from the INVENTORY_BACKORDER table. Name the first query Pr21Query1, the second query Pr21Query2, and so on. Name the queries to indicate the order in which they must be executed so that all necessary foreign key references are deleted in the correct order.

CASE PROJECTS

1. Create a subfolder named Ashland in the Chapter3 folder on your Data Disk. Open the Ashland Valley Soccer League database that you created in Chapter 2, Case Project 1, save it as Ch3Case1.mdb in the Chapter3\Ashland folder, and then do the following:
   a. Create queries to insert one record in each table, using the INSERT command.
   b. Create queries to update each of the records that you inserted in Step a.
   c. Create queries to delete each of the records that you inserted in Step a.
   d. Create two queries that use a search condition to display some of the data in the database.
   e. Create two queries that join at least two database tables to display some of the data in the database.
   f. Create two queries that join at least two database tables and also use a search condition to display some of the data in the database.

2. Create a subfolder named Waynes in the Chapter3 folder on your Data Disk. Open the Wayne's Auto World database that you created in Chapter 2, Case Project 2, save it as Ch3Case2.mdb in the Chapter3\Waynes folder, and then do the following:
   a. Create queries to insert one record in each table, using the INSERT command.
   b. Create queries to update each of the records that you inserted in Step a.
   c. Create queries to delete each of the records that you inserted in Step a.
   d. Create two queries that use a search condition to display some of the data in the database.
   e. Create two queries that join at least two database tables to display some of the data in the database.
   f. Create two queries that join at least two database tables and also use a search condition to display some of the data in the database.

3. Create a subfolder named Sunray in the Chapter3 folder on your Data Disk. Open the Sun-Ray Video database that you created in Chapter 2, Case Project 3, save it as Ch3Case3.mdb in the Chapter3\Sunray folder, and then do the following:
   a. Create queries to insert one record in each table, using the INSERT command.
   b. Create queries to update each of the records that you inserted in Step a.
   c. Create queries to delete each of the records that you inserted in Step a.
   d. Create two queries that use a search condition to display some of the data in the database.
   e. Create two queries that join at least two database tables to display some of the data in the database.
   f. Create two queries that join at least two database tables and also use a search condition to display some of the data in the database.

4

INTRODUCTION TO HTML

In this chapter, you will:

♦ Learn basic HTML commands
♦ Discover how to display graphic image objects in Web pages
♦ Create HTML tables
♦ Create hyperlinks in HTML documents

Recall that a Web page is a file with an .htm or .html extension that contains Hypertext Markup Language (HTML) commands and text that is displayed by a Web browser. The .htm extension is used with older, DOS-based file systems that can only handle three-character file extensions, while the .html extension is used with newer file systems that can handle longer extensions. HTML is a document-layout language with hypertext-specification capabilities. In a **document-layout language**, the user embeds special formatting symbols within a text document to control the document's appearance. Specific codes are used to specify text position, size, style, and formatting for objects such as tables, lists, and figures. The document is then viewed or printed using a program that interprets the codes and formats the output.

Hypertext provides a way to navigate through a document or series of documents by following links represented by keywords or other Web page objects. HTML is not a programming language, although it can contain embedded programming commands. HTML's primary task is to define the structure and appearance of Web pages and to allow Web pages to contain embedded hypertext links to other documents, Web pages, or programs.

HTML documents are text files that you can create using a text editor such as Windows Notepad. You can also create HTML documents using an **HTML converter**, which takes text in one format and converts it to an HTML file. For example, you could create a source document in Microsoft Word, and then convert it to an HTML document that can be displayed as a Web page. Or, you can use an **HTML editor**, such as Microsoft FrontPage, which allows you to create a formatted document in a word-processing environment. FrontPage then automatically inserts HTML commands for creating a formatted HTML document. While HTML converters and editors speed up the process of creating Web pages, neither approach provides the flexibility that most programmers need for specifying exactly how a Web page looks and works. To do this, programmers must enter and modify the HTML commands directly, using a text editor. In this book, you will use a text editor to create text files that contain HTML commands. In this chapter, you will become familiar with basic HTML commands, and you will learn how to create HTML tables, which will be used in later chapters to display database data. You will also learn how to create hyperlinks within HTML documents that reference objects within a Web page, objects on different Web pages, and e-mail addresses. This chapter is not intended to be a comprehensive overview of HTML, but it covers the commands you will need to use in later chapters to create database-driven Web pages.

BASIC HTML COMMANDS

The first step in creating a Web page is to visualize how the page will look when it is displayed in a browser. Figure 4-1 shows a design diagram for a home page for Clearwater Traders that contains many basic Web page elements, including different heading levels, a bulleted list, a graphic image, a horizontal rule, and formatted text.

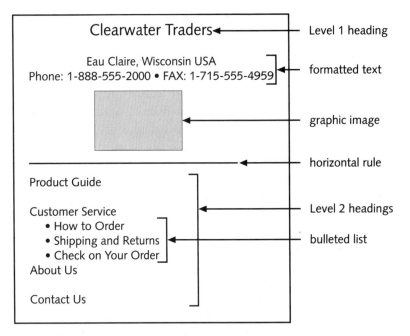

Figure 4-1   Design diagram for Clearwater Traders home page

Now you will create the HTML document for this home page, learn about the structure of an HTML document, and learn how to use HTML to create and format basic Web page elements.

HTML Tags

An HTML document that defines a Web page consists of the **Web page content**, which is the text that is displayed on the Web page, and HTML **tags**, which are codes that define how a particular line or section of the document content is displayed. HTML tags are normally used in pairs, enclosed in angle brackets (< >), and usually take the form `<tag name>text formatted by tag</tag name>`. Tags that are used in pairs are called **two-sided tags**. The first tag is called the **opening tag**, and the second tag is called the **closing tag**. For some tags, only the opening tag is required. This kind of tag is called a **one-sided tag**. You can enclose formatted text in multiple tags to specify different formatting properties. When you enclose text in multiple tags, the opening and closing tags can be in any order. HTML tags are not case sensitive, although it is a good practice to place tags in all uppercase letters to distinguish the tags from the Web page content. Many tags can be modified by **attributes**, which instruct the tag to behave a certain way. For example, Web page headings by default are left-justified on the Web page, but a heading tag's **ALIGN** attribute can optionally instruct the browser to display the heading center- or right-justified. When a browser encounters a tag that it doesn't recognize, or that is misspelled, the browser treats the tag as part of the Web page text, and displays the text of the tag.

HTML Document Structure

The following code shows the basic format of an HTML document:

```
<HTML>
<HEAD>
<TITLE>[Web page title text]</TITLE>
</HEAD>
<BODY>
[Web page content text and tags]
</BODY>
</HTML>
```

The beginning `<HTML>` and ending `</HTML>` paired tags tell the Web browser that the enclosed text is to be treated as an HTML document. The `<HEAD>...</HEAD>` tags enclose the document's header section. The **header section** contains information about the Web page that is used by the Web browser, but is not displayed on the Web page. Some search engines (such as AltaVista or Yahoo!) use header information when performing searches. One item that is usually included in the header section is the Web page **title**, which is the text that will be displayed in the title bar of the user's browser window, and is enclosed in `<TITLE>...</TITLE>` tags.

 TIP The title text is saved as the Web page's description when a user saves a link to the Web page using a Netscape bookmark, or as a "favorite" using Microsoft Internet Explorer.

The <BODY>...</BODY> tags enclose the text and tags that compose the **body** of the Web page, which is the Web page content that is displayed by the user's browser and the HTML tags used to format the Web page content. Now you will start Notepad (or another text editor on your workstation), and start creating the HTML document for the Clearwater Traders home page.

To start creating the home page HTML document:

1. Start Notepad (or another text editor on your workstation), and type the code shown in Figure 4-2 to create the Clearwater Traders HTML document and define the Web page title.

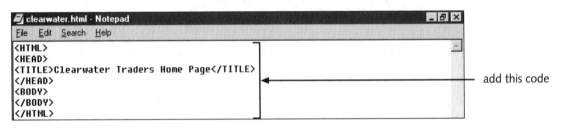

Figure 4-2   Defining an HTML document

 If you are using Wordpad, Word, or another word processor, be sure to save your file as a text file.

2. Save the file as **clearwater.html** in the Chapter4 folder on your Data Disk.

Now you will view the HTML document as a Web page in Internet Explorer. Recall that when you are developing new Web pages, you can view a Web page by specifying a file URL, which consists of the system drive letter, folder path, and name of the HTML file that you want to view.

To view the HTML document:

1. Start Internet Explorer, click **File** on the menu bar, click **Open**, click **Browse**, and then navigate to the Chapter4 folder on your Data Disk. Select **clearwater.html**, click **Open**, and then click **OK**. The current Clearwater Traders home page is displayed, as shown in Figure 4-3.

 All of the figures in this book show a computer screen that is set at a 640 x 480 screen resolution. If your screen is set at a different resolution, your screen might look slightly different.

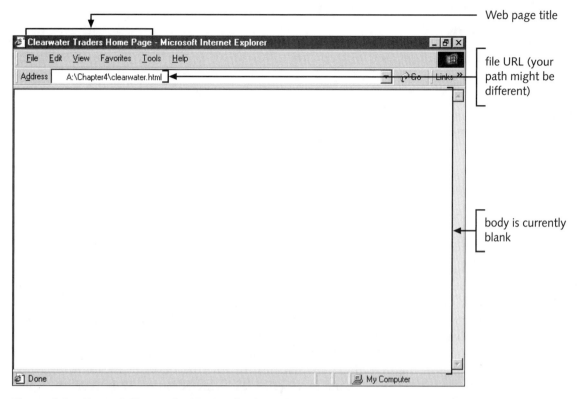

Web page title

file URL (your
path might be
different)

4

body is currently
blank

Figure 4-3   Current Clearwater Traders home page

Note that the Web page title is displayed in the window title bar. The Web page is currently blank, because you have not yet defined the Web page content in the body section of the HTML file.

HTML Headings

First you will create the Level 1 and Level 2 headings shown in Figure 4-1. HTML headings organize a Web page into sections. To create a heading, you use a **heading tag**, which has the following general format: `<H[heading level number]>[heading text]</H[heading level number]>`. HTML supports six levels of headings, numbered from H1 to H6. The heading level indicates the amount of emphasis that should be placed on the enclosed text. H1 headings use the largest font size, while H6 headings use a very small font. Figure 4-4 shows the relative sizes of HTML headings, as well as the size of regular text that is not within a heading tag. Actual font sizes might be displayed differently in different Web browsers.

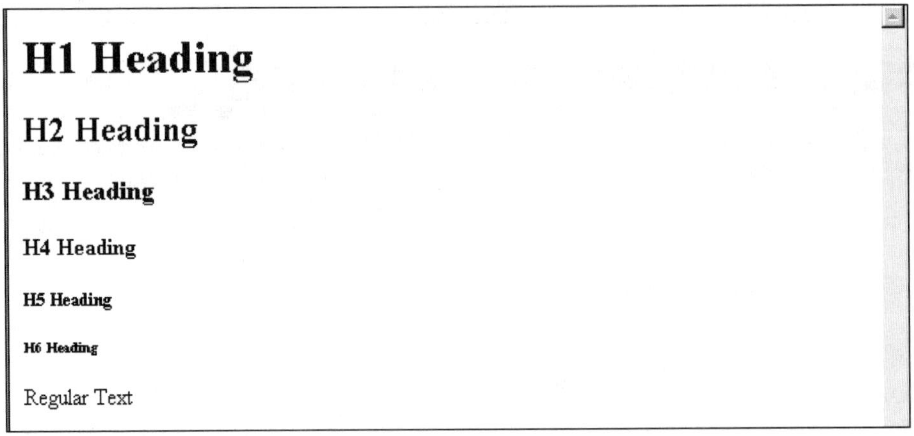

H1 Heading

H2 Heading

H3 Heading

H4 Heading

H5 Heading

H6 Heading

Regular Text

Figure 4-4   Relative sizes of HTML headings

Headings use two-sided tags, and they are always placed in the body section of the Web page. Headings always contain text, and they can be combined with other tags to indicate hyperlinks, text formatting, and so on. By default, headings are always left-justified, but you can specify a different alignment by using the HTML **ALIGN** attribute within the opening heading tag. The basic format of an opening Level 1 heading tag with the ALIGN attribute set is `<H1 ALIGN=[desired alignment]>`. Desired alignment values can be CENTER, RIGHT, or LEFT. For example, to create the Level 1 "Clearwater Traders" heading shown in Figure 4-1 and specify that it is centered on the Web page, you would use the following heading tag: `<H1 ALIGN=CENTER>Clearwater Traders</H1>`. Now you will add the Level 1 and Level 2 headings to the Clearwater Traders home page.

To add the Level 1 and Level 2 headings:

1. Switch back to Notepad, and within the clearwater.html file, add the heading and alignment tags and document text within the `<BODY>...</BODY>` tags, as shown in Figure 4-5, and then save the file.

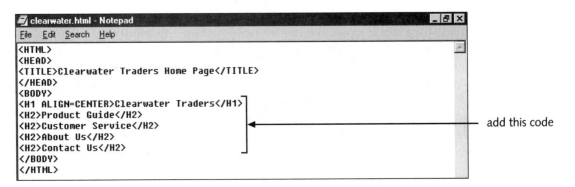

add this code

Figure 4-5   HTML code to specify Web page headings

2. Switch to Internet Explorer, click **View** on the menu bar, and then click **Refresh** to reload the HTML file and display your changes. Your Web page headings are displayed, as shown in Figure 4-6.

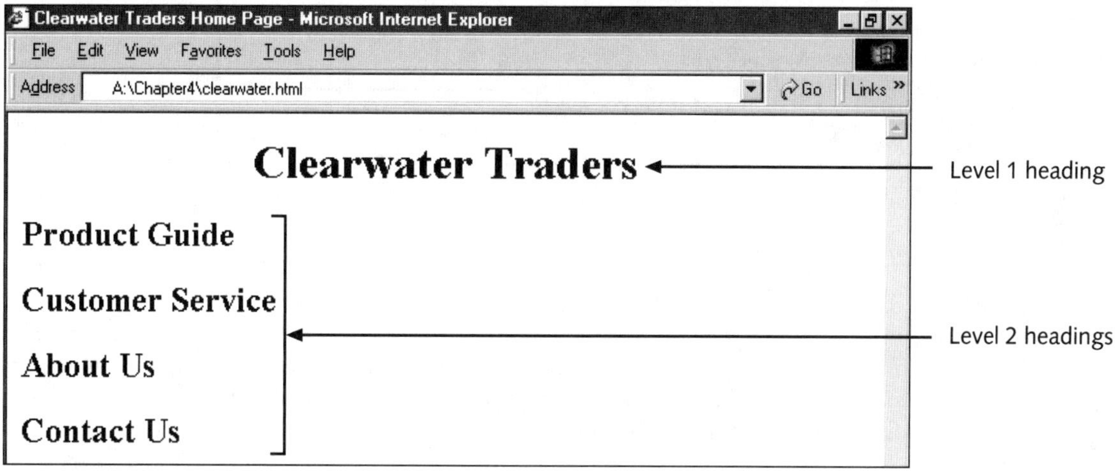

Figure 4-6 Web page headings

Text Formatting Commands

Next, you will add the formatted text under the Clearwater Traders Level 1 heading. You will enter the location text ("Eau Claire, Wisconsin, USA") and the text for the telephone numbers into your HTML document and view the result. For now, you will insert an asterisk (*) in place of the bullet between the telephone numbers. You will learn how to insert special characters such as bullets later in this chapter.

To enter the location and telephone number text:

1. Switch back to Notepad, add the location and telephone number text as shown in Figure 4-7, and then save the file. Note that there should be five blank spaces before and after the asterisk between the two numbers.

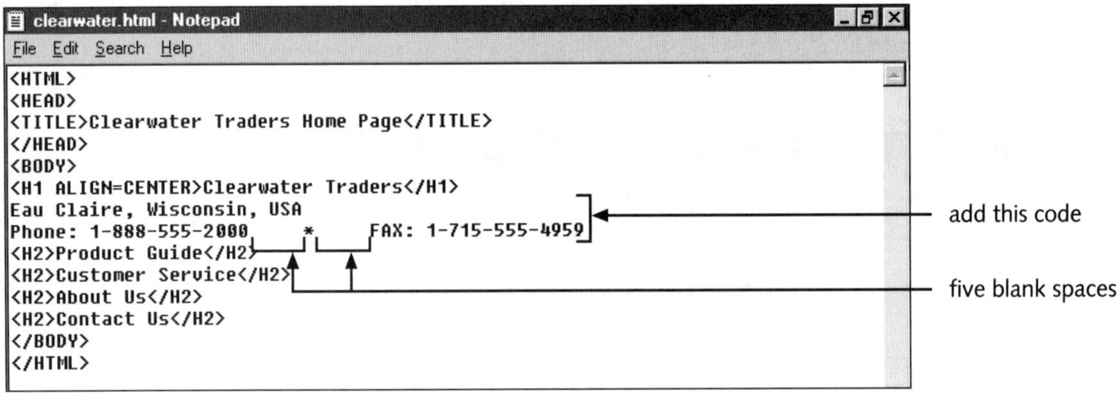

Figure 4-7   HTML code to specify location and phone numbers

2. Switch to Internet Explorer, click **View** on the menu bar, and then click **Refresh** to reload the HTML file and display your changes. Your Web page text is displayed, as shown in Figure 4-8.

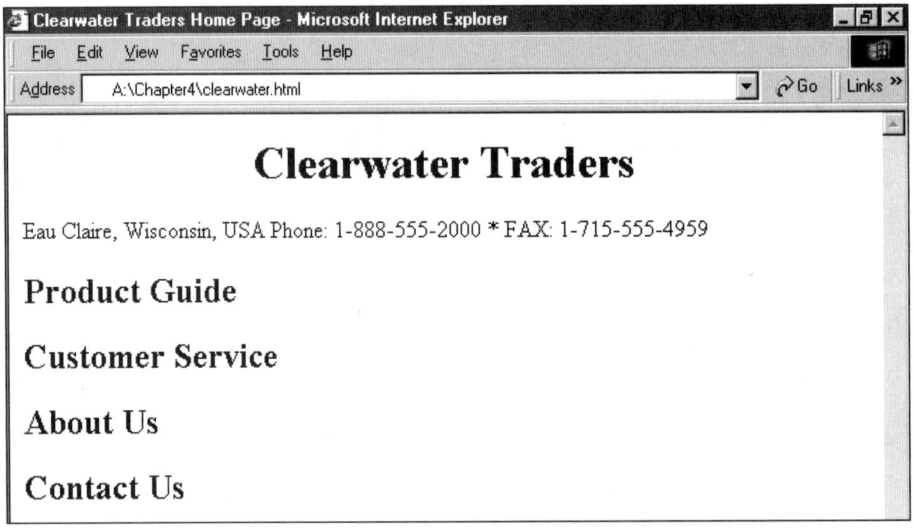

Figure 4-8   Web page with location and phone numbers

Note that the text is displayed left-justified and all on one line, even though you specified the text on two separate lines in the HTML code. Also, note that all of the extra blank spaces that you entered before and after the asterisk are displayed as a single blank space. Browsers ignore blank spaces and line breaks within HTML code. Tags and special characters are required to add blank spaces to document text, and special characters are needed to add nonkeyboard text such as bullets. Now you will learn how to format text line spacing and justification, insert special characters, and enhance text appearance.

Text Line Spacing and Justification

When you include nonheading text in an HTML document, the text appears in a continuous paragraph with no line breaks unless special tags are included to indicate paragraphs and line breaks. The **paragraph tag** (<P>) is a two-sided tag used to signal the beginning of a new paragraph within Web page text. A blank line is inserted between the previous text and the text that follows the <P> tag. Text within the paragraph tags will wrap to the next line. The exact way that the line breaks occur will depend on the size of the browser window, and will vary among different browsers.

The **line break tag** (<BR>) is a one-sided tag used within a paragraph to insert a line break. The text immediately following the line break tag is displayed on the line immediately below the previous text. Figure 4-9 illustrates Web page body text coded as a new paragraph, and including a line break.

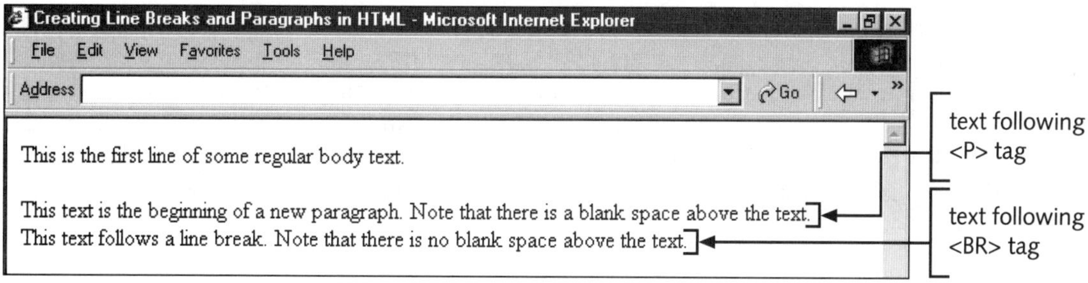

Figure 4-9 Web page body text with paragraph and line breaks

By default, Web page body text, like Web page heading text, is left-justified. The paragraph tag can also use the ALIGN attribute to specify the paragraph alignment. The basic format of the opening paragraph tag with the ALIGN attribute is <P ALIGN=[desired alignment]>. The tags used to specify line breaks and justified paragraph text are summarized in Table 4-1.

Table 4-1 Tags to specify line breaks, paragraphs, and paragraph alignment

Tag	Description
 	Creates a line break
<P> or <P ALIGN=LEFT>	Creates a new left-justified paragraph
<P ALIGN=CENTER>	Creates a new center-justified paragraph
<P ALIGN=RIGHT>	Creates a new right-justified paragraph

Now you will add the tags to place the location and phone number text in a center-justified paragraph, and to create a line break between the location and the phone numbers.

To add the paragraph and line break:

1. Switch back to Notepad, and add paragraph and line break tags to the location and phone number text as follows:

```
<P ALIGN=CENTER>Eau Claire, Wisconsin, USA
<BR>Phone: 1-888-555-2000   *   FAX: 1-715-555-4959</P>
```

2. Save the file, then switch to Internet Explorer, and refresh your browser display to view your changes. Your Web page text should be displayed with the location and phone number text centered and displayed on separate lines.

HTML Character Entities

Sometimes you need to include special characters in a Web page that are not on your computer keyboard. For example, the Clearwater Traders telephone numbers are separated by a bullet and extra blank spaces that cannot be represented directly in the text, but must be displayed using character entities. **Character entities** are special character codes composed of numbers or character strings that are always preceded by an ampersand (&), and are inserted directly into the Web page body text. Some character entities have been assigned both a number code and a character code, and you can use either one. Number codes are always preceded by an ampersand (&) followed by a pound sign (#). Some of the commonly used HTML character entities and their corresponding number and/or character codes are listed in Table 4-2.

Table 4-2   Common HTML character entity codes

Character	Description	Number Code	Character Code
●	Bullet	&#149	
·	Middle dot	&#183	&middot
©	Copyright symbol	&#169	&copy
®	Registered trademark	&#174	&reg
[blank space]	Nonbreaking space, used to add several blank spaces within text		

You can combine character entity codes by separating the individual codes by a semicolon (;). For example, the code to create a bullet followed by two blank spaces is written as • . Now you will modify the Web page HTML code to include the bullet between the telephone and fax numbers, and the five extra blank spaces before and after the bullet. Every   special character code inserts a single blank space, so you will include five   codes before the bullet code, and five   codes after the bullet code.

To add the bullet and blank spaces between the telephone and fax numbers:

1. Switch back to Notepad, add the special character codes shown in Figure 4-10, and then save the file.

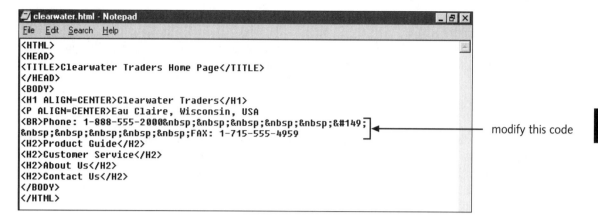

Figure 4-10   HTML code with character entities

2. Switch to Internet Explorer and refresh your browser display to view your changes. Your Web page text is displayed with the blank spaces and the bullet between the telephone and fax numbers, as shown in Figure 4-11.

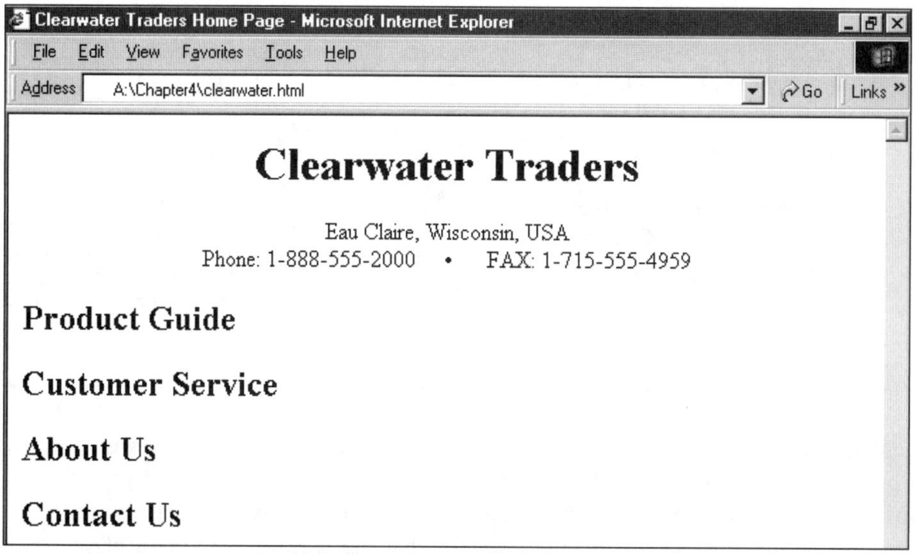

Figure 4-11   Web page with character entities

Character Tags

You will display the location text on the Clearwater Traders home page ("Eau Claire, WI USA") in a larger font than the telephone and fax numbers, and in a bold font style. The telephone and fax numbers will be displayed in an italic font style. You can use HTML **character tags** to specify the characteristics of individual characters. There are two kinds of character tags: content-based tags and physical-style tags. **Content-based character tags** are two-sided tags that format the enclosed text according to the text content. For example, a content-based tag might indicate that the text is computer code, which is displayed using a small, fixed-width font, or a bibliographic citation from a book or magazine, which is displayed using an italic font. Different browsers might display content-based tags using slightly different font types and styles.

Physical-style character tags are two-sided tags that allow the Web page developer to specify exact text properties, such as boldface, superscript, or italic text. You can usually achieve the same or similar results using content-based tags and physical-style tags. Content-based and physical-style tags simply provide two different ways to format text, and you can use either tag type according to your formatting needs and preferences. Table 4-3 summarizes some commonly used content-based character tags, and Table 4-4 summarizes some commonly used physical-style character tags.

Table 4-3   Content-based character tags

Tag	Description	Usage	Display Style
`<EM>`	Enclosed characters should be emphasized, usually displayed using italics	`<EM>Emphasized text</EM>`	*Emphasized text*
`<STRONG>`	Enclosed characters should be emphasized more strongly than `<EM>`, usually displayed using boldface	`<STRONG>Strongly emphasized text</STRONG>`	**Strongly emphasized text**
`<CODE>`	Enclosed characters are computer code and are usually displayed in a fixed-width font such as Courier	`<CODE>N = N + 1</CODE>`	`N = N + 1`
`<CITE>`	Enclosed characters are a bibliographic citation, usually displayed using italics	`<CITE>A Guide to Oracle8, Course Technology, 2000, pp. 1-12</CITE>`	*A Guide to Oracle8, Course Technology, 2000, pp. 1-12*

You can enclose text in multiple character tags to specify multiple formatting instructions. For example, you would use the following HTML code to display text with emphasis, using a bold font: `<EM><B>Bold italic text</B></EM>`. Now you will add character tags to the location and phone number text. You will specify that the location is to be displayed with emphasis, using the `<STRONG>` content-based tag, and you will specify that it is displayed using a bold font by using the `<B>` physical-style tag. You will specify that the telephone numbers are displayed using a small italic font, using the `<I>` and the `<SMALL>` physical-style character tags.

Table 4-4   Physical style character tags

Tag	Description	Usage	Display Style
`<B>`	Bold font	`<B>Bold font</B>`	**Bold font**
`<I>`	Italic font	`<I>Italic font</I>`	*Italic font*
`<U>`	Underlined font	`<U>Underlined text</U>`	<u>Underlined text</u>
`<BIG>`	Increased font size	`<BIG>Bigger text</BIG>`	Bigger text
`<SMALL>`	Smaller font size	`<SMALL>Smaller text<SMALL>`	Smaller font
`<SUB>`	Subscript text	`<SUB>Sub</SUB>script text`	$_{Sub}$script text
`<SUP>`	Superscript text	`<SUP>Super</SUP>script text`	^{Super}script text
`<BLINK>`	Alternating foreground and background colors	`<BLINK>Blinking text</BLINK>`	Blinking text
`<S>` or `<STRIKE>`	Strikethrough text	`<STRIKE>Strikethrough text</STRIKE>`	~~Strikethrough text~~
`<TT>`	Teletype-style (fixed-width font)	`<TT>Fixed-width text</TT>`	`Fixed-width text`

To add character tags to the location and phone number text:

1. Switch back to Notepad, add the character tags as shown in Figure 4-12, and then save the file.

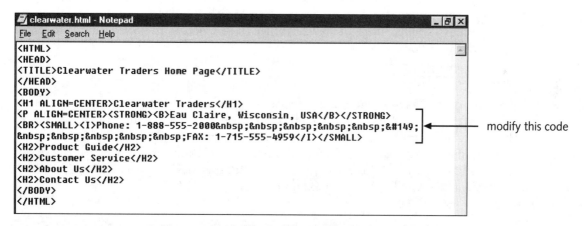

modify this code

Figure 4-12   HTML code with character tags

2. Switch to Internet Explorer, and refresh your browser display to view your changes. The Web page text is displayed with the bold and italic text style changes, as shown in Figure 4-13.

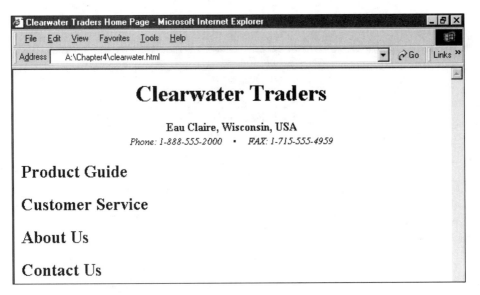

Figure 4-13   Web page with character tag formatting

Graphic Objects

Web pages often contain graphic images and other graphic objects to make the pages more appealing and easier to read and understand. In Figure 4-1, the Clearwater Traders home page contains a graphic image of the Clearwater Traders logo, and a horizontal rule to divide the page into sections.

Graphic Images

The Clearwater Traders logo will be displayed as an **inline image** that appears directly on the Web page, and is loaded when the Web page is loaded in the user's browser. To display a graphic image in a Web page, you use the **image tag**, which is a one-sided tag that specifies the filename of the graphic image. The basic format of the image tag is `<IMG SRC="[image filename]">`, where `SRC` specifies the image source file, which is a graphic file with a .gif or .jpg extension.

> Most Web browsers that can display graphics support two types of graphic images: GIF (Graphics Interchange Format) and JPEG (Joint Photographic Experts Group). Before you can display an image on a Web page, you must convert the image to one of these file types, using a graphic art software application.

The image filename can be specified using an absolute path or a relative path. An **absolute path** specifies the exact location of a file in the user's file system, including the drive letter, folder path, and filename. In an absolute path, the names of different folders within the folder path are separated by front slashes (/). An example of an absolute path to the clearlogo.jpg file that is stored in the Chapter8 folder on your Data Disk is A:/Chapter8/clearlogo.jpg (this path assumes that your Data Disk is a floppy disk and that your floppy drive is drive A).

> In DOS or Windows file system commands, folder names in paths are separated by **back slashes** (\). In HTML commands, folder names are separated by **front slashes** (/). Microsoft Internet Explorer Version 5 accepts either front slashes or back slashes in HTML folder path specifications. Netscape Navigator only recognizes front slashes in path specifications.

4

A **relative path** specifies a file location in relation to the location of the current HTML Web page file, which is called the **current working directory**. To reference a folder that is above the current working directory in a relative path, type two periods (..). To reference a folder that is below the current working directory, type the name of the folder. To reference a subfolder of the folder either above or below the current working directory, type a front slash, followed by the folder name. To illustrate relative paths, Figure 4-14 shows a hypothetical directory structure on your Data Disk.

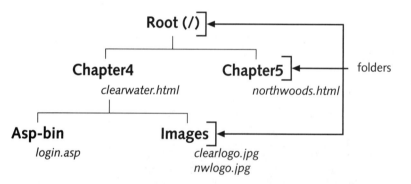
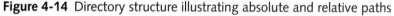

Figure 4-14 Directory structure illustrating absolute and relative paths

Figure 4-14 shows that the root directory of this Data Disk contains two folders, Chapter4 and Chapter5. The Chapter4 folder contains a file named clearwater.html, and the Chapter5 folder contains a file named northwoods.html. The Chapter4 folder also contains subfolders named Asp-bin and Images. Each of these folders contains the files shown in the figure. Table 4-5 shows the absolute and relative path addresses to different target files in the directory structure assuming that the Chapter4 folder is the current working directory.

Table 4-5 Examples of absolute and relative path addresses

Current Working Directory	Target File	Absolute Path	Relative Path
Chapter4	clearlogo.jpg	Chapter4/Images/clearlogo.jpg	Images/clearlogo.jpg
Chapter4	northwoods.html	Chapter5/northwoods.html	../Chapter5/northwoods.html

By default, images are displayed on the left edge of the Web page. There are two ways to control image alignment. One way is to use the ALIGN attribute directly in the image tag, using the following general format. Recall that the desired alignment value can be LEFT, CENTER, or RIGHT.

```
<IMG SRC="[image filename]" ALIGN=[desired alignment]>
```

This approach places the image in the same paragraph as the text that precedes it. A second approach is to place the image in a new paragraph, and then specify the paragraph alignment using the paragraph tag's ALIGN attribute. The advantage of using the new paragraph approach is that blank space is added above and below the image. You will use the new paragraph approach to center the Clearwater Traders logo on your Web page, and to create white space above and below the image. The logo source file is named clearlogo.jpg, and it is stored in the Chapter4 folder on your Data Disk. Since this is the current working directory (the same folder in which your Web page is stored), you will specify the image source file using a relative path that includes just the filename.

To add the image to the Web page:

1. Switch back to Notepad and add the following HTML code immediately below the program line that specifies the telephone and fax numbers and just above the `<H2>Product Guide</H2>` program line.

   ```
   <P ALIGN=CENTER><IMG SRC="clearlogo.jpg"></P>
   ```

2. Save the file, then switch to Internet Explorer and refresh your browser display to view your changes. The Web page text is displayed with the Clearwater Traders logo immediately below the telephone and fax numbers, as shown in Figure 4-15.

> **TIP** If your graphic image is displayed as a picture icon 🖻 instead of the actual image, then you made an error either in the image tag command or in the path to the source filename. Check your code and make sure it exactly matches the code specified in Step 1 above and make sure that the clearlogo.jpg file is in the Chapter4 folder on your Data Disk.

Currently, the Web browser determines the display size of the graphic image. The exact image display size can be specified directly within the image tag. You should always specify the image size within an image tag. If you do not specify the image size, the Web browser has to open the image source file, determine the image size, and then format the page and display the image. If you specify the image size directly in the image tag, the Web browser simply formats the page and displays the image so it fits on the page. To specify the size of an image, you use the **WIDTH** and **HEIGHT attributes** within the image tag, using the following general format: `<IMG SRC="filename" WIDTH=[desired display width] HEIGHT=[desired display height]>`. The desired display width and height can be specified as either a numerical value in pixels or a percentage of the Web page width and height. The following commands are used to specify the size of an image file named sample.jpg using both methods:

```
<IMG SRC="sample.jpg" WIDTH=100 HEIGHT=75>
<IMG SRC="sample.jpg" WIDTH="40%" HEIGHT="15%">
```

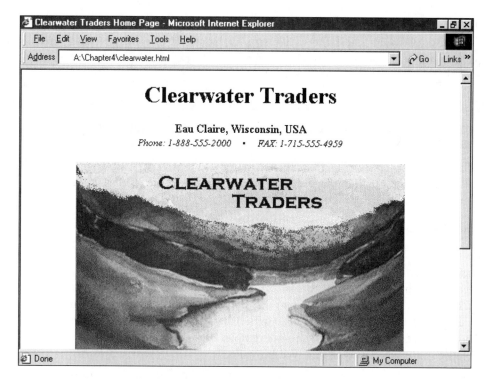

Figure 4-15 Web page with graphic image

Note that when you specify a size value as a percentage of the Web page size, the percentage value is enclosed in quotation marks.

 Indicating the number of pixels, or picture elements, is a method for specifying the size of graphic images when they are displayed on computer screens.

Determining the correct image size on a Web page is usually a trial-and-error process. The image size specified in the image tag can be different from the image size that is specified when you create or edit the image in a graphic arts program, but the aspect ratio of the new height and width should be the same as the aspect ratio for the original graphic image. Otherwise, the graphic image might be distorted when it is displayed.

 The aspect ratio of a graphic image is the ratio of the width to the height. For example, for a graphic image that is 320 pixels wide and 200 pixels high, the aspect ratio is 1.6 to 1.

Currently, the Clearwater Traders logo is larger than the logo in the design diagram in Figure 4-1. Now you will adjust the image size by specifying the image display size, in pixels, in the image tag.

To specify the image display size:

1. Switch back to Notepad and modify the image tag, using the following code:

```
<P ALIGN=CENTER><IMG SRC="clearlogo.jpg" WIDTH=240
HEIGHT=160></P>
```

2. Save the file, then switch to Internet Explorer and refresh the Web page display. The size of the graphic image should now be similar to the graphic image size in the design diagram in Figure 4-1.

Horizontal Rules

Horizontal rules provide a way to visually separate a Web page into different sections and make it easier to read. To create a horizontal rule, you use the **horizontal rule tag**, which is a one-sided tag with the following format: <HR>. A horizontal rule creates a simple line break, and is displayed directly below the text that precedes it, with no extra space added. You can include extra attributes within the horizontal rule tag to specify the line's thickness, shading, width, and alignment. Figure 4-16 shows examples of the way horizontal rules with different attribute values are displayed in a Web browser.

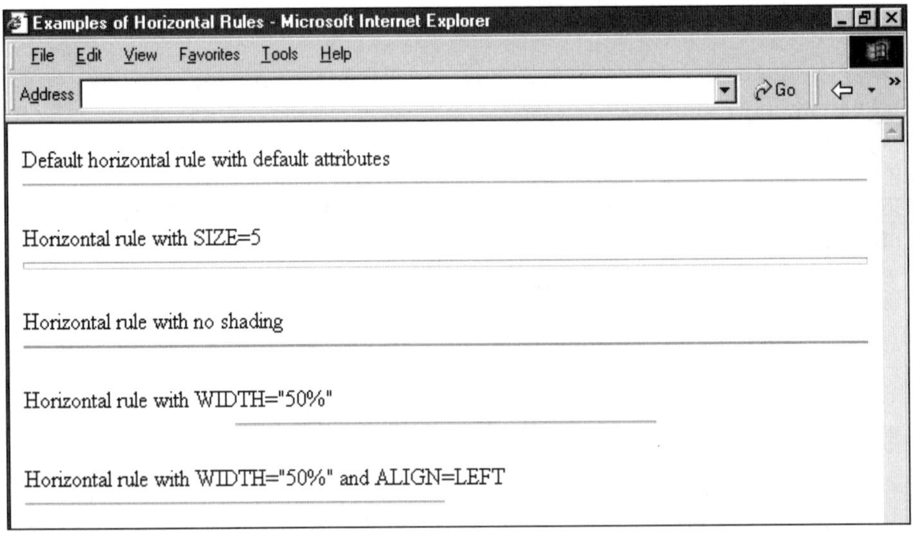

Figure 4-16   Horizontal rules with different attributes

By default, horizontal rules are 3 pixels high, displayed center-justified across the entire Web page width, and are shaded so that they appear to be inset within the Web page. You can modify the rule size, remove the shading so the rule appears as a two-dimensional flat line on the Web page, change the width to a specific pixel length, extend the rule across a specific percentage of the Web page, and/or change the rule alignment. Table 4-6 summarizes how the attributes of horizontal rules can be modified.

Table 4-6   Horizontal rule attributes

Property	Attribute	Example
Line thickness	SIZE	<HR SIZE=5>
No shading	NOSHADE	<HR NOSHADE>
Width	WIDTH=[number of pixels] WIDTH="[percent of Web page width]"	WIDTH=32 WIDTH="50%"
Alignment	ALIGN=[desired alignment]	ALIGN=LEFT

You can combine attributes by listing them sequentially in the horizontal rule tag. Now you will create the horizontal rule in the Clearwater Traders Web page. The rule will be 5 pixels thick, have no shading, and be centered across the width of the entire Web page.

To create the horizontal rule:

1. Switch to Notepad, and add the following command between the code for the image tag and the line that contains the code `<H2>Product Guide</H2>`.

   ```
   <HR SIZE=5 NOSHADE>
   ```

2. Save the file, then switch to Internet Explorer and refresh the display to view your changes. Your Web page with the horizontal rule should be displayed as shown in Figure 4-17.

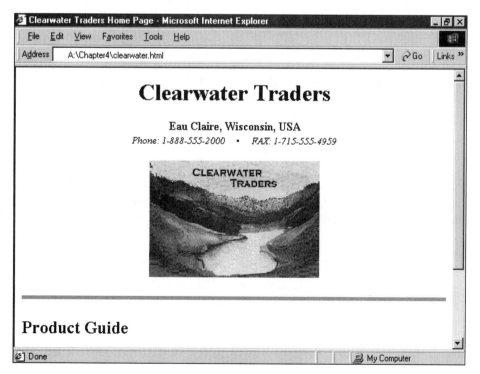

Figure 4-17   Web page with horizontal rule

HTML Lists

Now you need to create the bulleted list that is displayed under the "Customer Service" Level 2 heading in Figure 4-1. HTML allows you to create formatted lists for grouping and formatting related text items. You can create **unordered lists**, in which the list items have no particular order. Unordered lists are usually used for bulleted items or other nonsequential items, such as links to other Web pages. You can also create **ordered lists**, in which a number for each list item is displayed automatically. Ordered lists are usually used for sequential items, such as a table of contents or an instruction sequence.

Unordered Lists

An unordered list is defined by using the two-sided **unordered list tag**, which has the format <UL>. Each individual list item is then defined within the opening and closing unordered list tag, using the one-sided **list item tag** <LI>. The code for an unordered list has the following general format:

```
<UL>
        <LI>[text for item]
        <LI>[text for next item]
        ...
</UL>
```

It is a good practice to indent the individual list items within the HTML code so that the code is easier to understand. By default, Web browsers add a leading bullet to each unordered list item and place each item on a new line. Now you will add the unordered list to your Clearwater Traders Web page.

To add the unordered list:

1. Switch to Notepad, and add the following commands directly below the <H2>Customer Service</H2> code line.

```
<UL>
  <LI>How to Order
  <LI>Shipping and Returns
  <LI>Check on Your Order
</UL>
```

2. Save the file, then switch to Internet Explorer and refresh the display to view your changes. Your bulleted list should be displayed as shown in Figure 4-18.

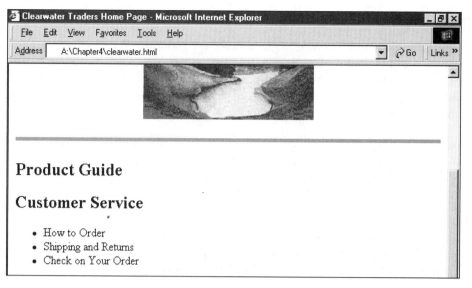

Figure 4-18   Web page bulleted list

Ordered Lists

An ordered list is defined by using the two-sided **ordered list tag**, which has the format `<OL>`. As with an unordered list, each individual list item is defined within the opening and closing ordered list tag by using the list item tag. With an ordered list, you can specify the **TYPE attribute**, which specifies the numbering style.

By default, ordered lists use Arabic (standard English-style) numbers and start with the number 1. You can also specify the start value of the first list item using the **START attribute**. The start attribute has the following format: `START=[Arabic number of desired start value]`. Table 4-7 shows the different ordered list numbering styles, list definitions including the TYPE and START attributes, and the resulting numbering sequence. For example, to define an ordered list using lowercase Roman numerals with a start value of vi, you would use the following ordered list tag:

```
<OL TYPE="i" START=6>
```

Table 4-7   Ordered list styles

Numbering Style	Type Definition	Sample Sequence
Arabic numbers	`<OL TYPE="1" START=3>`	3, 4, 5, 6, …
Capital letters	`<OL TYPE="A" START=3>`	C, D, E, F, …
Lowercase letters	`<OL TYPE="a" START=3>`	c, d, e, f, …
Roman numerals	`<OL TYPE="I" START=3>`	III, IV, V, VI, …
Lowercase Roman numerals	`<OL TYPE="i" START=3>`	iii, iv, v, vi, …

Comments in HTML Code

As you've probably noticed by now, HTML code for even a simple Web page can quickly become complex and difficult to understand. It is a good practice to add comment tags to internally document different Web page sections. Comments are not visible when the Web page is displayed in a Web browser, but anyone can view the HTML source code for the page and read the comments.

 TIP You can view the HTML source code for any Web page by clicking View on your browser's menu bar and then clicking Source. You might want to view the source code of a Web page to see how a developer achieved a certain formatting layout.

Comment tags are two-sided tags. An **opening comment tag** uses the format **<!--** (an angle bracket, then an exclamation point followed by two hyphens). A **closing comment tag** uses the format **-->** (two hyphens followed by an angle bracket). Now you will add comment tags to the HTML document to make it more readable.

To add comments to your HTML document:

1. Switch to Notepad, and add the comments and blank lines, as shown in Figure 4-19.

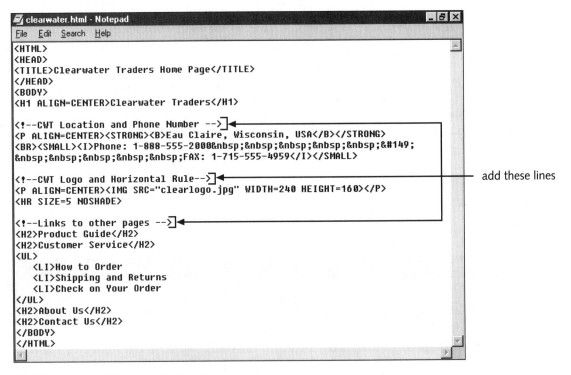

Figure 4-19   HTML document with comments

2. Save the file, then switch to Internet Explorer and refresh the display to confirm that your Web page display has not been changed.

3. Switch back to Notepad, and close the **clearwater.html** file.

TABLES IN WEB PAGES

Recall that data in a relational database are stored in a tabular format. When you create Web pages to display database data, often it is desirable to display the data in a table. Figure 4-20 illustrates a design diagram for the Clearwater Traders Product Guide Web page, which shows data about Clearwater Traders products from the ITEM table in Figure 2-4.

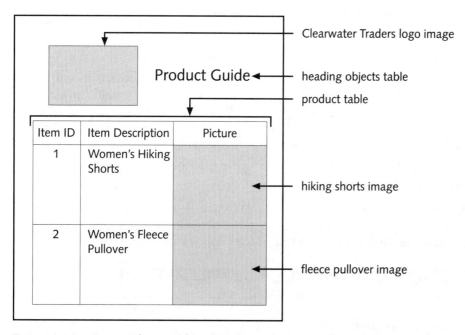

Figure 4-20   Design diagram for Clearwater Traders Product Guide Web page

This Web page contains two tables. The first table contains the page's heading objects. It has only one row and does not display row or column lines. Its first column contains the Clearwater Traders logo, and its second column contains the "Product Guide" text. The heading objects were placed in a table rather than as separate objects on the Web page because tables provide an easy way to display text next to graphic images. The second table displays the data for each product, which includes the item ID, item description, and a graphic image showing a picture of each product. Now you will learn how to create and format HTML tables.

HTML Table Definition Tags

An HTML table is defined by using the **table tag**, which is a two-sided tag with the following format: `<TABLE>[table contents]</TABLE>`. Individual rows in an HTML table are defined using the **table row tag** `<TR>`, and individual data items within each row are defined using the **table data tag** `<TD>` and the following general structure:

```
<TABLE>
     <TR>
          <TD>[Contents of first column in first row]</TD>
          <TD>[Contents of second column in first row]</TD>
     </TR>
      <TR>
          <TD>[Contents of first column in second row]</TD>
          <TD>[Contents of second column in second row]</TD>
     </TR>
</TABLE>
```

You should always indent the table row and data tags in your HTML code, as shown, so that you can easily identify the individual table rows and cells. To insert a graphic image into a table cell, you place the image tag directly in the cell. You can specify image properties, and format text within a table, just as with any Web page text. Now you will create the Product Guide Web page shown in Figure 4-20, and create the heading objects table that contains the Clearwater Traders logo and the "Product Guide" heading text.

To create the Product Guide Web page:

1. Create a new file in Notepad, type the HTML code shown in Figure 4-21 to define the Product Guide Web page and the table for the logo and heading text, and save the file as **products.html** in the Chapter4 folder on your Data Disk.

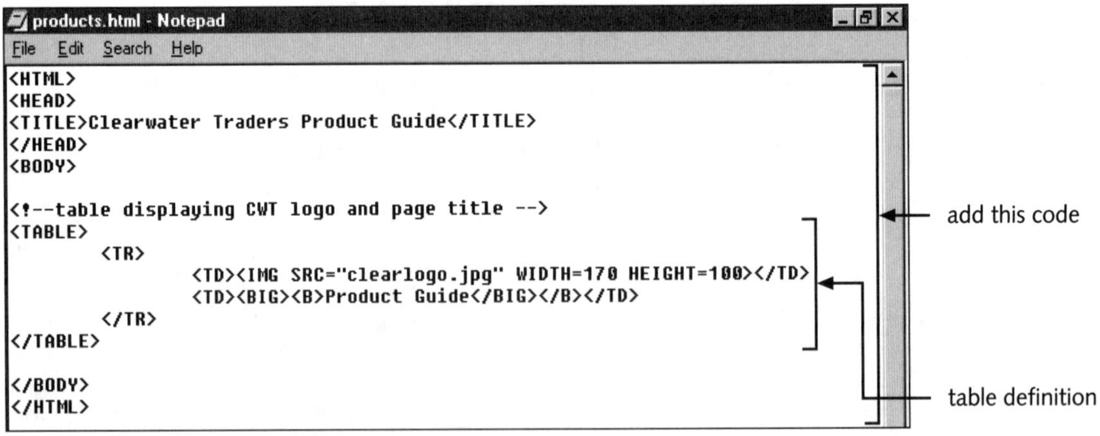

```
<HTML>
<HEAD>
<TITLE>Clearwater Traders Product Guide</TITLE>
</HEAD>
<BODY>

<!--table displaying CWT logo and page title -->
<TABLE>
        <TR>
                <TD><IMG SRC="clearlogo.jpg" WIDTH=170 HEIGHT=100></TD>
                <TD><BIG><B>Product Guide</BIG></B></TD>
        </TR>
</TABLE>

</BODY>
</HTML>
```


Figure 4-21 Code to define Product Guide Web page

2. Switch to Internet Explorer and open **products.html** from the Chapter4 folder on your Data Disk. The Web page with the heading objects table is displayed, as shown in Figure 4-22.

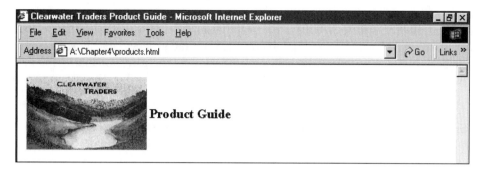

Figure 4-22   Heading objects table

Table Size and Alignment

By default, the width of a table is determined by the widths of the data values in the individual table columns, and the height is determined by the number of table rows. Alternately, you can specify a specific table size using the WIDTH and HEIGHT attributes within the table tag. (Recall that you used these attributes previously to specify the sizes of inline image objects.) Usually when you are creating tables that contain database records, you omit the HEIGHT property and only specify a value for the table's WIDTH property. This allows the table to grow vertically according to the number of records displayed. As before, you can specify the table size in pixels, or as a percentage of the Web page display area.

By default, tables are aligned on the left edge of the Web page. You can use the ALIGN attribute (`ALIGN=[desired alignment]`) within the table tag to change the table alignment. Now you will modify the table specification so that the table is centered on the Web page and spans 60 percent of the available Web page width.

To modify the table size and alignment:

1. Switch back to Notepad, and modify the opening table tag using the following code:

   `<TABLE ALIGN=CENTER WIDTH="60%">`

2. Save the file, and then switch to Internet Explorer and refresh your display to view the centered and resized table.

Column Headings

Next, you will create the table that contains the product information. For now, you will hard-code, or directly enter, the table values. In later chapters, you will learn how to write programs to retrieve these values from the database and display them in a Web page table. From Figure 4-20, you can see that the product table has a heading row. The column headings should be displayed in a large, boldface font. You can create a heading row in a table using the **table heading tag** `<TH>` in place of the table data tag for the first column row. By default, table headings are displayed in a large, boldface font, and they are centered within table columns. A table can have multiple heading rows if desired.

Now you will create the product table that contains the item IDs, item descriptions, and item images. You will place this table in a new paragraph, using the paragraph tag <P>, so that there is a blank space between the heading objects table and the product table. Then you will enter the code to create the row for the column headings, and the rows containing the first two Clearwater Traders products.

To create the product table:

1. Switch back to Notepad, add the code shown in Figure 4-23 to create the product table, and save the file.

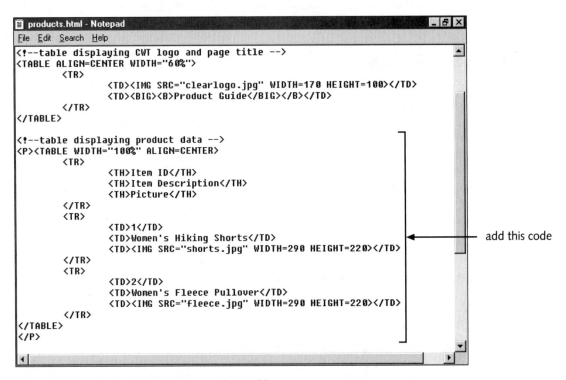

Figure 4-23   Code to create the product table

2. Switch to Internet Explorer and refresh your display to view the product table. Your table should look like the one shown in Figure 4-24.

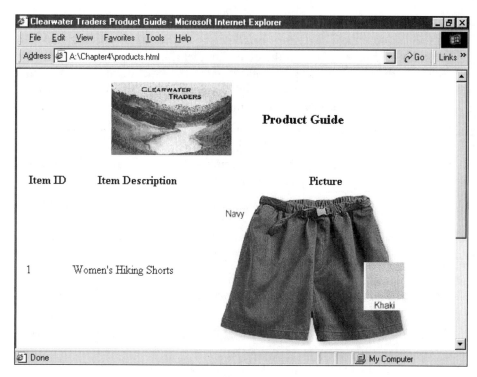

Figure 4-24   Web page product table

Table Borders and Cell Spacing

The current product table is hard to read because borders are needed to delineate the different table columns. To specify table borders, you use the BORDER, CELL SPACING, and CELL PADDING table tag attributes. These attributes are illustrated in Figure 4-25.

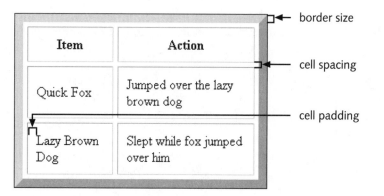

Figure 4-25   Table BORDER, CELL SPACING, and CELL PADDING attributes

The **BORDER attribute** is used to add borders to table columns and rows and has the following general format: BORDER=[desired border thickness]. By default, tables are displayed as three-dimensional objects, and the desired border thickness property, specified in pixels, controls the depth of the box that surrounds the table. The border lines around individual cells are always 1 pixel wide. If you do not specify a value for the desired border thickness and simply enter BORDER in the table tag, the outside border size will be 1 pixel.

The **CELL SPACING attribute** determines the amount of space, in pixels, between the inside border lines of adjacent table cells. It uses the following general format: CELLSPACING=[desired cell spacing]. To remove the space between the inside cell border lines, you can set the cell spacing equal to zero.

The **CELL PADDING attribute** determines the amount of space, in pixels, between the inside cell border and the object or text within the cell. When an object is left-justified within a table cell, the cell padding determines the space between the object and the top and left edges of the cell.

It is a good idea to display borders in a table while you are creating it in HTML, even if the finished table will not have borders that are displayed. The borders make it easier to visualize and adjust the cell spacing and cell padding.

Now you will add a border and modify the CELL SPACING and CELL PADDING attributes of the product table.

To modify the table borders:

1. Switch back to Notepad, and modify the table tag code for the product table as follows:

   ```
   <P><TABLE WIDTH="100%" ALIGN=CENTER BORDER=5 CELLSPACING=3
   CELLPADDING=5>
   ```

2. Save the file, then switch to Internet Explorer and refresh your display to view the product table. The table is now displayed with borders, as shown in Figure 4-26.

Figure 4-26   Product table with borders

Specifying the Widths of Table Columns

Web browsers automatically calculate the width of table columns according to the data values they contain. For example, in Figure 4-26, the first column is wide enough to accommodate the longest data value, which is the column title "Item ID," without wrapping it to two lines. The same approach is used to determine the width of all of the other columns. The last table column has extra space on its right edge because the data values do not require the entire column width. As before, when you do not specify an item's size, the Web browser has to perform extra processing to determine the size, and this causes the Web page to load more slowly. You should always specify the width of table columns to help make tables load and display more quickly.

To specify the widths of table columns, you can add the WIDTH attribute to the table header tag for each column in the first row of the table. (If a table does not have a table header in the first row, you add the WIDTH attribute to the table data tag for each column in the first row.) When you specify the widths for the columns in the first row, the width is automatically specified for all table rows. As always, the WIDTH attribute can be specified in pixels or as a percentage of the table display width. If you specify the column width as a percentage of the table display width, the sum of the WIDTH attribute values for all of the columns must equal 100 percent. Now you will specify the column widths in the product table.

To specify the column widths in the product table:

1. Switch back to Notepad, and modify the table heading tag code for each column in the heading row in the product table as follows:

```
<TH WIDTH="10%">Item ID</TH>
<TH WIDTH="40%">Item Description</TH>
<TH WIDTH="50%">Picture</TH>
```

2. Save the file, then switch to Internet Explorer, and refresh your display to view the product table. The table is now displayed with different column widths, as shown in Figure 4-27. The Item ID and Picture columns are narrower, and the Item Description column is wider.

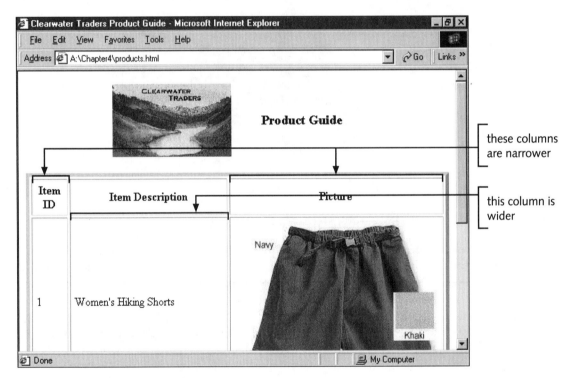

Figure 4-27   Product table with modified column widths

Aligning Table Objects

By default, table objects are left-justified and vertically centered within table cells. You can control the alignment of individual table objects by using the ALIGN attribute and the VERTICAL ALIGN attribute. These attributes must be placed in the table data tag (<TD>) for each data object. Recall that the general format of the ALIGN attribute is ALIGN=[desired alignment], and the desired alignment can be LEFT, CENTER, or RIGHT. The general format of the **VERTICAL ALIGN attribute** is VALIGN=[desired vertical alignment]. The desired vertical alignment can be TOP or BOTTOM. To center a data object vertically, simply omit the VERTICAL ALIGN attribute in the table data tag.

Now you will modify the alignments of some of your cell objects. You will specify that the item ID values will be horizontally centered and vertically aligned at the top of their cells. You will also align the item descriptions at the top of their cells, and align the Item Description header cell text on the left side of its cell.

To modify the table object alignments:

1. Switch back to Notepad, and modify the table data tag codes for the product table as shown in Figure 4-28.

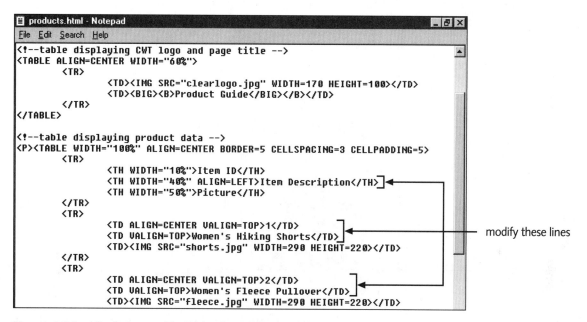

Figure 4-28   Code to modify table object alignments

2. Save the file, then switch to Internet Explorer, and refresh your display to view the product table with the modified column alignments.

HYPERLINKS

A **hyperlink** is a reference in an HTML document that enables you to jump to another location. The hyperlink can be associated with a single keyword, a group of words, or a graphic object. The text associated with a hyperlink is usually underlined on the Web page, and it is displayed in a different color from the rest of the Web page text. The associated location, called the **anchor**, might be an object on the same Web page or a separate HTML document. The hyperlink could also be associated with a computer program that creates a dynamic Web page. Or, the hyperlink could start an e-mail program that automatically inserts an e-mail address specified in the reference.

Hyperlinks to Anchors on the Same Web Page

On the Clearwater Traders Product Guide page, the user has to scroll down the page to view all of the products. Now you will create a bulleted list showing the product names at the top of the Product Guide page. Each list item will have a hyperlink, so that when the user clicks the list item, the Web page display will jump to that item in the table. The revised Product Guide page, with the bulleted list and hyperlinks, is shown in Figure 4-29.

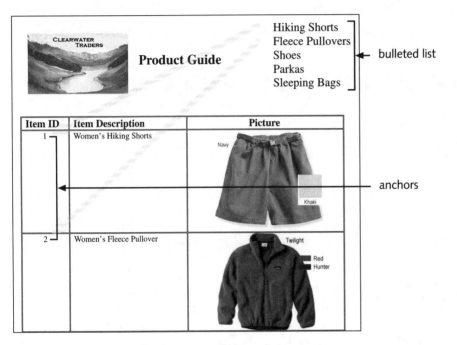

Figure 4-29   Product Guide page with hyperlinks

To create a hyperlink to an anchor on the same Web page, you first create the anchor, and then create the hyperlink to reference the anchor. To create an anchor, you use an **anchor tag**, which has the following general format: `<A NAME="[anchor name]">[anchor text or object]</A>`. The anchor name is a text string used to identify the anchor. Now you will create anchors to item ID 1 and item ID 2 in the product table.

To create the anchors:

1. Switch back to Notepad, and add anchor tags to the table data tags for item ID 1 and item ID 2 in the product table, as shown in Figure 4-30.

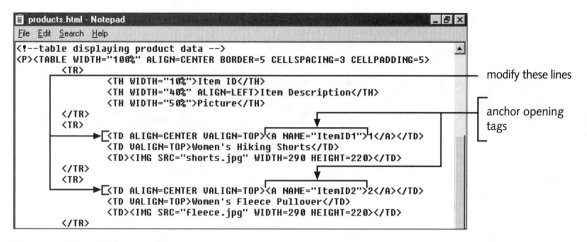

Figure 4-30   Adding anchor tags

To create a hyperlink that references an anchor, you use the **link tag**, which has the following general format: **<A HREF="#[anchor name]">[link text or object]</A>**. Note that you must preface the anchor name with a pound sign (#). Now you will create the bulleted list in the heading objects table (see Figure 4-29) that lists the products in the product table. You will also create a hyperlink that references the anchor for item ID 1 for the first list item, and a hyperlink that references the anchor for item ID 2 for the second list item.

To create the bulleted list and hyperlinks:

1. Modify the table width of the heading objects table, and add the code lines to create the bulleted list of product items and the associated hyperlinks, as shown in Figure 4-31.

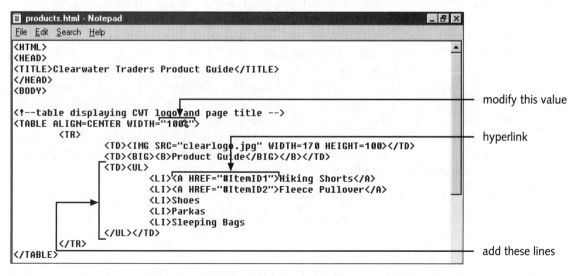

Figure 4-31   Code to add bulleted list and hyperlinks

2. Save the file, then switch to Internet Explorer and refresh the display to view the bulleted list. Note that the list items with hyperlinks are highlighted, as shown in Figure 4–32.

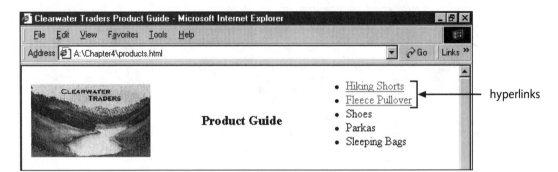

Figure 4-32   Bulleted list display with hyperlinks

3. Click the **Hiking Shorts** hyperlink. Your Web page display moves to item ID 1 in the product table.

> **TIP**
> If a Web page titled "This page cannot be displayed" is displayed instead of item ID 1 in the product table, you have made a mistake in creating either the anchor or hyperlink. Examine your code carefully and make sure that it exactly matches the code shown in Figures 4-30 and 4-31.

Hyperlinks That Reference Different Web Pages

To create a hyperlink to a different Web page, you use the link tag, but substitute the name of the second Web page's HTML file for the anchor name. For example, to create a hyperlink to an HTML file named referencedfilename.html, you would use the following opening link tag: `<A HREF="referencedfilename.html">`. Filenames within quotation marks are not case sensitive. As with graphic image references, if the referenced Web page file is in the current working directory (which is the same folder as the Web page file that contains the hyperlink), you simply list the filename, without any drive letter or folder path information. If the referenced Web page file is in another folder, you must list the absolute or relative path to the referenced file. Now you will open the HTML file for the Clearwater Traders home page that you created earlier in this chapter and create a hyperlink between the Product Guide heading and the Product Guide page you just created.

To create a hyperlink to a different Web page:

1. Switch back to Notepad and open the **clearwater.html** file in the Chapter4 folder on your Data Disk.

2. Modify the `<H2>Product Guide</H2>` tag to reference the products.html file by adding a link tag, using the following code:

```
<H2><A HREF="products.html">Product Guide</A></H2>
```

3. Save the file, then switch to Internet Explorer, click **File** on the menu bar, click **Open**, navigate to the **clearwater.html** file in the Chapter4 folder on your Data Disk, and open the file so that it is displayed in your Web browser. The Product Guide heading is highlighted to indicate that it contains a hyperlink reference.

4. Click the **Product Guide** heading on the Clearwater Traders home page. The Product Guide Web page is displayed.

Hyperlinks to E-mail Addresses

Sometimes Web pages contain hyperlinks to e-mail addresses. When a user clicks an e-mail hyperlink, the Web browser starts the user's default e-mail application, where a new message is displayed that is addressed to an e-mail address specified in the hyperlink. The general format for an e-mail hyperlink is as follows: `<A HREF="mailto:[e-mail address]">`. For example, to create an e-mail hyperlink to cwt@course.com, you would use the following link tag: `<A HREF="mailto:cwt@course.com">`. Now you will create an e-mail hyperlink in the Clearwater Traders home page. You will attach the link to the Contact Us heading, and specify that e-mail messages will be sent to your e-mail address.

To create an e-mail hyperlink:

1. Switch back to Notepad, and add an e-mail hyperlink to the `<H2>Contact Us</H2>` heading code as follows:

    ```
    <H2><A HREF="mailto:[your e-mail ID]">Contact Us</A></H2>
    ```

2. Save the file, then switch to Internet Explorer and click the **Back** button ⟵ on the browser toolbar so that the Clearwater Traders home page is displayed. Refresh the display, then click the **Contact Us** heading. Your e-mail application starts and displays an e-mail message addressed to your e-mail account.

3. Close Internet Explorer.

4. Switch to Notepad, and close Notepad and all other open applications.

SUMMARY

❐ HTML is a document-layout language with hypertext-specification capabilities. HTML is not a programming language, although it can contain embedded programming commands. HTML's primary task is to define the structure and appearance of Web pages and to allow Web pages to contain embedded hypertext links to other documents and/or Web pages. An HTML document that defines a Web page contains the Web page content, which is the text that is displayed on the Web page, and HTML tags, which are codes that define how a particular line or section of the document content is displayed. An HTML document consists of a header section, which contains information about the Web page that is used by the Web browser, and a body section, which contains the text that is displayed in the Web browser.

❏ You can create HTML headings to organize a Web page into sections. By default, text in a Web page is displayed left-justified and all on one line. Tags are required to add line breaks and blank lines to Web pages, and character entities are required to add blank spaces or nonkeyboard text such as bullets. Character tags can be used to format individual characters. Content-based character tags specify text appearance based on the text content, and physical-style character tags format text appearance on the basis of specific text display properties. You can apply multiple character tags to the same text to specify multiple formatting instructions.

❏ Web pages contain images and other graphics objects to make the pages appealing and easier to read and understand. Graphic images can be displayed as inline images that appear directly on the Web page and are loaded when the Web page is loaded in the user's browser. To create an inline image, you use the image tag, which specifies the image's source file, as well as properties such as image size and alignment. The location of the image's source file can be specified using an absolute path, which specifies the exact folder location of the file, or using a relative path, which specifies the location of the file in relation to the current working directory. Horizontal rules provide a way to visually separate a Web page into different sections and make it easier to read. To create a horizontal rule, you use the horizontal rule tag, which can be used to specify the rule's size and appearance. HTML supports commands for easily creating unordered and ordered lists. An unordered list can be a bulleted list, or any other list in which the items do not appear in a definite sequential order. In an ordered list, HTML automatically prefaces list items with numbers.

❏ When you create Web pages to display database data, it is desirable to display the data using an HTML table. Tables also provide an easy way to display graphic objects with text beside them. You can specify the table's size, alignment, border style, and cell padding and spacing properties. You can also specify the width and alignment of individual cells within a table.

❏ HTML hyperlinks can reference a variety of things, including a location in the same Web page, a different Web page, or an e-mail address. To create a hyperlink that references a location on the same Web page, you must create a named anchor at the location, and then reference the anchor in the link tag. To create a hyperlink that references a different Web page, the link tag must reference the HTML filename of the referenced Web page.

REVIEW QUESTIONS

1. What is the difference between a file with an .htm extension and a file with an .html extension?

2. What is the advantage of using a text editor to write HTML documents?

3. What is a tag attribute? List two tag attributes.

4. What are the two main sections of an HTML document?

5. Explain the difference between a Web page title and a heading.

6. What is the difference between the <P> and the <BR> tags?

7. Explain the purpose of the   character entity.

8. What is the difference between a content-based character tag and a physical-style character tag?

9. What is the current working directory of a Web page?

10. Write the relative path specification for a file named myfile.jpg that is in a folder named myparent that is directly above the current working folder.

11. Write the relative path specification for a file named myfile.jpg that is in a folder named mychild that is directly below the current working directory.

12. If a graphics icon is displayed instead of an image when you display HTML code in your Web browser, what probably happened?

13. Explain the difference between how ordered and unordered lists are displayed.

14. What is an aspect ratio?

15. Write a tag to display a block of text that is right-justified.

16. Write a tag to create a comment in an HTML document.

17. What is the <A> tag used for?

18. Why are tables useful for displaying data from a database?

19. When does a hyperlink need an associated anchor?

20. When should you use an e-mail hyperlink?

HANDS-ON PROJECTS

1. In this project, you will modify the Product Guide Web page that you created in the chapter tutorial so that it displays all of the products in the Clearwater Traders ITEM table (Figure 2-4). Your completed Product Guide Web page will look like Figure 4-33.

    a. Open the products.html file from the Chapter4 folder on your Data Disk, and save the file as Ch4Pr1.html.

    b. Add rows to the products table to display the data for the Airstream Canvas Shoes, All-Weather Mountain Parka, and Goose Down Sleeping Bag, as shown in Figure 4-33. (The image files for these items are stored in the Chapter4 folder on your Data Disk as shoes.jpg, parka.jpg, and bags.jpg.)

    c. Create anchors for the item ID in each of the new data rows.

    d. Create hyperlinks from the items in the bulleted list in the heading objects table to the associated objects in the product table.

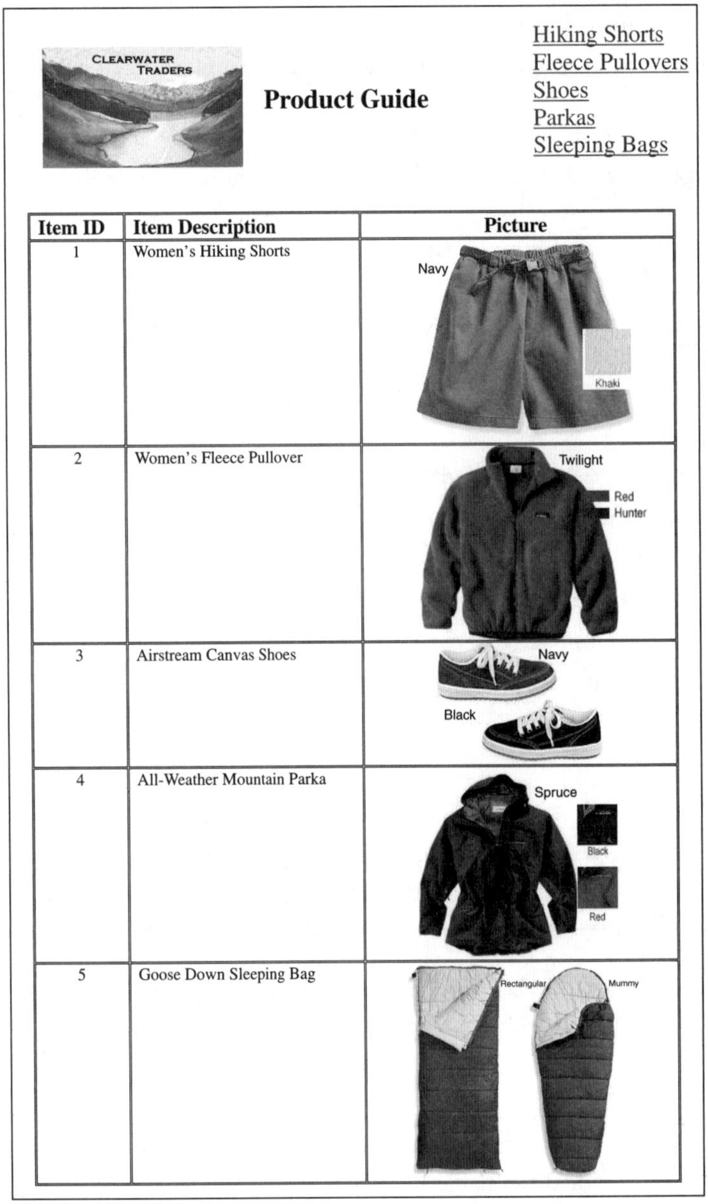

CLEARWATER TRADERS **Product Guide**		<u>Hiking Shorts</u> <u>Fleece Pullovers</u> <u>Shoes</u> <u>Parkas</u> <u>Sleeping Bags</u>

Item ID	Item Description	Picture
1	Women's Hiking Shorts	Navy Khaki
2	Women's Fleece Pullover	Twilight Red Hunter
3	Airstream Canvas Shoes	Navy Black
4	All-Weather Mountain Parka	Spruce Black Red
5	Goose Down Sleeping Bag	Rectangular Mummy

Figure 4-33

2. In this project, you will create the Northwoods University home page, as shown in Figure 4-34. Use the nwlogo.jpg file in the Chapter4 folder on your Data Disk to create the graphic image, and place the image and its adjacent text in a table. Use the unordered list tag to create the two side-by-side bulleted lists. Create a table with one row and two columns to format the lists. Format the list text as Level 2 headings. Save the finished Web page as Ch4Pr2.html in the Chapter4 folder on your Data Disk.

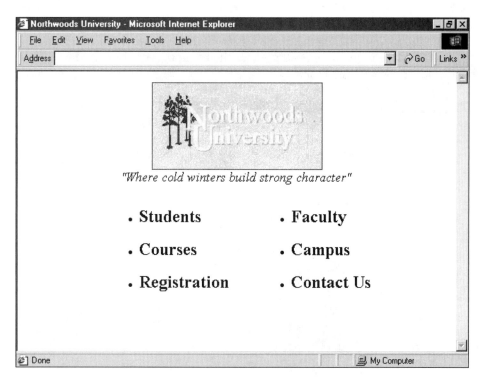

Figure 4-34

3. In this project, you will create the Northwoods University Student Directory, shown in Figure 4–35. Use the nwlogo.jpg file in the Chapter4 folder on your Data Disk to create the graphic image, and place the image and its adjacent text in a table. Create a table to display the student data as shown, and enter the data for the first two student records. Save the file as Ch4Pr3.html in the Chapter4 folder on your Data Disk.

Northwoods University Students

Name	Address	City	State	ZIP Code	Phone Number	Class
Sarah M. Miller	144 Windridge Blvd.	Eau Claire	WI	54703	715-555-9876	SR
Brian Umato	454 St. John's Place	Eau Claire	WI	54702	715-555-2345	SR

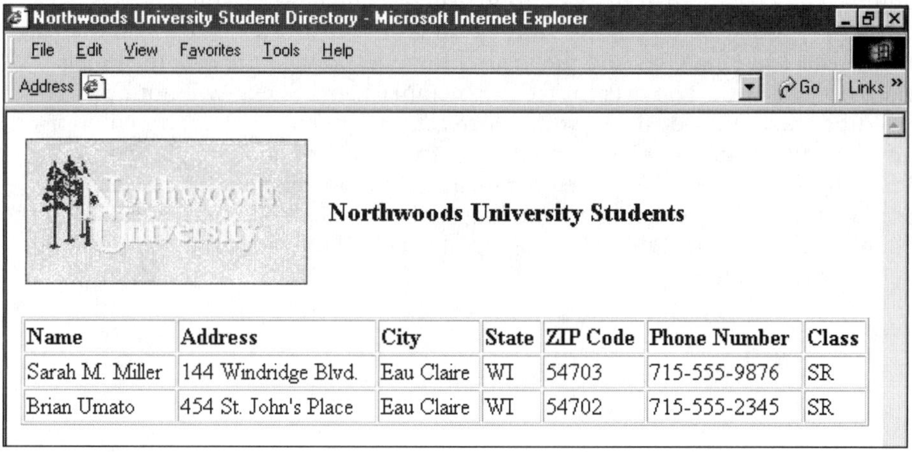

Figure 4-35

4. In this project, you will create the Northwoods University Faculty Web page shown in Figure 4-36. Use the nwlogo.jpg file in the Chapter4 folder on your Data Disk to create the graphic image in the page heading. Save the file as Ch4Pr4.html in the Chapter4 folder on your Data Disk.

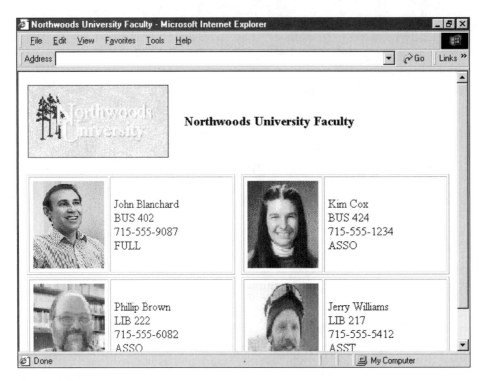

Figure 4-36

To format the faculty data so that the Web page matches Figure 4–36, you will need to create a table that contains two columns and two rows. The first row will contain the data for John Blanchard and Kim Cox, and the second row will contain the data for Phillip Brown and Jerry Williams. (The data for faculty member Laura Sheng will not be included.) Within each individual cell, you will create a second table with two columns and one row. The first column will contain the faculty member's photograph, and the second column will contain the faculty member's name, location, telephone number, and rank. A graphic image file containing a photograph of each faculty member is stored in the Chapter4 folder on your Data Disk. The graphic file name is the same as the associated faculty member's last name.

5. In this project, you will create the Northwoods University Courses page, as shown in Figure 4-37.

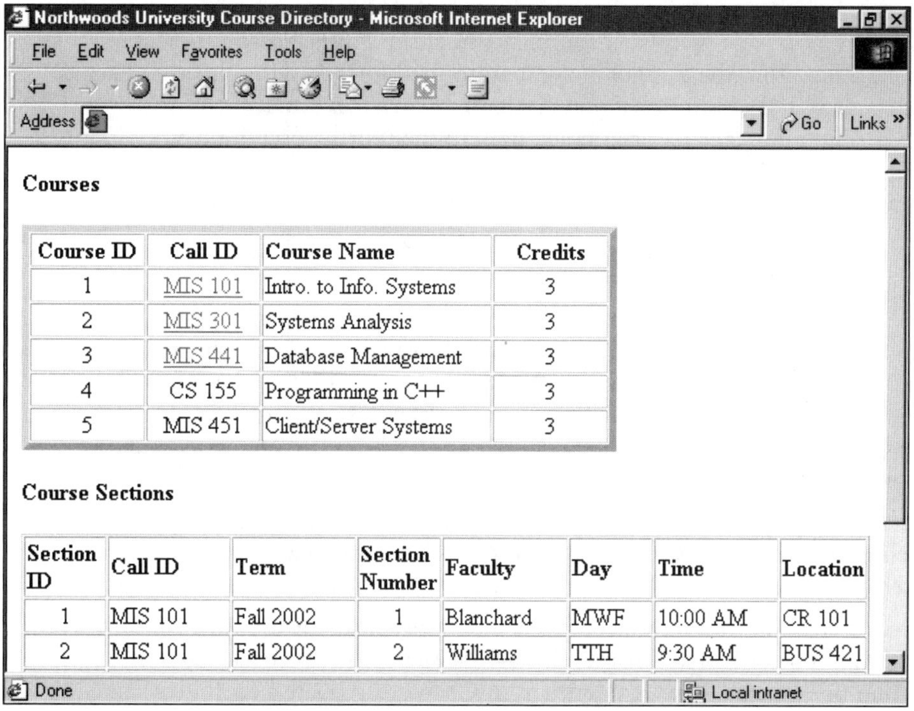

Courses

Course ID	Call ID	Course Name	Credits
1	MIS 101	Intro. to Info. Systems	3
2	MIS 301	Systems Analysis	3
3	MIS 441	Database Management	3
4	CS 155	Programming in C++	3
5	MIS 451	Client/Server Systems	3

Course Sections

Section ID	Call ID	Term	Section Number	Faculty	Day	Time	Location
1	MIS 101	Fall 2002	1	Blanchard	MWF	10:00 AM	CR 101
2	MIS 101	Fall 2002	2	Williams	TTH	9:30 AM	BUS 421

Figure 4-37

a. Create a new HTML document, and save it as Ch4Pr5.html in the Chapter4 folder on your Data Disk.
b. Create a table that displays all of the records in the COURSE table, as shown in Figure 4-37. Format the table as shown in the figure.
c. Create a second table to display the first six records from the COURSE_SECTION table, as shown in Figure 4-37. (Some of the records are displayed off-screen. The required data values are listed in Figure 2-5.) Format the table as shown in the figure.
d. Create hyperlinks and associated anchors so that when the user clicks one of the first three call IDs in the Courses table, the Web page display jumps to the first occurrence of that call ID in the Course Sections table. For example, when the user clicks "MIS 101" in the Courses table, the Web page display jumps to the first record in the Course Sections table. When the user clicks "MIS 301" in the Courses table, the Web page display jumps to the fourth record (the first record associated with MIS 301) in the Course Sections table.

6. Open the Ch4Pr2.html file that contains the Northwoods University home page that you created in Hands-on Project 2, and save it as Ch4Pr6.html. Then, create the following hyperlinks:
   a. Create a link from the Students bullet item to the Northwoods University Student Directory Web page (Ch4Pr3.html) that you created in Hands-on Project 3.
   b. Create a link from the Faculty bullet item to the Northwoods University Faculty Web page (Ch4Pr4.html) that you created in Hands-on Project 4.
   c. Create a link from the Courses bullet item to the Northwoods University Courses Web page (Ch4Pr5.html) that you created in Hands-on Project 5.
   d. Create an e-mail link from the Contact Us bullet item to your e-mail address.

CASE PROJECTS

1. Design and create at least three Web pages that display data for the Ashland Valley Soccer League, which is described in Chapter 2, Case Project 1. Use the data values that you inserted in the database tables you created in Chapter 2. Create a subfolder named Ashland in the Chapter4 folder on your Data Disk. Save your Web pages in the Chapter4\Ashland folder.

2. Create a home page for the Ashland Valley Soccer League that contains hyperlinks to the Web pages that you created in Case Project 1. Save the home page in the Chapter4\Ashland folder.

3. Design and create at least three Web pages that display data for the Wayne's Auto World database that is described in Chapter 2, Case Project 1. Use the data values that you inserted in the database tables you created in Chapter 2. Create a subfolder named Waynes in the Chapter4 folder on your Data Disk. Save your Web pages in the Chapter4\Waynes folder.

4. Create a home page for Wayne's Auto World that contains hyperlinks to the Web pages that you created in Case Project 3. Save the home page in the Chapter4\Waynes folder.

5. Design and create at least three Web pages that display data for the Sun-Ray Video database that is described in Chapter 2, Case Project 1. Use the data values that you inserted in the database tables you created in Chapter 2. Create a subfolder named Sunray in the Chapter4 folder on your Data Disk. Save your Web pages in the Chapter4\Sunray folder.

6. Create a home page for Sun-Ray Video that contains hyperlinks to the Web pages you created in Case Project 5. Save the home page in the Chapter4\Sunray folder.

5

WEB SERVERS

In this chapter, you will:

♦ Learn about the Microsoft Personal Web Server Software
♦ Learn how to improve Web site performance
♦ Learn about absolute and relative URL addresses
♦ Compare Personal Web Server to other Web servers

In Chapter 1, you learned that Web servers are computers that are connected to the Internet and run special Web server software. This software includes a component called a listener. The listener monitors for Web page requests that are sent to the Web server from client browsers. When a browser requests a particular Web page from a Web server, the Web server sends the HTML file for the Web page to the client browser. The Web server also processes server-side programs that create dynamic Web pages. Sometimes, these programs send queries to a database server that retrieve database data. In this chapter, you will configure and administer your own Web server, using the Microsoft Personal Web Server software. You will run both the Web server software and the client browser software on the same workstation.

PERSONAL WEB SERVER

Personal Web Server (PWS) is software that is designed to create and manage a Web server, also called a **Web site**, on a desktop computer. It can be used to learn how to set up and administer a Web site, and it can also serve as a site for testing dynamic Web pages. When you first start programming dynamic Web pages, you might make a mistake that causes your Web server to lock up and not service **visitors**, who are users who use browsers to make connections and request Web pages. If you test dynamic Web pages using your own personal Web site rather than a Web site that serves many users besides yourself, errors of this kind won't affect other Web programmers and users. PWS has most of the same functionality as Microsoft Internet Information Server (IIS), which is the Web server software that many companies use to manage their commercial Web sites.

The main difference between PWS and IIS is that PWS can support only 10 Web server connections at one time. A **Web server connection** corresponds to a socket on the Web server. A **socket** is an endpoint of a communications connection. Each connection between a client and a server creates a socket on the server and a socket on the client. Each socket has a corresponding memory location that specifies information about the connection, such as the network domain name and communication protocol. Each Web server socket also has another corresponding memory location that stores incoming data requests from the user's Web browser. Every visitor request for a Web page uses a Web server connection. Furthermore, every image file reference within a Web page uses a separate connection. To make Web pages appear faster, many Web browsers can create up to four simultaneous connections to a Web site. For example, if a Web page contains references to three graphic image files, a single request for that Web page would use a total of four Web server connections. This means that a PWS Web site cannot service Web page requests from more than two or three simultaneous visitors in a timely manner, and cannot be used for large-scale commercial Web sites. However, PWS provides an excellent environment for setting up a personal Web server for publishing information on an intranet, for learning about Web server administration, and for testing Web programs before moving the programs to a **production Web server**, which is a Web server that can be accessed by anyone who is connected to the Internet.

When PWS is running on your computer, the Tray icon is usually displayed on the right side of the taskbar on your Windows desktop. When you right-click this icon, a menu is displayed that allows you to start and shut down the PWS listener process. This menu also allows you to access a PWS utility called Personal Web Manager, which allows you to modify the configuration of PWS. You only start Personal Web Manager when you need to change a configuration setting. Now you will right-click the Tray icon , and start the PWS listener process if it is not already running. Then you will open Personal Web Manager, and view the current configuration settings.

To start PWS and open Personal Web Manager:

1. Right-click the **Tray** icon on your Windows desktop taskbar. The icon is usually displayed beside the date and time in the lower-right corner of your screen. If the Start Service menu selection is available, then the PWS listener is not started, and you should click **Start Service**. If the Start Service menu selection is not available, then the PWS listener is already running.

> TIP If the Tray icon is not displayed on your desktop, start Windows Explorer. Windows 95 and Windows 98 users should navigate to the Windows\System\Inetsrv folder, and then double-click pws.exe to start Personal Web Manager. (Windows NT Workstation and Windows 2000 users should navigate to the Winnt\Systems32\Inetsrv folder.) If this file is not on your workstation, then PWS might not be installed on your computer, and you need to ask your instructor or technical support person for help. After you have started Personal Web Manager, click Properties on the menu bar, and then click Show Tray icon to display the Tray icon on your taskbar.

5

> TIP You can also start Personal Web Manager by double-clicking.

2. If necessary, right-click, and then click **Properties**. The Personal Web Manager Main page is displayed (Figure 5-1). If the Tip of the Day window is displayed, click **Close**. If necessary, click **Start** to start the listener process and display the PWS components as shown.

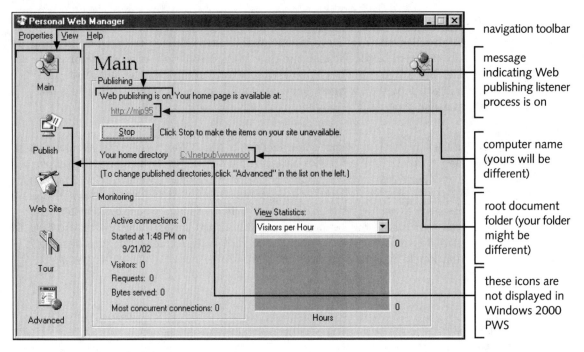

navigation toolbar

message indicating Web publishing listener process is on

computer name (yours will be different)

root document folder (your folder might be different)

these icons are not displayed in Windows 2000 PWS

Figure 5-1   Personal Web Manager Main page

A navigation toolbar lets you move to different pages within the Personal Web Manager application. Currently, the Main page is displayed. The Main page shows the URL for your PWS, which is the name of your computer as it is identified on its network. The Main page also shows the drive letter and folder path to Personal Web Server's root document folder. Recall that the root document folder is the folder on a Web server that contains the Web server's default home page, which is the page that is automatically displayed if a Web page request from a user does not specify an HTML Web page file. The Main page also has a Monitoring section for monitoring visitor activity at the Web site, which will be discussed later.

The Publish page and the Web Site pages have wizards that automate the process of creating and editing HTML documents and creating links to documents. (These wizards are not available for Windows 2000 PWS users.) Since you will be creating your own custom HTML documents and hyperlinks, you will not use these PWS features. The Tour page provides a basic overview of PWS. The Advanced page allows you to specify the Web server's root document directory and default document filenames, and to configure other Web server properties. Now you will view the Advanced page and examine the configuration properties.

To view the Advanced page and examine the PWS configuration properties:

1. Click **Advanced** on the Web Manager navigation bar. The Advanced Options page is displayed, as shown in Figure 5-2.

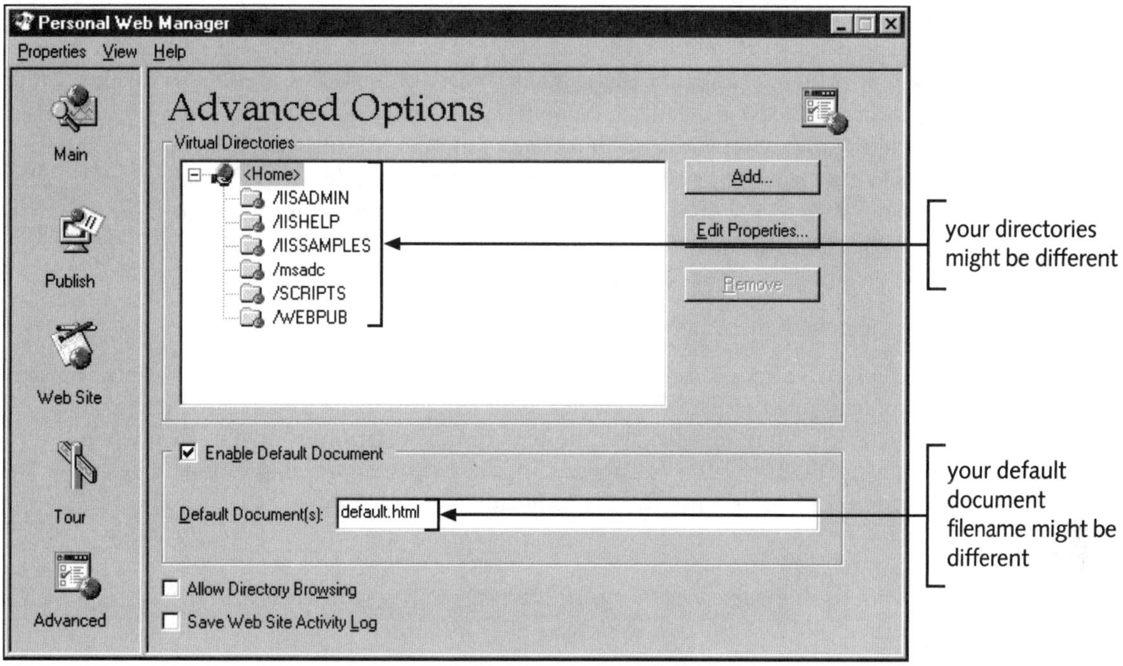

your directories might be different

your default document filename might be different

Figure 5-2   Advanced Options page

The Web Server Root Document Directory and Default Document

A Web server's **root document folder** is the central folder that contains all of the Web pages, graphic images, programs, and all other files that are available from the Web site. The root document folder can be located anywhere in the Web server's file system. Now you will modify the root document folder of your PWS so that it is the Chapter5 folder on your Data Disk.

To modify your PWS root document folder:

1. If necessary, click **<Home>**, which is the first entry in the Virtual Directories list on the Advanced Options page. Home refers to the root document folder.

2. Click **Edit Properties**, click **Browse**, navigate to the Chapter5 folder on your Data Disk, click **OK**, and then click **OK** again to change the root document folder specification.

3. Click **Main** on the navigation bar, and confirm that the root document directory specification next to "Your home directory" on the Main page specifies the Chapter5 folder on your Data Disk.

Recall that when a visitor specifies in his or her Web browser a URL that contains a Web server domain name or IP address, but no HTML Web page filename, the Web server returns the HTML document that has been specified as the Web server's **default document**. If the Web server does not have a default document, visitors can still connect to the Web server, but they must know the folder path and the name of the HTML file they wish to view, and they must include it as part of the URL. If they do not know the folder path and document filename, and the Web server does not have a default document, then the visitor's browser will display an error message when the visitor tries to connect to the Web site. Now you will specify the default document filename on the Advanced Options page.

To specify the default document filename:

1. Click **Advanced** on the Navigation toolbar to display the Advanced Options page, confirm that the Enable Default Document box is checked, delete the current Default Document filename, and type **default.html**, as shown in Figure 5-2. Changes on the PWS Advanced Options page are applied as soon as they are entered, so you do not need to explicitly save new values.

 With some Web servers, filenames are case sensitive. Filenames are not case sensitive with any of Microsoft's Web servers.

To make Web pages appear faster, most Web browsers are configured to **cache**, or save, recently viewed Web pages on the local hard drive. This way, the file does not have to be transmitted across the network each time it is viewed. When you are developing and displaying new Web pages, it is a good idea to configure your browser so that it does not cache any Web pages, but always reloads the most recent version of a page. This way, you can be sure that you are always viewing your most recent Web pages. Now you will start the Internet Explorer Web browser, delete all of the cached files, and change the configuration so that no Web pages are cached.

To configure your browser so that no Web pages are cached:

1. Start Internet Explorer, click **Tools** on the menu bar, and then click **Internet Options**. The Internet Options dialog box is displayed.

2. Under Temporary Internet Files, click **Delete Files**. The Delete Files dialog box is displayed.

3. Check the **Delete all offline content** check box, and then click **OK**.

4. Under Temporary Internet Files, click **Settings**, click the **Every visit to the page** option button, and then click **OK**.

5. Under History, click **Clear History**, and then click **OK**.

6. Change Days to keep pages in history to **0**, and then click **OK**.

Every computer that connects to the Internet must have a unique IP address. Some computers have **static IP addresses**, which are IP addresses that never change and always refer only to a specific computer. Static IP addresses are assigned to organizations or to Internet service providers (ISPs), who in turn can assign these static addresses to individual computers. Static IP addresses should only be assigned to computers that stay at the same physical location, or to computers that are servers, such as Web servers or database servers. Client programs are often configured to look for a server at a specific IP address.

The reason that static IP addresses should only be used for computers that stay in the same place is that some of the values in an IP address indicate the physical network to which the computer is attached. When a computer with a static IP address is moved to a new physical location, the computer's network settings must be manually reconfigured. Web servers should always use static IP addresses so that their URL remains the same, and visitors can always find them.

Computers that are connected to the Internet through large company networks or using ISPs and that are not servers and do not have to be at a specific IP address often have dynamic IP addresses. A **dynamic IP address** is assigned to a computer from a list of available addresses each time the computer is booted and its Internet access software is loaded. A dynamic IP address might change each time the computer is booted. Using dynamic IP addresses utilizes IP addresses more efficiently than using static IP addresses does because you reallocate idle IP addresses, thus stretching a limited pool of IP addresses to cover a larger pool of computers that need IP addresses.

Recall that when you request a Web page from a Web server, the URL is the Web server's IP address or domain name, followed by the name of the HTML document. (Remember that if you do not specify the name of an HTML document, then the Web server displays its default document.) To request the default document from your PWS, you need to type the IP address of your computer (which is where the PWS listener process is running) in the Address box on your Web browser. Since your computer might have a dynamic IP address, you need a way to specify the IP address of your PWS in a URL. One way is to use a special URL called http://localhost/. The http://localhost/ URL is associated with the reserved IP address of 127.0.0.1, which always refers to the local computer. This identifier allows you to request Web pages from your PWS and to create hyperlinks to other Web pages on your workstation without having to specify the actual IP address of your computer in the Web page URL.

The Web server default document is stored in the PWS root document folder that you specified earlier, which is the Chapter5 folder on your Data Disk. Now you will request the default document from your PWS using the http://localhost/ URL in your Web browser.

To view the PWS default document:

1. In Internet Explorer, type **http://localhost/** in the Address box, and then press the **Enter** key. The default.html document is displayed, which is the Clearwater Traders home page shown in Figure 5-3.

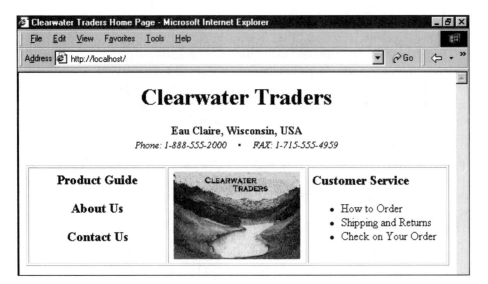

Figure 5-3   PWS default document

> **TIP**
>
> If a message is displayed stating that the Web page cannot be found, make sure that you changed the root document folder to the Chapter5 folder on your Data Disk. Also, make sure that default.html is the Default Document filename specified on the Personal Web Manager Advanced Options page, and that default.html is in the Chapter5 folder on your Data Disk.

> **TIP**
>
> If the message is displayed that states that the Internet site http://localhost/ cannot be found, confirm that the PWS listener process is running by opening the Main page in Personal Web Manager and confirming that Web publishing is on. If Web publishing is on and you still can't connect using the http://localhost/ URL, then ask your instructor or technical support person for help.

PWS allows you to specify multiple default document filenames by listing the filenames separated by commas. When you connect to PWS using your Web browser, the PWS looks for the first default document filename on the list. If it cannot find the file in the root document folder, it then looks for the next filename, and continues looking for successive names in the list until it finds a file. If it does not find a default document file, a Web page is displayed that states that access is denied. Now, you will specify multiple default document filenames and then connect to the Web server to see the results.

To specify multiple default document filenames:

1. Switch back to the Personal Web Manager Advanced Options page, and change the Default Document name to **home.html,default.html** to specify home.html as the first default document name, and default.html as the second default document filename.

2. Switch back to Internet Explorer, and press **F5** to refresh the display. The home.html default document, which is the Northwoods University home page, is displayed.

 If the Northwoods University home page is not displayed, click Tools on the menu bar, click Internet Options, click Delete Files, check Delete all offline content, click OK, click OK again, and then refresh the browser display. Repeat these steps whenever your Web page is not refreshed correctly.

3. Switch back to Personal Web Manager and delete the entry in the Default Document text box, so that no Default Document is specified.

4. Switch back to Internet Explorer, and refresh the display. The error message "Directory Listing Denied – This Virtual Directory does not allow contents to be listed" is displayed, indicating that there is no default document specified for PWS.

Directory Browsing

You can configure PWS to enable **directory browsing**, which allows Web site visitors to use a folder listing to navigate to different files on the Web server. When directory browsing is enabled, PWS will display a list of all of the files in the root document folder if the default document file is not specified or found. To enable directory browsing, you must check the Allow Directory Browsing check box on the Advanced Options page in Personal Web Manager. Then, visitors to your Web site can display, download, or print files displayed in the list. Now you will enable directory browsing.

To enable directory browsing:

1. Switch to the Personal Web Manager Advanced Options page, check the **Allow Directory Browsing** check box, and clear the **Enable Default Documents** check box. (A folder listing will not be displayed if a default document is specified and available.)

2. Switch to Internet Explorer, and refresh your display. A listing of the PWS root document folder contents is displayed, as shown in Figure 5-4.

```
 localhost - / - Microsoft Internet Explorer                    _ 8 X
  File   Edit  View  Favorites  Tools  Help                       

 Address    http://localhost/                               ▼  ∂ Go
```

localhost - /

```
9/11/99   4:22 PM        42127  bags.jpg
9/18/01   3:46 PM        46654  clearlogo.jpg
9/18/01   3:23 PM          859  default.html
9/23/02   9:40 AM        <dir>  Exercises
9/12/99   7:39 AM         9568  fleece.jpg
9/18/01   3:47 PM          651  home.html
9/18/01   3:46 PM         6189  nwlogo.jpg
9/11/99   4:23 PM        14139  parka.jpg
9/11/99   4:23 PM         9189  shoes.jpg
9/11/99   4:23 PM        11505  shorts.jpg
9/19/01   3:07 PM        <dir>  Tutorials
```

Figure 5-4   Listing of PWS root document folder contents

3. Click the **clearlogo.jpg** link. The Clearwater Traders logo is displayed in your Web browser. Note that the URL displayed in the browser Address box is now http://localhost/clearlogo.jpg. This indicates that you are displaying the clearlogo.jpg file in the Web server's root document folder.

4. Click the **Back** button ⇦ on the Browser toolbar to return to the folder listing.

5. Click the **default.html** link. The Clearwater Traders home page is displayed. Note that the URL is now http://localhost/default.html, indicating that you have navigated to the default.html file in the root document folder. Click the **Back** button ⇦ on the Browser toolbar to return to the folder listing.

6. Right-click the **clearlogo.jpg** link, and then click **Save Target As**. The Save As dialog box opens, which allows you to save clearlogo.jpg to a folder on your local workstation. Click **Cancel**.

A Web site visitor can use a URL that specifies the name of a folder within the root document folder. If a copy of the Web server default document file is not in that folder, and directory browsing is enabled, then the Web server will display the folder listing of the specified folder, and allow the visitor to navigate to other folders within the root document folder. If the visitor navigates to a folder that contains a copy of the default document, then the default document Web page is displayed, and directory browsing is not available to the visitor until he or she specifies a different URL that contains a folder path. To help you understand this, you will now restore default.html and home.html as the Web server default documents. Then you will create two folders within the root document folder, and connect directly to one of these folders by specifying a folder path in the Web site URL. Then you will see how you can browse within the Web site folders.

To browse among folders within the root document folder:

1. Switch to the Personal Web Manager, and check the Enable Default Document check box. Type **default.html** and **home.html** as the default document filenames.

2. Start Windows Explorer, and navigate to the Chapter5 folder on your Data Disk, which is the root document folder. Create a subfolder named **Graphics**, and a second subfolder named **Pages**.

3. Copy **clearlogo.jpg** and **nwlogo.jpg** from the Chapter5 folder to the Graphics subfolder.

4. Copy **default.html** and **home.html** from the Chapter5 folder to the Pages subfolder.

5. Switch to Internet Explorer, type **http://localhost/graphics/** in the Address box, and then press the **Enter** key. The folder listing for the Graphics subfolder is displayed (Figure 5-5) instead of the default document, because there is not a copy of the default document files (default.html and home.html) in the Graphics subfolder.

```
localhost - /graphics/ - Microsoft Internet Explorer          _ 8 X

 File   Edit   View   Favorites   Tools   Help

 Address [@] http://localhost/graphics/                    ▼  ⌀ Go    ⇦ ▾  »

localhost - /graphics/
_____

[To Parent Directory]
     9/10/99   3:58 PM          46654  clearlogo.jpg
     9/18/01   3:46 PM           6189  nwlogo.jpg
```

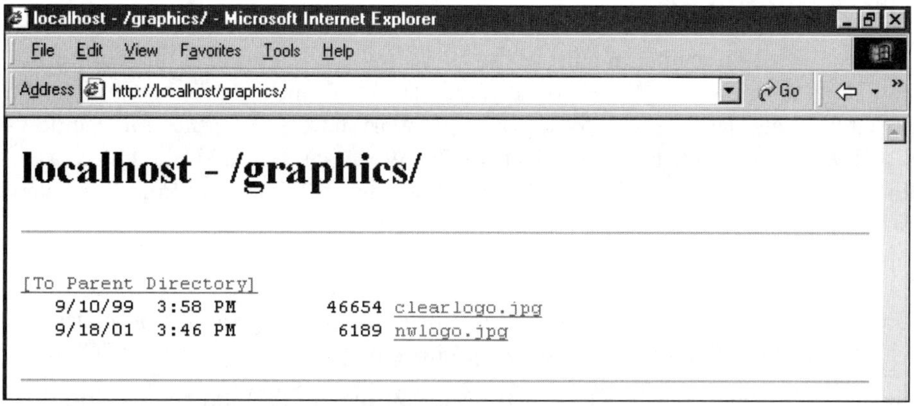

Figure 5-5   Graphics subfolder listing

 TIP If the folder listing is not displayed, make sure that the Enable Directory Browsing check box is checked on the Personal Web Manager Advanced Options page, and that default.html and home.html are not in the Graphics subfolder within your root document folder.

6. Click the **To Parent Directory** hyperlink. The Clearwater Traders home page (Figure 5-3), which is the default document file (default.html), is displayed rather than the folder listing. If a default document file exists within a folder, then the default document is displayed rather than the folder listing, and directory browsing is disabled.

7. Type **http://localhost/pages/** in the Address box, then press the **Enter** key. The Clearwater Traders home page, which is the default document file (default.html), is displayed, but the Clearwater Traders logo is not displayed on the Web page, because the graphics object (clearlogo.jpg) is not in the Pages folder. Again, directory browsing is disabled.

8. Switch to Windows Explorer, and delete the Graphics and Pages folders from the Chapter5 folder on your Data Disk.

It is useful to enable directory browsing if you want to use your Web site to distribute files to visitors. However, if you enable directory browsing, you should avoid placing sensitive files in your Web site folders. Although placing a default document in a folder disables directory browsing, a Web site usually has many folders, and it is easy to forget to put a default document and all of its associated graphic objects in every folder. Any folder that is accessible to your Web server that does not contain a default document file has its contents available to every user of the Web.

The Web Site Activity Log

The Web Site Activity Log maintains a list of the IP addresses of computers that connect to your Web site. A new log file is created each month and saved in the Windows\System\LogFiles\W3svc1 folder on your workstation. (Log files for Windows NT users and Windows 2000 users are saved in the Winnt\System32\LogFiles\W3svc1 folder.) Now you will enable the Web Site Activity Log and use Windows Explorer to view the log file.

To enable the Web Site Activity Log and view the log file:

1. Switch to the Personal Web Manager Advanced Options page and, if necessary, check the **Save Web Site Activity Log** check box.

2. Switch to Internet Explorer, type **http://localhost/** in the Address box, and then press the **Enter** key to request the PWS default document and cause an entry to be written to the log file.

3. Close all applications, and then reboot your computer. The log file entry is not written until PWS is shut down by rebooting.

4. Start Windows Explorer, and navigate to the **Windows\System\LogFiles\ W3svc1** folder, and display its contents. (Windows NT users and Windows 2000 users will navigate to the \Winnt\System32\LogFiles\W3svc1 folder.) A log file should be displayed, as shown in Figure 5-6.

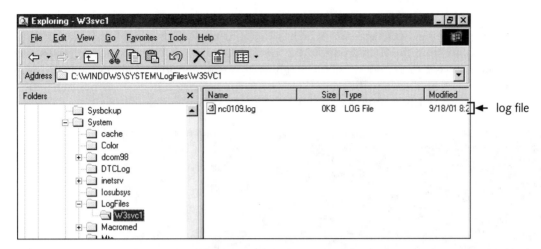

←— log file

Figure 5-6   Web Site Activity Log file

The first two letters of the log filename describe the log file format. The nc format signifies that the file is written using fixed ASCII characters. The fixed ASCII (nc) format is the only format that is available with Windows95 or Windows98 PWS. With Windows NT Workstation and Windows 2000 PWS, you can use the Internet Service Manager to select among four other log file formats. Usually, the fixed ASCII (nc) file format is used. The next two numbers (01 in Figure 5-6) refer to the last two digits of the current year (2001 on this system). The final two numbers (09 in Figure 5-6) refer to the number of the current month (September). A new log file is created on the first day of each month by Windows 95, Windows 98, and Windows NT PWS. A new log file is created every day by Windows 2000 PWS.

You can view the log file contents using any text editor or word processor. In order to view the log file, you must restart your computer, and then view the log file before any new connections are made to the Web server. Otherwise, the file is designated as in use by another application, and access is denied. Figure 5-7 shows the contents of a typical activity log. The first entry records the IP address of a site visitor, the date and time when the visitor accessed it, and the documents that were requested. The requests in Figure 5-7 were from a browser running on the same workstation as the Web server (localhost, which has the IP address 127.0.0.1).

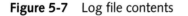

Figure 5-7   Log file contents

As you can see, the activity log reveals the names of files that are being accessed on your Web site, and when they were accessed, which is useful to know. Can you tell who is accessing your Web site from the IP addresses in the log file? Usually not. Recall that computers can have static or dynamic IP addresses. Currently, visitors with dynamic IP addresses usually cannot be identified. Visitors with static IP addresses and associated domain names can sometimes be identified, using a utility named Nslookup, as shown in Figure 5-8.

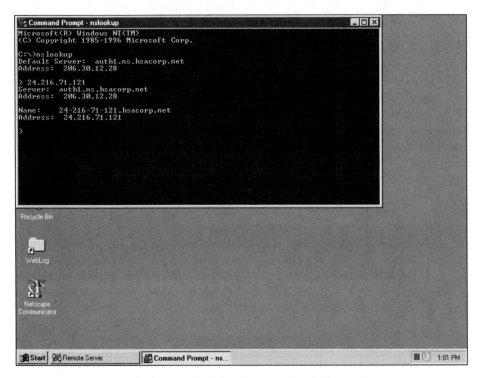

Figure 5-8   Using Nslookup to find the identity of a Web site visitor

To use this utility, Windows NT users can start a command prompt session, type nslookup on the command line, and then type an IP address. The domain name associated with the IP address is then displayed. For example, suppose that your activity log indicates that a Web site visitor with the IP address 24.216.71.121 visited your Web site. Figure 5-8 shows that the domain name associated with this IP address is hsacorp.net.

Further information about this domain name can be located using Web-based services that maintain information about domain names. An example of one of these services can be found at http://www.networksolutions.com/cgi-bin/whois/whois. (If this Web site is not available, you can find similar sites by performing an Internet search using "domain name find" as the search string.) These services allow you to enter a search string for a domain name or Web host. For example, searching on the domain name "hsacorp.net" returns the name and address of the entity to whom the domain name is registered, as shown in Figure 5-9. Using an Activity Log, this is about as much information as you can gather about visitors accessing your Web site.

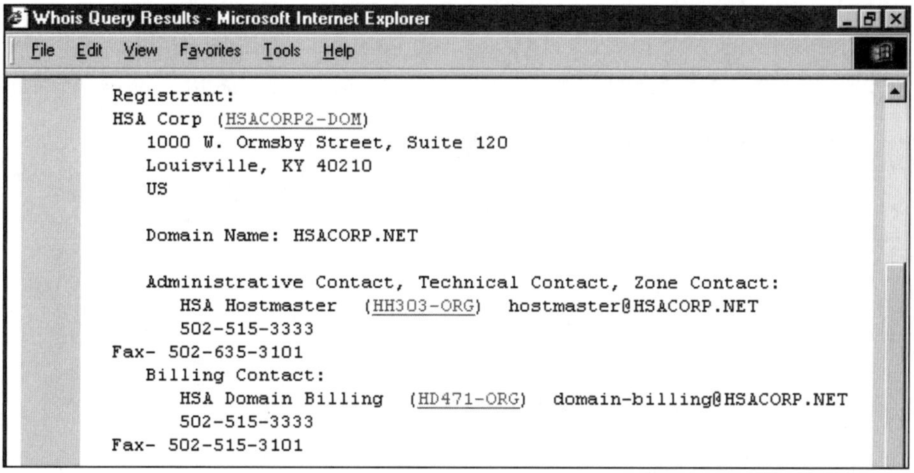

```
Whois Query Results - Microsoft Internet Explorer                    _ [8] [X]
 File  Edit  View  Favorites  Tools  Help

    Registrant:
    HSA Corp (HSACORP2-DOM)
       1000 W. Ormsby Street, Suite 120
       Louisville, KY 40210
       US

    Domain Name: HSACORP.NET

    Administrative Contact, Technical Contact, Zone Contact:
       HSA Hostmaster  (HH303-ORG)  hostmaster@HSACORP.NET
       502-515-3333
    Fax- 502-635-3101
    Billing Contact:
       HSA Domain Billing  (HD471-ORG)  domain-billing@HSACORP.NET
       502-515-3333
    Fax- 502-515-3101
```

Figure 5-9   Information about a Web site visitor's domain name

Creating Virtual Directories

Your Web site's root document folder is the central location for the files that are available on your Web site. You can create virtual directories to access Web pages and other files stored outside of the root document folder and its subfolders. A **virtual directory** is a folder that does not have to be physically within the root document folder, but always appears to client browsers as though it is. A virtual directory is associated with a physical folder within the Web server's file system. For example, you could create a virtual directory so that you could directly access files in the Chapter5/Tutorials folder on your Data Disk, which is on drive A of your computer or on the network drive to which you are currently attached.

Each virtual directory has an associated **alias**, which is a name that client browsers can use to access that directory. Web site visitors can use the Web site IP address or domain name plus the virtual directory alias within a URL to access files within the virtual directory. An alias is usually shorter than the folder pathname and is more convenient for users to type. An alias is also more secure, since visitors do not need to know the names of the folders where your server files are physically located. Now you will view the properties of a virtual directory on your Personal Web Server, and view the files in a virtual directory, using a URL that contains a virtual directory alias.

To use a virtual directory:

1. Start Personal Web Manager, open the Advanced Options page, click **/IISAdmin** in the Virtual Directories list, then click **Edit Properties**. The Edit Directory dialog box is displayed (Figure 5-10), which shows the physical folder path and alias of the virtual directory. Notice that the physical folder path (C:\WINDOWS\SYSTEM\inetsrv\iisadmin) is not a subfolder of the root document folder. Click **Cancel**.

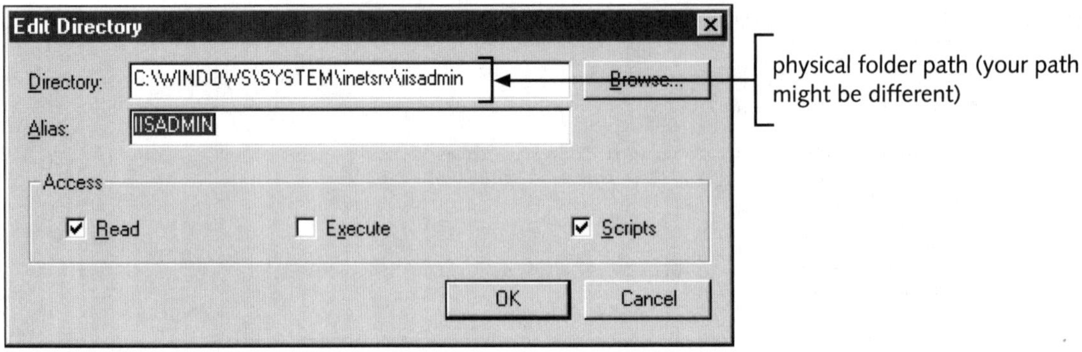

Figure 5-10   Virtual directory properties

> 💡 **TIP**   If /IISADMIN is not on your Virtual Directories list, select another directory on the list.

2. Be sure that the Allow Directory Browsing check box is checked.

3. Start Internet Explorer, type **http://localhost/iisadmin/** in the Address box, then press the **Enter** key. The folder listing for your workstation's C:\WINDOWS\SYSTEM\inetsrv\iisadmin folder is displayed, as shown in Figure 5-11. Recall that a folder listing is displayed when a default document file is not present in the folder specified in a URL.

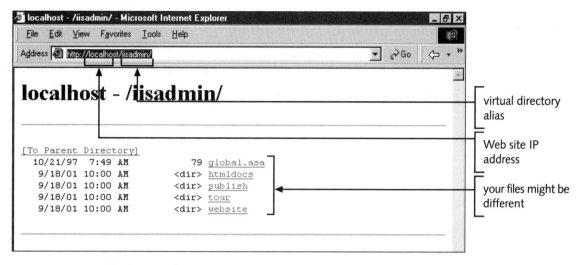

Figure 5-11   Folder listing of a virtual directory

4. Click the **To Parent Directory** hyperlink. The Clearwater Traders home page is displayed, and the URL changes to http://localhost/ in the browser Address box. Note that a virtual directory behaves like a subfolder of the root document folder.

An alias should be a short, descriptive text string with no blank spaces. Now you will create a virtual directory to the Clearwater subfolder on your Data Disk, and then display a Web page by specifying the virtual directory alias plus the name of the Web page HTML file. You will specify the word "Clearwater" as the virtual directory's alias.

To create a virtual directory:

1. Switch to the Personal Web Manager Advanced Options page, and click **<Home>** in the virtual directory list. If another directory is selected in the Virtual Directories list when you create a new virtual directory, then the URL of the new virtual directory will be a subfolder of the virtual directory that is currently selected.

2. Click **Add** to create a new virtual directory. The Add Directory dialog box is displayed.

3. Click **Browse**, navigate to the Chapter5\Tutorials folder on your Data Disk, and then click **OK**. The physical folder path to the Chapter5\Tutorials folder is displayed as the directory folder path.

4. Delete the current alias text, and then type **Clearwater** for the alias text. Your completed virtual directory specification should look like Figure 5-12.

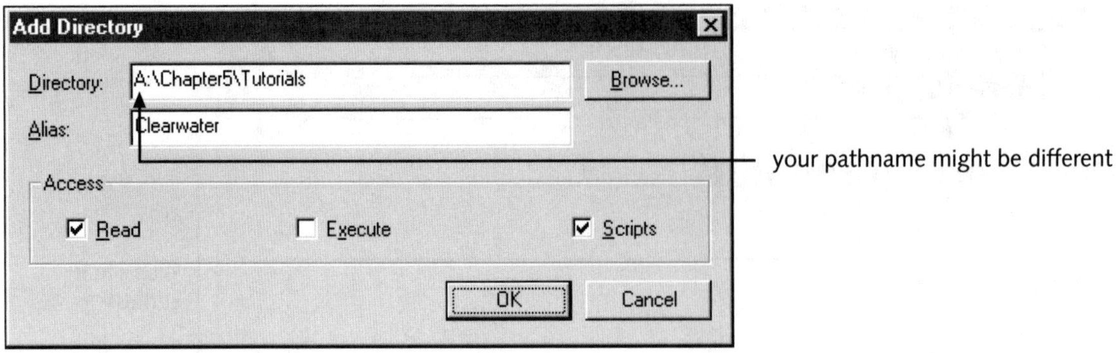

your pathname might be different

Figure 5-12   Creating a virtual directory

5. Click **OK** to create the virtual directory. The Clearwater virtual directory is displayed in the Virtual Directory list on the Advanced Options page.

6. Switch to Internet Explorer, type **http://localhost/Clearwater/products.html** in the Address box, and then press the **Enter** key. The products.html Web page, which is located in the Chapter5\Tutorials folder on your Data Disk, is displayed, using the virtual directory specification in the URL.

Virtual directories allow you to change the physical location of Web page files on your Web server without changing the URLs that visitors use to access the files. Suppose you decide to move the products.html Web page file to the Projects subfolder of the Chapter5 folder on your Data Disk. However, visitors are used to accessing the products.html page by specifying that the file is in the Clearwater virtual directory. In the next set of steps, you will move the products.html file to a new physical location, and then modify the virtual directory specification so that visitors can still view the file using the same URL.

To change the file location and virtual directory specification:

1. Switch to Windows Explorer, and move the **products.html** file from the Chapter5\Tutorials folder to the Chapter5\Projects folder.

2. Switch to the Personal Web Manager Advanced Options page, click the **Clearwater** virtual directory, and then click **Edit Properties**. The Edit Directory dialog box is displayed.

3. Click **Browse**, navigate to the **Chapter5\Projects** folder on your Data Disk, click **OK** to associate the Clearwater virtual directory with the Projects subfolder and then click **OK** again to close the Edit Directory dialog box.

4. Switch to Internet Explorer, type **http://localhost/Clearwater/products.html** in the Address box, and then press the **Enter** key. The products.html Web page is displayed using the same URL as before, even though the file's physical location has changed. Note that the graphic objects within the Products Web page are not displayed because the graphic source files are not in the Projects subfolder.

Managing Virtual Directory Access Privileges

Virtual directories can be used to specify how files within a virtual directory folder can be accessed and processed. In Figure 5-12, note that the Read and Scripts access properties for the Clearwater virtual directory are checked, and that the Execute property is not checked. **Read access** enables a visitor's Web browser to read or download files stored in a virtual directory. If a visitor's browser sends a request for a file that is in a virtual directory that does not have Read access, the Web server returns an error message. Generally, Read access is given to virtual directories that contain Web page HTML files or graphics files. You should disable the Read permission for directories that contain compiled Web applications designed to run on your Web server to prevent site visitors from downloading the application files and running them on other Web servers—effectively "stealing" your applications.

Execute access enables Web clients to run compiled (executable) Web applications as well as server-side scripts stored in a virtual directory. (Recall that a script is an uncompiled program that is compiled and processed while it runs, and that a server-side script runs on the Web server.) If a client sends a request to a Web server to run a program or a script in a virtual directory that does not have Execute access, the Web server returns an error message. **Scripts access** is more restrictive than Execute access, and enables a visitor's browser to run only scripts that are stored in the virtual directory, not executable programs. If Execute access is set, then Scripts access is automatically set also. You would use Scripts access for virtual directories that contain Active Server Page scripts or other server-side scripts. Table 5-1 summarizes the different directory access privilege types and the types of files you would store with the associated privileges.

> TIP
>
> Windows 2000 PWS allows users to specify access permissions and applications processing permissions for a virtual directory independently of each other. Access permissions include: Read, which allows visitors to only read directory contents; Write, which allows visitors to upload files to a virtual directory; and Script Source Access, which allows visitors to view and download source files for scripts. Application permission options include Name, Scripts, or Execute (including scripts).

Table 5-1 Virtual directory privilege types and associated file types

Privilege	File Types	Sample File Extensions
Read	HTML documents Graphics files	.html .jpg
Execute	Executable programs Server-side scripts	.exe .asp (Active Server Pages)
Scripts	Server-side scripts	.asp

Now you will create a virtual directory named cgi-bin, and change its access property so that files can be executed but not read. You will use this virtual directory to store compiled Web applications that you will create in a later chapter.

To create the cgi-bin virtual directory:

1. Switch to the Personal Web Manager Advanced Options page if necessary, select **<Home>** in the Virtual Directories list, and then click **Add**.

 If a virtual directory named cgi-bin already exists in your Virtual Directories list, select it, and then click the Edit Properties button and modify its properties if necessary, using the following steps.

2. Type **[*the path to your Data Disk*]\cgi-bin** in the Directory text box, and type **cgi-bin** in the Alias text box. Clear all of the check boxes, and then check the **Execute** access check box. (Windows 2000 PWS users will clear all of the Access permission check boxes and select the Execute [including scripts] option button.) Your virtual directory specification should look like Figure 5-13.

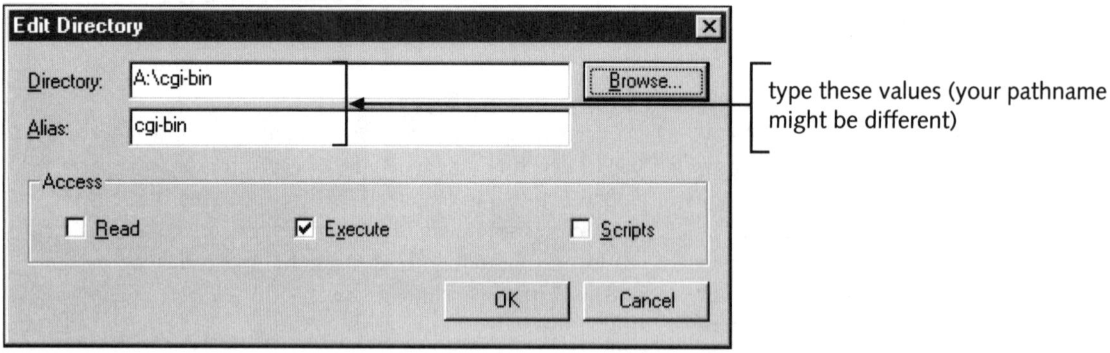

Edit Directory

Directory: A:\cgi-bin   Browse...

Alias: cgi-bin

Access
☐ Read   ☑ Execute   ☐ Scripts

OK   Cancel

type these values (your pathname might be different)

Figure 5-13 Creating the cgi-bin virtual directory

3. Click **OK**. When the message is displayed that states that the cgi-bin folder does not exist on your Data Disk and asks if you want to create it, click **Yes**. The cgi-bin virtual directory is now displayed in the Virtual Directories list, and the cgi-bin folder has been created on your Data Disk.

 TIP If a message is displayed stating that a virtual directory named cgi-bin already exists, change the alias of your new virtual directory to cgi-bin1.

5

When you create CGI (Common Gateway Interface) programs in Chapter 9, you will make them available to visitors in the cgi-bin virtual directory rather than in the root document directory. This provides better security, because the root document directory always has both Read and Execute access. Storing the programs in the root document directory would enable visitors to read and download your CGI programs.

The Remove button on the Advanced Options page allows you to remove a virtual directory specification from the Web site. Removing a virtual directory does not delete the associated folder or its files, but just removes the association between the folder and the Web server and makes the folder's contents unavailable to Web site visitors. Now you will remove the Clearwater virtual directory. Then you will try to access its contents to see what happens.

To remove the Clearwater virtual directory:

1. Switch to the Personal Web Manager Advanced Options page if necessary, select **Clearwater** in the Virtual Directories list, click **Remove**, and then click **Yes** to confirm removing the virtual directory. The Clearwater virtual directory is no longer displayed in the Virtual Directories list.

2. Switch to Internet Explorer, type **http://localhost/Clearwater/** in the Address box, and then press the **Enter** key. A Web page is displayed stating that the specified Web page cannot be found.

3. To remake the Clearwater virtual directory, switch back to the Personal Web Manager Advanced Options page, make sure that <Home> is selected in the Virtual Directories list, click **Add**, navigate to the **Chapter5\Projects** folder on your Data Disk, click **OK**, type **Clearwater** for the alias, and click **OK**.

Monitoring Web Site Performance

Recall that the Personal Web Manager Main page has a Monitoring section to allow you to monitor statistics about visits to your Web site. Now you will switch to the Main page, and view the statistics.

To switch to the Main page and view the statistics:

1. Switch to Personal Web Manager if necessary, and click **Main**. The monitoring statistics are displayed in the lower half of the Main page.

Data are collected about following items:

- **Active connections**, which represent the number of active server connections that are currently being used to transfer data to visitor browsers. Recall that PWS is limited to 10 active connections at a time.

- **Started at** shows when the server was last started.

- **Visitors** shows the number of unique IP addresses that have connected to the server since the workstation was last restarted. Repeated requests from the same IP address are only counted once. A total of 50 addresses are stored for comparison, and repeat visitors will be counted again in the usage statistics if more than 50 unique addresses have been added to the list since the last visit by a particular address.

- **Requests** shows the number of requests received since the computer was last restarted.

- **Bytes served** shows the total amount of data sent since the computer was last restarted.

- **Most concurrent connections** shows the number of connections opened to the server simultaneously since the computer was last started.

The View Statistics graph on the right side of the Monitoring display allows you to display four graphical views of Web site activity, based on Requests per day, Requests per hour, Visitors per day, and Visitors per hour. These statistics are reset each time your computer is rebooted. Now you will reboot your computer, and then view the Monitoring statistics.

To reboot your computer and view the monitoring statistics:

1. Close all of your open applications, and then reboot your workstation.

2. Start Personal Web Manager, view the Main page, confirm that Web publishing is on, and confirm that the Monitoring statistics have been reset. Your monitoring statistics should look like those in Figure 5-1, with no active connections, visitors, requests, bytes served, or most concurrent connections. (Your Started At date and time and home directory will be different.)

3. Start Internet Explorer, and then type **http://localhost/** to connect to your PWS and display the default document, which is the Clearwater Traders home page (Figure 5-3).

4. Switch back to Personal Web Manager, and view the updated monitoring statistics, which should be similar to the statistics shown in Figure 5-14. The exact values will depend on the configurations of individual systems.

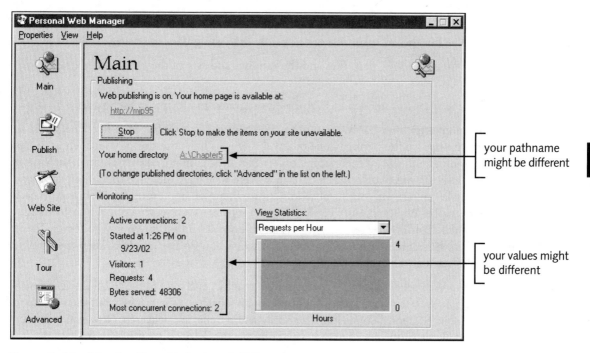

your pathname might be different

5

your values might be different

Figure 5-14   Viewing the monitoring statistics

There should be at least one active connection, since you just connected to the Web site and requested a Web page. (Your browser will automatically terminate the connection after a specific time interval if you do not request any more files from the Web site, so your Active connections property might be zero.) The other monitoring properties show that one visitor has visited the Web site, and made multiple requests for the Web page files and graphics files. The statistics also show that there have been a maximum of two concurrent connections.

5. Switch back to Internet Explorer, and refresh your display.

6. Switch back to Personal Web Manager, and view the updated statistics. Your monitoring information should now show that there have been additional requests, and that the number of bytes served have increased from the previous amount.

FACTORS AFFECTING WEB SITE PERFORMANCE

Anyone who visits Web sites frequently has experienced delays while waiting for a requested Web page to be displayed. Some of the factors that affect the time it takes for a Web site to service a visitor request include:

- The speed of the Web server's network connection

- The amount of main memory that a Web server has allocated to process Web page requests

- The Web server's processor speed
- The number of other visitors currently requesting Web site pages or files
- The size of Web page files and the number and size of their embedded graphic object files
- The resources needed by Web-based programs and scripts in Web pages

Aside from getting faster hardware, more main memory, or running on a faster network, an easy way to improve the performance of a Web site is to limit the size of your Web page files and the number and size of the graphic object files they contain. Always assume that visitors will have fairly slow network connections that make Web page files take much longer to load than they take to load on your local workstation when you are testing the Web page. Recall that each graphic object in an HTML file uses a separate Web server connection to transfer the file to the visitor's browser, which puts an additional burden on your Web server. Try to use graphics sparingly in your Web pages, and when you do use graphics, keep the graphic object files as small as possible.

Recall that a Web page containing more than 10 graphics will exceed the PWS active connection limit. The Web server will send all of the graphic objects to the browser, but there will be a delay while the additional connections are made and the files are delivered. Now you will open a Web page file that contains 11 graphics and observe the delay on your local workstation.

To open the Web page file with 11 graphics:

1. Switch to Internet Explorer, type **http://localhost/lotsagraphics.html** in the Address box, and then press the **Enter** key. You will probably notice a delay in displaying the Web page, because of the large number of graphic objects on the Web page. This delay would be more pronounced if the requested Web page had to be transmitted over a slow network connection. However, all of the graphics are displayed eventually.

On a production Web server, all of the available connections might be in use, and a Web page with multiple graphic objects might have to wait an unacceptable amount of time until additional connections become available to download graphic objects on a Web page.

REFERENCING FILES ON A WEB SERVER

Recall from Chapter 4 that when a Web page contains references to graphic objects or hyperlinks to other Web pages, these objects or pages must be in same folder as the current Web page file. Recall that the folder that contains the Web page that is currently displayed is called the Web browser's current working directory. Similarly, when you reference an object on a Web page that is stored on a Web server, the referenced object must be in the same folder as the Web page that is currently displayed. Saving copies of all Web pages and their associated graphic objects in multiple folders on a Web server is not an effective way to use disk space. Furthermore, when you change a Web page HTML file, you might not remember to update all the copies of the page file if they are stored in multiple places. A better way to manage referenced objects is by specifying object locations using absolute or relative URL addresses, which are similar to the absolute and relative path addresses you used in Chapter 4.

Absolute URL Addresses

Recall from Chapter 4 that an absolute path specifies a file location using the drive letter and complete folder path to show a file's physical location. Similarly, an absolute URL address can be used in a browser's Address box or in a hyperlink tag to specify the complete path location of a Web page file. An **absolute URL address** includes the Web server IP address or domain name, the complete folder path or virtual directory path to the Web page file, and the name of the Web page file. Figure 5-15 shows some examples of absolute URL addresses.

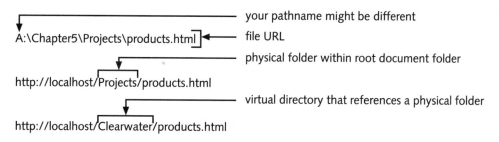

Figure 5-15 shows:
- your pathname might be different
- A:\Chapter5\Projects\products.html — file URL
- physical folder within root document folder
- http://localhost/Projects/products.html
- virtual directory that references a physical folder
- http://localhost/Clearwater/products.html

Figure 5-15   Absolute URL addresses

The first example in Figure 5-15 shows a file URL that uses an absolute path to show the actual physical location of the products.html Web page file. The second URL references the Projects subfolder within the root document directory, which contains the products.html Web page file. The third URL shows how the Clearwater virtual directory, which is associated with the Projects physical folder, can be used instead of the physical folder name in an absolute URL. Now you will use these different absolute URL addresses to display the same Web page file.

To display the products.html Web page file using different absolute URL addresses:

1. Switch to Internet Explorer, type **A:\Chapter5\Projects\products.html** in the Address box, and then press the **Enter** key. (The drive letter and path to your Data Disk might be different.) The Products page is displayed using the file URL. (Again note that the graphic objects are not displayed because their associated files are not located in the \Chapter5\Projects folder on your Data Disk. You will fix this problem later.)

2. In Internet Explorer, type **http://localhost/Projects/products.html** in the Address box, and then press the **Enter** key. The Products page is displayed using the absolute URL, which references the physical folder path within the root document folder. Again, the graphic objects are not displayed, because their files are not located in the current working directory.

3. Type **http://localhost/Clearwater/products.html** in the Address box, and then press the **Enter** key. This URL references the virtual directory associated with the Projects subfolder on your Data Disk. Once again, the graphic objects are not displayed.

Now you will modify the products.html file in the Chapter5\Clearwater folder on your Data Disk so that the reference to the Clearwater Traders logo graphics object uses an absolute URL. A copy of the file for the Clearwater Traders logo is stored in the Chapter5 folder on your Data Disk, which is the root document folder. You will use the absolute URL http://localhost/clearlogo.jpg to specify the image file that is stored in the root document folder of the Web server.

To modify products.html to use an absolute URL for the graphic object reference:

1. Start Notepad, and open **products.html** from the Chapter5\Projects folder on your Data Disk.

2. Change the 10th line of the file as follows so that the image source reference for the logo file is an absolute URL:

```
<TD><IMG SRC=http://localhost/clearlogo.jpg WIDTH=170 HEIGHT
 =100></TD>
```

3. Save the file, switch to Internet Explorer, and refresh the display. The Clearwater Traders logo image is now displayed.

If the logo is not displayed, make sure that the clearlogo.jpg file is located in the Chapter5 folder on your Data Disk, and that you modified the image source reference as shown in Step 2 in the previous set of steps. You might also need to delete all of your cached files again.

Whenever you change the structure of the folders that contain Web pages or graphic objects, you must change the absolute URL references in every HTML file whose path was altered by the change in the folder structure. For example, suppose that you decide to move all of the graphic objects in your Web pages into a folder named Graphics that is within the root document folder. You would need to change the absolute URL for the Clearwater Traders logo to http://localhost/graphics/clearlogo.jpg. Then you would have to change the URL for every other graphic image source reference on all of your Web pages to reflect the new path. To avoid this problem, it is a good idea to use relative URL addresses.

Relative URL Addresses

A **relative URL address** specifies the location of a file relative to the current working directory. To reference a file that is in a folder that is a subfolder of the current working directory, you list the subfolder name, a front slash (/), and then the filename, using the following format: [*subfolder name*]/[*filename*]. Do not preface the subfolder name with a slash. If you do, the relative path will start at the root document folder.

To reference a file that is in a parent folder of the current working directory, you specify the parent folder using two periods (..) followed by a front slash (/), using the following general format: `../[filename]`. Suppose that your Web server has the folder structure and files shown in Figure 5-16. The root document folder contains a file named default.html. There are virtual directories named Clearwater and Northwoods directly below the root document folder, and the Northwoods virtual directory contains a file named students.html. The Clearwater virtual directory contains a subfolder named Pages, and a second subfolder named Graphics. These subfolders contain the files shown in the figure.

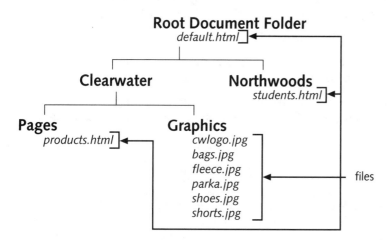

Figure 5-16   Sample Web server folder structure

Table 5-2 shows the relative path addresses that can be used to reference different files, depending on the Web browser's current working directory.

Table 5-2   Relative path addresses

Browser Current Working Directory	Target File	Relative Path Address
Root Document Folder	shorts.jpg	Clearwater/Graphics/shorts.jpg
Pages	fleece.jpg	../Graphics/fleece.jpg
Pages	students.html	../../Northwoods/students.html

For example, if the current working directory is the root document folder, and you want to reference the shorts.jpg file in an HTML document, you would specify the relative path as Clearwater/Graphics/shorts.jpg. This moves from the root document folder to the Clearwater folder, and then moves to the Graphics subfolder, where the shorts.jpg file is located. Similarly, to reference the fleece.jpg file when the current working directory is Pages, you would first move to the parent directory of pages (which is Clearwater), and then move down to the Graphics folder, where fleece.jpg is located.

Note that relative path addresses can be used to specify file addresses that are below, above, and across a folder structure. The third example in the table shows a combination of using the parent directory indicator (..) two times to move up to the Root Document folder, and then down to the Northwoods folder.

Earlier, you modified the image source reference for the Clearwater Traders logo on the Product Guide page so that it used an absolute URL to specify that the image file was located in the root document directory. Now you will modify the other graphic image source references in the products.html file, but this time you will use relative URLs to specify that the image files are stored in the parent folder of the folder that contains the products.html Web page file.

To modify the image references using relative URL addresses:

1. Switch to Notepad, and if necessary, navigate to the Projects folder in the Chapter5 folder on your Data Disk, and open **products.html**.

2. Scroll down to the table that displays the product data, and change the image source references as follows to show that the graphic files are in the parent folder of the Web page file:

Current Image Source Reference	Updated Reference
shorts.jpg	**..\shorts.jpg**
fleece.jpg	**..\fleece.jpg**

3. Save the file, switch to Internet Explorer, and refresh the display to display the updated HTML file using the virtual directory URL. The graphic objects are now displayed.

Now you can move the Chapter5 folder and its contents anywhere in the Web server file system, and as long as the graphic files in the table on the Web page remain in the parent folder of the products.html Web page file, the graphic objects will be displayed on the Web page.

COMPARING PWS TO OTHER WEB SERVERS

One of the main functions of Personal Web Server is to provide an environment where Web programmers can test their programs and Web pages. Therefore, PWS supports the most common server-side programming approaches that can be used with production Web servers such as Microsoft Internet Information Server (IIS). PWS can run CGI programs or scripts and Active Server Pages (ASPs). ASPs, in turn, can call compiled ActiveX programs written in C, C++, Visual Basic, and many other programming languages. (You will learn how to create ActiveX programs in Chapter 6 and Chapter 9.) This makes PWS an excellent learning and testing environment for Web programming.

One difference between PWS and IIS is that IIS has many more sophisticated administrative features. For example, IIS provides a utility that generates more detailed monitoring reports on how your Web site is being accessed by visitors. Additionally, the Internet Service Manager (ISM) utility within IIS provides the following additional Web site configuration features:

- Supports directory browsing that can be enabled or disabled for specific directories rather than for the entire Web site

- Provides Write access for virtual directories. (Recall that PWS only supports Read, Script, and Execute access.) Write access allows visitor browsers to upload as well as download files to a Web server, effectively turning the Web server into an FTP server that enables users to upload and download files.

- Allows the Web server administrator to tune the Web site for the number of expected hits per day. Web server memory is allocated to service visitor requests, and a Web site that receives a high volume of requests needs more main memory for servicing these requests than one that receives fewer requests. When main memory is allocated to service visitor requests, it cannot be used for other processing tasks, which slows down the overall Web service response time.

- Provides a higher level of security through NT file system permissions

Writing scripts and programs for Web servers is conceptually the same regardless of the Web server listener process. The primary difference involves the Web server operating system. Some Web programs cannot run on some operating systems; for example, Visual Basic programs will not run on a UNIX-based Web server. The entire Web server and Web browser industry is going through rapid changes. In this book, we focus on Microsoft technologies since we are using the Windows operating systems and Personal Web Server to illustrate Web programming concepts. However, the concepts presented in this book apply to all operating systems and Web servers.

SUMMARY

- ❑ Personal Web Server (PWS) is software that is designed to create and manage a Web server on a desktop computer. An important difference between PWS and production Web servers is that PWS can support only 10 Web server connections at one time. You can access Web pages on your PWS by using the IP Web address http://localhost/.

- ❑ Personal Web Manager is a utility that is used to configure and monitor PWS. Personal Web Manager is used to specify the Web site root document directory, and the name of the default document, which is the HTML Web page file that is displayed if a visitor request does not specify a particular HTML file. A Web site can have multiple default document filenames. PWS supports directory browsing, which means that a visitor can view a list of the contents of a folder on the Web server if the folder does not contain a copy of the default document. PWS collects monitoring statistics about the Web site, reporting how many visitors, requests, connections, and bytes have been provided to Web site visitors. Personal Web Manager is also used to create virtual directories. A virtual directory is a folder that is not physically contained within the root document folder, but appears to client browsers as though it were. Virtual directories can be used in URL addresses just like physical folder paths.

❑ A Web browser's current working directory is the folder that contains the Web page that is currently displayed. To specify Web page addresses and reference objects on a Web server, you can use absolute URL addresses, which include the Web server's IP address or domain name, and the full folder path of the Web page or object, or you can use relative paths, which specify the location of the Web page or object relative to the Web browser's current working directory. PWS provides an excellent environment for learning about Web servers, and for testing Web programs and new Web pages. Full-featured Web servers, such as Microsoft Internet Information Server, provide more functions to control Web server administration tasks and Web server security.

REVIEW QUESTIONS

1. How many Web server connections are required to display a Web page that contains five graphic objects?

2. True or False: if a Web page contains more that 10 graphic objects, it cannot be displayed by PWS.

3. Suppose that a Web server does not have a default document, and directory browsing is not enabled. A visitor types a URL in the Address box on his or her Web browser that specifies the Web server's IP address, but does not specify a Web page file. What is displayed in the visitor's browser?

4. In the scenario described in Question 3, what will be displayed in the visitor's browser if directory browsing is enabled on the Web server?

5. What is a socket?

6. What is the difference between static and dynamic IP addresses?

7. When should a computer have a static IP address?

8. When should a computer have a dynamic IP address?

9. To what IP address does the domain name localhost refer?

10. What is the purpose of the localhost identifier?

11. True or False: a Web server can only have one default document file, and it must be located in the root document folder.

12. What is a virtual directory? List two benefits of using virtual directories.

13. What is the difference between Execute access and Scripts access privileges in a virtual directory?

14. True or False: Web server monitoring statistics are reset every time the Web server is stopped and then restarted.

15. List three ways to speed up the amount of time it takes for a Web server to process visitor Web page requests.

5

16. Figure 5-17 shows the folder structure for the root document folder on a Web server.

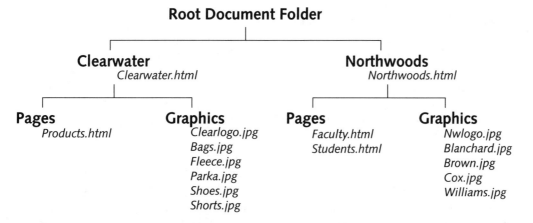

Figure 5-17

Specify the absolute URL addresses for the following files, using localhost as the Web server domain name:

a. clearwater.html

b. fleece.jpg

c. faculty.html

d. nwlogo.jpg

17. Using Figure 5-17 as the Web server folder structure, specify the relative URL addresses for the following target files, based on the specified current working directory:

Target File	Current Working Directory
products.html	Root Document Folder
northwoods.html	Northwoods
clearwater.html	Northwoods
clearlogo.html	Northwoods/Pages

Hands-On
Project

HANDS-ON PROJECTS

1. The folder structure below the Root Document Folder shown in Figure 5-17 has been created in the Projects folder in the Chapter5 folder on your Data Disk. Use this folder structure for all of the projects in this chapter. Create a virtual directory with the alias Ch5Pr1 that is associated with the Chapter5\Projects\Clearwater folder on your Data Disk. Specify that the directory has Read access only. Then, display the clearwater.html Web page file that is stored in the Clearwater folder in your Web browser, using an absolute URL address that includes the Ch5Pr1 virtual directory. Write down the URL address you use.

2. Modify the clearwater.html Web page file that is stored in the Clearwater folder so that it references the clearlogo.jpg image file that is in the Projects\Clearwater\Graphics sub-folder using an absolute URL address that includes the Ch5Pr1 virtual directory.

3. Create a hyperlink in the clearwater.html Web page file that is stored in the Clearwater folder so the Product Guide text is linked to the products.html Web page file that is stored in the Projects\Clearwater\Pages subfolder. Use a relative URL address to create the hyperlink.

4. Open the products.html Web page file that is stored in the Chapter5\Projects\Clearwater\Pages subfolder on your Data Disk, and modify the references to the graphic object files in the products.html Web page file, using relative URL addresses that reference the graphics files in the Clearwater\Graphics subfolder. View the modified page in Internet Explorer to confirm that your paths are correct.

5. Modify the products.html page that is stored in the Clearwater\Pages subfolder by cre-ating a new item that has the text "Clearwater Traders Home Page" in the bulleted list in the top-right corner of the page. When a visitor clicks this hyperlink, the Clearwater Traders home page should be displayed. Create a hyperlink so that the text is linked to the clearwater.html Web page file that is stored in the Clearwater folder, using a relative URL address.

6. Create a virtual directory with the alias Ch5Pr6 that is associated with the Projects\Northwoods subfolder in the Chapter5 folder on your Data Disk. Specify that the directory has Read access only. Display the northwoods.html Web page file in your Web browser, using an absolute URL address that includes the Ch5Pr6 virtual directory. Write down the URL address you use.

7. Modify the northwoods.html Web page file so that it references the nwlogo.jpg image file in the Projects\Northwoods\Graphics subfolder, using an absolute URL address.

8. Modify the Students and Faculty hyperlinks in the northwoods.html Web page file so that the text is linked to the students.html and faculty.html Web page files that are stored in the Projects\Northwoods\Pages subfolder. Use relative URL addresses to create the links.

9. Open the faculty.html Web page file that is stored in the Chapter5\Projects\Northwoods\Pages subfolder on your Data Disk, and modify the ref-erences to the image files so that they use relative URL addresses to reference the files that are stored in the Projects\Northwoods\Graphics subfolder on your Data Disk. View the modified page in Internet Explorer to confirm that your paths are correct.

10. Open the students.html Web page file that is stored in the Chapter5\Projects\Northwoods\Pages subfolder on your Data Disk, and modify the reference to the Northwoods University logo file so it uses an absolute URL address to reference the nwlogo.jpg file. The absolute URL address should include the Ch5Pr6 virtual directory. View the modified page in Internet Explorer to confirm that your path is correct.

11. Create a new text item at the bottom of the Students page (students.html) that has the text "Northwoods University Home Page." When a visitor clicks this link, the Northwoods University home page is displayed. Create a hyperlink so that the text is linked to the northwoods.html Web page file, using a relative URL address.

5

CASE PROJECTS

1. Create a folder named Ashland in the Chapter5 folder on your Data Disk. Store the Ashland Valley Soccer League home page that you created in Chapter 4, Case Project 2, in the Ashland folder. Create subfolders named Pages and Graphics within the Ashland folder. Store the Web pages that you created in Chapter 4, Case Project 1, in the Pages folder, and store any graphics files that you used in these Web pages in the Graphics folder. Then, create a virtual directory on your PWS named Ashland that corresponds to the Chapter5\Ashland folder on your Data Disk. Modify your Web pages so that they use relative paths to reference Web page documents and graphics files.

2. Create a folder named Waynes in the Chapter5 folder on your Data Disk. Store the Wayne's Auto World home page that you created in Chapter 4, Case Project 4, in the Waynes folder. Create subfolders named Pages and Graphics within the Waynes folder. Store the Web pages that you created in Chapter 4, Case Project 3, in the Pages folder, and store any graphics files that you used in these pages in the Graphics folder. Then, create a virtual directory on your PWS named Waynes that corresponds to the Chapter5\Waynes folder on your Data Disk. Modify your Web pages so they use relative paths to reference Web page documents and graphics files.

3. Create a folder named Sunray in the Chapter5 folder on your Data Disk. Store the Sun-Ray Video home page that you created in Chapter 4, Case Project 6, in the Sunray folder. Store the Web pages that you created in Chapter 4, Case Project 5, in the Pages folder, and store any graphics files that you used in these pages in the Graphics folder. Then, create a virtual directory on your PWS named Chapter5\Sunray that corresponds to the Sunray folder on your Data Disk. Modify your Web pages so that they use relative paths to reference Web page documents and graphics files.

6

USING VISUAL BASIC 6.0 TO CREATE WEB-BASED DATABASE APPLICATIONS

In this chapter, you will:

♦ Learn about the Visual Basic development environment
♦ Learn about the components of a Visual Basic database application
♦ Create a Visual Basic application using the ADO data control to display database data
♦ Create programmatic data controls to process data in a Visual Basic program
♦ Create a Visual Basic ActiveX document that is run from a Web page

Microsoft Visual Basic (VB) is a development language that enables programmers to create Windows-based programs. VB has a rich set of tools to support database operations. For example, you could create a program that would allow a customer to view the items in the Clearwater Traders database, and then select an item and place an order. To do this, the Visual Basic application connects to the database and composes a data query. The database server processes the query and returns the retrieved data, which are then displayed in the Visual Basic application.

This VB application can be converted to an **ActiveX document**, which is a program that users can download from a Web site and install on their computers. One of the Clearwater Traders Web pages can have a hyperlink that calls this program. The first time that the user clicks this link, a message is displayed asking the user if he or she wants to install the program on his or her workstation. If the user agrees, then the Web server sends the installation program to the user's workstation, where the program is installed and then run. This process is shown in Figure 6-1.

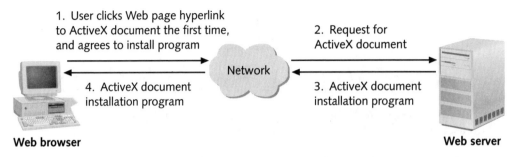

1. User clicks Web page hyperlink
to ActiveX document the first time,
and agrees to install program

2. Request for
ActiveX document

Network

4. ActiveX document
installation program

3. ActiveX document
installation program

Web browser

Web server

Figure 6-1   Installing an ActiveX document

When the user clicks this hyperlink on subsequent visits, the program is not reinstalled; instead, the program simply runs on the user's workstation. Depending on how the ActiveX document is written, the interface can look as if it is displayed in the Microsoft Internet Explorer Web browser, or it can look like a standard Windows application.

In this chapter, you will learn about the components of a VB program, become familiar with the VB programming environment, and create a VB application that interacts with database tables. Then, you will learn how to convert this application to an ActiveX document that can be installed and run from a Web page.

This chapter assumes that you have prior Visual Basic programming experience. It provides a rapid Visual Basic overview that focuses on creating database applications and ActiveX documents.

OVERVIEW OF VISUAL BASIC

Visual Basic can be used to create almost any kind of Windows-based program, from a database application to a video game. Visual Basic is an **event-driven** programming language, which means that program statements execute in response to user actions, such as clicking a command button, or to system actions, such as loading a program. The following paragraphs provide a brief overview of VB and an introduction to the VB programming environment.

Components of a Visual Basic Program

Every VB program has an individual **project file**, which has a .vbp extension. The project file specifies properties of the program and the names of the individual components of the program, which are stored in separate files. The main components of a VB project are forms, which are stored in files with an .frm extension, and standard modules, which are stored in files with a .bas extension. A **form** has two parts: the visible interface that the user sees and interacts with, and the associated code that responds to user and system actions. A **standard module** contains only code, and this code can be used by many forms. A standard module is used to store declarations for variables that are used in multiple forms. (In most programming languages, variables have to be declared, which means specifying the variable name and its data type, before the variable can be used in program statements. Declaring a variable causes the program to reserve an area in the computer's main memory for storing the variable's value.) The standard module also stores procedures and functions, which are independent code components that can be used by multiple forms. A **procedure** manipulates variable values, and a **function** returns a single value based on parameters that are passed to the function. **Controls** are the visible items on a form, such as command buttons, option buttons, and text boxes. Figure 6-2 shows some of the common controls that are often used in VB forms.

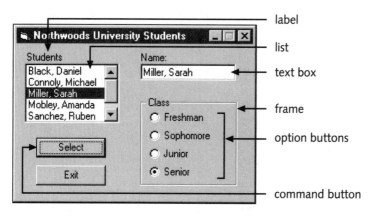

Figure 6-2   Form controls

Visual Basic Projects

When VB is started, a new project is created, which corresponds to an individual user application. When you create a new project, you can select the type of project it will be, which specifies how the project file is compiled. Figure 6-3 shows the New Project dialog box, which illustrates some of the different VB project types.

Figure 6-3 Visual Basic project types

VB projects can be compiled as standard executable files, which are Windows-based programs that can be run independently of other applications. VB projects can also be created using different ActiveX options to make programs that can be called within Web pages. These Web pages must be displayed using the Microsoft Internet Explorer Web browser. (Recall that ActiveX is a term that identifies a variety of technologies that integrate software components in Web-based systems.) To become familiar with performing database operations using Visual Basic, you will first create a standard executable project that lets you view inventory data about items in the Clearwater Traders inventory database. Later in the chapter, you will create a similar project that can be displayed in a Web browser using the ActiveX document project option.

Since ActiveX documents can only be displayed using Microsoft Internet Explorer, you must use Internet Explorer when you work with the Web-based tutorials and projects in this chapter.

THE VISUAL BASIC DEVELOPMENT ENVIRONMENT

Visual Basic has an integrated development environment (IDE) that is used to create and integrate the components of a VB project. An **IDE** is an environment for developing programs; it has multiple windows that can be displayed or hidden, as needed. The VB IDE windows can be used to manage the project, create the forms and their associated code, and create code modules. Figure 6-4 displays some of the components of the VB IDE. (Your IDE might look slightly different, depending on the windows that are currently open.)

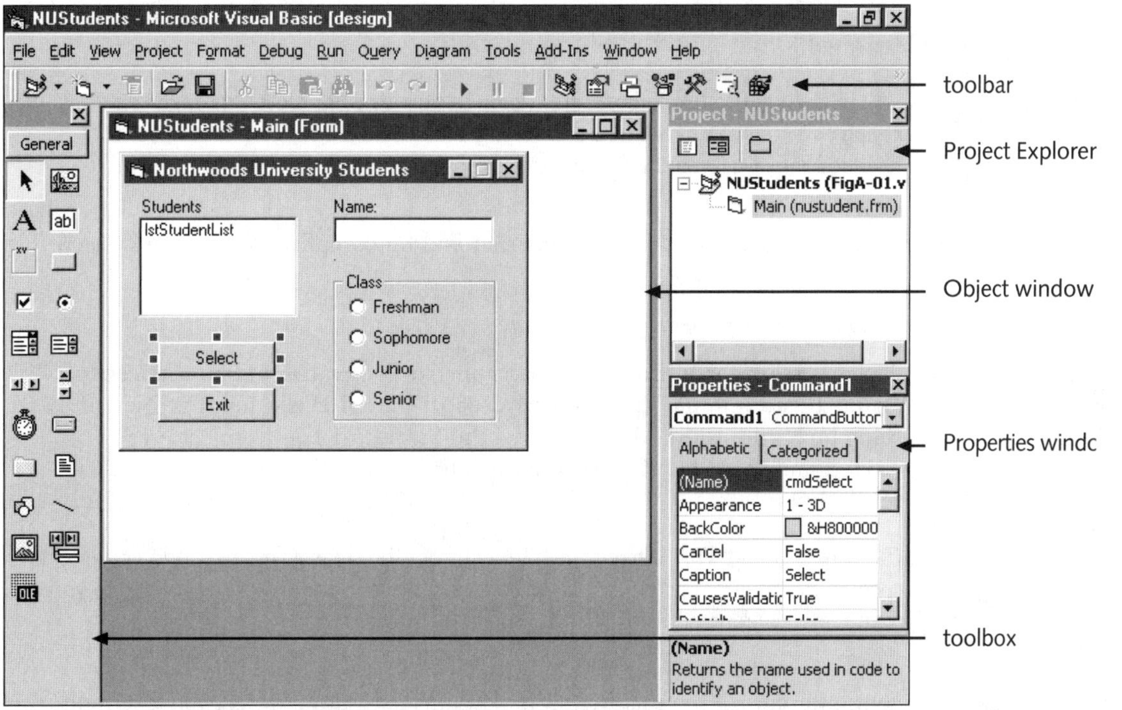

Figure 6-4   VB IDE components

The main IDE components include:

- The **toolbar**, which provides quick access to menu bar commands for opening, designing, and running VB projects, as well as ways to configure the VB IDE

- The **Object window**, which shows the form and the positions of the controls on the form

- The **toolbox**, which contains icons that are used to create form controls

- The **Project Explorer**, which displays a hierarchical list of the components of the current project

- The **Properties window**, which is used to assign and display the properties of the object that is currently selected in the Form window. (An object might be a control, like a command button or an option button, or the form itself.) Note that in Figure 6-4, the Select command button is selected in the Form window, and the Properties window displays the Select button's properties.

The VB IDE can be customized to display multiple windows, which can be sized and positioned according to your personal preferences. The IDE also supports **docking**, which allows the borders of windows to be attached, or docked, to other windows. When two windows are docked, they can be moved and resized as a single unit. The IDE configuration information is stored in a configuration file with a .vbw extension. When a new project is created, the default IDE configuration is used. When an existing project is opened, the IDE configuration stored in the .vbw file in the current working directory (which is the folder that contains the project file) is used.

You might want to take a break from time to time as you proceed through this chapter's tutorials. You can take a break any time you are instructed to save your changes or exit a form, then come back later and pick up where you left off.

Now you will start VB, create a new project that will be compiled as a standard executable file, and configure your VB IDE.

To start VB, create a new project, and configure the VB IDE:

1. Click **Start** on the Windows taskbar, point to **Programs**, point to **Microsoft Visual Basic 6.0**, and then click **Microsoft Visual Basic 6.0**. The New Project dialog box is displayed. Make sure that the **Standard EXE** project type is selected, and then click **Open**. The VB IDE is displayed.

The way you start VB 6.0 might be different from the steps given here, and you might need to ask your instructor or technical support person for instructions specific to your computing environment.

2. Configure the IDE so that the toolbox, Object window, Project Explorer, and Properties window are displayed. (To display a window that is not currently displayed, click View on the menu bar, and then click the name of the component.) If necessary, maximize the Object window, and move and resize the windows so that your IDE looks like Figure 6-5.

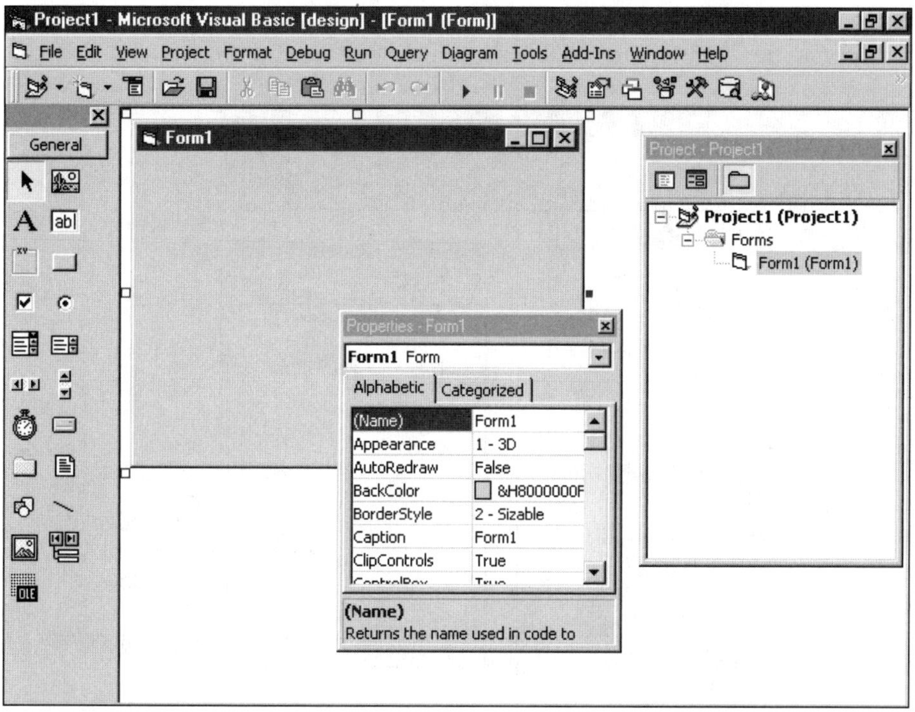

Figure 6-5   Configuring the VB IDE

> **TIP**
> If your windows are docked, you can right-click the window, and then click Dockable to detach them.

> **TIP**
> Sometimes when you move a window to the right edge of the screen, the window is automatically resized so that it fills the entire width of the screen. If this happens, drag the window to the lower-right corner of the screen until its border becomes a thick gray line. Then the window will be resized so that it is smaller, and you can modify its size and position as desired.

3. Click **Tools** on the menu bar, click **Options**, click the **Docking** tab, make sure that the Properties window and Project Explorer check boxes are checked, and then click **OK**.

4. To dock the top border of the Properties window to the bottom border of the Project Explorer, select the **Properties** window, and drag it to the lower-right corner of the screen so that it is on top of the Project Explorer window and its border changes to a thick gray line. Continue dragging the window to the bottom of the Project Explorer window until the border changes to a thin dashed line and

the border is approximately on top of the lower border of the Project Explorer window, as shown in Figure 6-6. Then, release the mouse button.

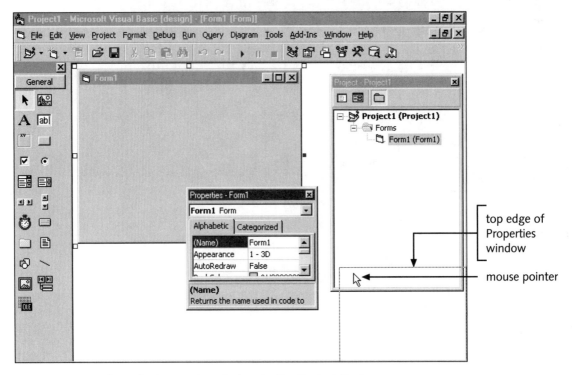

top edge of Properties window

mouse pointer

Figure 6-6   Docking the Properties window to the Project Explorer

5. Place the mouse pointer on the top edge of the Properties window so that the pointer changes to ⇕, and then resize the Properties window and the Project Explorer so that the top edge of the Properties window is docked to the bottom edge of the Project Explorer, as shown in Figure 6-7.

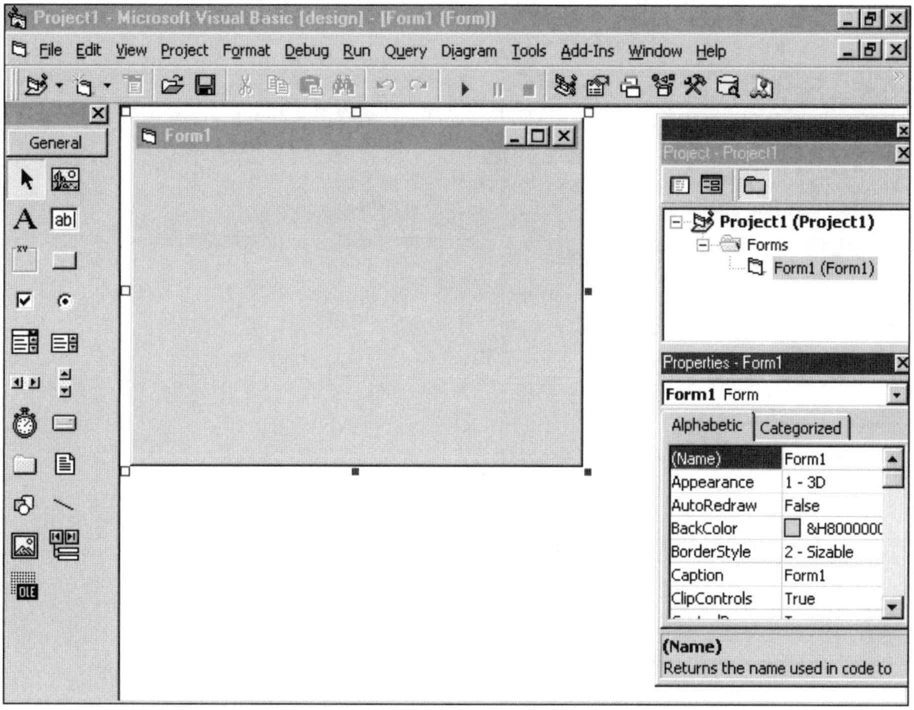

Figure 6-7   Finished IDE configuration

CREATING A VISUAL BASIC DATABASE APPLICATION

Now you will create an Inventory Maintenance application that will run on the Clearwater Traders intranet. The design sketch for this application is shown in Figure 6-8.

The first form that is displayed is the Items form, which displays the fields from a single record in the ITEMS table. The user can click the **data control**, which is a form control that is attached to a database table and is used to sequentially step through the records to view the items. The user can also use the form's command buttons to create and save new ITEM records and update or delete existing records. When the user clicks the "View Inventory" button, the Inventory form is displayed. This form shows in a grid display the related INVENTORY records for the item that is currently displayed, and shows all of the table fields and records on the form at the same time. The user can insert new inventory records or select an existing inventory record and update or delete it. When the user clicks the "View Shipments" button, the Shipments form is displayed, which shows all of the pending (unreceived) incoming shipments for the inventory record that is selected on the Inventory form. When the user clicks the Exit button on the Shipments form, the Inventory form is displayed. When the user clicks the Exit button on the Inventory form, the Items form is displayed.

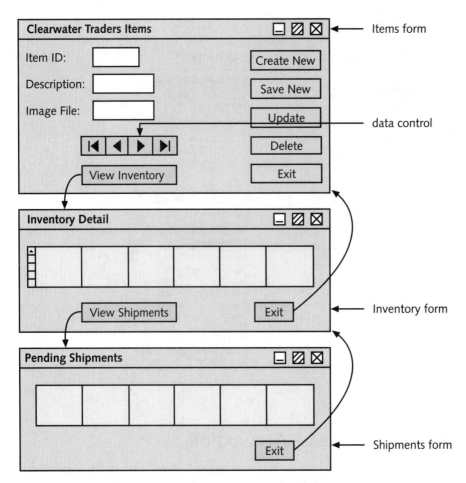

Figure 6-8   Clearwater Traders Inventory Maintenance application

You will create this application as a standard executable file so that you can become familiar with creating forms and code modules and using database controls and commands within VB. Later, you will use the components that you create in this project to make a Web-based application.

Modifying Form Properties

Currently, your VB IDE should look like Figure 6-7, with a single form (Form1) displayed. The first step is to modify the properties of this form. The **properties** of a VB object specify the object's appearance and behavior. For example, a form has a Caption property, which specifies the text that is displayed in its title bar. A form also has a Border Style property, which can be set as *sizeable* or *fixed*. If the border style is sizeable, users can resize the form window; if the border style is fixed, users cannot resize the form window.

You can assign property values when you design an application by modifying the object's properties using the Properties window. The Properties window shows a list of the properties for the object that is currently selected in the Form window. You can scroll in the Properties window to view the form properties. The property name is listed in the first column, and its current value is listed in the second column.

The first property you will change is the form's Name. The **Name** property determines how objects are internally identified within the project. The Name property must begin with a letter and can contain characters, numbers, or underscores. Object names should be descriptive, and should start with a three-letter prefix that identifies the object type. Table 6-1 shows some of the common object name prefixes that you will use.

Table 6-1   VB object name prefixes

Object Type	Prefix	Sample Name
ADO data control	ado	adoInventory
Check box	chk	chkTextBox
Command button	cmd	cmdExit
DataGrid	dbg	dbgInventory
Form	frm	frmItem
Option button	opt	optFreshman
Text box	txt	txtName

Now you will change the form name to frmItems.

To change the form Name property:

1. Make sure that Form1 is selected in the Object window. The selected form should have selection handles on its borders, as shown in Figure 6-7.

2. Scroll to the top of the Properties window list, if necessary, until you find the Name property. Delete the current value (which is Form1), type **frmItems**, and then click another property to apply the change. Note that the form's name is now modified in the Project Explorer window.

To follow accepted Windows application design guidelines, you should always modify the following form properties:

- **BorderStyle**, which determines whether the user can resize the form. In general, you should not allow users to resize a form, since resizing might cause some form controls to be clipped off or to be displayed off-center on the screen.

- **Caption**, which is the form description that is displayed in the form's title bar

- **MaxButton**, which allows the user to maximize the form so that it is displayed full-screen. In general, you should not allow users to maximize a form, since form objects might appear off-center in a maximized form.

- **MinButton**, which allows the user to minimize the form. It is a good practice to always allow users to minimize a form.

- **StartUpPosition**, which determines where the form is displayed on the screen when the application is running. Usually, the application should be displayed in the center of the user's screen.

Now you will modify these properties on the Items form.

To modify the other form properties:

1. Make sure that frmItems is selected in the Forms window, and then change the following properties to the specified value in the frmItems Properties window. When you are finished, your form should look like the form shown in Figure 6-9.

Property	Value
BorderStyle	**1 – Fixed Single**
Caption	**Clearwater Traders Items**
MaxButton	**False**
MinButton	**True**
StartUpPosition	**2 – CenterScreen**

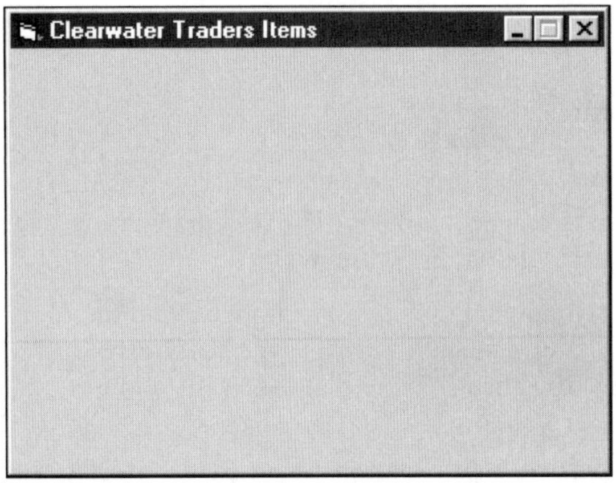

Figure 6-9   Form with modified properties

Saving Visual Basic Projects

Now you will save the project and the Items form. Recall that a VB project is saved in a file with a .vbp extension, and forms are saved in files with an .frm extension. The project file is a text file that specifies information about the project type, lists the names of the form files and other project components, and contains other project information that is used by the VB environment. When you create a new project, it is very important to always save the project (.vbp) file and the form (.frm) files in the same folder in your file system. If you do not, then the project file will specify the absolute path information (including drive letter and full folder path) to the form file. If the form file is moved, or if the .vbp file is run on a different computer with a different folder structure, then the project will not be able to find the form, and an error message will be displayed. If the project and form files are always saved in the same folder, no path information is saved in the project file, and the project file will always look in the current working directory (which is the folder where the .vbp file is located) for the form files.

To save the project and form file:

1. Click the **Save Project** button 🖫. When the Save File As dialog box opens, navigate to the Chapter6 folder on your Data Disk, make sure that the form file name is frmItems.frm, and then click **Save**.

2. When the Save Project As dialog box is displayed, do not change to a different folder. Change the project filename to **CWItems.vbp**, and then click **Save**.

Creating Form Controls

6

Now you will create the text boxes, labels, and command buttons on the Items form, as shown in Figure 6-8. First you will create the text boxes that will display the item ID, its description, and the name of the item's image file, and their corresponding labels. Then you will change the names of the new text boxes and modify the Text property of the text boxes. The Text property of a text box specifies the text that is currently displayed in the text box. When the form is first displayed, the text boxes should be blank, so you will delete the current value of the Text property. You will also modify the Caption property of the labels, which is the label text. Generally, you don't need to modify the Name property of a label unless the label's caption is changed while the form is running.

To create the text boxes and labels:

1. Click the **TextBox** tool 🔳 in the toolbox, and draw three text boxes on the Items form, as shown in Figure 6-10. (You might need to resize your form.)

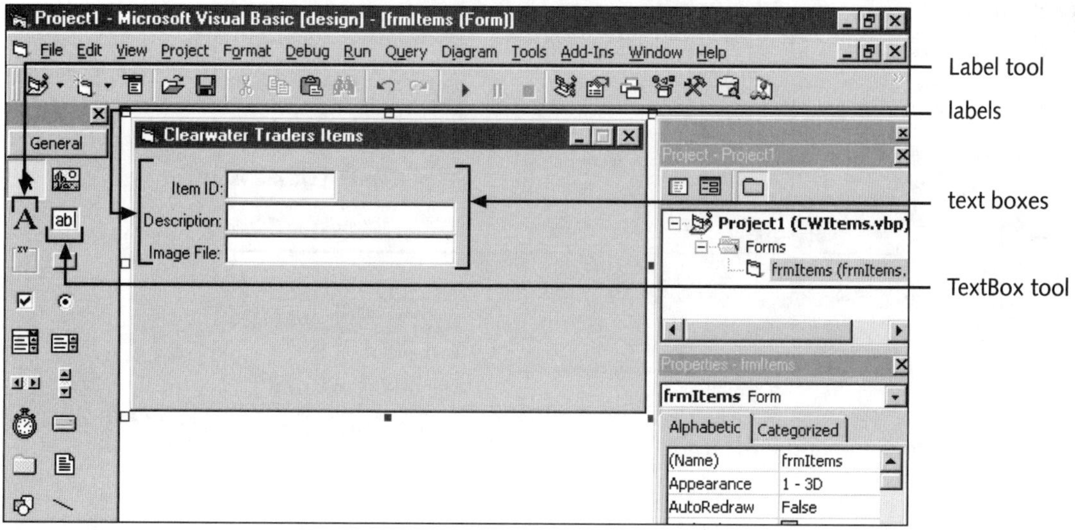

Figure 6-10   Form text boxes and labels

2. Click the **Label** tool $\boxed{A}$ and draw a label on the left edge of each text box.

3. Select the first text box, change its Name property to **txtItemID**, and delete the current value of its Text property.

4. Select the label on the right edge of the txtItemID text box, and change its Caption property to **Item ID:**.

5. Change the Name and Text properties and associated labels' Caption properties of the other two text boxes as follows:

Name	Text	Label Caption
txtItemDesc	[deleted]	**Description:**
txtItemImage	[deleted]	**Image File:**

6. Resize and reposition the text boxes and labels as necessary so that your form looks like Figure 6-10. Click the **Save Project** button $\boxed{\blacksquare}$ to save the changes to the form.

Now you will add the command buttons to the form. You will draw the command buttons on the form using the **CommandButton** tool $\boxed{\ \square\ }$, and then you will modify the Name and Caption properties of the command buttons. The Caption property specifies the labels that are displayed on the buttons.

To add the command buttons:

1. Click the **CommandButton** tool $\boxed{\ \square\ }$ in the toolbox and draw the command buttons, as shown in Figure 6-11.

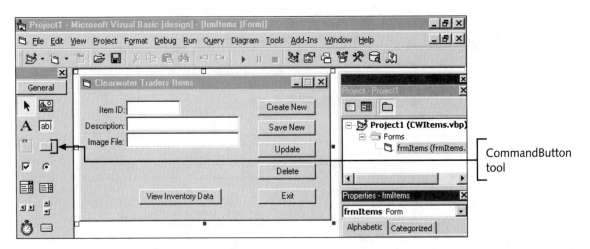

Figure 6-11 Form command buttons

2. Change the Name and Caption properties of the command buttons as follows:

Name	Caption
cmdCreate	**Create New**
cmdSave	**Save New**
cmdUpdate	**Update**
cmdDelete	**Delete**
cmdExit	**Exit**
cmdView	**View Inventory Data**

3. Save the project.

6

USING VISUAL BASIC WITH A DATABASE

Now that you have created a form with text boxes to display database data and command buttons to create, view, update, and delete records, the next step is to access the data in the database. To understand how this works, you need to understand how applications communicate with databases. When program developers first saw the need for applications that communicate with a variety of different databases, they created a technology called ODBC (Open Database Connectivity). Microsoft and database vendors developed ODBC drivers for a variety of different databases. An **ODBC driver** is a low-level program that translates messages from an application into the syntax expected by a specific database. Each different type of database (Access, Oracle, SQL Server, and so on) requires a different ODBC driver. The ODBC driver always runs on the client workstation.

Programs written in program development languages (such as Visual Basic and C++), as well as applications that access databases (such as Excel), need to be able to communicate with ODBC drivers. To simplify this communication, Microsoft has developed a variety of different data access technologies: **Data Access Objects (DAO)**, **Remote Data Objects (RDO)**, and **ActiveX Data Objects (ADO)**. DAO is available in most applications that support database connectivity, but it cannot support action queries that change the content in some databases. RDO is full-featured and very versatile, but is only available in Microsoft's high-end enterprise-level programming environments. ADO is also full-featured, is available in most Microsoft environments, and supports most types of queries. Figure 6-12 shows how the Microsoft data access technologies interact with ODBC drivers and databases.

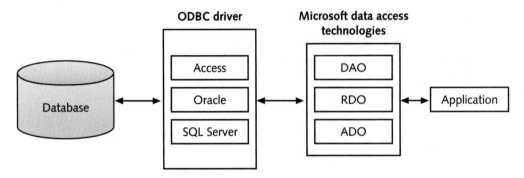

Figure 6-12 Microsoft data access architecture using ODBC

An application program uses one of the data access technologies (DAO, RDO, or ADO) to send a message to the ODBC driver associated with a particular database. The ODBC driver forwards the message to the database. If the command retrieves data, then the data are returned via the ODBC driver, and are displayed in the program using the appropriate data access technology.

Microsoft has developed a second approach for application/database connectivity using the ADO data access approach and a technology called OLE DB (Object Linking and Embedding Database), as shown in Figure 6-13.

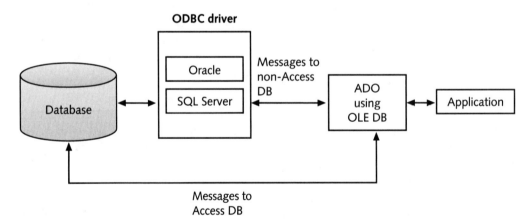
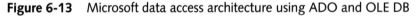

Figure 6-13 Microsoft data access architecture using ADO and OLE DB

With this approach, an application sends a message to a database using ADO along with OLE DB. If the database is an Access (Jet database engine) database, then the message is forwarded directly to the DBMS without using ODBC. If the database is a non-Jet database, then the message is forwarded to the ODBC driver, which then forwards the message to the database. The advantage of using this approach is that it allows developers to use some Jet-database-specific commands within programs.

Now you are ready to modify your Visual Basic program to interact with the Clearwater Traders database. You can do this in one of two ways. The first way to do this is to specify the properties of the database connection when you design the form. You can specify properties using an ActiveX data control within the form, which provides a button interface for stepping through the database records. This approach, which is described in the next section, is usually used when you create standard executable Visual Basic applications. In the second approach, you perform all of the database commands, such as creating a connection, retrieving records, and so on, using program code.

Note When you use Visual Basic programs to perform server-side processing of Web pages, the VB programs will not have a visible form component. If the programs have visible forms, the forms will be displayed on the Web server's screen rather than in the user's browser window, which is not very helpful to the user. Therefore, in Web applications that use server-side processing, you must use code rather than an ActiveX data control to process Web page inputs and specify outputs.

The following sections describe how to create an ActiveX data control and write code to connect and interact with the database.

Creating an ActiveX Data Control

An **ActiveX data control** is a control (like a command button or a text box) that is displayed on a form. It is different from an ordinary form control because it is associated with a **recordset**, which is a specific set of database records based on a SQL query. Text boxes on the form are then bound to specific fields within the data control's recordset. Figure 6-14 illustrates the relationships between a database, an ActiveX data control, and form text boxes.

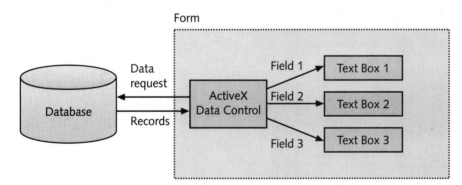

Figure 6-14 ActiveX data control

The ActiveX data control sends data requests to the database and receives records. It then associates the retrieved data values with form text boxes that are associated with specific data fields. In the frmItems form, you will create an ADO (ActiveX Data Object) data control, since ADO is the most versatile and readily available Microsoft data access technology.

To create an ADO data control, you must add a **type library** to your project, which is a library of code that has programs, such as additional controls, that you can add to the VB IDE and then use in your project. When you add the ADO type library to your project, a tool that is used to create an ADO data control will be displayed in the toolbox. Now you will add the ADO type library to your project.

To add the ADO type library and data control to your project:

1. Click **Project** on the menu bar, and then click **References**. The References dialog box is displayed.

2. Scroll down the Available References list, and check the **Microsoft ActiveX Data Objects 2.1 Library** check box. Do not clear the four check boxes that are already checked. Click **OK** to close the Available References list. The **Adodc** (ADO data control) tool is displayed in the toolbox.

 The ADO 2.1 Library is only available with the Visual Basic 6.0 Professional and Enterprise Editions. You might need to add the Microsoft ActiveX Data Objects 2.0 Library, depending on which version of Visual Basic 6.0 you are using.

TIP If the Adodc tool does not appear in the toolbox, you can add it by clicking Projects in the menu bar, then clicking Components. Check the Microsoft ADO Data Control 6.0 (OLEDB) check box, and click OK. should now be in the toolbox.

Now you will create the ADO data control on the Items form. You will create a database connection using the OLE DB approach shown in Figure 6-13. The data control will be associated with the clearwater.mdb database file that is in the Chapter6 folder on your Data Disk.

To create the data control:

1. Click the **Adodc** tool in the toolbox and draw the data control on the form, as shown in Figure 6-15.

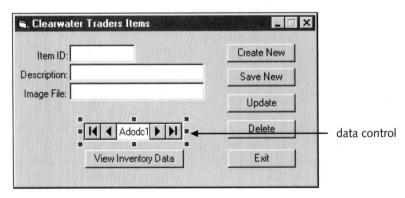

Figure 6-15   Creating the ADO data control

2. Change the data control's Name property to **adoItem** and the Caption property to **Items**.

3. Click the **ConnectionString** property in the Properties window, and then click the **Ellipsis** button . The Property Pages dialog box is displayed, which allows you to specify the database that is associated with the data control. You can specify the database connection using a file called a Data Link file, using ODBC with a source string, or using an ADO connection string, which uses OLE DB.

4. Make sure that the Use Connection String option button is selected, and then click **Build**. The Data Link Properties dialog box is displayed, which shows different databases that you can use to create the connection string.

5. Select **Microsoft Jet 4.0 OLE DB Provider**, and then click **Next**.

> 💡 **TIP**   If the Jet 4.0 OLE DB Provider is not available, you can use the Microsoft Jet 3.51 OLE DB Provider.

6. Click beside the Select or enter a database name text box, navigate to the Chapter6 folder on your Data Disk, select **clearwater.mdb**, and then click **Open**.

7. Click the **Test Connection** button. A message box stating "Test connection succeeded." should be displayed. Click **OK** to close the message box.

> 💡 **TIP**   If the test connection did not succeed, make sure that the clearwater.mdb file is in the Chapter6 folder on your Data Disk. If it is, open the clearwater.mdb file in Access to confirm that it is a valid database file.

8. Click **OK** to close the Data Link Properties dialog box, and then click **OK** again to close the Property Pages dialog box. Note that a connection string has now been entered into the ConnectionString property in the Properties window.

The next step is to specify the data control's recordset. Since the Items form will display all of the records in the ITEM table, the data control's recordset will be based on a SQL query that retrieves all of the records from the ITEM table.

To specify the data control's recordset:

1. Scroll down in the adoItems Properties window to the RecordSource property, click the **RecordSource** property, and then click the **Ellipsis** button beside the current RecordSource property. The Property Pages dialog box is displayed.

2. Type the following SQL query in the Command Text (SQL) text box:

```
SELECT * FROM item
```

3. Click **OK** to close the Property Pages dialog box and save the SQL query.

To finish the ActiveX data control, you must bind, or connect, the form text boxes to the data control by setting each text box's DataSource property to the data control. You must also specify the name of the data field that each text box will display. Then, you will run the form to test it and make sure that the ActiveX data control works correctly.

To bind the form text boxes to the data control and test the form:

1. Select the Item ID (txtItemID) text box on the form, click its **DataSource** property, open the list box, and select **adoItem**.

2. Select the Item ID (txtItemID) text box's **DataField** property, and open the list box. A list of the data fields that are retrieved by the ActiveX data control is displayed. The list should include ITEMID, ITEMDESC, and ITEMIMAGE. Select **ITEMID**.

3. Modify the properties of the other text boxes as follows:

Text Box Name	DataSource	DataField
Description (txtItemDesc)	**adoItem**	**ITEMDESC**
Image File (txtItemImage)	**adoItem**	**ITEMIMAGE**

4. Click the **Run Program** button ▶ on the toolbar to run the form. The first record in the ITEM table is displayed in the text boxes, as shown in Figure 6-16.

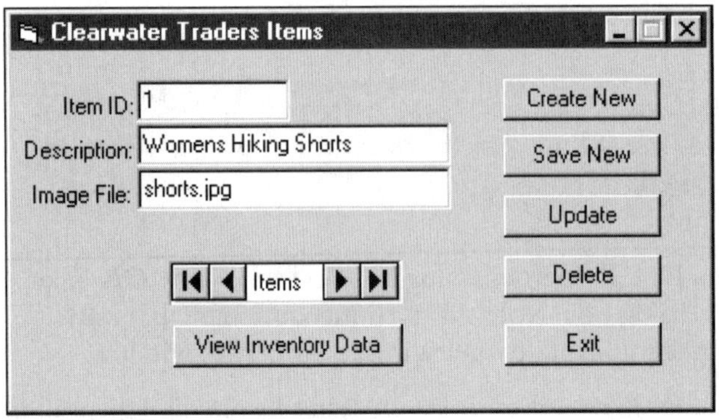

Figure 6-16 Displaying data using the ADO data control

5. Click the **Next Record** button ▶ on the ADO data control. The data for Item ID 2 (Women's Fleece Pullover) are displayed.

6. Click the **Last Record** button ▶I. The data for the last record in the ITEM table (Item ID 5, Goose Down Sleeping Bag) are displayed.

7. Click the **Previous Record** button ◀. The data for the record immediately before the last record (Item ID 4, All-Weather Mountain Parka) are displayed.

8. Click the **First Record** button I◀. The data for the first record (Item ID 1, Women's Hiking Shorts) are displayed again.

9. Click the **Close** button ✕ on the window title bar to close the form.

Using Program Code to Process Data

When you create a database connection using an ADO data control, the properties of the connection are specified in a control that is displayed on a form. The code that allows you to step through the database records is part of the control. With a **programmatic data connection**, all of the commands to create the connection and execute SQL commands are specified in a VB standard module. The user does not have to interact with a visible data control to perform database operations. Figure 6-17 illustrates how a programmatic data connection works.

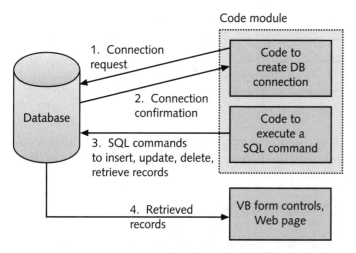

Figure 6-17   Creating a data connection programmatically

The code module first contains the commands for establishing the connection with the database. Then, it contains commands for executing SQL commands. The retrieved records could be displayed either in VB form controls or in Web pages.

Code in Visual Basic Programs

Recall that a VB project consists of forms and standard code modules. Every form and every code module has a section called the **General Declarations section**. This section contains declarations for variables, and the code for functions and procedures that are used in the form or code module. Forms also contain code that is executed when a specific event happens to a control, such as clicking a command button. Now you will examine the Visual Basic Code window and become familiar with its components.

To examine the VB Code window:

1. Click the **View Object** button 🔲 on the Project Explorer window toolbar, if necessary, to display the Object window. Select the **frmItems** form in the Object window, and then click the **View Code** button 🔲 on the Project Explorer toolbar. The Code window for the frmItems form is displayed, as shown in Figure 6-18. Currently, the insertion point is on the first line of the code window, which is the

start of the General Declarations section. Note that the Object list displays "(General)", and the Procedure/Event list displays "(Declarations)".

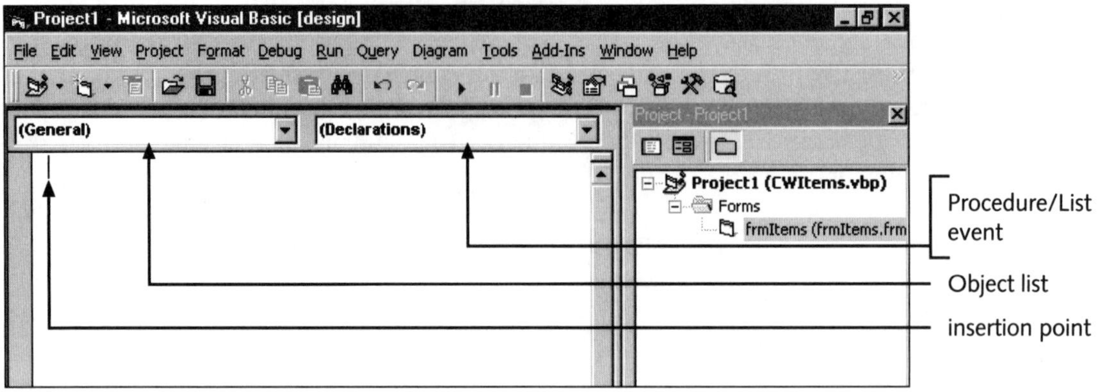

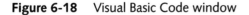

Figure 6-18 Visual Basic Code window

2. Open the Object list. All of the form controls are listed, along with the form itself. Click **cmdCreate**. A code template is displayed for the cmdCreate button's Click event, as shown in Figure 6-19.

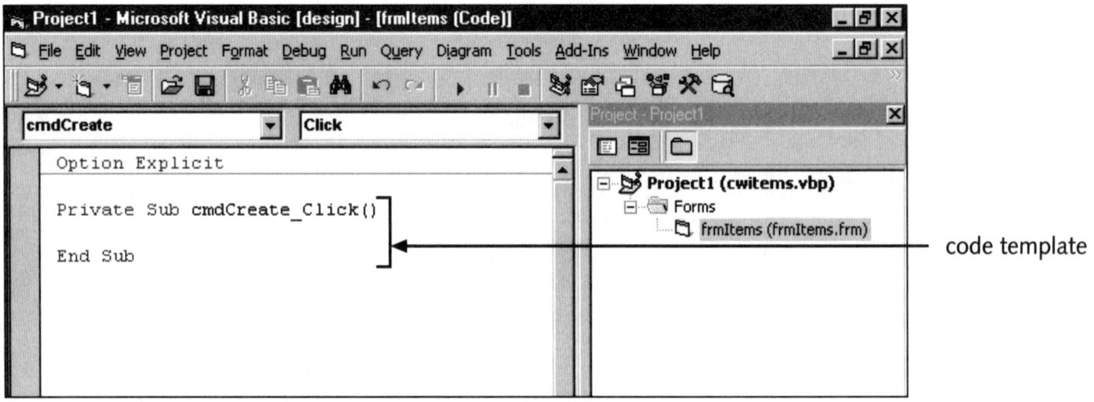

Figure 6-19 Code template for cmdCreate button

A **code template** provides the first and last lines of the code associated with an event procedure. The first line in a code template has the following format:

```
Private Sub [control name]_[event]()
```

The Private keyword indicates that the code is only visible to the current form. In this template, you enter code that is executed when the user clicks the cmdCreate button. Note that the Click event is now displayed in the Procedure/Event list.

3. Open the Procedure/Event list. A list of all of the events associated with a command button is displayed. Click **Click** so that the Click event is displayed in the Procedure/Event list again.

4. Click the **View Form** button on the Project Explorer toolbar to make the Form window the active window.

When the form is first loaded, the Save New (cmdSave) button is disabled, since a user cannot save a record until a new record has been added. To disable a command button, you set its Enabled property to False. You can set control properties programmatically using the following syntax: `[control name].[property name] = value`. Also, the Item ID (cmdItemID) text box is disabled, because the user should never be able to modify the value of the Item ID, since it is the table's primary key. Now you will create code for the Form Load event that sets the Enabled properties of the Save New button and the Item ID text box to False. You will also add comment lines to your VB code to internally document the code by prefacing the comment line with a single quotation mark (').

6

To create the Form Load event code:

1. Double-click anywhere on the form where there is not a control. This automatically opens the Code window and displays the code template for the Form Load event. A split bar is displayed between the code template for the cmdCreate_Click event and the new Sub Form_Load code.

 TIP   When you double-click the form in the Form window, a code template for the Form Load event is created. Form Load is the form's default event, or the form event for which developers most often write code, since often it is necessary to initialize program properties and variables before the form is displayed. When you double-click any other control on the form, a code template is displayed for the default (most common) event for that control.

TIP   Whenever a code template is created in the Code window, it remains there, even if the developer does not enter any code into the template.

2. Press the **Tab** key to indent the insertion point, type **'Disable Save New button and Text Item text box** to describe the code you are about to add, and then press **Enter** to move to the next line. It is a good practice to indent the commands within a code template to make the beginning and ending lines of the template easier to see, which makes the code easier to understand and debug.

3. Type **cmdSave.** (including the period), as shown in Figure 6-20. The member list box is displayed, which is a list of the properties for the cmdSave button that can be set in the code module.

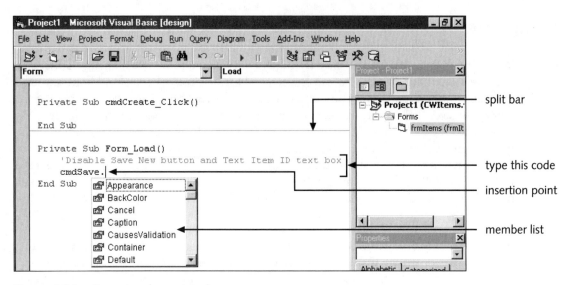

Figure 6-20   Form Load event code

4. Scroll down the list and double-click **Enabled** to insert the Enabled property into the code.

> **TIP** Another way to select a member list property is to type the first letter of the property so that the property is selected in the list, and then press the Tab key to enter the property in the code.

5. Type a blank space followed by an equal sign (=). Another member list is displayed, which shows the possible values for the cmdSave button's Enabled property. The value options are True or False.

6. Type **f** to select False, press the **Enter** key to insert "False" into the code, and then press **Enter** to create a new blank line in the Code window.

7. Type **txtItemID.**, press **e** to select the Enabled property from the member list, and then press the **Tab** key to insert "Enabled" into the code.

8. Type a blank space followed by an equal sign, type **f** to select False from the member list, and then press the **Tab** key to insert "False" into the code. The finished code should be:

```
Private Sub Form_Load()
    'Disable Save New button and Text Item ID text box
    cmdSave.Enabled = False
    txtItemID.Enabled = False
End Sub
```

9. Click the **Start** button ▶ to test the Form Load program code. The form should be displayed with the Save New button disabled. Click the **Item ID** text box to confirm that it is disabled also.

10. Close the form.

11. Click the **View Form** button 🖼 to redisplay the form in the Form window.

12. Save the project.

The code for the Create New (cmdCreate) command button will clear the Item ID, Description, and Image File text boxes so that a user can type a new data value by setting the Text property of the text boxes to a blank character string. The default property of a text box is the Text property. Therefore, when you set the text property of a text box, you can omit the property name using the following format: [text box name] = [text string]. The code for the Create New command button will also enable the Save New (cmdSave) command button and disable the Create New (cmdCreate), Update (cmdUpdate), and Delete (cmdDelete) command buttons.

The code for the Exit (cmdExit) command button will close the application by unloading the form from the computer's memory and then ending the application. To unload a form, you use the Unload command, which has the following general format: Unload [form name]. To end the application and release the computer memory locations that store program variables, you use the **End** command. Now you will write the code for the Create New and Exit command buttons.

To write the code for the Create New and Exit command buttons:

1. In the Form window, double-click the **Create New** button to display the Code window with a code template for the cmdCreate_Click event code.

2. Press the **Tab** key to indent the code, and then type the following code at the insertion point:

```
'initialize text box values to blank strings
txtItemID.Text = ""
txtItemDesc.Text = ""
txtItemImage.Text = ""
'disable all buttons except Save button
cmdCreate.Enabled = False
cmdSave.Enabled = True
cmdUpdate.Enabled = False
cmdDelete.Enabled = False
```

3. Open the Object list and select **cmdExit**. The code template for the Exit (cmdExit) command button's Click event is displayed.

4. Press the **Tab** key, and type the following code:

```
Unload frmItems
End
```

5. Run the form and then click the **Create New** button. Confirm that the form text boxes are cleared; that the Create New, Update, and Delete buttons are disabled; that the Save New button is enabled; and that the Item ID text box is disabled.

6. Click the **Exit** button to close the form.

7. Save the project.

Variables in Visual Basic Programs

Visual Basic code has variables and data types just like other programming languages. It is a good programming practice to always declare variables before using them. (Recall that declaring a variable assigns the variable name to a specific data type, and reserves a place in the computer's memory to store the variable value.) VB does not require you to declare variables, but allows you to assign a value to a variable without declaring it first. This can lead to errors. For example, suppose you write the following code:

```
StudentAge = 22
StudentAge = StdentAge + 1
```

Your intent is to increment the current StudentAge value by one, with the final value for StudentAge to be 23. However, note that in the second program statement, the second StudentAge variable reference is erroneously typed as StdentAge. VB thinks that StdentAge is a new variable. Since this variable has not been assigned a value previously, and is being used in a calculation, VB further assumes that its initial value is 0. Therefore, the resulting value for StudentAge is 1 instead of 23.

To avoid this kind of error, you can use the Option Explicit program statement to configure a VB form so that all variables must be declared prior to using them. When this statement is used as the first line of the General Declarations section of a form, the VB compiler checks to make sure that all variables are declared prior to their use. If it finds an undeclared variable, then an error message is displayed. If you do not specify Option Explicit in the form code module, then a variable is established in the program when the variable is first assigned a value, as described in the example above. Since this can lead to errors and unpredictable output, it is always a good practice to use Option Explicit to require all variables to be explicitly declared before they are used. Now you will configure your VB IDE to automatically place Option Explicit as the first command in the General Declarations section.

To require explicit variable definitions using Option Explicit:

1. Click **Tools** on the menu bar, click **Options**, make sure that the Editor tab is selected, make sure that the Require Variable Declaration check box is checked (do not clear or check any other check boxes), and then click **OK**.

2. Click the **View Code** button to open the form Code window, click **(General)** in the object list, and confirm that Option Explicit is the first line in the Code window. If it is not, type **Option Explicit** as the first code line.

To declare a variable in Visual Basic, you use the following general format: `[declaration keyword] [variable name] As [data type]`. Possible values for the declaration keyword are Public, Private, Dim, and Static. The declaration keyword that is used to declare a variable depends on the desired **scope** of the variable, which specifies how long the variable exists in memory, and what program components can assign and access the variable value. Variable declaration keywords are used as follows:

- The **Public** keyword is used to declare **global** variables, which are variables that are visible to all forms and modules within a project. Public variables can be declared within the General Declarations section of a standard module and are available as long as the project is running. Public variables can also be declared within the General Declarations section of a form. A Public variable is referenced within the same form in which it was declared simply by using the variable name. For example, if a Public variable named SampleVar is declared within a form named frmItems, the following code would be used to assign the value of SampleVar to the number 1 within the frmItems form:

```
SampleVar = 1
```

To reference a Public variable in any other form beyond the form where it was declared or in a standard module, the variable name must be prefaced with the form name. For example, to assign the value of SampleVar to a second variable named SecondSampleVar within another form, you would use the following code:

```
SecondSampleVar = frmItems.SampleVar
```

- The **Private** keyword is used to declare **form-level** and **standard module-level** variables, which are variables that are visible only to procedures and functions written within the form or standard module where the variable is declared. Form-level and standard module-level variables are declared within the General Declarations section of the form or standard module. Form-level variables only exist while a form is loaded, and cease to exist as soon as the form is unloaded. Standard module-level variables exist as long as the project is running, because standard modules remain in memory as long as the project is running.

- The **Dim** keyword is used to declare **local** variables, which are variables that are only visible in the function or procedure where they are declared. Local variables can be declared anywhere within a procedure, but are usually declared in the first program lines of the procedure. Local variables exist as long as the procedure is running, and do not exist after the procedure is exited.

 The Dim keyword can also be used in the General Declarations section to declare a form-level or standard module-level variable, but this is a practice that was supported in previous versions of Visual Basic, and is only supported in newer versions for backward compatibility. Since the semantics of the word Dim do not indicate whether the variable is private or public, it should not be used in the General Declarations section.

- The **Static** keyword is used to declare local variables whose values are only visible within the procedure where they are declared, but whose values still exist and can be accessed after the procedure is exited. Static variables can be declared anywhere within a procedure.

Visual Basic supports several predefined data types. VB has a naming convention in which the variable name is preceded with a three-letter prefix that identifies the variable's data type. Table 6-2 describes several VB data types, and lists the variable prefix and a sample variable declaration for each data type.

Table 6-2 Visual Basic data types

Data Type	Prefix	Values	Sample Declaration
Byte	byt	0 to 255	Dim bytCount As Byte
Boolean	bln	True or False	Private blnFlag As Boolean
Integer	int	-32,768 to 32,767	Public intCount As Integer
Date	dat	January 1, 100 to December 31, 9999	Static datToday As Date
Text String	str	0 to approximately 2 billion characters	Dim strName As String
Variant	vnt	[values will vary based on data type]	Private vntInput As on Variant

The **Variant** data type can store any type of data, and is used when the data type for a variable is not known before the program runs. Web-based applications that use VBScript support only the Variant data type.

Creating a Standard Module

To create a programmatic data connection, you will create a standard module that contains a function that establishes a connection to your Access database. This function will be called when the Items form is loaded in the Form Load event code. If the database connection is not successfully created, a message box will be displayed stating that the connection did not succeed. First, you will create the code module, and define a global variable within the code module that defines the ADO data connection.

To create the standard module:

1. Click **Project** on the menu bar, and then click **Add Module**. The Add Module dialog box is displayed.

2. Click **Open**. A new module named Module1 is displayed in the Project Explorer, and the Code window is displayed. The `Option Explicit` command is displayed in the General Declarations section of the code module.

Visual Basic Objects and Collections

In object-oriented programming languages, an **object** is an item that has a specific structure and behavior. In VB, forms and controls are examples of objects. For example, every form has the same properties and events, which can have associated code. Objects have associated **methods**, which are procedures that perform an operation on an object. A **collection** contains a set of related objects. For example, a forms collection contains all of the forms that are in a VB application. A forms collection has a single property called Count that represents the number of currently loaded forms in the application. Using VB code, you can create a new instance of a collection using the following general syntax:

```
[declaration keyword] [variable name] As New [collection type]
```

The declaration keyword is selected according to the object's scope: Public, Private, or Dim. The variable name is the name you choose for the variable, and usually has a prefix that describes the object type. A collection type can be predefined in VB or it can be user-defined. A predefined collection called ADODB.Connection is added to your project when you add a reference to the Microsoft ActiveX Data Objects 2.1 (or 2.0) Library in your project. Now you will programmatically create a new object instance of this collection in your code module.

To create the ADO data connection object:

1. Place the insertion point directly below `Option Explicit` in the Code window, and type the following program code to define the global variable that references the data connection:

```
Public connClearwaterDB As New ADODB.Connection
```

2. Click the **Save Project** button 🖫, and save the new code module as **cwconnection.bas** in the Chapter6 folder on your Data Disk.

3. If necessary, select the module in the Project Explorer and change the module Name property to **CWConnection** in the Properties window. Your screen should look like Figure 6-21.

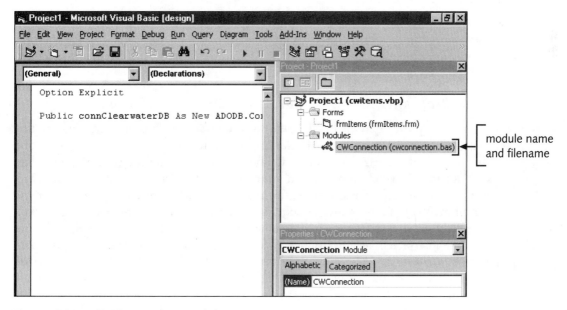

Figure 6-21   CWConnection module

Now you will write the function that creates the database connection. The general format for a Visual Basic function is as follows:

```
[variable declaration keyword] [function name] [parameter list] As [data type]
    [program statements]
    [function name] = [value]
    Exit Function
    [program statements]
End Function
```

In VB, functions, like variables, have scope that is determined by the variable declaration keyword. A function's variable declaration keyword can be Public, Private, or Static. If the Public keyword is used in the function declaration, then any code within the project can call the function. If the Private keyword is used, then the function can only be called by code within the code module in which the function is declared. If the Static keyword is used, then values that are used within the function's local variables are preserved after the function is exited. The function name can be any legal VB variable name. The parameter list is a list of variables that can be passed into the function. The data type of the function specifies the data type of the value that is returned by the function. Within the function body, the value that is returned by the function is assigned using the statement `[function name] = [value]`. The Exit Function statement causes the function to be exited immediately.

Often, functions include the On Error statement, which has the following general format:

```
On Error: GoTo [label name]
[program statements]
[label name]
[error handling statements]
```

The On Error statement is executed if an execution error (such as unsuccessfully creating a database connection or unsuccessfully processing a database query) occurs. When the error occurs, program execution is immediately transferred to the program statements following the label specified in the On Error statement.

Running Programs in the Visual Basic IDE

When you run a program in the VB IDE, the **source code**, which is the program code that you write, is **interpreted**, which means that the code is translated to machine language and executed one line at a time. After you have finished developing and debugging a VB program, it can be **compiled**, which means that all of the code is translated into machine language, and the machine-language version is then stored as an executable file. Every time you run the program in the VB IDE, the source code must be translated into machine language, which means that the interpreted program runs much more slowly than the compiled version. However, the interpreted version is much easier to debug, because as you execute the program one line at a time, you can watch how the variable values change. Since Visual Basic code is interpreted line by line in the VB IDE, each program statement must be on a single line. Sometimes you will have long program statements that might not be completely visible on your screen if you keep them on the same line. To signal to the VB interpreter that a program statement continues to the next line, you end the program statement with a blank space followed by an underscore (_). If the program statement is broken in the middle of a text string, you must use the concatenation operator (&), which joins two separate text strings into a single string.

Creating the Database Connection Using Program Code

Now you will create the function that creates the database connection using code. This will be a Public function, since it will need to be accessed by the Form Load event code. The function data type will be Boolean; if the function successfully creates a database connection, it will return the value True, and if it is unsuccessful, it will return the value False. The function will first declare an error handler, which will cause the function to return the value False if an error occurs within the function code. Then, the function will open the data connection. The ADODB.Connection object has a method named Open that opens the database connection and makes it available for database operations. This method has the following general syntax:

```
[connection object name].Open "[database connection information]"
```

The database connection information is stored in a text string, and can be specified in a variety of ways for different databases.

> You can find specific information about the database connection information for different databases by clicking Start on the Windows taskbar, pointing to Settings, clicking Control Panel, and then double-clicking ODBC data sources. You can also find examples of connection strings for specific databases in the documentation for the database.

In this exercise, you will specify the name of an ODBC driver for the Microsoft Access database, and then specify the absolute path to the Clearwater Traders database that is stored in the Chapter6 folder on your Data Disk, using the following database connection string:

```
"Driver={Microsoft Access Driver (*.mdb)};DBQ=[absolute path
to database .mdb file]"
```

Notice that the driver specification is enclosed in curly braces ({ }), and the filetype associated with the driver (*.mdb) is enclosed in parentheses. Now you will create the function that opens the database connection. You will specify the path to the database file as the folder path to the Chapter6 folder on your Data Disk.

To create the database connection function:

1. Click in the Code window, if necessary, to make the Code window the active window.

2. Click **Tools** on the menu bar, and then click **Add Procedure**. The Add Procedure dialog box is displayed.

3. Type **ADO_Connect** for the function name, select the **Function** option button to specify the procedure type, select the **Public** option button to specify the procedure scope if necessary, make sure the All Local variables as Statics check box is cleared, and then click **OK**. The code template for the new function is displayed in the Code window.

4. Type the function code within the function code template, as shown in Figure 6-22. Note that the command to open the database connection spans two program lines by concatenating two separate text strings.

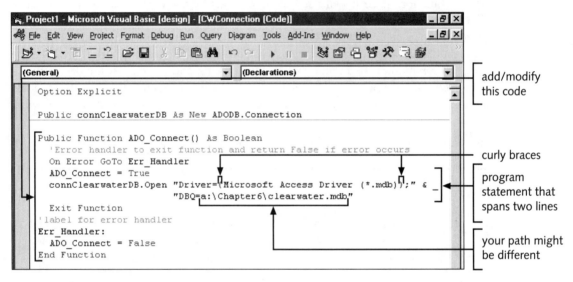

Figure 6-22   ADO_Connect function code

5. Save the project.

Now you will add the code in the Form Load event procedure to call the ADO_Connect function. If the connection is not successful, a message box will be displayed that states that the connection failed.

Message Boxes

A message box provides information to the user regarding the status of the program or current operation. Figure 6-23 shows an example of a message box. Note that the message box has a descriptive title in the title bar, an icon to alert the user to the nature of the message, a prompt, which is the text of the message, and one or more buttons.

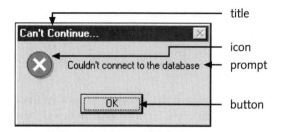

title

icon

prompt

button

Figure 6-23 Message box

A message box is displayed using the MsgBox function, which has the following format:

```
[return value] = MsgBox([prompt], [buttons], [title])
```

Return value is an integer value that corresponds to the button that the user clicks in response to the message box. Table 6-3 shows message box return values.

Table 6-3 Message box return values

Button Caption	Return Value
OK	1
Cancel	2
Yes	6
No	7

Prompt is a text string that specifies the message that is displayed in the message box.

Buttons defines the buttons that are displayed in the message box. Commonly used values include **vbOKOnly**, which displays a single OK button; **vbOKCancel**, which displays an OK button and a Cancel button; **vbYesNo**, which displays a Yes button and a No button; and **vbYesNoCancel**, which displays a Yes button, a No button, and a Cancel button. When you define the specific buttons, no icon is displayed on the message box. You can also use the predefined message box definitions shown in Table 6-4 to display a message box with a specific icon and an OK button.

Table 6-4 Predefined message box definitions

Message Box Definition	Icon
vbCritical	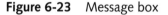
vbInformation	
vbQuestion	
vbExclamation	

6

Title is a text string that defines the text that is displayed in the message box title bar.

If you want to display an informational message box, you can use the message box procedure, which has the following format:

```
MsgBox [prompt], [buttons], [title]
```

The message box procedure works identically to the message box function, except that since no value is returned, the programmer cannot specify different options depending on the user's response. Notice that you do not place parentheses around the parameters when you use the MsgBox procedure.

Opening the Database Connection in the Form Load Event

If a database connection is not successfully made, the message box shown in Figure 6-23 will be displayed, and the program will be exited. To exit the program, you can programmatically call the event associated with clicking the Exit button by entering the following program line: `cmdExit_Click`. Now you will add the code to open the database connection by calling the ADO_Connect function.

To add the code for calling the ADO_Connect function:

1. Select **frmItems** in the Project Explorer, and then click the **View Object** button ⬚ to display the form.

2. Double-click on the background area of the form to display the Form Load event code, and then modify the Form Load event code as shown in Figure 6-24.

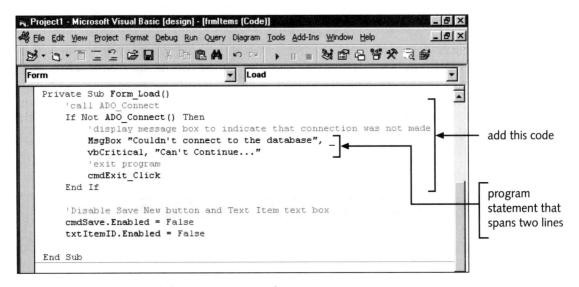

Figure 6-24   Code to call the ADO_Connect function

3. Save the project.

4. Run the form. If the form is displayed, then the programmatic connection was successfully made.

 If the message box is displayed, then the connection was not successfully made, and you need to double-check the Open method in the ADO_Connect function (Figure 6-22) to make sure that you typed the database connection information correctly, and that the clearwater.mdb database file is located in the folder path location specified in the command.

5. Click **Exit** to exit the form.

Processing SQL Queries Programmatically

6

Now you will create a function named ADO_Execute that will be used to process SQL queries using the programmatic data connection. The ADODB.Connection object has a method named Execute that sends a SQL query to the database for processing. This method has the following general syntax: `[connection object].Execute [SQL query string]`.

The SQL query string can be either an actual SQL command or a text variable that represents a SQL command.

The ADO_Execute function will receive a parameter that is a text string containing the SQL command to be executed. It will also call a procedure named DisplayErrors that displays any errors that might be generated if the query is not processed successfully.

To create the function to programmatically process SQL queries:

1. Double-click the **CWConnection** code module in the Project Explorer to display the module code, and then click the mouse pointer in the Code window so that it is the active window.

2. Click **Tools** on the menu bar, and then click **Add Procedure** to create a new function. Type **ADO_Execute** for the function name, select the **Function** option button to specify the procedure type, select the **Public** option button, if necessary, to specify the procedure scope, make sure the All Local variables as Statics check box is cleared, and then click **OK**. The code template for the new function is displayed in the Code window.

3. Type the function code, as shown in Figure 6-25, within the function code template.

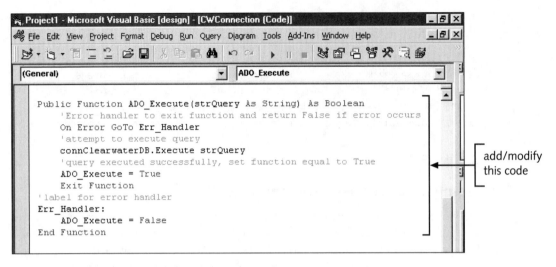

Figure 6-25   ADO_Execute function code

4. Save the project.

Creating Code to Insert, Execute, and Delete Records

Now you will write the code for the Save New (cmdSave), Update (cmdUpdate), and Delete (cmdDelete) command buttons on the Items form. These command buttons will compose the SQL query, call the ADO_Execute function, and pass the SQL query to the function as a parameter. First, you will create the code for the Save New button's Click event. This code will create a SQL INSERT command that uses the values that are currently in the Description (txtDescription) and Item Image (txtItemImage) text boxes. Since the ITEMID data field in the database uses the AutoNumber data type, no value will be inserted for Item ID, and the database will automatically insert the next Item ID value.

When you create the SQL command, you will have to insert the form text box values into the SQL command text, using the concatenation operator (&). Recall from Chapter 3 that data values in Text data fields in SQL commands must be enclosed in single quotation marks, so the single quotation marks will have to be part of the SQL command text. The following code is used to create the SQL text string that inserts a record into the ITEM table. This command inserts the value currently displayed in the txtDescription text box into the record's ITEMDESC field:

```
strSQL = "INSERT INTO ITEM (itemdesc) VALUES '" & txtDescription & "'"
```

Note that the single quotation mark that appears before the item description text variable is enclosed in the double quotation marks that enclose the first part of the SQL command, and that the closing single quotation mark is added after the item description text variable. After the code creates the SQL INSERT command text string, it executes the command using the ADO_Execute function. Then, the code issues a command to refresh the ActiveX data control, so its recordset is refreshed and is consistent with the database. Finally, program lines will be added to disable the Save New command button and reenable the Insert New (cmdInsert), Update (cmdUpdate), and Delete (cmdDelete) command buttons on the form.

To create the code for the Save New (cmdSave) command button Click event:

1. Select **frmItems** in the Project Explorer, and then click the **View Form** button to open the Form window.

2. Double-click the **Save New** button to create the code template for the button's Click event.

3. Type the program code shown in Figure 6-26.

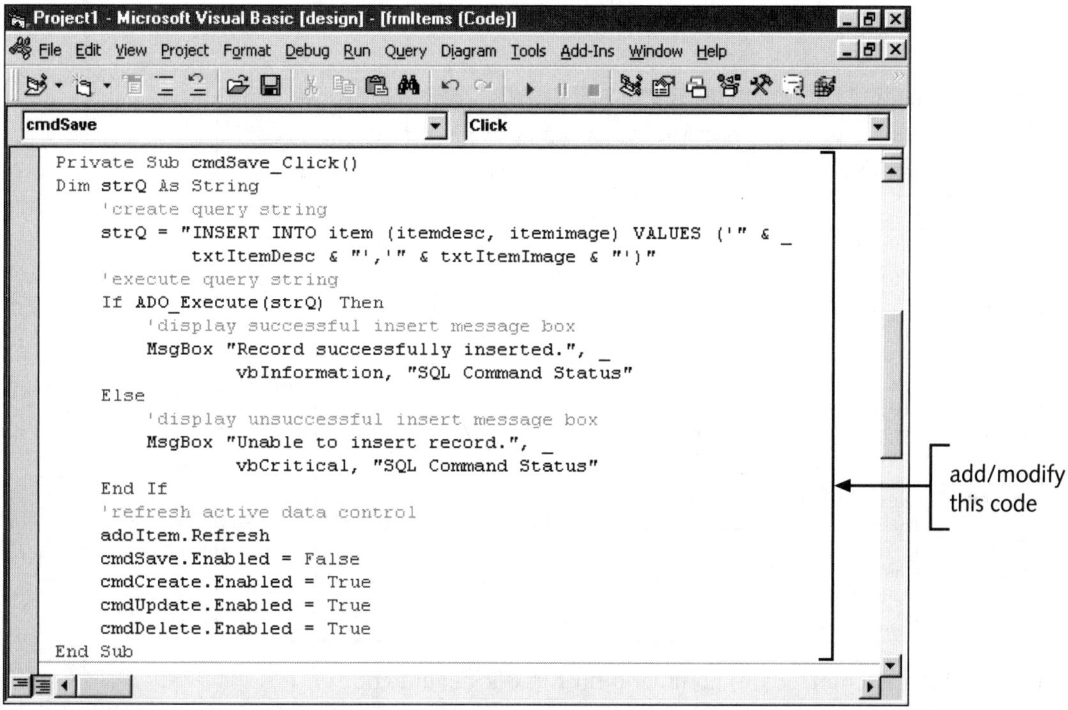

add/modify this code

Figure 6-26   Save New (cmdSave) command button Click event code

4. Save the project.

5. Run the project. The form is displayed with the data for item ID 1 (Women's Hiking Shorts) displayed.

6. Click **Create New**. The form text fields are cleared, and all of the form command buttons except the Save New and Exit buttons are disabled.

7. Type **Three-Season Tent** for the new item's description and **tent.jpg** for the new item's image filename, and then click **Save New**. The message box stating "Record successfully inserted." should be displayed.

8. Click **OK**. The Create New, Update, and Delete buttons should be reenabled, and the new item, including its item ID, should be displayed in the form.

9. Click **Exit** to exit the form.

Next, you will create the code for the Update (cmdUpdate) command button. This code will update the database by issuing a SQL UPDATE command to update the data for the record that is currently displayed.

To create the code for the Update command button:

1. Open the View Object window, and double-click the **Update** (cmdUpdate) button to create a code template for the button's Click event.

2. Type the code shown in Figure 6-27.

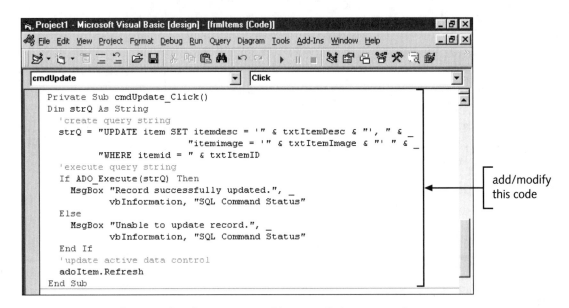

add/modify
this code

Figure 6-27   Update (cmdUpdate) command button Click event code

3. Save the project.

4. Run the project, and then use the ADO data control to navigate to item ID 3 (Airstream Canvas Shoes). Change the item description to **Airwalk Canvas Shoes**, and then click **Update**. The message box stating "Record successfully updated." is displayed.

5. Click **OK**, and then use the ADO data control to navigate back to Item ID 3 and confirm that the change was successful.

6. Click **Exit** to exit the form.

To finish the Items form, you will add the code for the Delete button's Click event. This code will delete the record that is currently displayed, clear the form text boxes, and then refresh the ADO data control's recordset.

To add the code for the Delete button:

1. Open the View Object window, and double-click the **Delete** (cmdDelete) button to create a code template for the button's Click event.

2. Create the Click event code for the Delete (cmdDelete) button using the code shown in Figure 6-28.

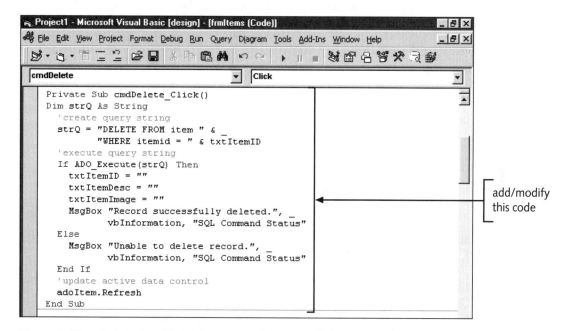

Figure 6-28   Delete (cmdDelete) command button Click event code

3. Save the project.

4. Run the form, and if necessary, use the data control to navigate to the Three-Season Tent record that you inserted earlier. Click **Delete** to delete the record. The message box stating that the record was successfully deleted is displayed.

5. Click **OK**. The text boxes are cleared, and the ADO data control recordset is refreshed.

6. Click **Exit** to exit the form.

USING A DATAGRID CONTROL

According to the design diagram for the Clearwater Traders intranet application (Figure 6-8), when the user clicks the View Inventory button on the Items form, the associated inventory fields are displayed on the Inventory form in a matrix with all inventory records displayed on the form. To display multiple database records on a Visual Basic form, you use a **DataGrid**. A DataGrid is always associated with an ADO control, which specifies the database connection and the SQL query that returns the records that are displayed in the grid. Now you will add a new form to the project that will display the inventory information and draw its controls.

To add the Inventory form:

1. Click **Project** on the menu bar, and then click **Add Form**. The Add Form dialog box is displayed. Make sure that Form is selected on the New tab, and then click **Open**. A new form (Form1) is displayed in the Object window and in the Project Explorer.

2. Modify the form properties as follows:

Property	Value
Name	**frmInventory**
BorderStyle	**1 – Fixed Single**
Caption	**Inventory Detail**
Height	**3450**
MaxButton	**False**
MinButton	**True**
StartUpPosition	**2 – Center Screen**
Width	**8925**

3. Click **Project** on the menu bar, click **Components**, scroll down the Components list and check the check box beside **Microsoft DataGrid Control 6.0 (OLEDB)**, and then click **OK**. The DataGrid control is now displayed in the toolbox.

> **TIP** If the DataGrid tool is not in the Toolbox, click Project on the menu bar, click Components, scroll down the Components list and check the check box beside the Microsoft DataGrid Control 6.0 (OLEDB), and then click OK.

4. Click in the toolbox, and then draw the DataGrid on the form, as shown in Figure 6-29.

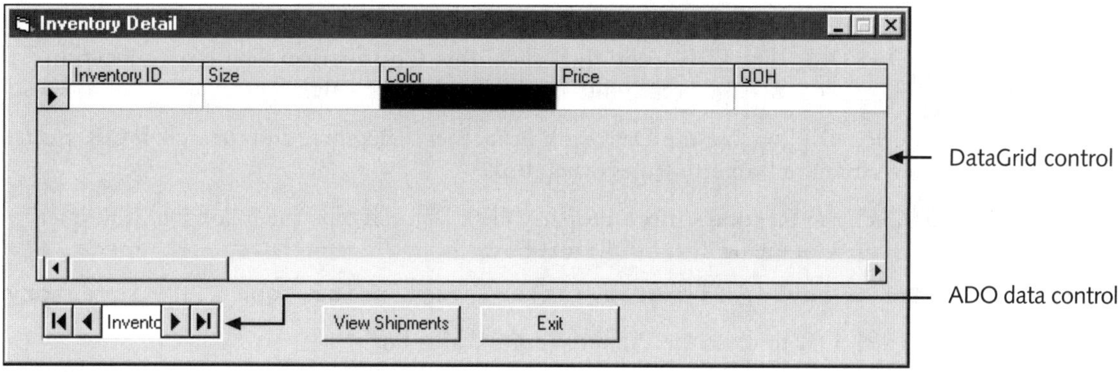

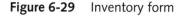

Figure 6-29   Inventory form

5. Click the **CommandButton** tool ▭ in the toolbox, and draw the two command buttons on the form. Position the command buttons as shown in Figure 6-29.

6. Click the **Adodc** tool ᵈ▫ in the toolbox, and draw the ActiveX data control, as shown in Figure 6-29.

7. Modify the properties of the command buttons as follows:

Button name	Caption
cmdShipments	**View Shipments**
cmdExit	**Exit**

8. Click the **Save Project** button 🖫 on the toolbar, and save the new form as **frmInventory.frm** in the Chapter6 folder on your Data Disk.

Using an ADO data control with a DataGrid is very similar to using an ADO data control with form text boxes: you first specify the properties of the ADO data control, then you change the DataGrid's DataSource property to the name of the ADO data control. Now you will specify the properties of the ADO data control. The ADO data control's connection will be to the clearwater.mdb database file on your Data Disk. Its RecordSource property will be a SQL query that retrieves all of the records in the INVENTORY table where the ITEMID value is the same as the Item ID displayed on the Items form. This property will be set programmatically at run time, because it references a value that changes while the program is running. However, you must specify a RecordSource property at design time; otherwise, an error message will be generated. For now, you will omit the search condition and specify that the RecordSource query will return all of the records in the INVENTORY table.

To specify the properties of the data control and DataGrid control:

1. Select the ADO data control on the form, change its Name property to **adoInventory**, and change its Caption property to **Inventory**.

2. Click the **ConnectionString** property, and then click the Ellipsis button […] to display the Property Pages dialog box. Click **Build**, select **Microsoft Jet 4.0 OLE DB Provider**, and then click **Next**.

3. Click ![icon], navigate to the **clearwater.mdb** file in the Chapter6 folder on your Data Disk, click **Open**, and then click **Test Connection**. The Test connection succeeded message box should be displayed. Click **OK**.

4. Click **OK** to close the Data Link Properties dialog box, and then click **OK** again to close the Property Pages dialog box.

5. Click the **RecordSource** property, click ![icon], and type the following SQL query in the Command Text (SQL) text box:

```
SELECT invid, itemsize, color, curr_price, qoh FROM inventory
```

6. Click **OK** to close the Property Pages dialog box.

7. Select the ADO data control's **Visible** property, and set its value to **False**. Since this ADO data control will be used with a DataGrid, and all of the data records are displayed on the form at once, the user will not use the ADO data control to navigate between records.

8. Select the DataGrid on the form and change its Name property to **dbgInventory**.

9. Scroll down in the DataGrid's Properties list to the DataSource property, open the list, and select **adoInventory**.

10. Save the project.

You can modify the field widths and column headings of a DataGrid at design time by updating the DataGrid after you have assigned a value to its DataSource. You will do this next.

To modify the DataGrid control field widths and column headings:

1. Select the **Inventory DataGrid** (dbgInventory), right-click, and then click **Retrieve fields**. Click **Yes** when the message box is displayed asking if you want to replace the current grid layout. The database fields corresponding to the data control SQL query are displayed.

2. Right-click the DataGrid again, and then click **Properties**.

3. Select the **Columns** tab, make sure that **Column0(invid)** is selected in the Column list, and change the Caption property to **Inventory ID**.

4. Select **Column1(itemsize)** from the Column list, and change the Caption to **Size**.

5. Change the captions of the other data fields as follows:

Column	Caption	Data Field
Column2	**Color**	color
Column3	**Price**	curr_price
Column4	**QOH**	qoh

6. Click **OK** to close the Property Pages dialog box.

7. Right-click on the DataGrid, and then click **Edit**. Place the mouse pointer on the dividing lines between the columns, and adjust the column widths so that your finished DataGrid looks like Figure 6-29.

8. Save the project.

Now you need to write the code that changes the ADO data control's RecordSource property so that it displays only the inventory records for the item that is currently displayed on the Items form. You will add this code to the Inventory form's Form Load event. You will specify that the adoInventory ADO data control's RecordSource property is a SQL command that retrieves all of the records in the INVENTORY table where the ITEMID field is equal to the item ID value that is currently displayed in the Items form. To reference a control that is on a different form, you must preface the control name with the form name, using the following format: [form name].[control name].

To update the data control's RecordSource at run time:

1. Double-click on the background of the Inventory form to open the Code window and create the Form_Load code template.

2. If `Option Explicit` is not displayed as the first line in the Code window, select **General** from the Objects list to move to the General Declarations section, and then type **Option Explicit**.

3. Type the code shown in Figure 6-30 for the Form Load event.

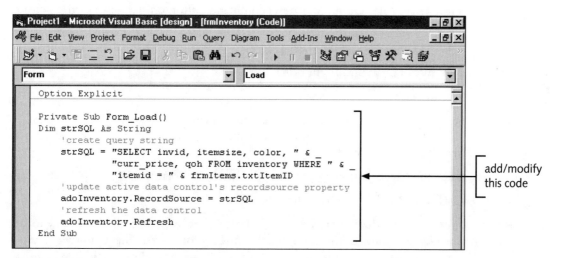

Figure 6-30   Code to update the ADO data control's recordset

4. Save the project.

Displaying and Hiding Forms in a Project

Now you need to add code to the View Inventory Data (cmdViewInv) command button on the Items form that displays the Inventory form. There are two ways to display a new form in a Visual Basic project. The first way is to use the Show method, which has the following format: `[new form name].Show`. The Show method both loads and displays the new form using a single command. The second way is to use the Load command, which has the following format: `Load [new form name]`. The Load command loads the form into memory, but does not actually display the form on the user's screen. The Load command is useful if you want to perform some processing using the form components prior to actually displaying the form. After you do this processing, you can then display the form using the Show method.

In Visual Basic, a form can be displayed as modal or modeless. When a form is displayed as **modeless**, the user can interact with other project forms while the form is displayed. This is useful for multitasking between multiple windows. When a form is displayed as **modal**, the user can interact with only the modal form, and cannot interact with any other project forms until the modal form is unloaded. By default, a form is displayed as modeless. To display a form as a modal form, you must modify the Show method as follows: `[form name].Show vbModal`. You will display the Inventory form as a modal form.

To display the Inventory form from the Items form:

1. Make sure that the Items form (frmItems) is the active window. Double-click the **View Inventory Data** (cmdView) command button on the Items form to create the Click event code template in the Code window.

2. Add the following code to the Click event:

   ```
   frmInventory.Show vbModal
   ```

3. Save the project.

4. Run the project, use the ADO data control to navigate to item ID 2 (Women's Fleece Pullover), and then click **View Inventory Data**. The inventory records for item ID 2 are displayed in the Inventory form.

5. Click the **Close** button ⊠ to close the Inventory form.

6. Click **Exit** to close the Items form.

Recall from Figure 6-8 that when the user clicks the Exit button on the Inventory form, the Inventory form is hidden, and the Items form is still displayed. There are two ways to hide a form in a Visual Basic application. The first way uses the Hide method, which has the following format: `[form name].Hide`. With the Hide method, the form is hidden on the user's screen, but the form is still loaded into memory, its objects can still be referenced by other forms, and its objects (such as the text boxes) still retain the values that were last displayed. The second way uses the Unload command, which has the following format: `Unload [form name]`. With this approach, the form is unloaded from memory, and must be reloaded to be displayed again or for form elements to be referenced by other forms. The values displayed on the Inventory form are specific to the current item ID value that is displayed on the Items form, and the values are updated when the form is loaded. You will use the Unload command in the Click event of the Exit button on the Inventory form, so that when the user clicks the Exit button, the form is unloaded from memory.

To add the code to the Click event on the Exit button on the Inventory form:

1. Make sure the Inventory form is the active window. Double-click the **Exit** button on the Inventory form to create a Click event code template in the Code window.

2. Type the following command for the Click event:

```
Unload frmInventory
```

3. Save the project.

To finish the project, you need to add the Shipments form, which displays the incoming shipments for a selected inventory item. This form will show all of the records in the INVENTORY_SHIPPING table for the inventory item that is currently selected on the Inventory Detail form where the DATE_RECEIVED field is NULL. First, you will create the Shipments form and add the form controls.

To create the Shipments form and add the form controls:

1. Add a new form to the project and modify the form properties as follows:

Property	Value
Name	**frmShipments**
BorderStyle	**1 – Fixed Single**
Caption	**Pending Shipments**
Height	**3570**
MaxButton	**False**
MinButton	**True**
StartUpPosition	**2 – Center Screen**
Width	**8370**

2. Click the **DataGrid** control ⊞ in the toolbox and draw the DataGrid on the form, as shown in Figure 6-31.

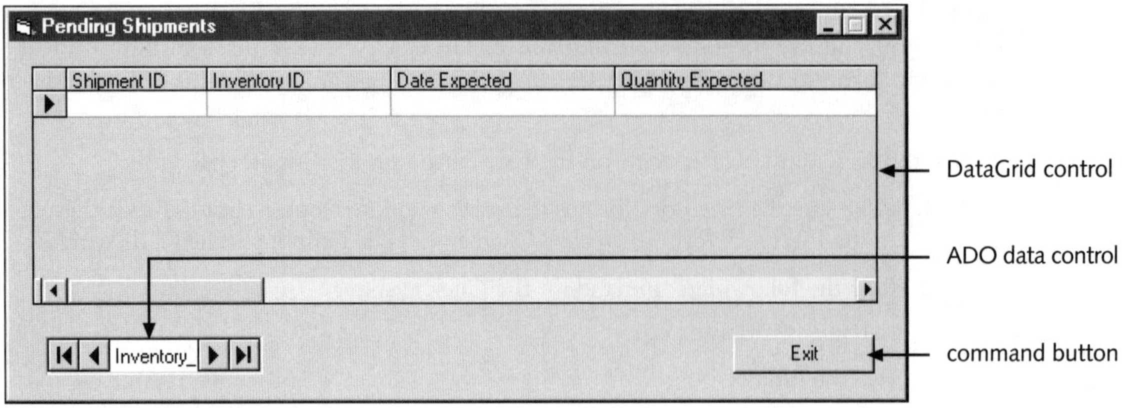

Figure 6-31 Shipments form

3. Click the **CommandButton** tool ▭ in the toolbox and draw the command button on the form, as shown in Figure 6-31.

4. Click the **Adodc** tool 🎱 in the toolbox and draw the ADO data control on the form, as shown in Figure 6-31.

5. Change the Name property of the command button to **cmdExit**, and change the Caption to **Exit**.

6. Create the Click event code for the Exit button, using the following code:

```
Unload frmShipments
```

7. Click the **Save Project** button 💾 and save the form as **frmShipments.frm** in the Chapter6 folder on your Data Disk.

Now you need to modify the properties of the DataGrid and the ADO data control. You will specify that the RecordSource property of the data control is a SQL query that retrieves all records in the INVENTORY_SHIPPING table where the DATE_RECEIVED field is NULL. When the form is loaded, the RecordSource property will be modified so that the query retrieves only the records for the current inventory item.

To modify the properties of the DataGrid and ADO data control:

1. Select the ADO data control on the Shipments form, and change its Name property to **adoInventory_Shipping**, its Caption property to **Inventory_Shipping**, and its Visible property to **False**.

2. Click the ADO data control's **ConnectionString** property and create a connection to the **clearwater.mdb** file in the Chapter6 folder on your Data Disk.

3. Click the **RecordSource** property, click the **ellipsis** button ⌗, and type the following SQL query in the Command Text (SQL) text box:

```
SELECT invshipid, invid, date_expected, quantity_expected
FROM inventory_shipping WHERE date_received IS NULL
```

4. Select the **DataGrid** control on the form, and change its Name property to **dbgShipping** and its DataSource property to **adoInventory_Shipping**.

5. Right-click the **DataGrid**, click **Retrieve fields**, and then click **Yes** to replace the current fields.

6. Modify the current column captions and field widths so that your DataGrid looks like Figure 6-31.

7. Save the project.

Now you will add the code to the View Shipments (cmdShipments) command button on the Inventory form that will display the Shipments form. This code will load the Shipments form using the Load command. It will then call a function that executes a SQL query that updates the ADO data control on the Shipments form. The SQL query searches for all incoming shipments for the currently selected Inventory item. If the Inventory item has pending shipments, then the Shipments form will be displayed using the Show method. If the Inventory item does not have any pending shipments, a message box will be displayed to inform the user that there are no shipments pending, and the Shipments form will be unloaded.

To add the code for the View Shipments command button:

1. On the Inventory form, double-click the **View Shipments** (cmdShipments) command button to create a Click event code template.

2. Add the code shown in Figure 6-32, then save the project.

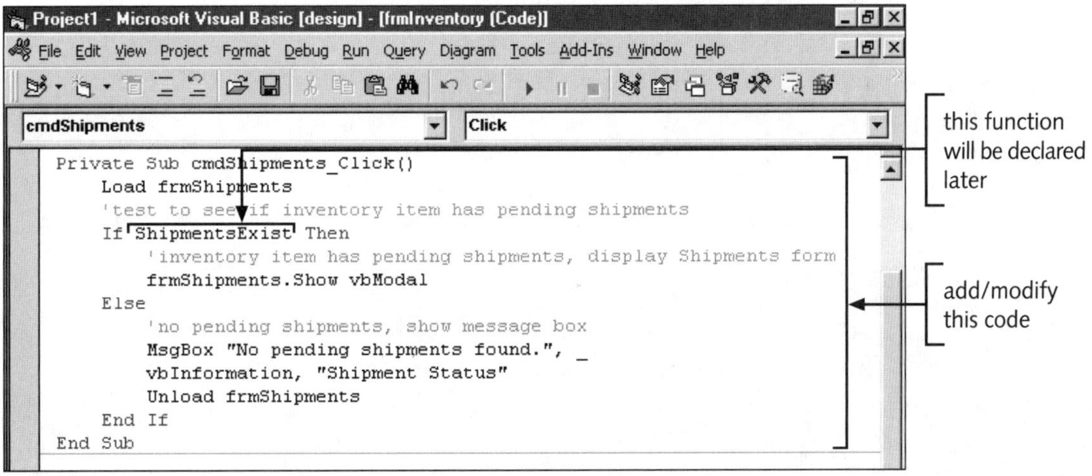

Figure 6-32 View Shipments (cmdShipments) Click event code

> **TIP** You will create the ShipmentsExist function in the next set of steps.

Now you will create the function to test if the current Inventory item has pending shipments in the INVENTORY_SHIPPING table. This will be a Private function that is written in the General Declarations section of the Inventory form, so it can only be called within the Inventory form. The SQL query that populates the recordset for the Shipping form will have a search condition that references the INVID value for the record that is currently selected in the DataGrid on the Inventory form. To reference the value of a field in the record that is currently selected in a recordset, you use the following general syntax; since this command contains square brackets ([ ]), the values that you insert are shown in angle brackets (< >):
`<data control name>.Recordset![<database field name>]`.

For example, to reference the value for INVID in the recordset of the adoInventory control, you use the expression:

```
adoInventory.Recordset![invid]
```

To determine if a recordset contains any records, you use the RecordCount method, which has the following general format: `[data control name].Recordset.RecordCount`. This method returns an integer value representing the number of records that currently exist in the recordset.

To create the function that determines if the current Inventory item has pending shipments:

1. Be sure the Inventory form code window is the active window, click **Tools** on the menu bar, and then click **Add Procedure**.

2. Create a Private function named ShipmentsExist, and then type the code shown in Figure 6-33 to create the function.

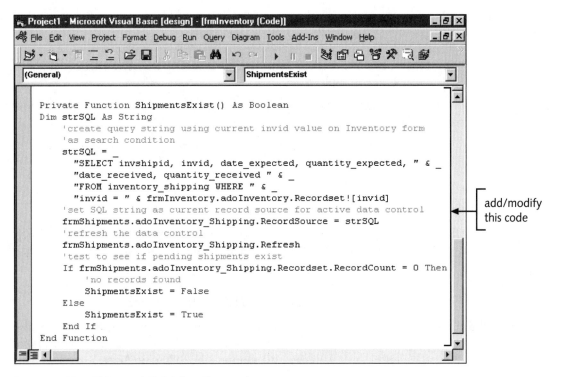

Figure 6-33   ShipmentsExist function code

3. Save the project, and then run the project.

4. Make sure that item ID 1 (Women's Hiking Shorts) is selected in the Items form, and then click **View Inventory Data**. The Inventory Detail form is displayed.

5. Click inventory ID **5** to select it, and then click **View Shipments** to view the related shipment data. The Pending Shipments form is displayed, showing the data for Shipment ID 213.

6. Click **Exit** to unload the Shipments form.

7. Click inventory ID **3** to select it, and then click **View Shipments** to view the related shipment data. Since this inventory item does not have any pending shipment, the message box stating "No pending shipments found." is displayed. Click **OK**.

8. Click **Exit** to exit the Inventory form.

9. Click **Exit** to exit the Items form.

The final step in creating a Visual Basic project is to compile the code into an executable file so that the application can be run independent of the VB IDE. Now you will create an executable file, and run it using Windows Explorer.

To create and run an executable file:

1. Select **Project1(CWItems.vbp)** in the Project Explorer.

2. Click **File** on the menu bar, and then click **Make CWItems.exe**. The Make Project dialog box is displayed.

3. If necessary, navigate to the Chapter6 folder on your Data Disk, and click **OK** to create CWItems.exe.

4. When the mouse pointer changes back to the normal pointer, open Windows Explorer, and navigate to the Chapter6 folder on your Data Disk.

5. Double-click **CWItems.exe**. The Items form is displayed.

6. Click **Exit**.

7. Click **File** on the menu bar, and then click **Remove Project** to remove the project from the VB IDE. Click **Yes** when you are asked if you want to save your changes.

DISPLAYING VISUAL BASIC PROGRAMS USING WEB PAGES

Recall that Visual Basic projects can be created to make standard executable files. They also can be created using different ActiveX options to make programs that can be installed and/or run by clicking a hyperlink on a Web page. VB supports the following ActiveX options:

- **ActiveX documents**, which have both a visual interface and code to process user inputs and actions. You will create an ActiveX document that duplicates the functionality of the Clearwater Traders Inventory Maintenance application that you just created in Visual Basic. An ActiveX document can be compiled either as an executable (.exe) file, which can be called directly within a Web page, or as a dynamic-link library (.dll) file.

 A dynamic-link library (DLL) is a block of compiled code that can be called and executed from other programs. A single DLL can be called and executed from multiple other programs at the same time with only one copy of the DLL loaded into main memory. You will learn how to create ActiveX DLLs in Chapter 9.

- **ActiveX programs**, which provide processing for other Web programs, but do not have a visual interface component. An ActiveX program could contain the code to create a database connection and retrieve database data, and then display the retrieved data in an HTML document. Like ActiveX documents, ActiveX programs can be compiled either as executable files or DLLs.

- **ActiveX controls**, which are used to create custom controls that can be used in other Web-based programming projects, just like ActiveX documents or ActiveX programs. For example, you could create an Exit button custom control that is a command button that always displays the text "Exit" and has the underlying code to exit the application whenever the user clicks the button.

Creating an ActiveX Document

Recall from Figure 6-1 that a user can click a hyperlink on a Web page that references an ActiveX document. If it is the first time that the user clicks the hyperlink, the user is asked if he or she wants to install the document on his or her computer. If the user agrees to install the document, then the ActiveX document program is downloaded from the Web server and installed on the user's computer. When the user clicks the hyperlink to the ActiveX document on subsequent visits to the Web page, the ActiveX document program is run on the user's computer.

Now you will modify the Inventory Maintenance application that you created earlier so that it is compiled as an ActiveX document. Then, you will modify a Web page so that it contains a hyperlink that allows the user to download and run the ActiveX document. To do this, you will create a new project that will be compiled as an ActiveX document, and then add the VB project components (forms and code modules) from the application you created earlier.

To create the new project as an ActiveX document:

1. Click **File** on the Visual Basic menu bar, and then click **New Project**. The New Project dialog box is displayed.

2. Select **Activex Document Exe**, and then click **OK**.

3. If necessary, click the **Toggle Folders** button 🗀 on the Project Explorer window toolbar to display the project components so that they are organized by object types. The User Documents folder is displayed.

A **user document** is a container object in an ActiveX document. A user document is similar to a form in the sense that it can contain controls and code, and has events similar to those in a form. A user document must be associated with, or **sited on**, an external application, which is called a **container**. In this case, the container is the Microsoft Internet Explorer Web browser. ActiveX documents cannot be displayed using other Web browsers. An ActiveX document is stored in a file with a .dob extension, which contains the form and code components of the document. The ActiveX project also has an associated Visual Basic project file with a .vbp extension that is automatically created when you create the ActiveX project. The project file is used to modify the project properties in the Visual Basic IDE. Now you will examine the user document within the new project, change its Name property, and save the project.

To examine the user document and save the project:

1. In the Project Explorer, open the User Document folder, and double-click **UserDocument1**. The document is displayed as a gray rectangle in the Object window.

2. In the Properties window, change the Name property to **CWItemsActiveX**, and then click another property to apply the change. Since the document will not be displayed, you will not modify any of its other properties.

3. Save the ActiveX document file as **CWItemsActiveX.dob** in the Chapter6 folder on your Data Disk.

4. Save the ActiveX document project file as **CWItemsActiveX.vbp** in the Chapter6 folder on your Data Disk.

Now you will add the forms and the code module to your project. You will also need to add the Microsoft ActiveX Data Objects 2.1 reference library to the project (or the 2.0 reference library, if appropriate) from the VB IDE, so that the ADO data controls and commands will work. You will also add code to the Initialize event of the user document, which is the event that occurs when the ActiveX document is first started. This code will display the Items form using the Show method, and will show the form as a modal form. In a user document, the code for the Show method to display a form as a modal form is slightly different from the code used in a form, and uses the following format: [form name].Show 1. Note that the vbModal parameter is replaced by the number 1.

To add the forms and code module to the project:

1. Click **Project** on the menu bar, click **Add Form**, click the **Existing** tab, navigate to the Chapter6 folder on your Data Disk, select **frmInventory.frm**, and then click **Open**. The Forms folder is displayed in the Project Explorer.

2. Open the Forms folder in the Project Explorer, and confirm that frmInventory has been added to the project.

3. Add the **frmItems.frm** and **frmShipments.frm** forms to the project.

4. Click **Project** on the menu bar, click **Add Module**, click the **Existing** tab, select **cwconnection.bas**, and then click **Open**. The Modules folder is displayed in the Project Explorer.

5. Open the Modules folder and confirm that cwconnection.bas has been added to the project.

6. Double-click the user document in the Object window to create the code template for the user document Initialize event, and then type the following code within the code template:

```
frmItems.Show 1
```

7. Click **Project** on the menu bar, and then click **References**. The References dialog box is displayed.

8. Scroll down the Available References list, and check the **Microsoft ActiveX Data Objects 2.1 Library** check box (or click the 2.0 library, if appropriate). Click **OK**.

9. Save the project.

You cannot run an ActiveX document directly in Visual Basic. Instead, you have to create an ActiveX executable file. When you create an ActiveX executable file, VB automatically generates a Visual Basic document (.vbd) file, which is the file that associates the ActiveX executable file with its container application (recall that the container is the application used to display the ActiveX document). In this case, the container application is Microsoft Internet Explorer. Now you will create the executable file and display the .vbd file, using Internet Explorer and a file URL.

To create an executable ActiveX document file and a VB document file and display the document file using Internet Explorer:

1. Click **File** on the menu bar, and then click **Make CWItemsActiveX.exe**. The Make Project dialog box is displayed.

2. If necessary, navigate to the Chapter6 folder on your Data Disk, and then click **OK** to save the CWItemsActiveX.exe file. It will take a few moments to generate the executable file.

3. Exit Visual Basic. Click **Yes** if you are asked if you want to save your project.

4. Switch to Windows Explorer, and note that the files CWItemsActiveX.exe and CWItemsActiveX.vbd have been added to the Chapter6 folder on your Data Disk.

5. Start Internet Explorer, click **File** on the menu bar, click **Open**, click **Browse**, navigate to the Chapter6 folder on your Data Disk, select **CWItemsActiveX.vbd**, click **Open**, and then click **OK**. The File Download dialog box is displayed.

 If the CWItemsActiveX.vbd file is not displayed, click View on the Internet Explorer menu bar, click Folder Options, click the View tab, and then click Show all files.

 If the Open With dialog box is displayed, type Visual Basic ActiveX Documents in the Description box, select Internet Explorer from the applications list, and then click OK. Close Internet Explorer, start it again, and open the CWActiveX.vbd file again.

6. Select the **Open this file from its current location** option button, and then click **OK**. The Items form is displayed.

7. Click **View Inventory Data**. The Inventory form is displayed.

8. Select inventory ID **5**, and then click **View Shipments**. The Shipments form is displayed.

9. Click **Exit** to close the Shipments form, click **Exit** again to close the Inventory form, and then click **Exit** once again to close the Items form.

Creating an Installation Package for Your ActiveX Document

The VB IDE enables programmers to create executable files that users can run independently of other applications. However, for a user to run one of these programs on his or her workstation, he or she needs to install dynamic-link libraries and create system Registry entries so that the application will work correctly. To do this, VB programmers create an **installation package**, which has the files needed to install an application on a user's workstation. Visual Basic provides a program called the Package and Deployment Wizard that leads developers through the steps needed to create an installation package.

You have successfully run the ActiveX document on your workstation using a file URL. To make an ActiveX document available to Web site visitors, you need to create an installation package for the application. You will do this next.

To create an installation package for the ActiveX document:

1. Click **Start** on the Windows taskbar, point to **Programs**, point to **Microsoft Visual Basic 6.0**, point to **Microsoft Visual Basic 6.0 Tools**, and then click **Package & Deployment Wizard**. The Package and Deployment Wizard window is displayed. This window allows you to create an installation package for a VB project, and then deploy the project, which sends the installation files to a Web server and makes them available to users.

2. Click **Browse**, navigate to the Chapter6 folder on your Data Disk, select **CWItemsActiveX.vbp**, and then click **Open**.

3. Click Package to create the installation package. The Package Type dialog box is displayed. If you are asked if you want to recompile the file, click **Yes**.

4. Click **Internet Package** from the Package type list, and then click **Next**. The Package Folder dialog box is displayed, which determines where the installation package will be stored. You will store the files in the Chapter6 folder on your Data Disk.

5. If necessary, navigate to the Chapter6 folder on your Data Disk, make sure that the package folder path is A:\Chapter6\Package (the drive letter and path to your Chapter6 folder might be different), and then click **Next**. When the message box is displayed asking if you want to create the A:\Chapter6\Package folder, click **Yes**.

6. When you are asked if the package will need the Remote Automation (RA) files, click **Yes**. The Included Files dialog box is displayed. Click **Next** to include the specified files.

 TIP   If one or more message boxes are displayed stating that a DLL file is missing, click OK in each message box to continue.

7. The File Source dialog box is displayed, which specifies where the application should locate files needed for the application. If necessary, click the **include in this cab** option button under File Source, and then click **Next**. The Safety Settings dialog box is displayed.

8. Click the mouse pointer in the Safe for Scripting column next to CWItemsActiveX, open the list, and select **Yes**. Click the mouse pointer in the Safe for Initialization column next to CWItemsActiveX, open the list, and select **Yes**, and then click **Next**. The Finished dialog box is displayed.

9. Type **CWPackage** for the package script name, and then click **Finish**.

10. When the Packaging Report is displayed, click **Close**, and then click **Close** again to close the Package and Deployment Wizard.

Displaying an ActiveX Document Using a Hyperlink

When you create an Internet package using the Package and Deployment Wizard, the Wizard creates an HTML file that contains the command for the hyperlink that references the ActiveX document .vbd file. Now you will open the HTML file and examine its contents.

To open the HTML file created by the Package and Deployment Wizard:

1. Start Notepad, navigate to the Chapter6\Package folder on your Data Disk, and open **cwitemsactivex.htm**. The link to the ActiveX document within the file is shown in Figure 6-34.

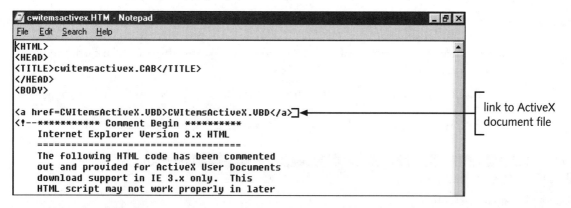

Figure 6-34   Link to ActiveX document file in HTML file created by Package and Deployment Wizard

Now you will view the Clearwater Traders intranet home page in Internet Explorer, and then copy the command for the hyperlink from the cwitemsactivex.htm file to the Clearwater Traders intranet home page HTML file, so that the Clearwater Traders HTML file has the command to link to the ActiveX document file.

To view and then modify the Clearwater Traders intranet home page:

1. Switch to Internet Explorer, and open the **CWintrahome.html** Web page file from the Chapter6 folder on your Data Disk. The Clearwater Traders intranet home page is displayed, as shown in Figure 6-35. You will first copy the code to create a hyperlink from the Inventory Maintenance list item to the CWItemsActiveX.vbd document.

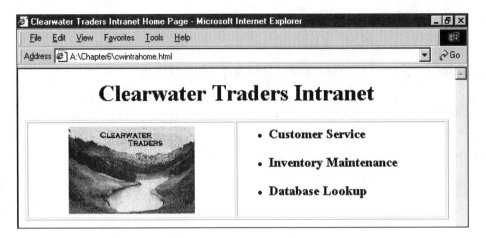

Figure 6-35 Clearwater Traders intranet home page

2. Start another session of Notepad, and open **CWIntrahome.html** from the Chapter6 folder on your Data Disk.

3. Copy the hyperlink reference for the CWItemsActiveX.vbd file from the cwitemsactivex.HTM file (see Figure 6-34), and paste the reference into the CWIntrahome.html file, as shown in Figure 6-36, and then save the file.

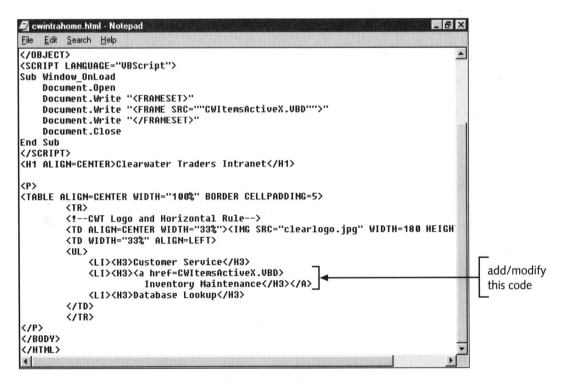

Figure 6-36 Hyperlink to the ActiveX document file

4. Switch to Internet Explorer, refresh your display, and then click the **Inventory Maintenance** hyperlink. The File Download dialog box is displayed.

5. Select the **Open this file from its current location** option button, and then click **OK**. The Items form is displayed. Click **Exit** to close the Items form.

6. Close Internet Explorer and all other open applications.

ActiveX Documents and Security Considerations

Recall that when a user clicks a hyperlink to an ActiveX document, the document file is downloaded to the user's workstation and is run on the user's workstation. From a security standpoint, it can be risky to load and execute programs that are downloaded from Web sites. These programs might corrupt your data, or introduce harmful viruses into your file systems. One approach to controlling and screening ActiveX programs is the use of verification certificates. Developers can obtain **verification certificates**, which certify that their software is from a trustworthy source, and users can be confident that the certified software will not harm their workstations. These certificates are issued by a company named VeriSign, which investigates the credentials of applicants and grants verification certificates. The verification certificate is then displayed when the user clicks the ActiveX document link.

6

SUMMARY

❑ Visual Basic is a development language used to create Windows-based applications. A VB project can have forms and code modules. A form has controls such as text boxes and command buttons. Visual Basic has an integrated development environment (IDE) with multiple windows for displaying and modifying project components. The main windows within the VB IDE are the Project Explorer, Form window, Code window, toolbox, and Properties window. Visual Basic forms and controls have properties, which determine how the forms and controls look and function. Forms and controls also have associated code, which is processed when an event occurs, such as clicking a command button or loading a form.

❑ An Open Database Connectivity (ODBC) driver is a program that allows an application to interact with a database. Microsoft has developed a variety of technologies to enable its applications to interact with ODBC drivers; these technologies include Data Access Objects (DAO), Remote Data Objects (RDO), and ActiveX Data Objects (ADO). A VB project can connect to a database using an ADO ActiveX data control, which is a form control whose properties are specified when the form is designed. A VB project can also connect to a database by using special ADO commands in the program code. A DataGrid is used to display multiple database records in a matrix format. You can create a VB project that is an ActiveX document, which has both visual components and code, and can be displayed as a Web page using the Microsoft Internet Explorer browser.

REVIEW QUESTIONS

1. When is an ActiveX document installed on a user's workstation?
2. What is an event? List examples of two common events in Windows-based programs.
3. What is a control? List examples of three controls that are commonly used in Windows-based programs.
4. What is the difference between the Name property and the Caption property for a VB command button control?
5. What are the main components of a VB project?
6. What property is used to reference a VB form control internally within a project?
7. What is the difference between a procedure and a function?
8. What is the purpose of docking windows within the VB IDE?
9. What form properties should you always change when you create a new form in a VB application, and what should their values be?
10. Why should you always save the .vbp file and project .frm files in the same folder?
11. What is an ODBC driver?
12. Describe DAO, RDO, and ADO.
13. What is OLE DB? What is the advantage of using OLE DB?
14. What is a code library?
15. What does the ConnectionString property of an ActiveX data control specify?
16. What is the purpose of the Option Explicit command?
17. What is the difference between a modal and a modeless form?
18. What is the difference between an ActiveX document and an ActiveX program?
19. When is the Visual Basic document (.vbd) file associated with an ActiveX document created?
20. How do you create a link to an ActiveX document in a Web page?

HANDS-ON PROJECTS

1. In this project, you will modify the Shipments form in the Inventory Maintenance application so that it displays the back-order records associated with the Shipping record that is currently selected, as shown in Figure 6-37.

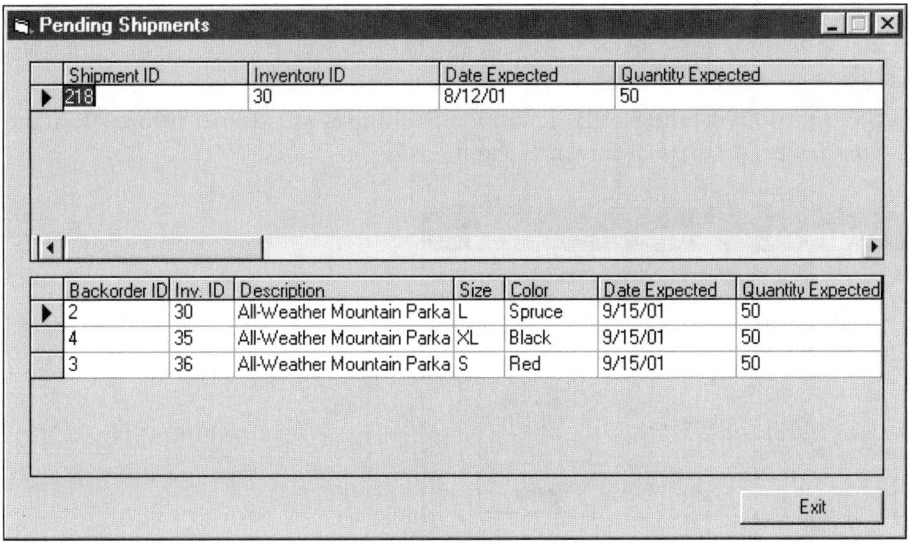

Figure 6-37

    a. Open the CWItems.vbp project file from the Chapter6 folder on your Data Disk, and save it as Ch6Pr1.vbp.

    b. Select the Shipments form (frmShipments.frm) file in the Project Explorer, click File, click Save frmShipments.frm As, and then save the form as frmShipPr1.frm in the Chapter6 folder on your Data Disk. Save the Inventory form as frmInvPr1.frm, and the Items form as frmItemsPr1.frm.

    c. Create a new ADO data control and associated DataGrid to display the INVEN-TORY_BACKORDER records that are associated with the record for the Shipment ID currently selected in the Shipping DataGrid. Only display records for back orders that have not yet been received (DATE_RECEIVED in the INVEN-TORY_BACKORDER table is NULL). Create the RecordSource SQL query so that the ADO data control retrieves all of the data fields shown in Figure 6-37. (*Hint*: You might need to create and debug your query using Access.) You will need to refresh your back-order DataGrid every time the user selects a different shipment using the DataGrid **Refresh** method. One way to refresh the DataGrid when the form is first displayed is to include in the code the Form **Paint** event, which occurs after the form is loaded but just before the form is displayed.

    d. Modify the other form properties as necessary so that your finished form looks like Figure 6-37. Be sure to give all new controls descriptive names using the correct control name prefixes.

2. In this project, you will create an ActiveX document file that incorporates the changes that you made in the previous exercise to the Inventory Maintenance application.

    a. Create a new project named CWWebPr2.vpb that is compiled as an ActiveX document. Add the modified forms you created in Project 1, and rename the user document CWItemsActiveXPr2. Create an executable ActiveX document file, and an associated .vbd file.

    b. Create an installation package for the ActiveX document.

    c. Open the CWIntrahome.html file in the Chapter6 folder on your Data Disk, and save it as CWIntrahomeEx2.html. Modify the HTML Web page file so that it has a hyperlink to the modified application file.

3. In this project, you will create a VB application that displays Customer records from the Clearwater Traders database, as shown in Figure 6-38.

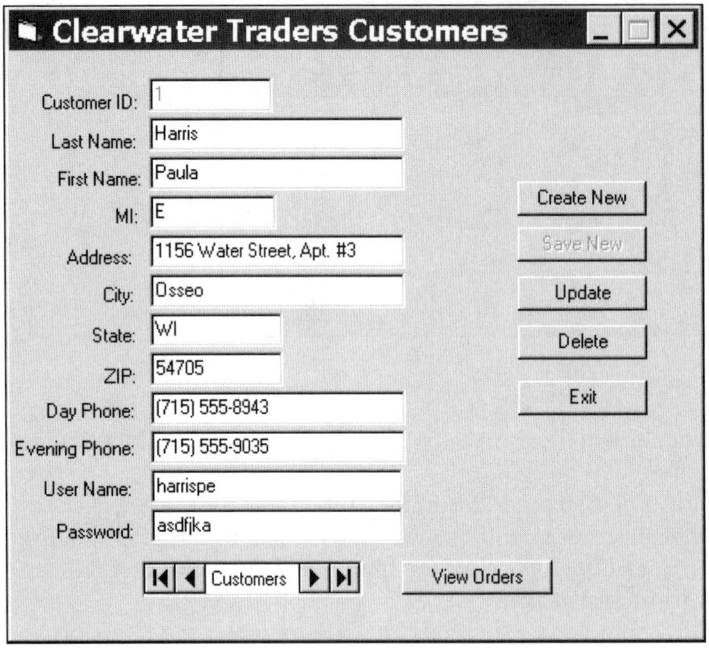

Figure 6-38

    a. Create a new form named frmCustomers, and add the controls shown in Figure 6-38. Save the form as frmcustomers.frm in the Chapter6 folder on your Data Disk, and save the project as Ch6Pr3.vbp in the Chapter6 folder on your Data Disk.

    b. Modify the properties of the data control so it retrieves all of the records from the CUSTOMER table in the Clearwater Traders database.

    c. Add the cwconnection.bas module to the project, and then add the code the user will use to create new records, update, and delete records using the command buttons on the form. (You will add the code for the View Orders command button in a later project.)

4. In this project, you will create an ActiveX document file corresponding to the Customer form that you created in the previous project.

    a. Create a new project named CWWebPr4.vbp that is compiled as an ActiveX document. Add the form you created in Project 3, and rename the user document CWCustActiveXPr4. Create an executable ActiveX document file and an associated .vbd file.

    b. Create an installation package for the ActiveX document.

c. Open the CWIntrahome.html file in the Chapter6 folder on your Data Disk, and save it as CWIntrahomePr4.html. Modify the HTML Web page file so that it has a hyperlink to the Customer form.

5. In this project, you will add the code for the View Orders command button in Figure 6-38.
   a. Open Ch6Pr3.vbp from the Chapter6 folder on your Data Disk, and save the file as Ch6Pr5.vbp. Save the frmCustomers.frm file as frmCustomersEx5.frm.
   b. Add a new form to the project named frmOrders, and save the form as frmorders.frm in the Chapter6 folder on your Data Disk.
   c. Add the controls to the form, as shown in Figure 6-39. When the user clicks the View Orders command button on the Customers form, the frmOrders form should display the customer order data for the customer that is currently selected in the Customer Orders DataGrid control. When the user selects a specific customer order, the order line information should be displayed in the Order Lines DataGrid control.

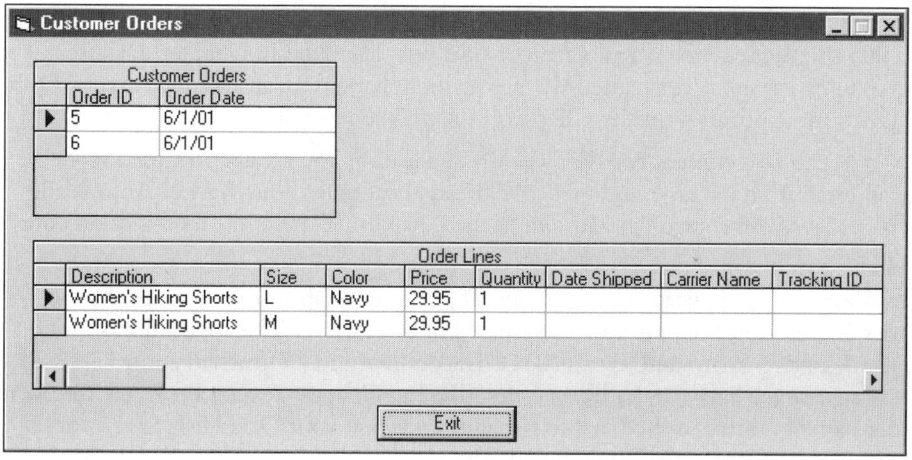

Figure 6-39

6. In this project, you will create an ActiveX document file corresponding to the modified Customer form that you created in the previous project.
   a. Create a new project named CWWebPr6.vpb that is compiled as an ActiveX document. Add the forms and modules for the project you created in Project 5, and rename the user document CWCustActiveXEx6. Create an executable ActiveX document file and an associated .vbd file.
   b. Create an installation package for the ActiveX document.
   c. Open the CWIntrahome.html file in the Chapter6 folder on your Data Disk, and save it as CWIntrahomePr6.html. Modify the HTML Web page file so that it has a hyperlink to the modified Customer form.

CASE PROJECTS

1. Create a Visual Basic application for the Ashland Valley Soccer League database that is similar to the Inventory Maintenance application you created in this chapter. The application should contain at least two forms and use an ADO data control and a DataGrid control. Recall that the database for the Ashland Valley Soccer League was described in Chapter 2, Case Project 1. Create a subfolder named Cases in the Chapter6 folder on your Data Disk. Create a subfolder named Ashland in the Chapter6\Cases folder on your Data Disk. Save your application in the Chapter6\Cases\Ashland folder.

2. Create an ActiveX document based on the VB application you created in Case Project 1. Create an installation package, and then link the application to your Ashland Valley Soccer League home page. Save your ActiveX document in the Chapter6\Cases\Ashland folder on your Data Disk.

3. Create a Visual Basic application for the Wayne's Auto World database that is similar to the Inventory Maintenance application you created in this chapter. The application should contain at least two forms and use an ADO data control and a DataGrid control. Recall that the database for Wayne's Auto World was described in Chapter 2, Case Project 2. Create a subfolder named Waynes in the Chapter6\Cases folder on your Data Disk. Save your application in the Chapter6\Cases\Waynes folder.

4. Create an ActiveX document based on the VB application you created in Case Project 3. Create an installation package, and then link the application to your Wayne's Auto World home page. Save your ActiveX document in the Chapter6\Cases\Waynes folder on your Data Disk.

5. Create a Visual Basic application for the Sun-Ray Video database that is similar to the Inventory Maintenance application you created in this chapter. The application should contain at least two forms and use an ADO data control and a DataGrid control. Recall that the database for Sun-Ray Video was described in Chapter 2, Case Project 3. Create a subfolder named Sunray in the Chapter6\Cases folder on your Data Disk. Save your application in the Chapter6\Cases\Sunray folder.

6. Create an ActiveX document based on the VB application you created in Case Project 5. Create an installation package, and then link the application to your Sun-Ray Video home page. Save your ActiveX document in the Chapter6\Cases\Sunray folder on your Data Disk.

7

CLIENT-SIDE SCRIPTS

In this chapter, you will:

♦ Create HTML forms
♦ Learn about client-side scripting languages
♦ Create a client-side script using VBScript
♦ Validate HTML form inputs using client-side scripts
♦ Create cookies using client-side scripts

A script is a file that contains source code that is **interpreted**, or translated into machine language, one line at a time. **Machine language** is the binary language understood by your computer's processor. In script processing, each line of code is translated and then executed one line at a time until all of the code lines in the script have been processed. Web applications often use **client-side scripts**, which are scripts that run on the user's workstation, and **server-side scripts**, which run on Web servers and are covered in Chapter 8. Client-side scripts are primarily used to validate user inputs entered on HTML forms, which are enhanced Web pages that provide ways for users to submit data. For example, a script running on the user's workstation might check the inputs that a user enters on a Web page that interacts with a database, to make sure that the user entered all the required data and entered appropriate data values. This approach avoids transmitting inputs to the Web server that are incomplete or have errors. Client-side scripts can also be used to create advanced Web page features, such as opening a new browser window to display an alternate Web page, or creating "cookies" that store data on a user's computer about his or her actions while browsing a Web page.

In this chapter, you will learn how to create HTML forms and client-side scripts. HTML forms have controls and properties that are similar to the ones used in Visual Basic. You will write client-side scripts using a language named VBScript. These scripts will be used to validate inputs into HTML forms that will be submitted to the Web server and used as data values in database queries.

HTML FORMS

To do business on the Web, a company needs to be able to interact with customers through its Web site. One technology that can be used for acquiring user inputs is **HTML forms**, which are enhanced HTML documents designed to collect user inputs and send them to a Web server. When a form is submitted to a Web server, a program running on the Web server processes the form inputs and dynamically composes a Web page reply. HTML forms allow users to input data using interface controls, which are also called form elements. These interface controls are very similar to the form controls that you used in Visual Basic. Table 7-1 outlines the most common HTML form interface controls and their functions. It also lists the names of the related Visual Basic form controls that perform similar functions.

Table 7-1   HTML form interface controls

HTML Form Interface Control	Related VB Form Control	Control Function
Input box	Text box	Entering text into a form
Radio button (or option button)	Option button	Selecting a single option from a predefined list
Selection list	List	Listing options in a list box
Submit command button	Command button	Submitting the form to the processing program
Reset command button	Command button	Returning the form to its original state by clearing all user inputs

 TIP   In this book, the terms "radio button" and "option button" are used interchangeably.

You can create a form anywhere within an HTML document using the form tag, which has the following format: `<FORM ACTION="[filename of processing program or script]" [form interface control tags]</FORM>`. A form tag's ACTION attribute specifies a URL or a relative path to an application saved on the Web server. (Recall that an attribute instructs an HTML tag to behave in a certain way.) This application processes submitted form data and returns a Web page response. After the ACTION attribute, you add the tags to create the form fields. Several commonly used form element tags are shown in Figure 7-1.

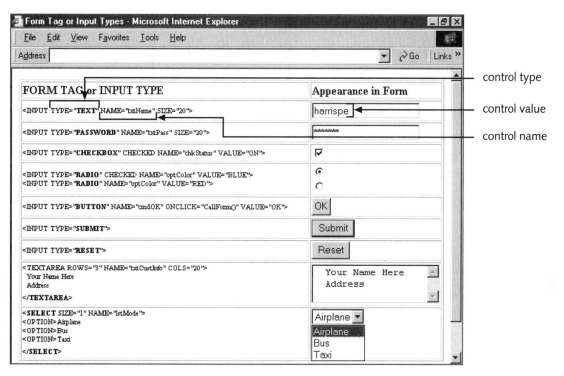

Figure 7-1   HTML form element tags

You can see in Figure 7-1 that form element tags are made up of several attributes. Each attribute specifies a characteristic of the form element that is described by the tag. The <INPUT> tag is used to create a new input box, check box, radio button, or command button. The TYPE attribute of the <INPUT> tag determines the type of input control that is being created. The NAME attribute specifies the field's internal identifier within the Web page. (The NAME attribute is similar to the Name property for Visual Basic controls.) In this book, you will use the Visual Basic form and control naming conventions for HTML forms and form elements. For example, you will preface form names with the frm prefix and command buttons with the cmd prefix. The VALUE attribute specifies the control's current or default value. For example, in a text box, the value is the current text that is displayed.

 TIP   Recall that the text for HTML tags is written in all uppercase letters in this book to distinguish HTML tags from other Web page text. In an HTML document, tag text is not case sensitive except when the text is enclosed in quotation marks (").

The TYPE attribute of the <INPUT> tag can have the following values:

- **TEXT**, which specifies that the input control is a text box where the user input is displayed exactly as it was entered. In Figure 7-1, the user input was "harrispe."

- **PASSWORD**, which creates an input box where the characters that the user types are masked, and an asterisk (*) is displayed in place of each typed character. In Figure 7-1, the actual user input was "asdfjka," but the input was displayed on the screen as asterisks.

- **CHECKBOX**, which specifies a check box control. If the **CHECKED** keyword is included, then the check box is checked when the form is first displayed. The **VALUE** attribute is associated with the CHECKED keyword, and specifies the value of the check box when it is checked. For example, in Figure 7-1, the value of the check box is "ON". This might be used on a Printing dialog box to indicate whether color printing is on or off.

- **RADIO**, which specifies a radio button control. If the CHECKED keyword is included, then the radio button is selected when the form is first displayed. The VALUE attribute indicates the value of the specific radio button. Note that in Figure 7-1 both radio buttons have the same NAME value ("optColor"), which indicates that both radio buttons are in the same **radio button group**. Only one radio button in a radio button group can be selected at a time, and the value of the radio button group corresponds to the value of the radio button that is selected.

- **BUTTON**, which specifies a command button. The **ONCLICK** attribute specifies the name of a program that is called when the user clicks the button. The default button caption is "Button", but you can add an optional **VALUE** attribute to specify a different button caption. For example, in Figure 7-1, a command button with the caption "OK" was created by adding the following VALUE attribute to the tag: VALUE="OK".

- **SUBMIT**, which specifies a command button with a "Submit" caption. When the user clicks this button, the values of the form fields are submitted as parameters to the form-processing program in a parameter list, which consists of the name of every form field along with its current value. A **parameter** is a variable value that is passed from one program to another program. The default button caption is "Submit"—but you can add an optional VALUE attribute to specify a different button caption, such as "Process Order".

- **RESET**, which specifies a command button with a "Reset" caption. When the user clicks this button, all form control values are cleared, and the form is returned to its default state. The default button caption is "Reset", but, as with the Submit button, you can add an optional VALUE attribute to specify a different button caption, such as "Clear".

An additional INPUT tag type is the **HIDDEN tag**, which is used to create a hidden form field that is not visible to the user, but can be used to submit data to the processing program that the user cannot see. These data might be used for internal programming documentation; for example, the hidden field might record the date on which the form HTML code was last modified, or it could include data that were entered in a previous form and that need to be submitted with the current form. An example of a HIDDEN form tag that specifies the date that the current form was last modified is as follows:

```
<INPUT TYPE="HIDDEN" NAME="DateModified" VALUE="11/15/2001">
```

Two additional types of form element tags are:

- **TEXTAREA**, which specifies an input box that can contain multiple lines of text. The **ROWS** and **COLS** attributes specify the size of the text box in terms of rows and number of characters.

- **SELECT**, which specifies a list box. The **SIZE** attribute specifies the number of list items that are displayed. When the SIZE attribute is "1", then the list box is a drop-down list box with only one item displayed. When the SIZE attribute is greater than one, the list box appears as a list with vertical scrollbars, which the user can scroll to display all of the list items.

Creating Web Forms

Now you will create two HTML forms. You will first create the Login – Order Tracking form shown in Figure 7-2, and then you will create the Order Tracking form shown in Figure 7-3.

Figure 7-2   Login - Order Tracking form

The Login – Order Tracking form will be used by Clearwater Traders customers to log on to the company's Web site. After a user enters his or her user ID and password and clicks the Login button, the Order Tracking form shown in Figure 7-3 is displayed.

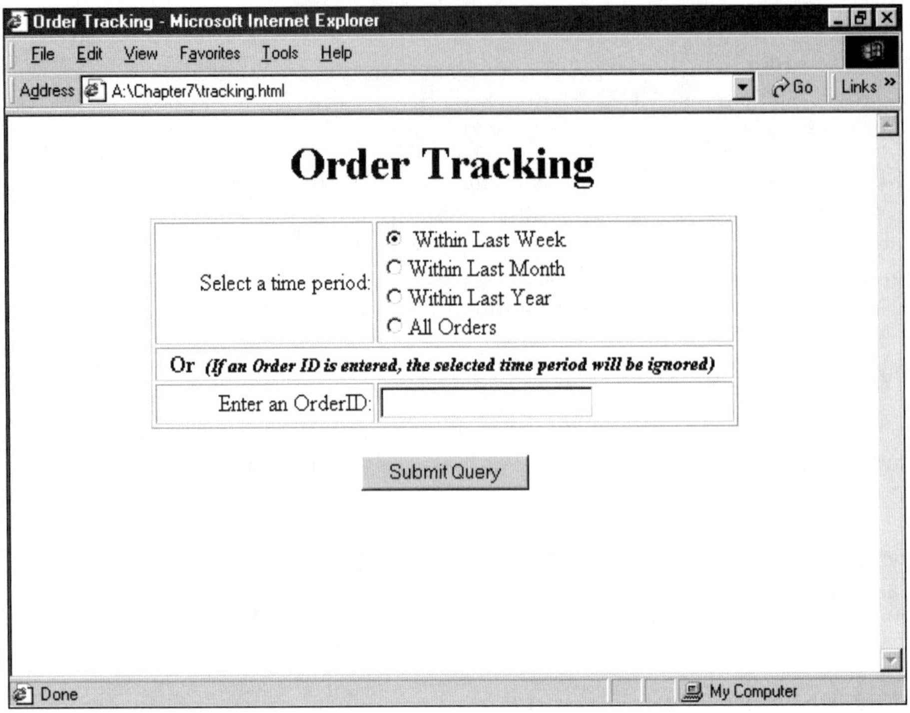

Figure 7-3   Order Tracking form

The Order Tracking form allows the user to search for orders by a specific time period, or by a specific Order ID. When the user clicks the Submit Query button, the user's orders, according to the specified search condition, are displayed.

Now, you will create the Login - Order Tracking form. For now, you will not worry about the form's ACTION attribute. (You will create it later in the chapter.) You will place the form fields in a table to align the input boxes. The "Login" button will be a command button, and later you will write the code to make this button work correctly. The form name will be frmLogin. This name will be used later to reference the form and its fields.

To create the form:

1. Start Notepad, type the code shown in Figure 7-4 to create the Login - Order Tracking HTML document, and save the file as **login_tracking.html** in the Chapter7 folder on your Data Disk.

2. Start Internet Explorer, click **File** on the menu bar, click **Open**, click **Browse**, and then navigate to the Chapter7 folder on your Data Disk. Select **login_tracking.html**, click **Open**, and then click **OK**. The current Login - Order Tracking form is displayed, as shown in Figure 7-2.

Now you will create the Order Tracking form shown in Figure 7-3. This form will be displayed after the user clicks the Login button on the Login - Order Tracking form.

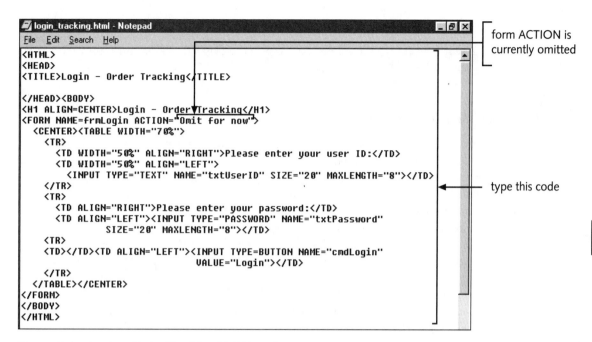

Figure 7-4   Login - Order Tracking HTML code

To create the Order Tracking form:

1. Switch to Notepad, create a new file, and type the code shown in Figure 7-5 to create the Order Tracking HTML document and define the Web page title.

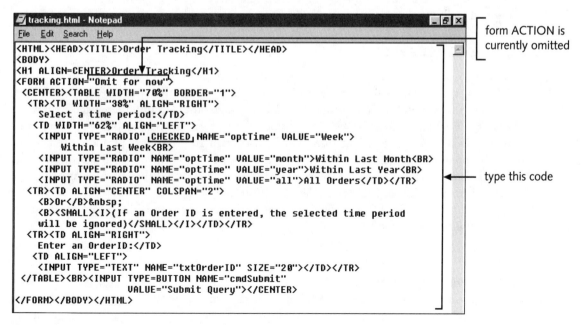

Figure 7-5   Order Tracking form HTML code

2. Save the file as **tracking.html** in the Chapter7 folder on your Data Disk.

3. Switch to Internet Explorer, and display the Order Tracking form. Your Web page should look like Figure 7-3.

INTRODUCTION TO SCRIPTS

The language you used to create the two forms in the previous section was HTML. Now you will learn how to use scripts to perform data validation within HTML forms. **Data validation** is the process of making sure that users type the correct data in a form input. Recall that scripts have commands that are interpreted into machine language each time the script is run. Applications created with scripts usually have a limited number of code lines—usually fewer than 100. Scripts are small because they are usually written in text editors, or in HTML development environments, such as Microsoft FrontPage, that do not have the project management and debugging support offered by more complex languages, such as Visual Basic, Java, or C++. Compiled programs are converted to machine language and then saved as machine language files. Since compiled programs do not have to be converted to machine language each time they are run, compiled programs execute more quickly than scripts. The question emerges: Why use scripts?

Scripts are desirable because, in many cases, processing HTML form inputs does not require large applications, and creating a script might be faster than creating a compiled program. In addition, you can quickly and easily modify a script using a text editor. To modify a compiled program, you must have the necessary programming environment installed on your workstation, you must have the program's original source code, and after you modify the source code you must recompile it. All these operations make modifying a compiled program more complicated and time-consuming than modifying a script.

Scripting Languages

In this book, you will create client-side scripts to process HTML form inputs using **VBScript**, and you will create server-side scripts using **Active Server Pages (ASPs)**. However, it is useful to have some knowledge about other scripting languages. **PERL** is probably used most often for Web server-side HTML form processing, but is not supported by any Web browsers for client-side scripts. **JavaScript** is the most commonly used client-side scripting language, because it is supported by Netscape Navigator and Microsoft Internet Explorer. (JavaScript can be used for server-side processing using Web-server-specific language derivatives: A version of JavaScript called LiveWire can be used on Netscape Web servers for server-side processing of form inputs. A Microsoft-specific version of JavaScript called Jscript can be used on Microsoft Web servers.)

PERL

PERL (Practical Extraction and Report Language) was developed by Larry Wall in 1987. It was originally intended to be a UNIX operating system scripting language for the purposes of text and file processing and system management. Since 1987, PERL has been expanded to run on a variety of operating systems, including Windows NT, Windows 2000, and the Macintosh operating systems. PERL has a combination of features from UNIX, C, and BASIC. PERL cannot be used for client-side scripts, because it does not run in a Web browser. It is used only on server-side scripts for processing data submitted from Web forms.

The current version of PERL is Version 5, which was released in 1994. PERL 5 easily handles binary file processing as well as text file processing. The language is terse, and many operations and commands are specified with one- or two-character commands. Special characters such as $, #, %, and / are heavily used to indicate data types and operations. The following code, which is a small excerpt from a much larger PERL script, illustrates how cryptic and difficult to understand PERL can be.

```
%bdgvar = (null => sub { $_[0] },
           'eval' => sub { $_[0] },
           identity => sub { $_[0] },
           ucwords =>
           sub {
              my $s = lc shift;
              $s =~ s/\b(\w)/\u$1/g;
              $s
           }
```

PERL has many functions for manipulating text strings and processing files that have descriptive names and make the code easier to understand and work with. Although it is possible to write well-documented and maintainable PERL scripts, the language encourages cryptic shortcuts.

JavaScript

JavaScript was developed in 1995 by Netscape as a server-side scripting language that was originally called LiveScript. Shortly thereafter, Netscape and Sun Microsystems formed an alliance and jointly announced that LiveScript would be renamed JavaScript and would be used in Web browsers as a client-side scripting language. The version of LiveScript that supports server-side scripting was renamed LiveWire and was retained by Netscape Web servers for processing HTML form data. When Microsoft introduced its Active Server Page technology for server-side processing, it chose to support JavaScript using an implementation called JScript.

JavaScript's syntax is similar to C, C++, and Java, but technically, functionally, and behaviorally, JavaScript is very different from these languages. JavaScript client-side scripts can be added to otherwise standard HTML Web pages using special HTML tags. Figure 7-6 shows the code for a JavaScript procedure that ensures that a user has entered his or her name in a form input box.

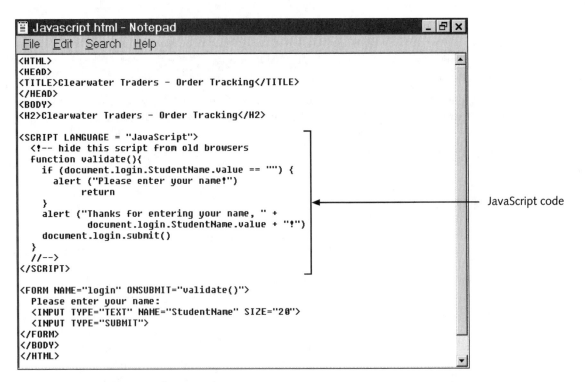

Figure 7-6 JavaScript code example

Client-side JavaScript procedures are often used in Web pages for data validation, which means ensuring that users fill out HTML form entries correctly and completely before submitting the form to the Web server. Another emerging use of JavaScript procedures is to create the pop-up browser windows filled with advertisements that are commonly seen in commercial Web pages.

VBScript and Active Server Pages

VBScript is one of Microsoft's technologies for creating client- and server-side scripts. In addition, VBScript is the default scripting language used in **Active Server Pages** (ASPs). An ASP contains script-processing commands and HTML commands. An ASP is processed on a Microsoft Web server, and its output is a dynamic Web page that is forwarded to the user's browser and then displayed. When Microsoft's Internet Information Server Web server (discussed in Chapter 5) encounters scripting commands in an ASP, commands are executed on the Web server, not on the client's browser.

VBScript is closely related to the Visual Basic programming language. VBScript is used in this book because of the similarity between VBScript syntax and that of Visual Basic. Creating scripts using VBScript can be challenging, because the scripts are typed into the HTML document using a text editor. Since you do not use an integrated development environment like the one provided with VB, there is often no good way to debug scripts, and script error messages are often cryptic or nonexistent. VBScript can be used for both client-side and server-side scripts, unlike PERL, which can only be used for server-side scripts. VBScript is also easier to read and understand than PERL, which shortens its learning curve and makes for more maintainable code.

If you plan to enhance Web pages using client-side scripts, and these pages will be accessed by a wide variety of users over the Internet, it is probably best to use JavaScript rather than VBScript. JavaScript is the only scripting language capable of running on nearly all of the browsers visiting your Web site. If your Web pages will be viewed on an intranet, and if the company has standardized on Microsoft's browser and Web server, VBScript is a satisfactory scripting language for creating client-side scripts. Regardless of the scripting language you use, the concepts for creating and using scripts are similar.

CREATING CLIENT-SIDE SCRIPTS USING VBSCRIPT

7

The code for a VBScript program is embedded within the header section of a Web page. The user's browser, which must be Microsoft Internet Explorer, is signaled to interpret the code as a VBScript program by the two-sided SCRIPT tag, which has the following syntax:

```
<SCRIPT LANGUAGE="VBSCRIPT">
[script program lines]
</SCRIPT>
```

Each VBScript program line must be on a separate physical line in the program code text, so sometimes your code lines might extend beyond the visible area on the right edge of your text editor. To avoid this, you can use the Visual Basic line continuation character, which is a blank space followed by an underscore (_) to continue a script command to the next line. To enter comment statements in VBScript, preface the comment text with a single quotation mark (').

Referencing Form Fields and Button Click Events

In VBScript, the HTML document where the script is located is referenced by the keyword Document. Each form within a document can be referenced using the command `Document.[form name]`. Scripts can reference values associated with HTML form fields using the following format: `Document.[form name].[field name].Value`. For example, to reference the value that the user enters in the User ID form input box on the Login - Order Tracking form shown in Figure 7-2, you use the following expression: `Document.frmLogin.txtUserID.Value`. (Recall from Figure 7-4 that the NAME attribute of the form is frmLogin, and that the NAME attribute of the input box where the user enters his or her user ID is txtUserID.)

VBScript commands are not case sensitive.

Scripts used within forms to validate user inputs are usually associated with a command button's Click event. Recall that HTML form input buttons have an associated ONCLICK attribute that can be used to specify the name of a processing program that is called when the user clicks the button. If an HTML form command button is of the type SUBMIT (see Figure 7-1), then its ONCLICK event always submits the form to the Web server for processing. If an HTML form command button is of the type BUTTON, then its ONCLICK event can be a procedure that is defined in a client-side script. You can create a procedure that is referenced by a form command button's ONCLICK attribute using the following code:

```
Sub [button name]_Click
    [procedure code]
End Sub
```

To create a procedure associated with the ONCLICK attribute of the Login button shown in Figure 7-2, you would use the following code template (recall that in VB, a code template defines the first and last lines of a procedure):

```
Sub cmdLogin_Click
    [procedure code]
End Sub
```

A procedure associated with the ONCLICK attribute usually contains a function that contains code to validate form inputs and display message boxes if the user enters an incorrect value or omits a required value.

Creating Functions

The code to create a VBScript function is very similar to the code for a Visual Basic function, and has the following syntax:

```
Function [function name](By Val [parameter list])
    [function program lines]
    [function name] = [function return value]
End Function
```

The function name is the name that you give to the function in the function code template. The parameter list is a list of variable values that are passed to the function from the command that calls the function. The function program lines are the commands that calculate the value that is returned by the function. The code line [function name] = [function return value] associates the function name with the value that the function returns after the program lines are processed. The code to create a VB function must always appear in the script before the program line that contains the **function call**, which is the code in another program that calls the function. If a function call is encountered before the code that creates the function, the script will not run, because the interpreter will not recognize the name of the function since it has not been previously created. The By Val keyword indicates that the actual parameter values are passed to the function.

> **TIP** Parameters in Visual Basic (and VBScript) functions can be passed in two ways: by reference (By Ref) and by value (By Val). Passing a parameter **by reference** means that the memory location where the parameter is stored is passed to the function. If the parameter value is modified within the function, then the modified value is stored in the memory location, and the modified value is available to procedures other than the function. Passing a parameter **by value** indicates that the actual parameter value is passed to the function. If the parameter value is modified within the function, the modified value will not be available to procedures other than the function.

VBScript Variables

Variables within VBScript functions and procedures are declared using the Dim keyword, just as in Visual Basic. As with Visual Basic, variables in VBScript programs do not have to be declared unless the Option Explicit command is issued at the beginning of the script. When you declare a variable in a VBScript program, you do not specify a data type, because all variables in VBScript have the Variant data type. (Recall that a variable with the Variant data type automatically adapts to the data type of whatever value it is assigned.) To assign a number to a VBScript variable, assign the number value without quotation marks. To assign a character to a VBScript variable, assign the character value enclosed in quotation marks. The following code example shows the variable declarations and assignment statements for two variables in a VBScript program:

```
Option Explicit
Dim intNumberFive
Dim strCharFive
intNumberFive = 5
strCharFive = "5"
```

If you are comparing two values in an If/Then operation, the values must be the same data type. For example, if you are making a comparison to determine if the value currently stored in the string variable strCharFive is equal to the integer number 5, you must first convert the string variable strCharFive to an integer using the CInt function, which has the following format: `CInt([variable being converted to an integer])`. The code for this If/Then comparison is as follows:

```
If CInt(strCharFive) = 5 Then
     [program statements]
Else
     [alternative program statements]
End If
```

Similarly, to compare a number value to a character string, you use the CStr function, which has the format `CStr([variable being converted to a string])`. Values stored in HTML form input boxes are string variables, so for input validation, they must be converted to numbers to check if they fall within a specific numerical range.

Scope of Variables in VBScript

Recall that the scope of a variable determines what program components can access a variable or assign values to it. In VBScript, scope is determined by the location where a variable is declared. If the variable is declared outside of a procedure or function, then it is a global variable that is visible to all procedures and functions. If a variable is declared within a procedure or function, then it is a local variable that is only visible within the procedure or function. The following code shows examples of global and local variables:

```
<SCRIPT LANGUAGE="VBSCRIPT">
Option Explicit
Dim GlobalVar
GlobalVar="Sample Data Value"
Function SampleFunction()
Dim LocalVar
    LocalVar = GlobalVar
    'associate function name with value that is returned by
    function when it is called
    SampleFunction = LocalVar
End Function
</SCRIPT>
```

In this code example, GlobalVar is declared outside of the function, so its value can be assigned within the function. LocalVar is declared within the function, so it is only visible and accessible within the function. Note that in the last program line of the function, the function name (SampleFunction) is assigned to the value that is returned by the function (LocalVar). Therefore, the function will return the text string "Sample Data Value".

Using Message Boxes in VBScript

Recall that in Visual Basic, a message box is displayed using the message box function, which has the following format: `[return value] = MsgBox([prompt], [buttons], [title])`. When you display a message box using the message box function, the function return value is associated with the button that the user clicked on the message box.

Also, recall that a message box can be displayed using the message box procedure, which has the following format: `MsgBox [prompt], [buttons], [title]`.

You usually use the message box procedure to display informational message boxes that only have one button (such as OK). Note that the values passed to the message box procedure are not enclosed in parentheses.

CREATING A SCRIPT TO VALIDATE HTML FORM INPUTS

Now you will create a script within the Login - Order Tracking form that will be used to ensure that a user has entered his or her user ID before submitting a form to a Web server. You will create a script within the Web page HTML file. This script has a function that checks to make sure that the user has entered a value in the User ID input box. You will also modify the Login button's ONCLICK attribute so it calls the script code associated with the button's Click event.

To create the script:

1. Switch to Notepad, open the **login_tracking.html** file from the Chapter7 folder on your Data Disk, add the code shown in Figure 7-7 to create the code for the validation function and the button Click event procedure, and save the file as **logintracking_vbs.html** in the Chapter7 folder on your Data Disk.

2. Scroll down in the logintracking_vbs.html file code and modify the program line that defines the Login command button as shown in Figure 7-8, so it includes the ONCLICK attribute.

3. Save the file.

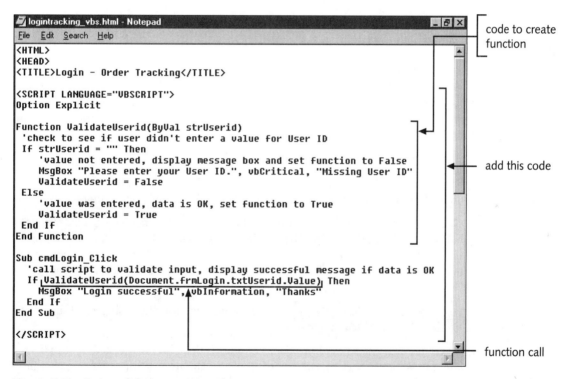

code to create function

add this code

function call

Figure 7-7   Data validation script code

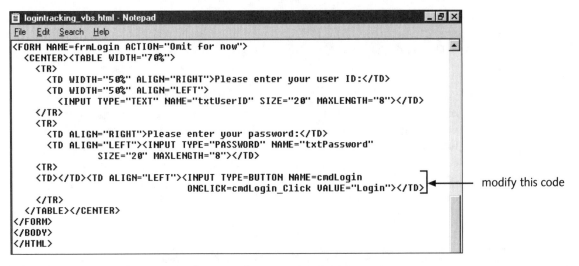

Figure 7-8 Calling the script in the Login button's ONCLICK event

Some client-side script commands must be viewed from Web pages that are requested from a Web server rather than by using a file URL. You will configure Personal Web Server so that the Chapter7 folder on your Data Disk is the Web server root document folder. And you will make sure that directory browsing is enabled, so that a listing of all files in the root document folder is displayed.

To configure PWS:

1. Start Personal Web Manager, and confirm that PWS is started and the message under Publishing frame on the Main page states that "Web publishing is on."

2. Click **Advanced** to open the Advanced Options page. If necessary, click **Home** in the Virtual Directories list, click **Edit Properties**, click **Browse**, navigate to the Chapter7 folder on your Data Disk, and then click **OK** to change the root document folder to the Chapter7 folder on your Data Disk. Click **OK** again to close the Edit Directory dialog box.

3. For now, you will display Web page files using Directory Browsing, so clear the **Enable Default Documents** check box.

4. Make sure that the Allow Directory Browsing check box is checked. Recall that when this box is checked, a listing of all files in the root document folder will be displayed if no default document file is found in the root document folder.

Now you are ready to test your script. You will switch to Internet Explorer and type the URL http://localhost/ to view the directory listing of the root document folder on PWS. Then, you will select the logintracking_vbs.html file that contains the data validation script.

To test the data validation script:

1. Switch to Internet Explorer, type **http://localhost/** in the Address box, and then press the **Enter** key. A listing of the root document folder contents is displayed.

2. Click **logintracking_vbs.html**. The Login – Order Tracking Web page form should be displayed, as shown in Figure 7-2.

3. Do not enter any text into the input boxes, and click **Login**. Since you didn't enter a value for User ID, the message box in Figure 7-9 is displayed. Note that the message box title is prefaced with the text "VBScript:".

VBScript: Missing User ID   ☒

❌ Please enter your User ID.

OK

Figure 7-9   Data entry error message box

7

> TIP   If an error message is displayed when you load the form or click the Login button, double-check your HTML file to make sure the modified code looks exactly like the code in Figures 7-7 and 7-8. If you still cannot find your error, proceed to the section titled "Debugging Client-side Scripts" to learn about debugging strategies.

4. Click **OK** to close the message box.

DEBUGGING CLIENT-SIDE SCRIPTS

As noted before, one of the disadvantages of creating client-side scripts is the absence of a development environment, like the one provided in Visual Basic, to help developers locate and correct program errors. One error programmers commonly make is to modify a file, and then forget to save the modified file. When you refresh the display in Internet Explorer, the Web page that is displayed was generated using the last saved version of the HTML source code file. To determine if unsaved changes are causing an error, view the Web page HTML source code by clicking View on the browser toolbar, and then clicking Source to view the HTML source code. Then, confirm that the source code is your most recent version. If it is not the most recent version, switch to Notepad and save the file, then press F5 to refresh your browser display and load the most recent version of the file.

If you are sure that you have saved the modified HTML source code, but the Web browser still displays an older version of the source code file, the problem might be that the Web browser is displaying a cached version of the Web page. (Recall from Chapter 5 that most Web browsers are configured to cache, or save, recently viewed Web pages on the local hard drive, so that the file does not have to be transmitted across the network each time it is viewed.) To be sure you are not viewing a cached version of a Web page, you should delete all previous saved versions from your workstation. To do this, click Tools on the browser menu bar, click Internet Options, click Delete Files, check the Delete all offline content check box, and then click OK.

When you are certain that you are viewing the latest source code, and it still isn't working, the next step is to find the code line that is causing the error by displaying the information in the Internet Explorer script error messages dialog box. Now you will intentionally add an error to the script code in the logintracking_vbs.html file, and view the error information.

To view the script error information:

1. Switch to Notepad, modify the logintracking_vbs.html file as shown in Figure 7-10 by deleting the single quotation mark (') in front of a comment statement in the script to intentionally cause an error, and then save the file.

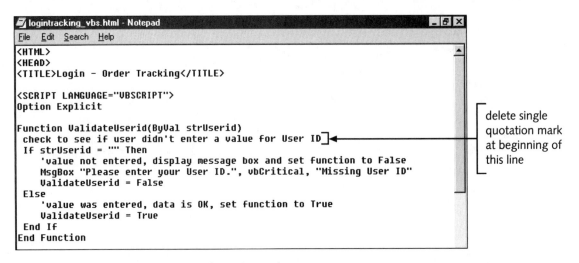

Figure 7-10   Creating an error in the script code

2. Switch to Internet Explorer, type **http://localhost/** in the Address box, press the **Enter** key, and then click **logintracking_vbs.html**. If necessary, check the Always display this message when a page contains errors check box, and click **Show Details**. The message box containing information about the error, shown in Figure 7-11, is displayed. The error details indicate the nature of the error ("Syntax error") and the location of the error (Line 9).

> TIP
> If you click OK on this message box when the Always display this message when a page contains errors check box is not checked, then your browser will be configured not to display script error messages, and the script error message dialog box will not be displayed when future scripts have errors. Instead, when an error is encountered, the script error icon 🔺 will be displayed in the Web browser status bar in the lower-left corner of the screen. To display the error message dialog box, double-click 🔺.

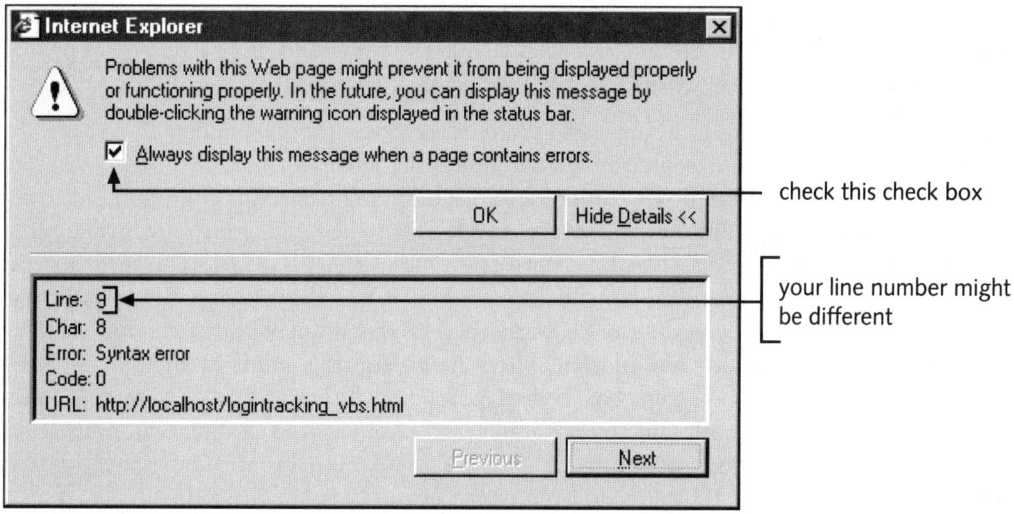

Figure 7-11   Internet Explorer script error message

> **TIP**
> If the script error message dialog box is not displayed, it means your browser is configured not to display script error messages. Instead, the script error icon ⚠ is displayed on the status bar on the lower-left corner of your screen. To display the error message dialog box, double-click ⚠. To configure your browser to always display the error message dialog box instead of the icon when an error is encountered, click Tools on the browser menu bar, click Internet Options, and then click the Advanced tab. Make sure that the Disable script debugging check box is cleared, and that the Display a notification about every script error check box is checked. Then, click OK to save the changes.

If a different error message is displayed, it means you have multiple errors in your script. Click the Previous or Next button on the error message dialog box until you see a message similar to the one in Figure 7-11. Often, a single error generates multiple error messages.

3. Click **OK** to close the message dialog box.

4. Switch back to Notepad. Place the insertion point on the first line of the file, and press the **down arrow** key eight times to move to Line 9. (If the error location displayed in the error message dialog box was different from line 9, then press the down arrow the number of times needed to move to the line number indicated in the error message that was displayed on your screen.) The insertion point should be on the line where you intentionally created the error in Step 1.

5. Correct the error by adding the single quotation mark back to the beginning of the comment line (see Figure 7–10), and save the file.

6. Switch back to Internet Explorer, then press **F5** to reload the file and refresh the display. The form should be displayed with no errors.

If your script code still contains errors, examine the line of code indicated in the error message, correct the error, save the file, and then refresh the browser display. Repeat this process until the Web page is correctly displayed.

Another useful debugging technique is to add message boxes for debugging that indicate the current line that is being executed in the script and the current values of specific variables. Now you will add message boxes to the logintracking_vbs.html script code to indicate the current execution point and the value of the user ID. These debugging message boxes will be removed when the program is working correctly. One message box will indicate when the execution point is in the cmdLogin_Click procedure. When this message box is displayed, you will know that code execution has proceeded to this point without encountering an error. A second message box will indicate when the execution point is in the ValidateUserid function; similarly, if this message box is displayed, you will know that execution has proceeded to this point without encountering an error. Another message box will indicate the value of the user ID that is passed to the ValidateUserid function. From this message box, you can determine if the user ID value has been passed correctly to the function.

To add debugging message boxes to the script code:

1. Switch to Notepad, add the message boxes as shown in Figure 7-12, and then save the file.

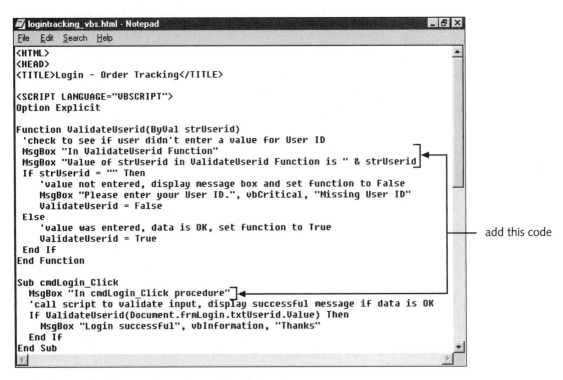

```
logintracking_vbs.html - Notepad

File  Edit  Search  Help

<HTML>
<HEAD>
<TITLE>Login - Order Tracking</TITLE>

<SCRIPT LANGUAGE="VBSCRIPT">
Option Explicit

Function ValidateUserid(ByVal strUserid)
  'check to see if user didn't enter a value for User ID
  MsgBox "In ValidateUserid Function"
  MsgBox "Value of strUserid in ValidateUserid Function is " & strUserid
  If strUserid = "" Then
     'value not entered, display message box and set function to False
     MsgBox "Please enter your User ID.", vbCritical, "Missing User ID"
     ValidateUserid = False
  Else
     'value was entered, data is OK, set function to True
     ValidateUserid = True
  End If
End Function

Sub cmdLogin_Click
  MsgBox "In cmdLogin_Click procedure"
  'call script to validate input, display successful message if data is OK
  If ValidateUserid(Document.frmLogin.txtUserid.Value) Then
     MsgBox "Login successful", vbInformation, "Thanks"
  End If
End Sub
```

add this code

Figure 7-12   Adding message boxes for debugging

2. Switch to Internet Explorer, type **http://localhost/** in the Address box, press the **Enter** key, and then click **logintracking_vbs.html**. Type **harrispe** for the user ID and **asdfjka** for the password, and then click **Login**. The VBScript message box "In cmdLogin_Click procedure" is displayed, indicating that execution has proceeded successfully to this point. If an error message had been displayed before this message box appeared, you would know that the error occurred before the cmdLogin_Click procedure was called.

3. Click **OK**. The VBScript message box "In ValidateUserid function" appears, indicating that execution has successfully proceeded to this point. If an error message box had been displayed before the VBScript message box "In ValidateUserid function" appeared, then you would know that the error occurred after the cmdLogin_Click procedure was called in the HTML form, but before the ValidateUserid function was called.

4. Click **OK**. The VBScript message box "Value of strUserid in ValidateUserid Function is harrispe" is displayed, showing the user ID variable value that was passed to the ValidateUserid function. From this message box, you can verify that the value for the user ID that was passed to the function is correct.

5. Click **OK**. The Login successful message box is displayed, indicating that the script ran successfully. Click **OK**.

6. Switch back to Notepad, delete the code lines that you added in Figure 7-12 to create the debugging message boxes, and then save the file.

Using message boxes to display variable values this way will pinpoint errors that might be made in passing parameters to functions and procedures, and in concatenating text strings.

In summary, use the following strategies to debug client-side scripts:

- View the script source code to make sure that you are viewing the correct source code file. If the source code is not the version you expected, save the source code file in Notepad, and then refresh the browser display.

- If the source code is not updated after saving the source code file, delete all of the cached files to make sure that you are not viewing a cached version of the HTML file.

- If the source code has an error, view the line number of the error in the Internet Explorer script error message dialog box, and try to spot the error visually. Always click the Previous and Next buttons in the error message dialog box, and examine each code line where an error is reported, since one error might generate multiple error messages.

- If you cannot spot the error visually, or if no browser error message box is displayed, add message boxes to your code to track execution progress and variable values.

USING CLIENT-SIDE SCRIPTS TO CREATE COOKIES

A **cookie** is a data file that is written on the user's workstation by a program within a Web page. A cookie contains information that is stored by a Web server on a Web site visitor's computer. Cookies are often used to store information about which pages a user has viewed on a Web site, how many times a user has visited a site, and what information a user has entered during past visits, such as name or shopping preferences. Cookies are also used to create "shopping carts," or information about items a visitor plans to purchase. Cookies provide a convenient way to pass variable values among different Web pages in the same application.

A cookie stores information in pairs of variable names and associated values, where each variable name has an associated value. Each cookie name/value pair is separated from the next by a semicolon (;). For example, a cookie that stores the user ID and password entered in the Login - Order Tracking form might have one cookie variable named userid that stores the value harrispe, and a second cookie variable named password that stores the value asdfjka. This information would be stored in the cookie in two name/value pairs, as follows:

```
userid=harrispe;password=asdfjka;
```

A single cookie can store a maximum of 20 name/value pairs, or a maximum of 4096 characters. If the 20-name/value-pair limit is reached before the cookie accumulates 4096 characters, then the most recent name/value pairs are stored, and the oldest pairs are dropped. If the 4096-character limit is reached before the 20-variable/value-pair limit, the cookie values cannot be read within a VBScript procedure.

There are two types of cookies: temporary and persistent. **Temporary cookies** store information in the main memory of the user's computer and are only valid during the browser session in which they are created. When the user exits his or her browser, this memory is reclaimed by the system, and the cookie information is no longer available. **Persistent cookies** store information in text files on the user's workstation, and this information is available in subsequent browser sessions, after the user exits his or her browser. Persistent cookies have an expiration date, and are deleted by the system after a specific time interval.

Information in cookies is essentially private. You cannot write a program to search for and read cookies written on a user's workstation, because cookies can only be read by the same Web site domain name or IP address that created them. Since persistent cookies are text files and not executable programs, viruses cannot be passed using cookies. Not all browsers support creating and maintaining cookies, and browsers that support cookies often allow users to configure the browser to prevent cookies from being saved. As a result, cookies are not always a reliable way to save information. However, many programs on commercial Web sites use cookies. In the following sections, you will learn to create temporary and persistent cookies.

Temporary Cookies

A cookie is associated with an HTML document, and can be referenced using the Cookie property of the document, as follows: `Document.Cookie`. A cookie is created within VBScript by assigning a value to the document's Cookie property. The value that is assigned to this property is the cookie variable name, an equal sign (=), and the data that are stored in the cookie, followed by a semicolon (;). Cookies are always stored as text strings. For example, to create a cookie with the cookie variable name userid that stores the value that is displayed in the txtUserID text box on the frmLogin form, you use the following code:

```
Document.Cookie = "userid=" & Document.frmLogin.txtUserID.Value & ";"
```

This string is created by concatenating the name of the cookie variable ("userid"), the equal sign ("="), and the variable that is stored in the cookie. A semicolon (";") is concatenated to the end of the cookie string text to signal the end of the cookie name/value pair.

To retrieve the contents of a cookie, you reference the Document.Cookie property to return the name of the cookie variable and the associated text string. Now you will create a temporary cookie that records the user ID in the Login – Order Tracking form that you created earlier, and then displays the cookie variable name ("userid") and the user ID typed by the user in a message box for confirmation. The purpose of this exercise is to practice using cookies. Later in this chapter, you will create an application that uses a cookie like this to store the user ID and password values, so these values can be passed to different Web pages in the application, and the user does not have to reenter his or her user ID and password multiple times.

To create a temporary cookie to store the user ID:

1. Switch to Notepad and save logintracking_vbs.html as **logintracking_cookie.html** in the Chapter7 folder on your Data Disk.

2. Modify the script code as shown in Figure 7-13 to create the cookie, and then save the file.

```
logintracking_cookie.html - Notepad
File  Edit  Search  Help
<HTML>
<HEAD>
<TITLE>Login - Order Tracking</TITLE>

<SCRIPT LANGUAGE="VBSCRIPT">
Option Explicit
Function ValidateUserid(ByVal strUserid)
 'check to see if user didn't enter a value for User ID
 If strUserid = "" Then
    'value not entered, display message box and set function to False
    MsgBox "Please enter your User ID.", vbCritical, "Missing User ID"
    ValidateUserid = False
 Else
    'value was entered, data is OK, set function to True
    ValidateUserid = True
 End If
End Function

Sub cmdLogin_Click
  'call script to validate input, display successful message if data is OK
  If ValidateUserid(Document.frmLogin.txtUserid.Value) Then
    'create a cookie to store the value of the user ID
    Document.Cookie = "userid=" & Document.frmLogin.txtUserid.Value & ";"  ◄──── add this code
    'display message box showing cookie variable name and value
    MsgBox Document.Cookie, vbInformation, "Cookie Alert"
    MsgBox "Login successful", vbInformation, "Thanks"
  End If
End Sub
```

Figure 7-13   Creating a temporary cookie

3. Switch to Internet Explorer, type **http://localhost/** in the Address box, and then click **logintracking_cookie.html** to display the Login Tracking document that contains the code to create the cookie.

4. Type **harrispe** for the user ID and **asdfjka** for the password, and then click **Login**. The message box shown in Figure 7-14 is displayed, showing the cookie variable name ("userid") and the value you typed for user ID. In a real application, this message box would not be displayed to a user. The message box is displayed here to demonstrate the code for retrieving the cookie variable name and value.

Figure 7-14   Message box displaying cookie

 If the message box showing the cookie name and value is not displayed, check to make sure your code looks exactly like the code in Figure 7-13. If you cannot find your error, use the debugging strategies discussed in the "Debugging Client-side Scripts" section of this chapter. Make sure that the text string that is assigned to the Document.Cookie property is formatted correctly.

5. Click **OK** to acknowledge the Cookie Alert, and then click **OK** again to acknowledge that the login was successful.

You can store multiple values in a single cookie by appending the new cookie variable name and value to the end of the existing cookie variable and value pairs. Recall that each variable name/value pair is separated from the next by a semicolon (;). To add an additional value to a cookie, you use the following code: `Document.Cookie = [new cookie variable name]=[new cookie value];`. This appends the variable name and value of the new cookie variable to the existing document cookie. Each new name/value pair must be assigned to the Document.Cookie variable using a separate command. Now you will modify the logintracking_cookie HTML file code so that the cookie has a second cookie variable named password that stores the password that the user enters in the Web page. To simplify the code, you will declare a variable named strFirstVal to hold the text string that will create the first cookie name/value pair, and a variable named strSecondVal to hold the text string that will create the second cookie name/value pair.

To modify the cookie to store two name/value pairs:

1. Switch to Notepad, save the logintracking_cookie.html file as **logintracking_cookie2.html**. Modify the program lines as shown in Figure 7-15, and then save the file. Note that the cookie now contains two cookie name/value pairs.

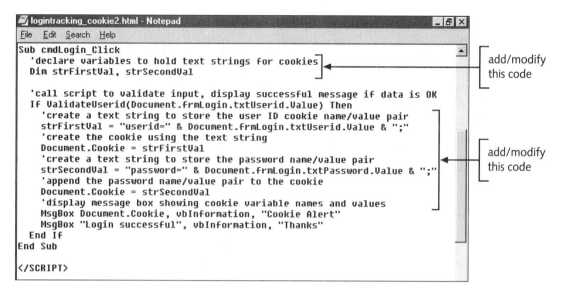

```
logintracking_cookie2.html - Notepad                              _ 8 X
File   Edit   Search   Help
Sub cmdLogin_Click
  'declare variables to hold text strings for cookies           add/modify
  Dim strFirstVal, strSecondVal                                  this code

  'call script to validate input, display successful message if data is OK
  If ValidateUserid(Document.frmLogin.txtUserid.Value) Then
    'create a text string to store the user ID cookie name/value pair
    strFirstVal = "userid=" & Document.frmLogin.txtUserid.Value & ";"
    'create the cookie using the text string
    Document.Cookie = strFirstVal                                add/modify
    'create a text string to store the password name/value pair  this code
    strSecondVal = "password=" & Document.frmLogin.txtPassword.Value & ";"
    'append the password name/value pair to the cookie
    Document.Cookie = strSecondVal
    'display message box showing cookie variable names and values
    MsgBox Document.Cookie, vbInformation, "Cookie Alert"
    MsgBox "Login successful", vbInformation, "Thanks"
  End If
End Sub

</SCRIPT>
```

Figure 7-15   Creating a cookie with two values

2. Switch to Internet Explorer, and type **http://localhost/** to display the updated file listing of your root document folder.

3. Click **logintracking_cookie2.html** in the file listing. The Login - Order Tracking form is displayed.

4. Type **harrispe** for the user ID, type **asdfjka** for the password, and then click **Login**. The message box shown in Figure 7-16 is displayed, showing both cookie values.

```
VBScript: Cookie Alert                    X
 (i)    userid=harrispe; password=asdfjka

        [        OK        ]
```

Figure 7-16   Message box showing two cookie values

5. Click **OK** to acknowledge the Cookie Alert, and then click **OK** again to acknowledge that the login was successful.

Persistent Cookies

Recall that a temporary cookie is only available to your Web pages until the user exits the current browser session. If you want to store cookie values that will be available to your Web pages when a user makes future visits to your Web site, you need to create a persistent cookie, which stores cookie name/value pairs in a text file on the user's workstation. To create a persistent cookie whose name/value pairs are available to future browser sessions, you create a cookie using the same syntax you used to create a temporary cookie, but you add an expiration date. Recall that cookies can only be read by the Web server that originally generated the cookie. When a cookie is created, the domain name of the Web server that created the cookie is automatically stored along with the cookie variables and values. Therefore, whenever a script creates a new cookie, the new cookie is added to the list of cookies already created by that Web server. Each cookie name/value pair can have a different expiration date, but the overall cookie will not expire until the expiration date that is specified on the cookie variable with the most distant expiration date. At the present time, most browsers are configured so that a user's workstation cannot store more than a total of 300 cookies.

To add an expiration date to a cookie, you use the following code:

```
Document.Cookie = [cookie variable name and value];expires=[date];
```

The date attribute must be written using the following date format:

```
day,dd-mmm-yy hh:mm:ss GMT
```

> **TIP** GMT stands for Greenwich Mean Time. The actual time that the cookie will be deleted will be converted to the corresponding time in your time zone.

To create a cookie that expires at 12:00 PM (GMT) on December 31, 2002, you would format the date for the expires attribute as follows:

```
Tuesday, 31-Dec-2002 12:00:00 GMT
```

Now you will modify the Login - Order Tracking form so that it creates a persistent cookie. You will set the expiration date for the userid cookie variable to be December 31, 2004, and the expiration date for the password cookie variable to be December 31, 2002. (In a real application, the user ID and password would probably be set to expire on the same date, but for this exercise, they will be set to expire on different dates to illustrate how different name/value pairs within the same cookie can have different expiration dates.) Then, you will display the Web page in Internet Explorer, create the cookie, and view the cookie file in your file system.

To create a persistent cookie and view the cookie file:

1. Switch to Notepad, open **logintracking_cookie2.html** from the Chapter7 folder on your Data Disk, and save the file as **logintracking_persistentcookie.html**.

2. Modify the script text for the Login button Click event as shown in Figure 7-17, to create the persistent cookie, and then save the file.

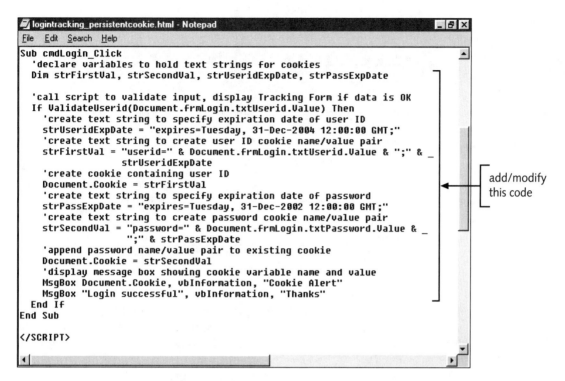

```
logintracking_persistentcookie.html - Notepad                    _ 8 X
File  Edit  Search  Help
Sub cmdLogin_Click                                                ▲
  'declare variables to hold text strings for cookies
  Dim strFirstVal, strSecondVal, strUseridExpDate, strPassExpDate

  'call script to validate input, display Tracking Form if data is OK
  If ValidateUserid(Document.frmLogin.txtUserid.Value) Then
    'create text string to specify expiration date of user ID
    strUseridExpDate = "expires=Tuesday, 31-Dec-2004 12:00:00 GMT;"
    'create text string to create user ID cookie name/value pair
    strFirstVal = "userid=" & Document.frmLogin.txtUserid.Value & ";" & _
                  strUseridExpDate
    'create cookie containing user ID
    Document.Cookie = strFirstVal
    'create text string to specify expiration date of password
    strPassExpDate = "expires=Tuesday, 31-Dec-2002 12:00:00 GMT;"
    'create text string to create password cookie name/value pair
    strSecondVal = "password=" & Document.frmLogin.txtPassword.Value & _
                  ";" & strPassExpDate
    'append password name/value pair to existing cookie
    Document.Cookie = strSecondVal
    'display message box showing cookie variable name and value
    MsgBox Document.Cookie, vbInformation, "Cookie Alert"
    MsgBox "Login successful", vbInformation, "Thanks"
  End If
End Sub

</SCRIPT>
                                                                  ▼
◄                                                                 ►
```

add/modify this code

Figure 7-17   Creating a persistent cookie

3. Switch to Internet Explorer, type **http://localhost/** in the Address box, and then click **logintracking_persistentcookie.html**. The Login - Order Tracking form is displayed.

4. Type **harrispe** for the user ID and **asdfjka** for the password, and then click **Login**. The Cookie Alert message box is displayed (see Figure 7-16), which shows the value for both of the cookie name/value pairs. Note that the cookie expiration dates are not displayed in the Document.Cookie property that is shown in the message box; this is because the expiration date is a property of the variable, but is not part of the actual variable value. Click **OK** to close the message box, and then click **OK** to close the Login successful message box.

5. Start Windows Explorer, navigate to the C:\Windows\Temporary Internet Files folder, which is the default directory where Internet Explorer stores persistent cookie files, and view your cookie files. (Windows NT users will find their temporary Internet files in the C:\Winnt\Temporary Internet Files folder. Windows 2000 users will find their temporary Internet files in the C:\Documents and Settings\[your username]\Local Settings\Temporary Internet Files folder.) Your file listing should look similar to Figure 7-18.

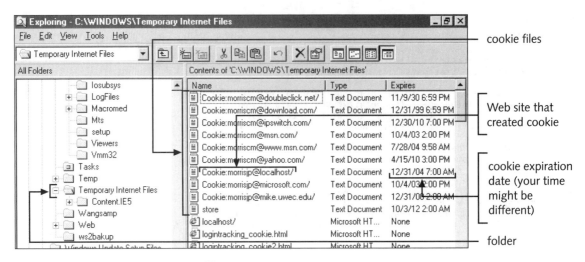

Figure 7-18 Temporary Internet files

> **TIP**
>
> If you do not have a folder named C:\Windows\Temporary Internet Files, or if there are no cookie files in the folder, it might be because your browser is set to save temporary files (such as cookie files) in a different folder. To find the folder where your browser saves temporary files, click Tools on the browser menu bar, click Internet Options, and then click Settings. The Settings dialog box displays the path to the Temporary Internet Files folder.

Note that each cookie file is associated with a different Web server domain name. For example, in Figure 7-18, there are cookie files from yahoo.com and microsoft.com, as well as other domains. There is also a cookie file from the localhost domain—this is the cookie file that you just created in the Login - Order Tracking form. Note that the expiration date for this cookie is December 31, 2004, which is the expiration date of the password cookie variable. The time is converted from 12:00 PM GMT to the equivalent time in your time zone. You can view the data in any cookie file, and you can manually delete any cookie file.

USING SCRIPTS TO DISPLAY DIFFERENT WEB PAGES AND SHARE COOKIE VALUES

In the previous section, you learned how to create and retrieve cookie values. Recall that an important application of cookies is sharing data values among different Web pages in an application. Now you will learn how to write the script code to display a new Web page from the current page, and to retrieve and display the values of a cookie that was written in a script in the current page. Currently, when the user clicks Login in the Login - Order Tracking Web page, the script creates the cookie containing the user ID and password. You will modify this Web page's script code so that after it creates the cookie, it displays the Order Tracking form shown in Figure 7-3. There are two ways to display a different Web page using a client-side script. You can start a new browser session and open a new browser window with the new Web page displayed, or you can display the new Web page in the current browser window.

Displaying a Web Page in a New Browser Window

Sometimes, it is desirable to open a new browser window to display a different Web page. This is usually done when the new Web page is unrelated to the current page or does not have to share data with the current Web page. For example, many commercial Web sites automatically open new browser windows to display advertisements. This allows the user to have multiple browser windows open at the same time, and to view multiple Web pages simultaneously.

Now you will modify the Login – Order Tracking form file so that it displays the Order Tracking form in a separate browser window. The keyword Window is used to reference the browser window. To open a new browser window using VBScript, you use the Open method. This method has the following format:

```
Window.Open [URL], [Target], [Option List]
```

The URL parameter is the address of the document that you want to display in the window. This could be a file URL, or a relative or absolute URL that references folders on the Web server. (Recall that a relative folder path specifies a folder path location that is relative to where the current Web page is located, and an absolute folder path specifies a folder path from the root document folder.) To display the Order Tracking form, you will specify the name of the HTML form file. Since this file is in the same folder as the current form, you will use a relative path and not specify folder path information.

The Target parameter is the name that you give to the new window. This name will be used to reference the window in other scripts or procedures, and it cannot contain any blank spaces. The Option List parameter allows you to specify the properties of the new browser window, as summarized in Table 7-2.

Table 7-2   New window Option List parameters

Option	Description	Sample Values
Toolbar	Displays browser toolbar	toolbar=yes toolbar=no
Location	Displays Address box in browser window to show form URL	location=yes location=no
Directories	Displays links to frequently used URLs in window title bar	directories=yes directories=no
Status	Shows the Web page status (loading, done loading) in the window status bar at the bottom edge of the window	status=yes status=no
Menubar	Displays the browser menu bar	menubar=yes menubar=no
Scrollbar	Displays scrollbars on the browser window	scrollbar=yes scrollbar=no

Table 7-2   New window Option List parameters (continued)

Option	Description	Sample Values
Resizeable	Allows the user to resize the window	resizeable=yes resizeable=no
Width, Height	Specifies the window width and height in pixels	width=300, height=200

Within a script, the desired window options are listed sequentially, with each option separated from the next by a comma (,). If no options are specified, then the browser window is opened with all options in the option list displayed. If any option value is specified in the command, then no other options are displayed unless you explicitly set the option to "yes."

Now you will modify the Login - Order Tracking form so it displays the Order Tracking form (tracking.html) in a new browser window. You will modify the window properties to change the window size, and to prevent the user from resizing the window.

To modify the Login - Order Tracking form to display the Order Tracking form:

1. Switch to Notepad, open the **logintracking_cookie2.html** file, and save the file as **logintracking_newwindow.html** in the Chapter7 folder on your Data Disk. Modify the file as shown in Figure 7-19, and save the file.

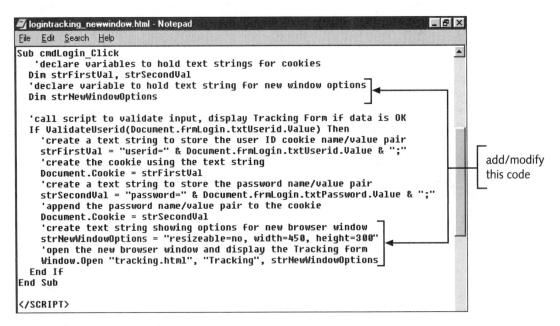

```
logintracking_newwindow.html - Notepad
File   Edit   Search   Help
Sub cmdLogin_Click
    'declare variables to hold text strings for cookies
    Dim strFirstVal, strSecondVal
    'declare variable to hold text string for new window options
    Dim strNewWindowOptions

    'call script to validate input, display Tracking Form if data is OK
    If ValidateUserid(Document.frmLogin.txtUserid.Value) Then
        'create a text string to store the user ID cookie name/value pair
        strFirstVal = "userid=" & Document.frmLogin.txtUserid.Value & ";"
        'create the cookie using the text string
        Document.Cookie = strFirstVal
        'create a text string to store the password name/value pair
        strSecondVal = "password=" & Document.frmLogin.txtPassword.Value & ";"
        'append the password name/value pair to the cookie
        Document.Cookie = strSecondVal
        'create text string showing options for new browser window
        strNewWindowOptions = "resizeable=no, width=450, height=300"
        'open the new browser window and display the Tracking form
        Window.Open "tracking.html", "Tracking", strNewWindowOptions
    End If
End Sub

</SCRIPT>
```

add/modify this code

Figure 7-19   Opening a new browser window

2. Switch to Internet Explorer, type **http://localhost/** in the Address box, and then click the hyperlink to the **logintracking_newwindow.html** file. The Login – Order Tracking form is displayed.

3. Type **harrispe** for the user ID and **asdfjka** for the password, and then click **Login**. The Order Tracking Web page is displayed in a new browser window.

4. Click the **Close** button ☒ on the title bar of the browser window that displays the Order Tracking form.

Navigating to a New Web Page in the Current Browser Window

Another way to display a new Web page programmatically within a VBScript program is to display the new page in the current browser window using the Navigate method. This method prevents you from having to close multiple browser windows and uses less space on the Windows taskbar. The Navigate method has the following format:

```
Navigate("[Web page URL]")
```

The Web page URL can use either a relative or absolute folder path. Now you will modify the Login – Order Tracking Web page so that when the user clicks the Login button, a client-side script runs that displays the Order Tracking form in the current browser window.

To modify the Login – Order Tracking page to navigate to the Order Tracking form:

1. Switch to Notepad, open **logintracking_cookie2.html** from the Chapter7 folder on your Data Disk, and save the file as **logintracking_newpage.html**.

2. Modify the file as shown in Figure 7-20, and then save the file.

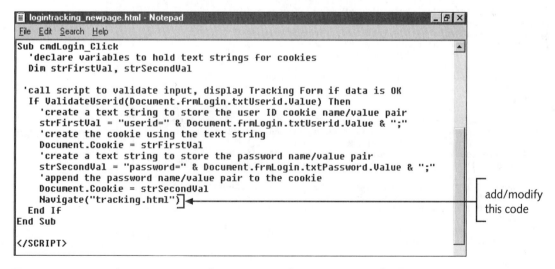

Figure 7-20   Displaying a new Web page using the Navigate method

3. Switch to Internet Explorer, type **http://localhost/** in the Address box, and then click the hyperlink to the **logintracking_newpage.html** file. The Login - Order Tracking form is displayed.

4. Type **harrispe** for the user ID and **asdfjka** for the password, and then click **Login**. The Order Tracking Web page is displayed in the current browser window.

Retrieving the Values of Individual Cookie Variables

So far, you have retrieved and displayed the entire contents of the cookie (all variable names and corresponding values) associated with your Web page process. In normal use, each cookie name/value pair is usually retrieved and processed individually. For example, you might create an application that would retrieve the value associated with the userid cookie variable, and then create a database query to confirm that the retrieved user ID matches a user ID that is stored in the Clearwater Traders database.

Now you will learn how to extract the values of individual cookie variables. To do this, you will add a script to the Order Tracking form to retrieve the cookie values stored by the Login - Order Tracking form. When the user clicks the Submit Query button on the Order Tracking form, a message box will appear that shows the value of each cookie variable separately. To do this, you will add a custom VBScript function named CookieValue to the Order Tracking form. The code for this function is shown in Figure 7-21.

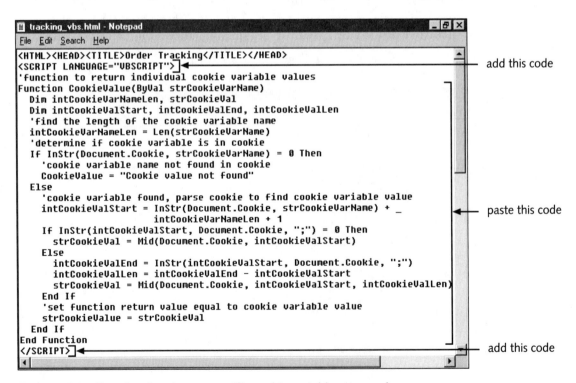

```
tracking_vbs.html - Notepad
File  Edit  Search  Help
<HTML><HEAD><TITLE>Order Tracking</TITLE></HEAD>
<SCRIPT LANGUAGE="VBSCRIPT">                                    ◄——— add this code
'function to return individual cookie variable values
Function CookieValue(ByVal strCookieVarName)
  Dim intCookieVarNameLen, strCookieVal
  Dim intCookieValStart, intCookieValEnd, intCookieValLen
  'find the length of the cookie variable name
  intCookieVarNameLen = Len(strCookieVarName)
  'determine if cookie variable is in cookie
  If InStr(Document.Cookie, strCookieVarName) = 0 Then
    'cookie variable name not found in cookie
    CookieValue = "Cookie value not found"
  Else
    'cookie variable found, parse cookie to find cookie variable value
    intCookieValStart = InStr(Document.Cookie, strCookieVarName) + _
                        intCookieVarNameLen + 1
    If InStr(intCookieValStart, Document.Cookie, ";") = 0 Then
      strCookieVal = Mid(Document.Cookie, intCookieValStart)
    Else
      intCookieValEnd = InStr(intCookieValStart, Document.Cookie, ";")
      intCookieValLen = intCookieValEnd - intCookieValStart
      strCookieVal = Mid(Document.Cookie, intCookieValStart, intCookieValLen)
    End If
    'set function return value equal to cookie variable value
    strCookieValue = strCookieVal
  End If
End Function
</SCRIPT>                                    ◄——— add this code
```
◄——— paste this code

Figure 7-21 Function to return a specific cookie variable name value

When this function is called, the program passes the name of a specific cookie variable as an input parameter. The function code then searches the document cookie and returns the value associated with the cookie input variable. Recall that the script in the Login - Order Tracking form creates a cookie with the following variables and associated values:

```
userid=[value for user ID];password=[value for user password];
```

If the text string "userid" is passed to the function, then the function returns the user ID value that the user entered on the Login - Order Tracking form. If the text string "password" is passed to the CookieValue function, then the function returns the password value that the user entered.

Now you will add the CookieValue function to the HTML file that contains the code for the Order Tracking form. You will copy this code from a text file named CookieValue.txt that is stored in the Chapter7 folder on your Data Disk.

7

To add the function to the Order Tracking form code:

1. Switch to Notepad, open **CookieValue.txt** from the Chapter7 folder on your Data Disk, and copy all of the function text.

 TIP The function text might exceed the size of the open Notepad window. Scroll down, if necessary, to make sure you have copied all of the text.

2. In Notepad, open **tracking.html** from the Chapter7 folder on your Data Disk, and save the file as **tracking_vbs.html**.

3. Place the insertion point at the end of the first line of the file, press **Enter**, and then type the script heading (**<SCRIPT LANGUAGE="VBSCRIPT">**) and the comment statement to describe the function, as shown in Figure 7-21.

4. Paste the code for the CookieValue function directly below the comment statement, as shown in Figure 7-21.

5. Add the closing script tag (**</SCRIPT>**) after the End Function command, as shown in Figure 7-21, and then save the file.

Now you will add the script code to call the function and pass it the value of the specific cookie variables ("userid" and "password") to be returned. This code will be in a procedure named cmdSubmit_Click, and will be associated with the Click event of the form's Submit Query button. The procedure will find the cookie values, and then display them in a message box. You will also add the ONCLICK attribute to the INPUT tag that defines the "Submit Query" button, so that when the user clicks the button, the cmdSubmit_Click procedure is called.

To add the code to find the cookie values and display them in a message box:

1. In the tracking_vbs.html file, add the code shown in Figure 7-22 directly below the function code you just added.

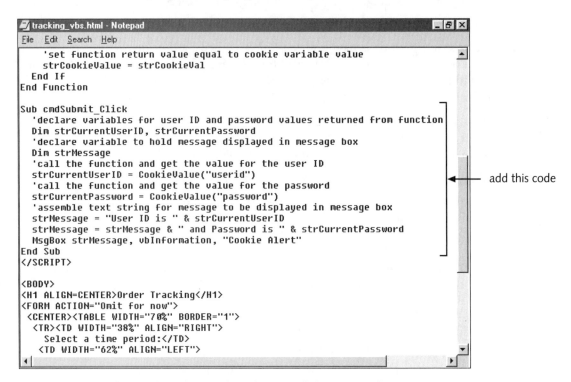

```
'set function return value equal to cookie variable value
    strCookieValue = strCookieVal
  End If
End Function

Sub cmdSubmit_Click
  'declare variables for user ID and password values returned from function
  Dim strCurrentUserID, strCurrentPassword
  'declare variable to hold message displayed in message box
  Dim strMessage
  'call the function and get the value for the user ID
  strCurrentUserID = CookieValue("userid")
  'call the function and get the value for the password
  strCurrentPassword = CookieValue("password")
  'assemble text string for message to be displayed in message box
  strMessage = "User ID is " & strCurrentUserID
  strMessage = strMessage & " and Password is " & strCurrentPassword
  MsgBox strMessage, vbInformation, "Cookie Alert"
End Sub
</SCRIPT>

<BODY>
<H1 ALIGN=CENTER>Order Tracking</H1>
<FORM ACTION="Omit for now">
 <CENTER><TABLE WIDTH="70%" BORDER="1">
  <TR><TD WIDTH="38%" ALIGN="RIGHT">
    Select a time period:</TD>
    <TD WIDTH="62%" ALIGN="LEFT">
```

add this code

Figure 7-22   Order Tracking form Submit button Click event code

2. Scroll down in the file, find the INPUT tag that defines the "Submit Query" button and add the following code to the tag, so the finished button tag looks like this:

```
<INPUT TYPE=BUTTON NAME=cmdSubmit

ONCLICK=cmdSubmit_Click VALUE="Submit Query">
```

3. Save the file.

Finally, you will need to modify the logintracking_newpage.html file so that when the user clicks the Login button, the tracking_vbs.html Web page file is displayed. (Currently, the Login button's ONCLICK event calls the tracking.html Web page file.) Then, you will test your changes.

To modify the logintracking_newpage.html file and test the changes:

1. In Notepad, open **logintracking_newpage.html** from the Chapter7 folder on your Data Disk, change the Navigate command as follows to display the tracking_vbs.html file, and then save the file:

```
Navigate("tracking_vbs.html")
```

2. Switch to Internet Explorer, type **http://localhost/** in the Address box, and then click **logintracking_newpage.html**. The Login - Order Tracking form is displayed.

3. Type **harrispe** for the user ID and **asdfjka** for the password, and then click **Login**. The Order Tracking form is displayed.

4. Click **Submit Query** on the Order Tracking form. The message box shown in Figure 7-23 is displayed, showing the retrieved cookie values. Recall that these cookie values were saved using the previous Web page. Note that the cookie variable names are not displayed, since you modified the code to retrieve and display each cookie variable name value separately.

VBScript: Cookie Alert

(i) User ID is harrispe and Password is asdfjka

OK

Figure 7-23   Message box showing cookie values

> **TIP** If the message box does not appear, it means that you have an error in your code. Double-check to make sure you made the modifications exactly as described in the previous set of steps, and debug your code using the debugging strategies provided earlier in this chapter.

5. Click **OK** to close the message box.

6. Close Notepad, Internet Explorer, and any other open applications.

SUMMARY

❏ A client-side script is uncompiled code that is interpreted on the user's workstation. Client-side scripts are primarily used to validate user inputs entered on HTML forms, open new browser windows, and create cookies, which store information about a user's actions in a Web page. HTML forms are enhanced HTML documents that collect user inputs using form elements such as input boxes, option buttons, and command buttons. You can also create hidden form elements that are not visible to the user, which are often used to store information.

❏ Scripts are small programs that can be created more rapidly than compiled programs, and can be easily modified using a text editor. Popular scripting languages include PERL, JavaScript, and VBScript. VBScript commands are enclosed in <SCRIPT>...</SCRIPT> tags within an HTML document and are similar to Visual Basic commands. Data validation within scripts can be performed using a script procedure that is associated with the ONCLICK attribute of a form command button. You can display message boxes in scripts just as in Visual Basic programs.

❏ A cookie contains information that is stored by a Web server on a Web site visitor's computer. A cookie stores information in ordered pairs of variables and associated values, with each separate name/value pair separated from the next by a semicolon (;). Temporary cookies store information in the main memory of the user's computer, and are not available after the user exits his or her browser. Persistent cookies store information in text files on the user's workstation, and this information is available even after the user exits the browser. Persistent cookies have an expiration date, and are deleted by the user's system when the expiration date is reached. Temporary and persistent cookies can only be read by the Web server that created the cookie. Cookies can be used to share data values among different Web pages that are downloaded from the same Web server.

❏ Scripts can also be used to open new browser windows, or to navigate to different Web pages within the current browser window. Cookie values can be shared by different Web pages in the same Web page application.

REVIEW QUESTIONS

1. What is the difference between a script and a compiled program?

2. What is the difference between a client-side script and a server-side script?

3. List two uses for client-side scripts.

4. What is the purpose of the Reset button in an HTML form?

5. What is the purpose of the ACTION attribute in an HTML form?

6. What is the purpose of the Submit button on an HTML form?

7. What does the VALUE attribute specify for an HTML form element?

8. In what part of an HTML document are form tags placed?

9. How do you make a cookie a persistent cookie?

10. Where in an HTML document file is the code for a VBScript procedure or function located?

11. Give an example of a situation in which you would use a cookie.

12. What type of event is usually used to activate a data validation script?

13. How are the data in an input field accessed in VBScript?

14. Which form input type lets you pass values the user doesn't see?

15. What is the advantage of using a script rather than a compiled program for validating user inputs or creating cookies?

16. What is the difference between passing parameters by reference and passing parameters by value?

17. True or False: a Web page cannot read a cookie created by a script in another Web page.

18. How many name/value pairs can a single cookie store?

19. True or False: you can manually delete a cookie file that is stored on your workstation.

20. What is the difference between displaying a new Web page from an existing Web page using the Window.Open method and displaying it using the Navigate method?

HANDS-ON PROJECTS

1. Write the HTML code to create the Web page form shown in Figure 7-24. This form displays the shoes.jpg image file and the text "Airstream Canvas Shoes" in a table, displays the information about the individual shoe sizes and colors in a second table, and then displays a "Desired Quantity" input box and an "Order Now" button in a third table. Save the file as Ch7Pr1.html in the Chapter7 folder on your Data Disk.

Figure 7-24

a. Use a relative path to reference the shoes.jpg image file, which is stored in the Chapter7 folder on your Data Disk.

b. Name the form "frmOrderItem," and code the FORM ACTION tag as "Omit for now".

c. Name the Desired Quantity input box txtOrderQuantity, and the Order Now command button cmdOrder.

d. Hard-code the data values exactly as shown in Figure 7-24. (Recall that hard-coding means entering the actual data values within the HTML text.)

2. Modify the code for the Web page that you created in Hands-on Project 1 so that when the user clicks the Order Now button, a script runs verifying that the user entered a value for the desired quantity, and that the value entered is a number greater than zero and less than 100. If the user did not enter a value at all, the script displays a message box stating "You forgot to enter an order quantity." If the user entered a value that is greater than zero and less than 100, the script displays a message box stating "Thank you for your order." If the user entered a number that is not greater than zero and less than 100, the script displays a message box stating "The order quantity that you specified is incorrect. Please check and make sure you entered a value greater than 0 and less than 100." Save the modified file as Ch7Pr2.html in the Chapter7 folder on your Data Disk. *(Hint:* Check to see if the desired quantity value is an empty text string. If it is not, check to see if it fits the specified number range. The value entered in the text input box is a text string; to check its value, you will need to convert it to an integer, using the CInt function. The solution does not need to be able to process negative numbers.)

3. Write the code to create the HTML form shown in Figure 7-25, which allows a student at Northwoods University to log on to the student registration system. Save the file as Ch7Pr3.html in the Chapter7 folder on your Data Disk.

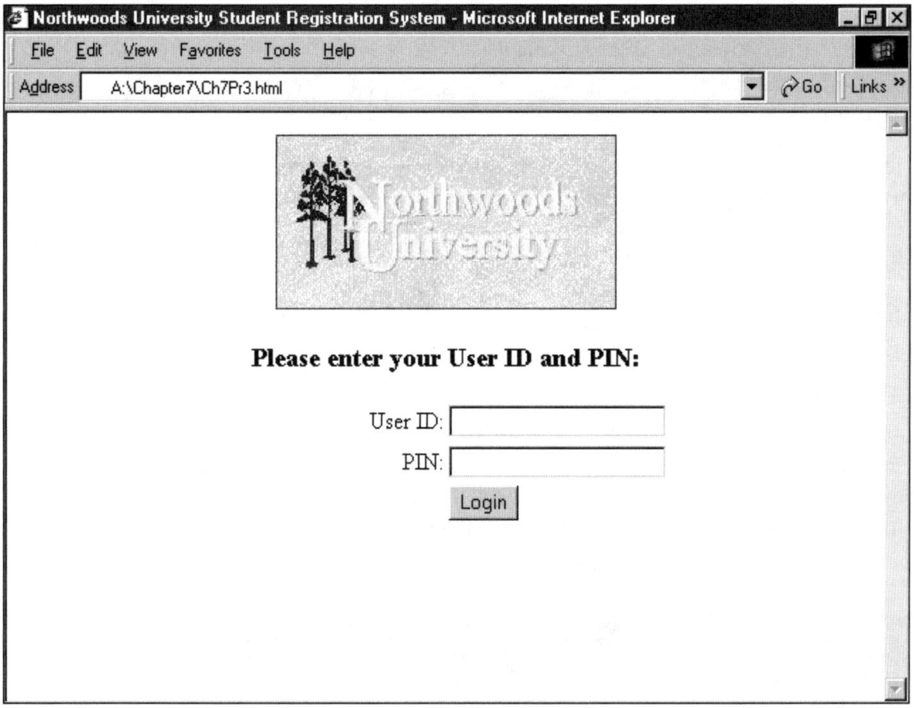

Figure 7-25

    a. Name the user ID input box txtUserID and the PIN input box txtPIN.

    b. Name the form frmStudentLogin, and set the FORM ACTION attribute as "Omit for now".

    c. Name the command button cmdSubmit and make it a SUBMIT input element.

4. In this project, you will modify the Student Login form you created in Project 3 by writing a client-side script that verifies that the user has entered values in the User ID and PIN input boxes, and writes a cookie that saves the User ID and PIN values.

    a. Open Ch7Pr3.html from the Chapter7 folder on your Data Disk, and save the file as Ch7Pr4.html.

    b. Modify the Submit button so that it is a BUTTON input, and modify its ONCLICK attribute so that it calls a procedure named cmdSubmit_Click.

    c. Create a VBScript procedure named cmdSubmit_Click that checks to see if the user has entered values for User ID and PIN. If the user entered the values, the script displays a message box stating "Values entered correctly." If the user did not enter the User ID, the script displays a message box stating "User ID not entered." If the user did not enter the PIN, the script displays a message box stating "PIN not entered."

    d. Create a temporary cookie that stores the User ID and PIN value, and then displays the values in a message box. Use the CookieValue function to retrieve the individual values so the message box text is formatted like Figure 7-23.

5. In this project, you will modify the code from Project 4 so that the script creates a persistent cookie that stores the User ID and PIN values within cookie variables.

   a. Open Ch7Pr4.html from the Chapter7 folder on your Data Disk and save the file as Ch7Pr5.html.

   b. Modify the code in the cmdSubmit_Click script to create a persistent cookie. Make the user ID cookie variable value expire on January 1, 2005, and make the PIN variable expire on January 1, 2002.

6. Write the code to create the HTML form shown in Figure 7-26. Save the form as Ch7Pr6.html in the Chapter7 folder on your Data Disk.

   a. Display the nwlogo.jpg image file and the title "Student Information" in a table at the top of the form.

   b. Create a table that displays all of the form elements shown. Make each element's name the same as its corresponding field name in the STUDENT table in the Northwoods University database, with the appropriate control prefix. (The Northwoods University database is shown in Figure 2-5.) For example, the code to specify the name of the "Last Name" input box would be **NAME=txtSLast**.

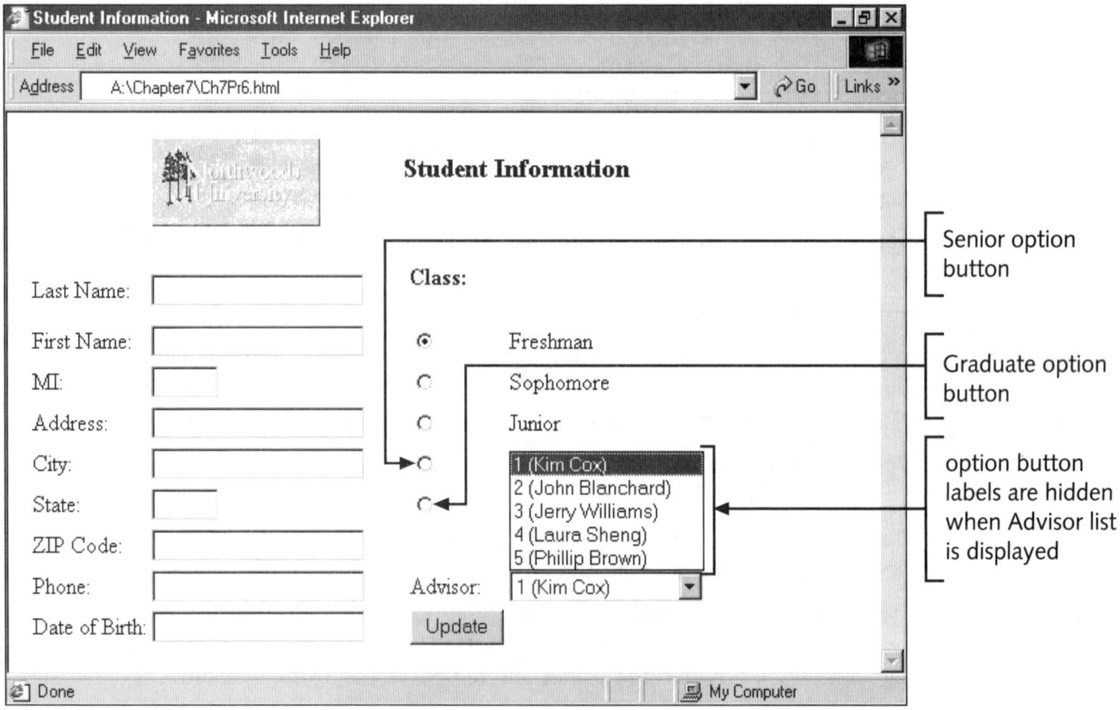

Figure 7-26

c. Specify that only the first radio button ("Freshman") is selected. Name the radio button group optSClass, and set the value of each individual radio button equal to the corresponding database value. For example, the value for the "Freshman" radio button would be "FR". (Note that in Figure 7–26, the labels for the Senior and Graduate option buttons are hidden by the faculty ID list.)

d. For the Advisor list, hard-code the values for each faculty member's FID and last name, as shown in Figure 7–26.

e. Name the command button cmdUpdate, and make it a BUTTON input element.

7. In this project, you will modify the Student Login form you created in Project 4 so that when the student successfully logs on to the system, the Student Information page shown in Figure 7–26 is displayed. First you will modify the form so the Student Information page is displayed in a new browser window. Then, you will modify the form so the Student Information page is displayed in the current browser window.

a. Open Ch7Pr4.html from the Chapter7 folder on your Data Disk, and save the file as Ch7Pr7a.html. Modify the script commands so that after the message box showing the cookie values is displayed, the Student Information (Ch7Pr6.html) Web page is displayed in a new browser window. Configure the window so that the browser toolbar, menu bar, and status bar are displayed in the window, but none of the other window options is enabled. Configure the window so the entire Student Information form is displayed.

b. Open Ch7Pr4.html from the Chapter7 folder on your Data Disk, and save the file as Ch7Pr7b.html. Use the Navigate command so the Student Information Web page (Ch7Pr6.html) is displayed in the same browser window. Use a relative path to specify the Web page filename.

CASE PROJECTS

1. Create at least two Web page forms to display or enter data that are stored in the Ashland Valley Soccer League database, which was described in Chapter 2, Case Project 1. Add data validation scripts to the pages and create a link so you can navigate from one of the pages to the other using an HTML form command button. (You do not need to actually insert data into the database at this time.) Create a folder named Cases in the Chapter7 folder on your Data Disk. Create a subfolder named Ashland in the Chapter7\Cases folder on your Data Disk. Save your work in the Chapter7\Cases\Ashland folder on your Data Disk.

2. Create at least two Web page forms to display or enter data that are stored in the Wayne's Auto World database, which was described in Chapter 2, Case Project 2. Add data validation scripts to the pages and create a link so you can navigate from one of the pages to the other using an HTML form command button. (You do not need to actually insert data into the database at this time.) Create a folder named Waynes in the Chapter7\Cases folder on your Data Disk. Save your work in the Chapter7\Cases\Waynes folder on your Data Disk.

3. Create at least two Web page forms to display or enter data that are stored in the Sun-Ray Video database, which was described in Chapter 2, Case Project 3. Add data validation scripts to the pages and create a link so you can navigate from one of the pages to the other using an HTML form command button. (You do not need to actually insert data into the database at this time.) Create a folder named Sunray in the Chapter7\Cases folder on your Data Disk. Save your work in the Chapter7\Cases\Sunray folder on your Data Disk.

In this chapter, you will:

♦ Create dynamic Web pages that retrieve and display database data using Active Server Pages

♦ Process form inputs using Active Server Pages

♦ Create a Web application using client- and server-side scripts

♦ Learn how to share data values among different pages in a Web application

♦ Insert, update, and delete database records using Active Server Pages

So far, the scripts that you have created have been client-side scripts that are processed by the user's browser. Web applications also use **server-side scripts**, which are scripts that are processed on the Web server. These scripts are used to create dynamic Web pages that retrieve and display database data and modify data records. The Web server retrieves the data from the database, inserts the retrieved data values into the Web page HTML commands, and then returns the formatted Web page to the user's browser. The architecture for Web processing using server-side scripts is illustrated in Figure 8-1.

In this chapter, you will learn how to create **Active Server Pages**, which are Microsoft-specific Web pages that contain server-side scripting commands to process user inputs and create dynamic Web pages that display database data. Since the Web server creates an HTML document that contains retrieved data values, the formatted Web page can be displayed by any browser—not only Microsoft Internet Explorer. You will also learn how to include client-side scripts within Active Server Pages to create a Web application that allows Clearwater Traders customers to view merchandise, determine if an item is in stock, and place an order. You will also learn how to update the database using an Active Server Page.

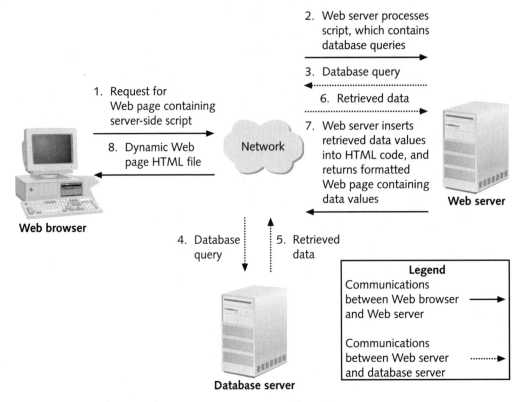

Figure 8-1   Web site architecture using a server-side script

ACTIVE SERVER PAGES

An Active Server Page (ASP) is a text file that has an .asp extension and contains server-side script commands that can perform a variety of tasks, such as inserting, updating, and retrieving data from a database. An ASP also usually contains HTML commands for creating a formatted Web page. If a script command involves retrieving database data, then the Web server retrieves the data values from the database and then inserts the retrieved data values into the HTML commands within the ASP to create a formatted HTML document. The formatted HTML document is then sent to the user's browser and displayed. Scripts within ASPs can be created using VBScript, which is the default ASP scripting language, and JScript, which is Microsoft's JavaScript implementation.

ASPs are a Microsoft-specific technology, and can only be processed on Microsoft Web servers (specifically, Microsoft Personal Web Server and Microsoft Internet Information Server). Netscape has a server-side scripting technology called LiveWire that is similar to Active Server Pages.

Since ASPs are processed on a Web server, ASP files must be stored and run from a folder on the Web server—they cannot be displayed from a folder on the user's workstation using a file URL.

Now you will create a folder in the Chapter8 folder on your Data Disk named asp-bin where you will store your ASPs.

> **TIP** Programmers often store program files in folders that are named "bin" or have the word "bin" as part of the folder name. The word "bin" is short for binary, which indicates that the folder contains machine-language (binary) files. Although script files are not translated to machine language until they are executed, including the suffix "bin" in the folder name indicates that the folder contains program files.

You will also modify Personal Web Server so that the root document folder is the Chapter8 folder on your Data Disk. Finally, you will create a virtual directory on Personal Web Server named asp-bin that corresponds with the physical asp-bin folder on your Data Disk. Recall from Chapter 5 that you can set the access privileges for a virtual directory according to the type of files that are stored there. Recall that access privileges that are available in PWS include **Read**, which only allows users to view HTML documents; **Execute**, which allows users to run Web pages that contain executable programs as well as scripts; and **Scripts**, which allows users to run Web pages that contain scripts, but not to run Web pages that contain executable programs. You will enable the Scripts privilege in the asp-bin virtual directory.

To create the asp-bin folder, modify the root document folder, and create the virtual directory:

1. Create a folder named **asp-bin** in the Chapter8 folder on your Data Disk.

2. Open Personal Web Manager, and change to the **Advanced** page, if necessary.

3. Click **Home** in the Virtual Directories list, click **Edit Properties**, click **Browse**, navigate to the Chapter8 folder on your Data Disk, and click **OK**. Make sure that the **Read** access check box is checked, and that the other check boxes are cleared, and then click **OK** again to set the root document folder to the Chapter8 folder on your Data Disk.

4. Confirm that clearwater.html is the Default Document name, and make sure that the Enable Default Document check box is checked.

5. Make sure that Home is selected in the Virtual Directories list, click **Add**, click **Browse**, navigate to the asp-bin folder on your Data Disk, and then click **OK**.

6. In the Add Directory dialog box, type **asp-bin** for the directory alias, make sure the Scripts check box is checked and the other check boxes are cleared, and then click **OK**. (Windows 2000 users should make sure that the Read check box is checked, and that the Scripts option button is selected.) The asp-bin virtual directory should be displayed in the Virtual Directories list.

7. Switch to the Main page, and confirm that the home directory is the Chapter8 folder on your Data Disk and that Web publishing is on. If Web publishing is off, click **Start**.

8. Start Internet Explorer and type **http://localhost/** in the Address box. The Clearwater Traders home page is displayed, as shown in Figure 8-2.

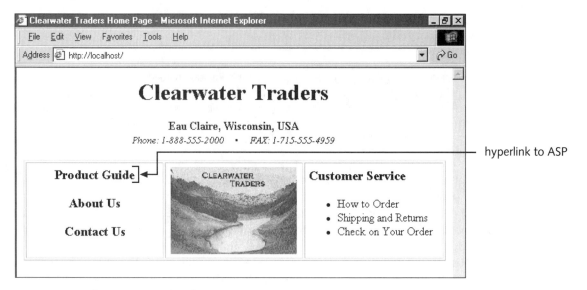

Figure 8-2   Clearwater Traders home page

When the user clicks the Product Guide hyperlink on the home page, an ASP will be processed that queries the Clearwater Traders database, and dynamically creates the Product Guide page by retrieving the descriptions of the items in the ITEM table, as shown in Figure 8-3.

Now you will create the Product Guide ASP that generates the text and HTML formatting tags for the Web page shown in Figure 8-3. This ASP will contain the script code to retrieve the database data, and create the formatted Web page. Whenever you create an ASP, it is a good practice to first create a static HTML Web page template file that contains all of the HTML tags and formatted text that you want to have displayed on the formatted Web page that is generated by the ASP. Then, you can add the script code for the dynamic components and be certain that the page's HTML formatting will be correct. A Web page template file named products_template.html has been created and stored on your Data Disk. This file contains the HTML code for the Product Guide Web page, with the first data record (Item ID 3, Airstream Canvas Shoes) hard-coded into the HTML code. (Recall that hard-coding data means typing data values directly into the code, rather than retrieving the data from a database.) Now you will display this Web page template file in your Web browser.

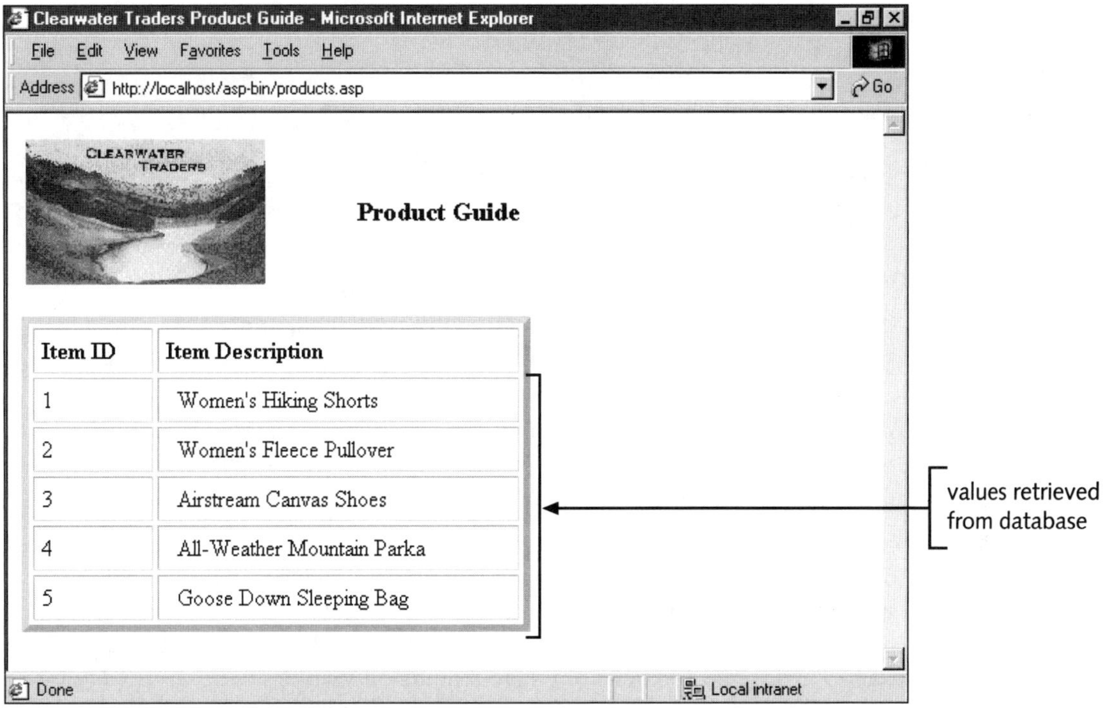

Figure 8-3   Product Guide Web page

To display the template file in your Web browser:

1. In Internet Explorer, click **File** on the menu bar, click **Open**, click **Browse**, navigate to the Chapter8 folder on your Data Disk, and open **product_template.html**. The Web page template file should look like Figure 8-4.

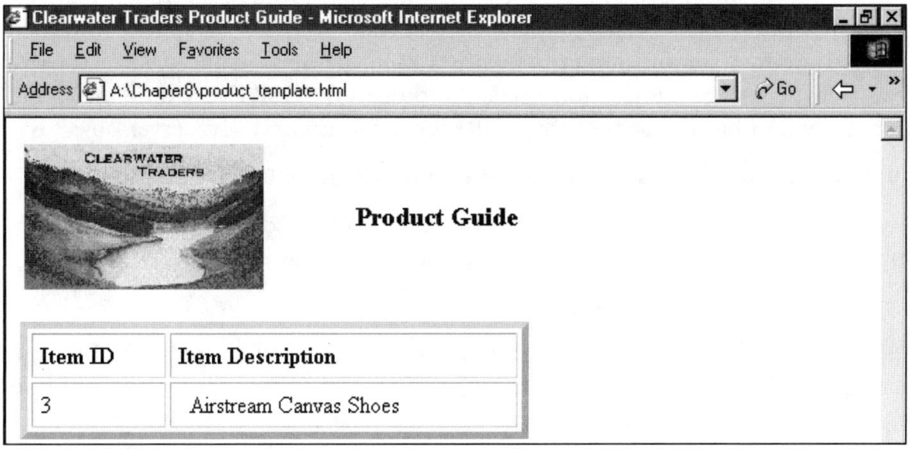

Figure 8-4   Product Guide template Web page

2. Start Notepad, open **product_template.html**, and save the file as **products.asp** in the asp–bin folder on your Data Disk.

 TIP If you do not change the file extension to .asp, the server-side script commands will not be processed by the Web server.

ASP Commands

The main difference between an ASP file and an HTML document file is that the ASP file contains ASP script code lines along with HTML commands in the Web page body. Script commands, like HTML commands, can span multiple lines. The beginning and ending points of ASP script code lines are signaled by **script delimiter tags**. The opening script delimiter tag is an opening angle bracket and a percent sign (<%). The closing script delimiter tag is a percent sign and a closing angle bracket (%>).

VBScript commands within server-side scripts are very similar to the VBScript commands you used to create client-side scripts in Chapter 7. Variables are declared using the Dim keyword, and all variables are declared using the Variant data type. (Recall that a variable with the Variant data type assumes the correct data type depending on the data value that is assigned to the variable.) The Option Explicit command requires all variables to be declared before a value can be assigned to the variable. In ASPs, the Option Explicit command must be placed in script delimiter tags, and it must be placed as the first line of the ASP file.

Displaying Database Data in an ASP

Now you will modify the products.asp file by adding script code to connect to the Clearwater Traders database, retrieve the records in the ITEM table, and then insert the retrieved item description records into the table on the Web page. First, you will create an ADO database connection object and use it to open the database. (Recall from Chapter 6 that ADO is a Microsoft data access technology.) To create an ADO database connection object, you must create a **server object**, which is a memory area on the Web server that stores the variables and other information needed to process the ASP. Every time the ASP is executed, a new server object must be created. The format to create a new server object is:

```
<% Set [connection variable name] = Server.CreateObject("ADODB.Connection") %>
```

Usually, the name of a database connection object variable is prefaced with the "conn" prefix. For example, the following code creates a database connection named connCW:

```
<% Set connCW = Server.CreateObject("ADODB.Connection")%>
```

The next step is to open the database connection. To do this, you must create an ODBC connection using an ODBC driver. Recall from Chapter 6 that an ODBC driver is a low-level program that translates messages from an application into the syntax expected by a specific database, and then forwards the translated message to the database. The code to open an

ODBC connection is very similar to the connection string code you used in Visual Basic to open a database connection. You must specify the name of the server object, and use the Open method to specify that the object is to be opened. You specify the database type (in this case, Microsoft Access) and the database location. For an Access database, the database location is the drive letter, folder path, and database filename. The code to open a connection named connCW that connects to the clearwater.mdb Access database file in the Chapter8 folder on your Data Disk is shown in Figure 8-5.

script
delimiters   ODBC driver

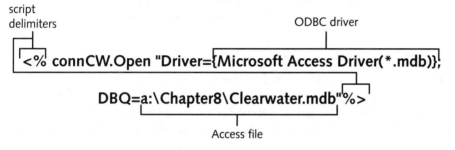

Access file

Figure 8-5 Code to open an Access database connection object

Notice that the ODBC driver information is enclosed in curly braces ({ }).

To retrieve data from a database, you create a recordset based on a SQL SELECT query using the database connection object's Execute function. This function passes a SQL query as a text string. For a SELECT query, the function's return value is a recordset that contains the retrieved data values. The code to call the Execute function for the connCW database connection using a SQL query that retrieves the ITEMID and ITEMDESC fields from the ITEM table is as follows:

```
<% Set rsItem = connCW.Execute("SELECT itemid, itemdesc FROM ITEM") %>
```

Note that the retrieved data records are stored in a recordset named rsItem. Usually, a recordset variable name uses the "rs" prefix.

To display an individual field in a recordset record within an HTML tag, you reference the field value using the following code:

```
<% =[recordset variable name]."fieldname" %>
```

To display all of the records that are retrieved by a query and stored in a recordset, you must use a Do While loop that displays the first record, and then continues to loop through and display records until the loop reaches the end of the recordset, which is marked with an end-of-file (EOF) marker. This loop has the following general format:

```
<% Do While Not [recordset name].EOF %>
    [program statements]
    <% [recordset name].MoveNext  %>
<% Loop %>
```

The following code creates a loop that displays values for the ITEMID and ITEMDESC fields for each record in the rsItem recordset and displays them in an HTML table:

```
< %Do While Not rsItem.EOF %>
    <TR><TD><% =rsItem.("ITEMID") %></TD>
    <TD><%= rsItem.("ITEMDESC") %></TD></TR>
    <% rsItem.MoveNext %>
<% Loop %>
```

When you are finished using a database connection object, you should close the database connection and make its resources available to other Web server processes. To close a database connection object, you use the following format:

```
<% [connection name].Close %>
```

Now you will modify the Product Guide ASP to create a server database connection object, open the database connection, retrieve the item IDs and description fields for all of the records in the ITEM table into a recordset, and display the recordset results on the Web page. You will use the Option Explicit command to ensure that all variables are declared prior to being used.

To modify the Product Guide ASP:

1. In Notepad, add the following code to the first line of the products.asp file:

```
<% Option Explicit %>
```

2. Add the rest of the script commands to the products.asp file as shown in Figure 8-6, and then save the file.

> **TIP** In this code, each individual script line is enclosed in script tags (<% ... %>). However, you can enclose contiguous script commands in a single set of script tags, as shown in Figure 8-7.

Figure 8-6   Script to display ITEM records

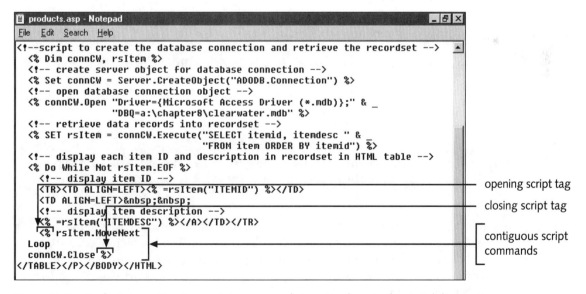

Figure 8-7   Enclosing contiguous script commands in a single set of script delimiter tags

Now, you will modify the Clearwater Traders home page so that the Product Guide list item includes a hyperlink that calls the Product Guide ASP. Then, you will test the hyperlink and the ASP.

To add the hyperlink and test the ASP:

1. In Notepad, open the **clearwater.html** file from the Chapter8 folder on your Data Disk. Modify the Product Guide list item by adding the hyperlink reference to display the products.asp Web page when the user clicks the Product Guide hyperlink, as shown in Figure 8-8, and then save the file.

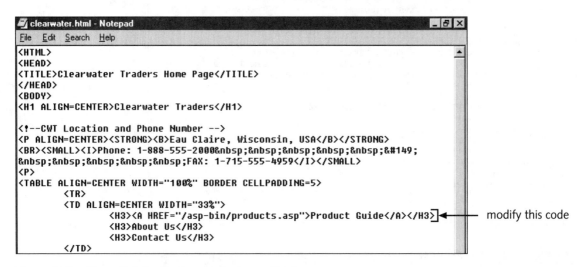

```
clearwater.html - Notepad                                      _ 8 X
File  Edit  Search  Help
<HTML>
<HEAD>
<TITLE>Clearwater Traders Home Page</TITLE>
</HEAD>
<BODY>
<H1 ALIGN=CENTER>Clearwater Traders</H1>

<!--CWT Location and Phone Number -->
<P ALIGN=CENTER><STRONG><B>Eau Claire, Wisconsin, USA</B></STRONG>
<BR><SMALL><I>Phone: 1-888-555-2000     &#149;
     FAX: 1-715-555-4959</I></SMALL>
<P>
<TABLE ALIGN=CENTER WIDTH="100%" BORDER CELLPADDING=5>
        <TR>
        <TD ALIGN=CENTER WIDTH="33%">
                <H3><A HREF="/asp-bin/products.asp">Product Guide</A></H3>   ◄────── modify this code
                <H3>About Us</H3>
                <H3>Contact Us</H3>
        </TD>
```

Figure 8-8   Hyperlink to display products.asp Web page

2. Switch to Internet Explorer, and type **http://localhost/** in the Address box. The Clearwater Traders home page is displayed. Click the **Product Guide** hyperlink. The Product Guide Web page appears with the retrieved data values displayed, as shown in Figure 8-3.

TIP   If the Product Guide Web page is not displayed, or if it is displayed with errors, proceed to the section titled "Debugging ASP Scripts" later in this chapter.

In a Web page with server-side scripts, all of the server-side commands enclosed in <% ... %> script delimiter tags are removed by the Web server when the Web page is processed. Only the finished HTML commands, which might include retrieved data values, are sent to the user's browser for display. Now you will view the source code for the Product Guide Web page in your Web browser. The source code shows the HTML commands that the browser uses to compose the Web page.

To view the ASP source code:

1. In Internet Explorer, click **View** on the menu bar, and then click **Source**. The HTML code for the Product Guide Web page is displayed in Notepad (or your browser's default text editor), as shown in Figure 8-9. Note that the server-side script commands have been replaced by the actual data values that were retrieved from the database.

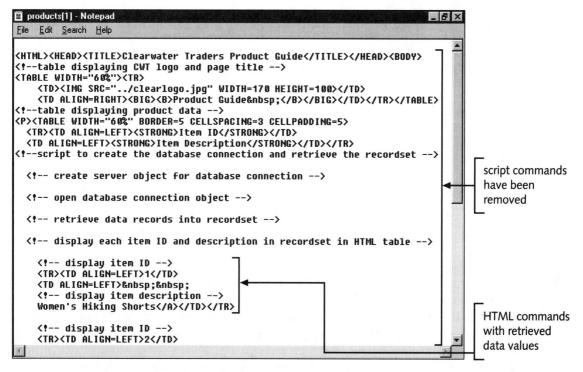

Figure 8-9   Product Guide Web page source code

Passing URL Parameters to an ASP

When the user clicks one of the item descriptions shown in Figure 8-3, the system displays a Web page that describes the inventory information for the specific item, including the available colors and sizes, the associated price, and the item's in-stock status. For example, if the user clicks "Goose Down Sleeping Bag," the associated Order Items Web page shown in Figure 8-10 is displayed.

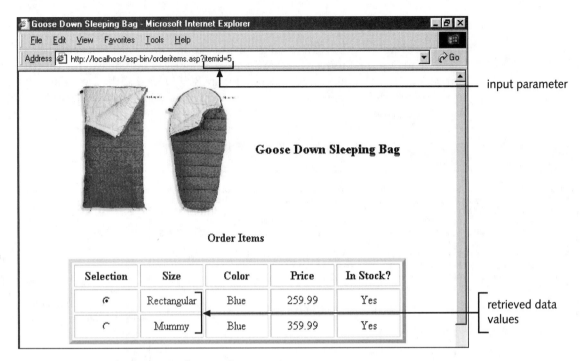

Figure 8-10   Order Items Web page for item ID 5

To create this Web page, you will make an Order Items ASP named orderitems.asp that retrieves the data about the selected item ID from the database, and displays it on the Web page. To display this Web page, you must create a hyperlink from each item description entry on the Product Guide Web page to the Order Items ASP. Since you want to display inventory information for a particular item, you must pass the item ID of the selected item as a URL parameter in the hyperlink. A **URL parameter** is a parameter that is passed to a target ASP as part of the ASP's URL. (Recall that a parameter is a variable value that is passed from one program to another.) Each URL parameter consists of a name/value pair, which consists of the name of the parameter variable, an equal sign (=), and the current parameter value. The general format for the code for a hyperlink that passes a parameter to an ASP is as follows:

```
<A HREF=[ASP filename]?[parameter name]=[parameter value]>
[item hyperlink is attached to]</A>
```

Note that the parameter list is separated from the ASP filename with a question mark (?). This indicates to the Web server that the values that follow are parameters. If there are multiple URL parameter name/value pairs, each pair is separated from the next by an ampersand (&). When you are passing a parameter that will be used as a search condition in a SQL query, it is a good practice to give the parameter the same name as the corresponding database field, to keep parameter names from becoming confusing.

Often, the URL parameter variable value is a value that must be inserted within the hyperlink tag. For example, to create the hyperlink between the Product Guide Web page and the

Order Items ASP, you will need to insert the current ITEMID value from the rsItem record-set as a URL parameter named itemid. Recall that the script command to reference the current ITEMID value in the rsItem recordset is `<% =rsItem("ITEMID") %>`. The hyperlink tag that calls the orderitems.asp file and passes the itemid variable as a URL parameter is formed as follows:

```
<A HREF=orderitems.asp?itemid=<% =rsItem("ITEMID") %>
```

Now you will modify the Product Guide Web page so that each item description has a hyperlink to orderitems.asp, which you will create in the next section. This hyperlink will pass the value of the current item description's associated item ID as a URL parameter within the hyperlink. The parameter variable value name will be itemid, which is the same as the corresponding database field name. The parameter value will be inserted using a script tag that retrieves the current ITEMID value from the rsItem recordset.

To create hyperlinks with dynamic URL parameter values on the Product Guide Web page:

1. Switch to Notepad, and modify the Do While loop in the products.asp file to create a hyperlink for each item description, as shown in Figure 8-11.

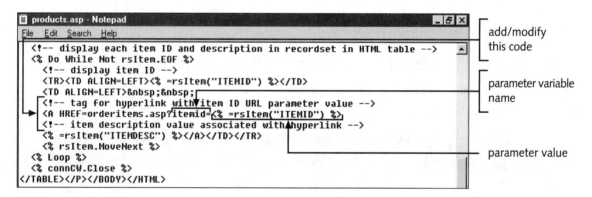

Figure 8-11   Creating a hyperlink with a dynamic URL parameter

2. Save the file, switch to Internet Explorer, and refresh the display. Each item description entry should now be displayed as a hyperlink.

3. Place the mouse pointer on **Women's Hiking Shorts**, but *do not click the hyperlink*. The hyperlink filename and URL parameter value are displayed in the status bar at the bottom of the browser window, as shown in Figure 8-12.

Clearwater Traders Product Guide - Microsoft Internet Explorer

File   Edit   View   Favorites   Tools   Help

Address   http://localhost/asp-bin/products.asp   Go

CLEARWATER TRADERS

Product Guide

Item ID	Item Description
1	Women's Hiking Shorts
2	Women's Fleece Pullover
3	Airstream Canvas Shoes
4	All-Weather Mountain Parka
5	Goose Down Sleeping Bag

mouse pointer

hyperlink filename
and URL
parameter value

http://localhost/asp-bin/orderitems.asp?itemid=1   Local intranet

Figure 8-12   Product Guide Web page with hyperlinks

TIP
If the status bar is not displayed on the Internet Explorer window, click View on the menu bar, and then click Status Bar.

TIP
If your hyperlink filename and/or URL parameter value are not the same as the ones shown in Figure 8-12, recheck the modifications you made to the products.asp file and make sure they look exactly like the ones shown in Figure 8-11.

Retrieving Input Parameters into an ASP

To create the Order Items Web page shown in Figure 8-10, you will create an ASP based on an HTML Web page template file named orderitems_template.html, which is stored in the Chapter8 folder on your Data Disk. You will add server-side script commands to retrieve the item ID data value passed as a URL parameter from the Product Guide Web page (see Figure 8-12). First, you will open the orderitems_template HTML file and save it as an ASP file named orderitems.asp in the asp-bin folder on your Data Disk.

To open the template file:

1. Switch to Notepad, open **orderitems_template.html** from the Chapter8 folder on your Data Disk, and save the file as **orderitems.asp** in the Chapter8\asp-bin folder on your Data Disk.

2. Switch to Internet Explorer, and click the **Women's Hiking Shorts** hyperlink. The Order Items Web page is displayed, as shown in Figure 8-13. Currently, the data values displayed on the page are hard-coded.

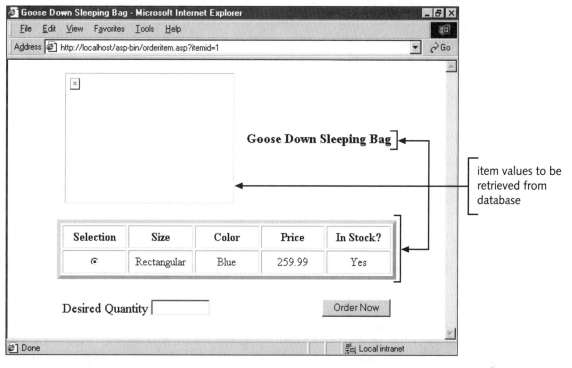

Figure 8-13   Order Items Web page template

3. Click the **Back** button ⇐ on the browser toolbar to return to the Product Guide Web page.

The Order Items Web page shown in Figure 8-13 retrieves the inventory detail records for the item ID that was passed to the page as a URL parameter. It allows the user to view the selected item's available sizes and colors, and see whether a particular item is in stock. If the user decides to purchase an item, he or she selects the option button associated with the desired item, specifies an order quantity in the Desired Quantity input box, and then clicks the Order Now button to submit the order to Clearwater Traders. In Figure 8-13, the item's graphic image is not yet displayed, because you need to query the database to specify the image filename. Also, the data values for item ID 5 (Goose Down Sleeping Bag) are currently hard-coded into the Web page, so these values are displayed regardless of which hyperlink you click on the Product Guide Web page.

To retrieve the data values from the database and display them on the Order Items Web page, you will retrieve the itemid URL parameter that is passed from the Product Guide Web page, and assign the value to a variable within the Order Items ASP script code. Then, you will use this variable as part of a query search condition to retrieve the inventory information that is displayed on the Order Items Web page.

To retrieve the value of a variable that is passed as a URL parameter, you use the Request object, which is an object within an ASP that stores information that is sent from a user's browser to the Web server. The Request object has a Querystring property, which contains the name of the variable whose value will be retrieved as a URL parameter. To retrieve a URL variable value using the Request object's Querystring property, you use the following syntax:

```
<% =Request.Querystring("[parameter variable name]") %>
```

For example, to retrieve the value of a URL parameter named itemid that was passed to an ASP as a URL parameter, you would use the following code:

```
<% =Request.Querystring("itemid") %>
```

The parameter name within the quotation marks is case sensitive. In this book, URL parameter variable names are always written in lowercase letters.

Now you will add a command to the Order Items ASP to retrieve the item ID value that is passed to the ASP as a URL parameter. The parameter value will be stored in a variable named intItemID in the ASP. You will also add code to create a database connection object, open the connection, and retrieve the associated item description and item image into a recordset named rsItem, using a SQL query that uses the retrieved item ID as a search condition. Since the retrieved item ID is stored as a variable, the variable must be concatenated to the SQL query string.

It can be tricky to create SQL queries that use URL parameters, because you must concatenate text strings, blank spaces, and variable values together so that the variable string is formatted correctly. Therefore, whenever you create a SQL query in an ASP that requires concatenating variable values into the text of the SQL query, it is a good practice to create a string variable, and then assign the text that constitutes the query to the string variable. This enables you to view the query string by displaying the string variable value on your Web page. (You will learn how to display a string variable value on a Web page in the section on debugging ASP script code later in this chapter.)

After you have retrieved the inventory data values into the rsItem recordset, you will display the retrieved item description value in the Web page's <TITLE> tag, insert the name of the graphic image file in the <IMG SRC> tag, and insert the name of the item description in the table heading row.

To retrieve the item description and image file based on the URL parameter value:

1. Switch to Notepad, modify the orderitems.asp file as shown in Figure 8-14, and then save the file.

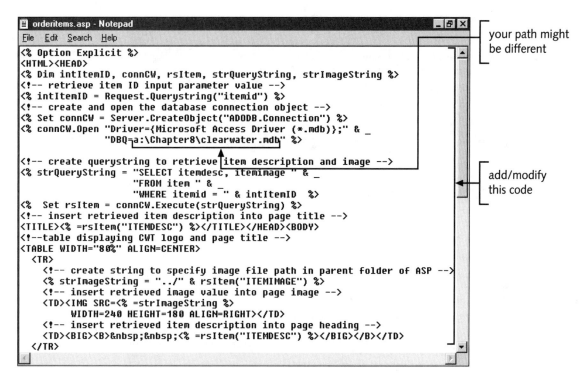

your path might
be different

add/modify
this code

Figure 8-14 Code to retrieve URL parameter into Order Items ASP

2. Switch to Internet Explorer, and click **Women's Hiking Shorts**. The Order Items Web page is displayed, as shown in Figure 8-15. The item image and description are dynamically updated on the basis of the input parameter value. (The inventory data records in the table at the bottom of the Web page still display data for the Goose Down Sleeping Bag, which are hard-coded data values.)

TIP

If the Web page shown in Figure 8-15 is not displayed, or if an error message is displayed, go to the next section on debugging ASP scripts.

3. Click the **Back** button ⬅ on the browser toolbar to return to the Product Guide Web page, and click **Women's Fleece Pullover**. The Order Items Web page is updated to show the Women's Fleece Pullover data in the page heading.

4. Click ⬅ to return to the Product Guide Web page.

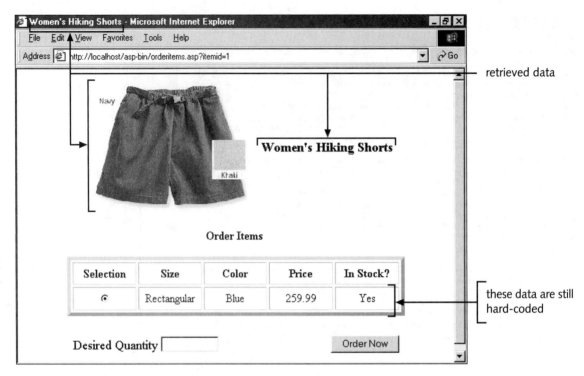

Figure 8-15   Order Items Web page with retrieved data

Debugging ASP Scripts

Debugging strategies for ASP scripts are similar to the debugging strategies you learned in Chapter 7 for client-side scripts. The common errors of forgetting to save a modified ASP file, or displaying a cached version of a previous file, apply to ASPs as well as client-side scripts. Recall that the first step in debugging is to view the Web page HTML source code in the browser, and confirm that the source code that is being used to create the Web page is the most recent version. If you are sure that you have saved the most recent version of your source code, but the correct source code is still not being used to create the Web page, you must make sure you are not viewing a cached version of a Web page. Do this by deleting all previous saved versions from your workstation. (Recall that to delete all previous saved versions, you need to click Tools on the browser menu bar, click Internet Options, click Delete Files, check the Delete all offline content check box, and then click OK.)

When you call an ASP from another Web page and pass URL parameter values, you should always confirm that the parameter name/value pairs are passed correctly by viewing the URL of the hyperlink that calls the ASP. As you saw in Figure 8-12, when you place the mouse pointer on a hyperlink, the name of the file that is called by the hyperlink and the list of URL parameter name/value pairs are displayed in the browser status bar.

Another common error in ASP scripts occurs when you inadvertently omit an opening or closing script delimiter tag. Figure 8-16 shows an example of the Order Items ASP source code in which the closing script delimiter tag for the command that opens the database connection has been omitted. Figure 8-17 shows the error message that is displayed as a result of this error.

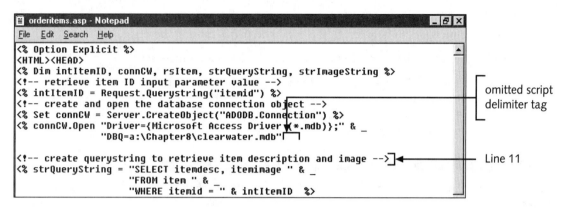

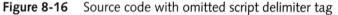

Figure 8-16   Source code with omitted script delimiter tag

Figure 8-17   Error message resulting from omitted script delimiter tag

The error message reports that the error occurs on Line 11 of the source code, although the script delimiter tag was omitted on Line 9. When looking for the causes of errors, always look at the code lines immediately before the line reported in the error message.

If you cannot locate the error visually, the next step is to systematically locate the code line that is causing the error. In an ASP, you can track script execution by adding debugging messages. These message are displayed directly on the Web page. Each debugging message should describe the script code line that was just executed, and should be terminated with a <BR> tag, so that each debugging message will be displayed on a separate line on the Web page. The debugging messages for code lines that retrieve URL parameter values or create SQL query strings should display the value of the retrieved variable or concatenated text string. To display a script variable value in the text on a Web page, you use the following syntax:

```
<% =[variable name] %>
```

For example, to create a debugging message that displays the current value of the strQueryString variable, you would use the following code:

```
Current value of strQueryString = <% =strQueryString %>
```

Now, you will create an error in the source code for the Order Items ASP, and you will add debugging messages to help locate the code line that is causing the error.

To add an error to the Order Items ASP and add debugging messages:

1. Switch to Notepad, modify the code line that inserts the retrieved item description into the page title, as shown in Figure 8-18, by deleting the leading equal sign (=) in the reference to the ITEMDESC field in the rsItem recordset (which introduces a syntax error), and then save the file.

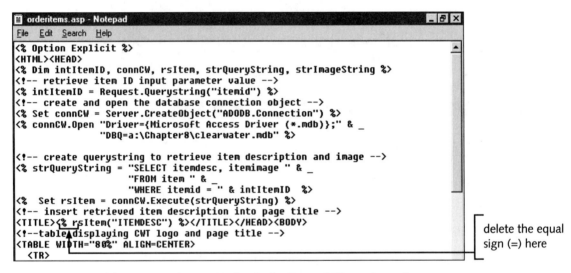

Figure 8-18   Adding a syntax error to the Order Items ASP source code

2. Switch to Internet Explorer, and click **Women's Hiking Shorts**. A blank Web page is displayed, unless you have other errors in your code. Since no error message appears that reports the line number of the source code command causing the error, you will need to add debugging messages to locate the error. Click the **Back** button on the browser toolbar to redisplay the Product Guide Web page.

3. Switch back to Notepad, add the six debugging messages shown in Figure 8-19, and then save the file.

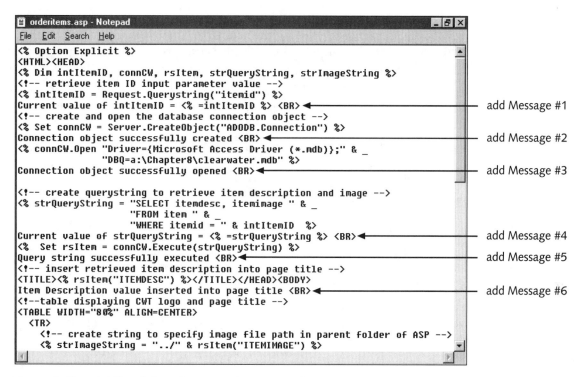

```
orderitems.asp - Notepad
File  Edit  Search  Help
<% Option Explicit %>
<HTML><HEAD>
<% Dim intItemID, connCW, rsItem, strQueryString, strImageString %>
<!-- retrieve item ID input parameter value -->
<% intItemID = Request.Querystring("itemid") %>
Current value of intItemID = <% =intItemID %> <BR>                     add Message #1
<!-- create and open the database connection object -->
<% Set connCW = Server.CreateObject("ADODB.Connection") %>
Connection object successfully created <BR>                           add Message #2
<% connCW.Open "Driver={Microsoft Access Driver (*.mdb)};" & _
               "DBQ=a:\Chapter8\clearwater.mdb" %>
Connection object successfully opened <BR>                            add Message #3

<!-- create querystring to retrieve item description and image -->
<% strQueryString = "SELECT itemdesc, itemimage " & _
                    "FROM item " & _
                    "WHERE itemid = " & intItemID  %>
Current value of strQueryString = <% =strQueryString %> <BR>          add Message #4
<%  Set rsItem = connCW.Execute(strQueryString) %>
Query string successfully executed <BR>                               add Message #5
<!-- insert retrieved item description into page title -->
<TITLE><% rsItem("ITEMDESC") %></TITLE></HEAD><BODY>
Item Description value inserted into page title <BR>                  add Message #6
<!--table displaying CWT logo and page title -->
<TABLE WIDTH="80%" ALIGN=CENTER>
  <TR>
    <!-- create string to specify image file path in parent folder of ASP -->
    <% strImageString = "../" & rsItem("ITEMIMAGE") %>
```

Figure 8-19 Adding debugging messages to an ASP

4. Switch back to Internet Explorer, and click **Women's Hiking Shorts** again to reload the modified Order Items ASP. The debugging messages are displayed as Web page text, as shown in Figure 8-20.

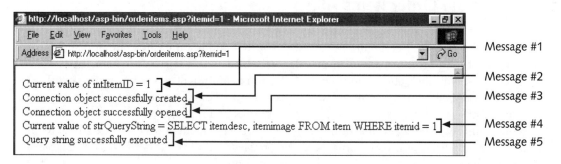

Figure 8-20 Order Items Web page with debugging messages displayed

Note that the first five debugging messages are displayed, but the sixth message (which is below the code line that displays the item description in the Web page title) is not displayed. This indicates that execution proceeded normally through the commands before Message #5, but then execution stopped. Therefore, you know that the error is probably on the code line before Message #6, which is the code line in which you intentionally created the error in Step 1. Also, note that the URL input parameter value for the item ID is correctly displayed as the number 1, and that the SQL query string is formed correctly.

5. Switch back to Notepad, correct the error that you created in the code shown in Figure 8-18, and remove the debugging messages from the orderitems.asp file so that the file looks like Figure 8-14 again. Correct any other errors you find, and then save the file.

6. Switch back to Internet Explorer, click the **Back** button ⬅ to redisplay the Product Guide Web page, and then click any of the hyperlinks and confirm that the Order Items Web page is displayed correctly.

7. Click ⬅ to redisplay the Product Guide Web page.

In summary, use the following strategies to debug server-side scripts:

- View the script source code to make sure that you are viewing the correct source code file. If the source code is not the version you expected, save the source code file in Notepad, and then refresh the display.

- If the source code is not updated after saving the source code file, delete all of the cached files to make sure that you are not viewing a cached version of the HTML file.

- If a code line containing an error is reported by the Web server, examine the code line reported in the error message as well as the code lines above the line with the reported error, and try to spot the error visually.

- If you cannot spot the error visually, or if no error message box is displayed, add debugging messages to your code to track execution progress and variable values.

Finishing the Order Items ASP

Recall that currently the information about each inventory item on the Order Items Web page is hard-coded (see Figure 8-15). Now you will modify the Order Items ASP so that it displays the information for each product associated with the selected item ID. The value associated with the option button in the Selection column will be the inventory ID value for each product. The other columns will display the size, color, current price, and in-stock status. (You will determine whether the inventory selection is in stock a little later.) You will use the connCW database connection that you created earlier, but you will create a new recordset named rsInv that is based on a query that retrieves all of the INVENTORY table fields, using the selected item ID value as the search condition.

To modify the Order Items ASP to display the inventory records:

1. Switch to Notepad, modify the orderitems.asp file as shown in Figure 8-21, and then save the file.

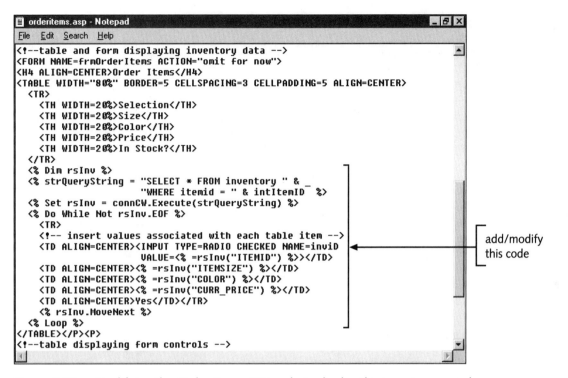

Figure 8-21   Modifying the Order Items ASP code to display the inventory records

2. Switch to Internet Explorer, and click **Women's Hiking Shorts**. The selected item's inventory data should appear in the Web page table, as shown in Figure 8-22.

3. Click the **Back** button ⬅ on the browser toolbar to redisplay the Product Guide Web page, and click **Women's Fleece Pullover**. Note that the inventory records are updated to show the data for the new item.

4. Click ⬅ to display the Product Guide Web page again.

Note that in Figure 8-22, the In Stock? column values are all hard-coded as Yes. You can embed HTML commands within an If/Then/Else conditional structure so that if a condition is true, a specific HTML command will be placed in the Web page source code; if the condition is false, then a different HTML command will be placed in the Web page source code. You will add the commands to determine if the quantity on hand for each item is greater than zero. If it is, then the item's In Stock? value will be Yes. If the quantity on hand is equal to zero, then the item's In Stock? value will be No.

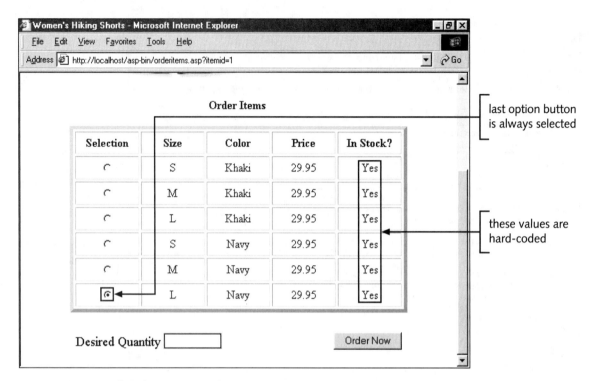

Figure 8-22　Updated inventory values

Also, note that the Selection option button, which is used by the customer to select an item to be ordered, is always selected for the last inventory item in the list. This occurs because as the inventory items are written on the Web page, the option button for each successive item is selected. Since only one option button in an option button group can be selected, the option button for the record that was most recently written is always selected. You will add a loop counter to the code so that the option button will be selected for only the first record.

To modify the script to check the item quantity on hand and select the first option button:

1. Switch to Notepad, modify the orderitems.asp file as shown in Figure 8-23, and then save the file.

2. Switch to Internet Explorer, and click **Women's Hiking Shorts**. The first option button in the table should now be selected, and the In Stock? value for Size L, Color Khaki should now be No.

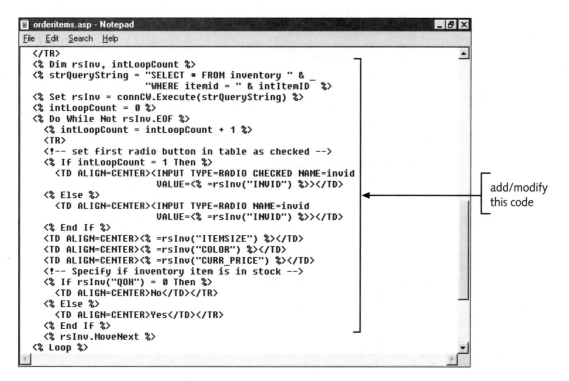

```
orderitems.asp - Notepad                                    _ 8 X
File   Edit   Search   Help
</TR>
<% Dim rsInv, intLoopCount %>
<% strQueryString = "SELECT * FROM inventory " & _
                    "WHERE itemid = " & intItemID  %>
<% Set rsInv = connCW.Execute(strQueryString) %>
<% intLoopCount = 0 %>
<% Do While Not rsInv.EOF %>
   <% intLoopCount = intLoopCount + 1 %>
   <TR>
   <!-- set first radio button in table as checked -->
   <% If intLoopCount = 1 Then %>
     <TD ALIGN=CENTER><INPUT TYPE=RADIO CHECKED NAME=invid
                        VALUE=<% =rsInv("INVID") %>></TD>
   <% Else %>
     <TD ALIGN=CENTER><INPUT TYPE=RADIO NAME=invid
                        VALUE=<% =rsInv("INVID") %>></TD>
   <% End If %>
   <TD ALIGN=CENTER><% =rsInv("ITEMSIZE") %></TD>
   <TD ALIGN=CENTER><% =rsInv("COLOR") %></TD>
   <TD ALIGN=CENTER><% =rsInv("CURR_PRICE") %></TD>
   <!-- Specify if inventory item is in stock -->
   <% If rsInv("QOH") = 0 Then %>
     <TD ALIGN=CENTER>No</TD></TR>
   <% Else %>
     <TD ALIGN=CENTER>Yes</TD></TR>
   <% End If %>
   <% rsInv.MoveNext %>
<% Loop %>
```

add/modify
this code

Figure 8-23   Code to select first option button and determine in-stock status

CREATING A WEB APPLICATION WITH CLIENT-SIDE AND SERVER-SIDE SCRIPTS

Now you will create an application to process Clearwater Traders customer orders. This application will contain both client- and server-side scripts to process orders, display Web pages, and validate user inputs. Figure 8-24 shows the Web pages in this application. All of the Web pages will be created by ASPs. The Order Items and Login Web pages will contain client-side scripts for creating cookies and performing data validation.

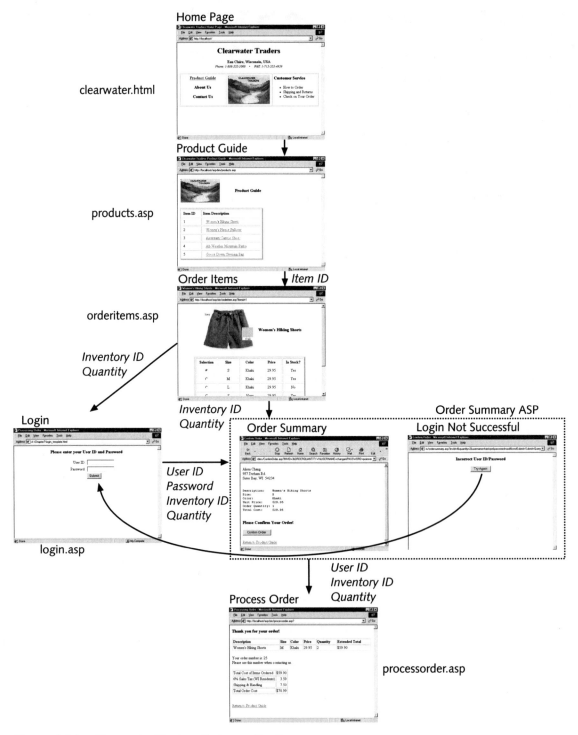

Figure 8-24 Clearwater Traders Order application

You have already created the Clearwater Traders home page, the Product Guide page, and the Order Items page. When the user selects an item on the Order Items page and enters a quantity to purchase, the Login form is displayed. On this form, the user enters his or her user ID and password, and clicks the Submit button, which calls the ordersummary.asp Active Server Page. This ASP is unique because it displays different Web page elements depending on the inputs it receives. If the user logs on successfully, the Order Summary Web page is displayed, which summarizes the customer information and the information about the item that was just ordered. The user can then confirm the order, which inserts the order information data into the database, or return to the Product Guide page and continue shopping. Once the user has successfully entered his or her username and password on the Login form, the Login form will be bypassed whenever he or she adds a new item to the order. If the user does not log on successfully, then the Login Not Successful Web page is displayed. The Login Not Successful Web page tells the user that his or her user ID and/or password is incorrect, and allows the user to link back to the Login Web page to try to log on again.

Figure 8-24 also shows the parameter values that must be passed from one page to another. The Product Guide page passes the item ID of the selected item to the Order Items page. The Order Items page passes the selected inventory ID and the desired quantity to the Order Summary page, and the Login page passes the user ID, password, inventory ID, and quantity to the ordersummary.asp ASP. When a login attempt is successful, the Order Summary page passes the user ID, inventory ID, and quantity to the Process Order page.

Sharing Data Values Among Multiple ASPs

Web applications with multiple pages usually share data values. One approach is to pass data values from one Web page to a second Web page as URL parameters. (Recall that a URL parameter is passed within a hyperlink reference, and that the URL parameter variable names and values are separated from the Web page address or ASP filename in the URL by a question mark. You used a URL parameter when you passed the item ID from the Product Guide Web page to the Order Items Web page.)

A second way to share data values among ASPs is to use **form parameters**. Recall that an HTML form has elements such as text input boxes and radio buttons. When the user clicks a SUBMIT button on an HTML form, the values of all of the form inputs are passed to the Web server as form parameters. Form parameters are similar to URL parameters in the sense that they consist of name/value pairs, and each parameter name/value pair is separated from the next parameter name/value pair by an ampersand (&). Like URL parameters, form parameter values can be processed by a server-side program, or passed to another Web page and used as input variables. Form parameters are more convenient to use than URL parameters for passing form input values from one Web page to another, because you do not have to explicitly specify the variable name and value of each form item within the HREF attribute of the hyperlink tag.

A problem with passing parameters either as URL parameters or as form parameters is that it forces the pages to be viewed in a certain order to ensure that the correct parameters are always passed. For example, the Order Summary page expects to receive the user ID, password, inventory ID, and order quantity as input parameters. However, the user ID and password values are only passed to the Order Summary page for the first order item—when the user orders a second item, he or she is routed directly to the Order Summary page and bypasses the Login page, so the user ID and password values are not available as form parameters. A way to solve this dilemma is to store the user ID as a cookie, since cookie values are available to all of the Web pages in the application.

Calling the Login Form from the Order Items ASP Files

You will first open the HTML template for the Login form and save it as an ASP.

To open the Login form template:

1. Switch to Notepad, and open the **login_template.html** file from the Chapter8 folder on your Data Disk.

2. Save the file as **login.asp** in the asp-bin folder in the Chapter8 folder on your Data Disk.

Next, you will modify the ACTION attribute in the FORM tag on the Order Items Web page to specify the Login ASP as the program that runs when the Order Items ASP is submitted to the Web server. (Note that the "Order Now" button is a SUBMIT form element.)

To modify the Order Items form ACTION attribute:

1. Switch to Notepad, and open **orderitems.asp** from the asp-bin folder on your Data Disk.

2. Scroll down to the `<FORM ACTION "omit for now">` tag, and modify the tag as follows:

   `<FORM NAME=frmOrderItems ACTION=login.asp>`

3. Save the file, switch to Internet Explorer, where the orderitems.asp Web page is currently displayed, and refresh the display.

4. Select the second option button in the table (size M, color Khaki), type **2** for Desired Quantity, and then click **Order Now**. The Login form is displayed, as shown in Figure 8-25.

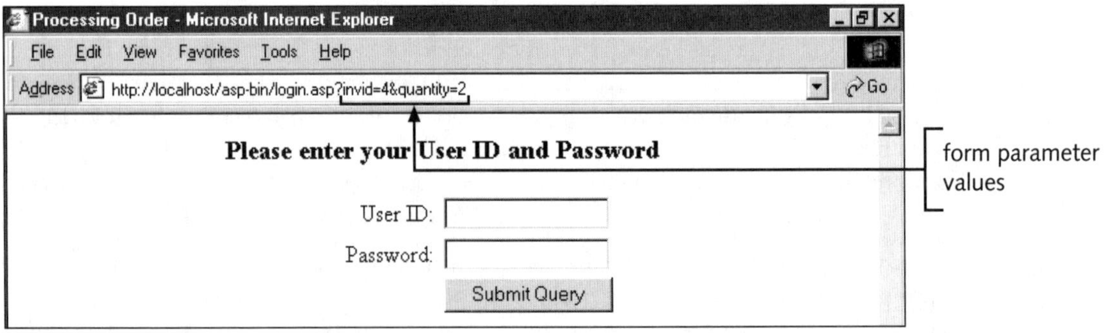

Figure 8-25   Login Web page with form parameters from previous Web page

Note the parameter values that are displayed in the Address box of your Web browser. These values were passed to the Login Web page from the Order Items Web page as form parameters. Recall that the HTML form on the Order Items Web page has two form elements: invid, which is the radio button group that determines which inventory item the user selects, and quantity, which is the text box that displays the desired order quantity. The radio button value corresponds to the inventory ID value in the INVENTORY table for the item that is selected on the Order Items form. (Recall that you selected Women's Hiking Shorts, size M, color Khaki, on the Order Items form.) The form parameter value for invid that was passed to the Web server is 4, which is the inventory ID value for this item in the INVENTORY table in the Clearwater Traders database. Since you typed 2 for the desired order quantity, the parameter value for the quantity form element that was passed to the Web server is 2.

 Sometimes you do not want to display all form parameters in the Address box. You will learn how to suppress the display of form parameter values later in this chapter. While you are developing Web pages, it is a good idea to display the parameter values to aid in debugging.

Creating the Login Form ASP

Figure 8-24 shows that the Login Web page receives the selected inventory ID and order quantity as form parameters, and then passes the selected inventory ID and order quantity to the Order Summary page as form parameters. To pass these values, you must create a form on the Login ASP that retrieves and stores these form parameter values, and then passes the values to the Order Summary page as form parameters. Since you do not want to display the inventory ID and order quantity values on the Login Web page, you will store the form parameter values in hidden form fields.

Storing Form Parameter Values in Hidden Form Fields

Now you will create the hidden form fields to store the inventory ID and desired quantity. You will create these fields, and then assign their VALUE attribute to the values passed as form parameters to the Login Web page. As you learned earlier, to retrieve the value of an individual input parameter string item that is passed to an ASP, you use the Request.Querystring object property. Recall that you used Request.Querystring to retrieve the form URL value that was passed from the Product Guide Web page to the Order Items Web page, and that it had the following general format:

```
<% =Request.Querystring("[parameter variable name]") %>
```

The format of the command is the same for form parameters. The code to retrieve the value for the invid form parameter that was passed from the Order Items form is as follows:

```
<% =Request.Querystring("invid") %>
```

Recall that the text within the quotation marks is case sensitive, so the variable name must *exactly* match the name of the form element in the form that is passing the parameter to the Web server. For example, the commands Request.Querystring("Invid") or Request.Querystring("InvID") will not assign the passed form parameter to the new form field. In this book, form fields are always named using all lowercase letters to simplify the matching process.

To create the hidden form items and store the form input parameter values:

1. Switch to Notepad, and open **login.asp** from the asp-bin folder in the Chapter8 folder on your Data Disk.

2. Add the code shown in Figure 8-26 to create the hidden form fields, and then save the file.

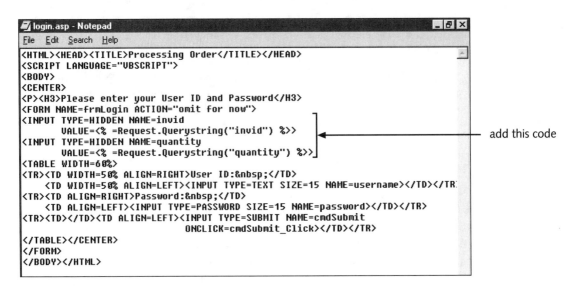

add this code

Figure 8-26 Creating hidden form fields to share form parameter values

Creating an ASP to Verify the Username and Password and Summarize the Order Data

As you saw in Figure 8-24, the user enters his or her username and password in the Login Web page, and clicks the Submit button. This calls the Order Summary ASP. The Order Summary ASP is unique, because the Web page elements it displays depend on the user ID and password values that it receives. The Order Summary ASP has code that verifies that the user ID and password are correct. If these values are valid, then the Order Summary Web page elements summarizing the user information and the details for the item just ordered are displayed, as shown in Figure 8-27.

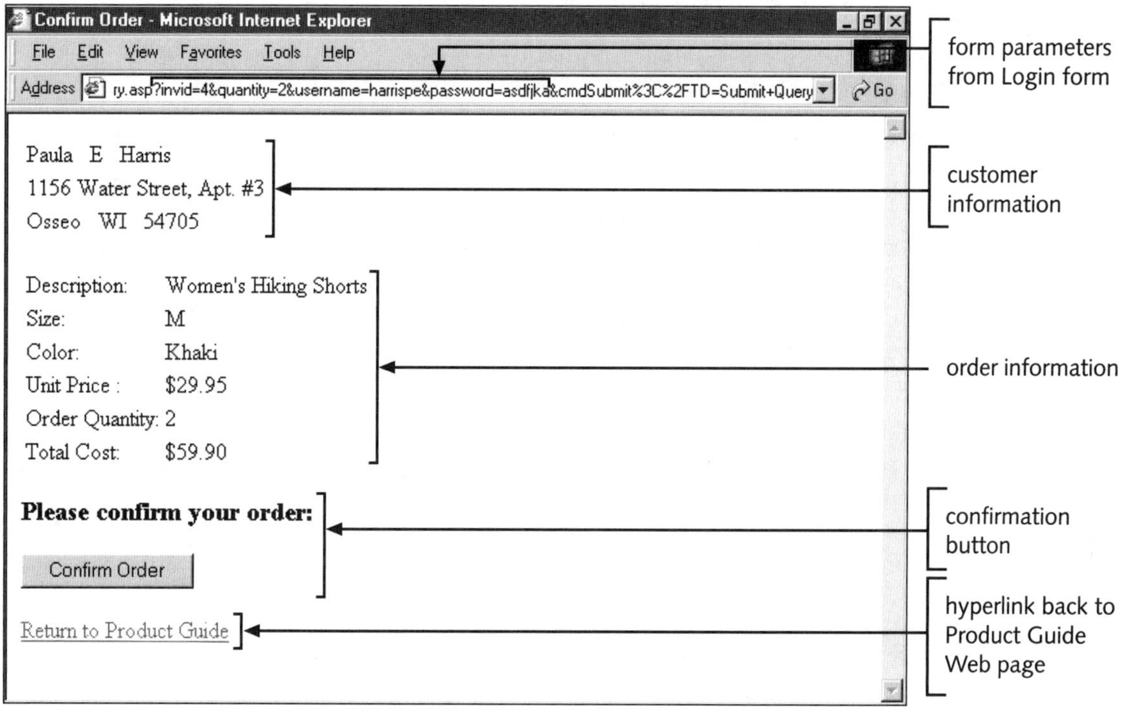

Figure 8-27   Order Summary Web page elements

If the user ID/password combination is not correct, then the Web page elements shown in Figure 8-28 are displayed. When the user clicks "Try Again," the Login Web page is redisplayed.

Figure 8-28   Web page elements informing user of unsuccessful login attempt

First, you will modify the ACTION attribute of the form tag in the Login Web page HTML code so that it calls the Order Summary ASP when the user clicks the Submit button.

To modify the Login form's ACTION attribute:

1. In Notepad, modify the ACTION attribute in the Login form as follows, and then save the file:

```
<FORM NAME=frmLogin ACTION=ordersummary.asp>
```

Now you will write the code for the Order Summary ASP. First, you will write the code to retrieve the user ID, password, inventory ID, and order quantity values that are passed as form parameters to the ASP. These values will be retrieved into variables within the ASP, using the Request.Querystring property. Then, you will create a database connection object, open the connection, and create a SQL query string that retrieves all of the fields from the CUSTOMER table for the customer record associated with the user ID and password values that were received as form parameters.

Creating this query string is a bit tricky, because the username and password fields that will be used as search conditions in the query are text fields. Recall that a search condition value that is a text string must be enclosed in single quotation marks in a SQL query. Since you are creating a concatenated text string based on variable values for the username and password that are stored as ASP variables, you must include the single quotation marks as the literal part of the SELECT query.

For example, suppose that you want to create the following SQL query string:

```
SELECT custid FROM customer WHERE username = 'harrispe' AND
password = 'asdfjka'
```

If the search condition values ("harrispe" and "asdfjka") are referenced as variables, you must concatenate the single quotation marks that enclose the search condition value into the text on either side of the search condition. Suppose that the username value is referenced using a variable named strUsername, and the password value is referenced using a variable named strPassword. The code to create a SQL query string referenced by a variable named strQuery that creates the query shown above, using variables for the user ID and password values, is as follows:

```
strQueryString = "SELECT custid FROM customer WHERE username
= '" & strUsername & "' AND password = '" & strPassword &
"'"
```

Note that the opening single quotation marks for each search variable are included in the query string text just before the variable names, and that the closing single quotation marks are included in the query string text just after the variable names.

Now you will create the Order Summary ASP code to retrieve the user ID and password form parameters, create and open the database connection object, and create and execute the SQL query string. For now, the only output on the Web page will be the customer ID of the customer record that was retrieved on the basis of the user ID and password values entered by the user. This output will confirm that the query is working correctly. (You will add the code to display the correct Web page elements later.)

To write the Order Summary ASP code:

1. In Notepad, create a new file, type the commands shown in Figure 8-29, and then save the file as **ordersummary.asp** in the Chapter8\asp-bin folder on your Data Disk.

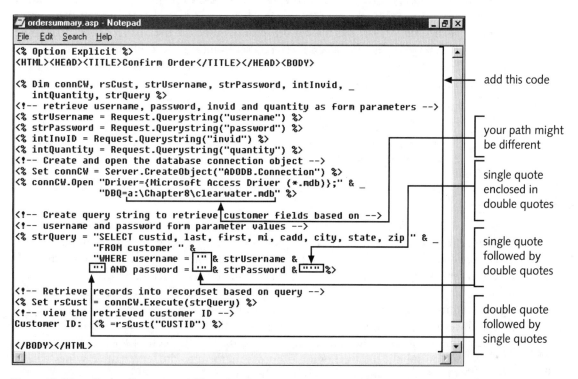

```
ordersummary.asp - Notepad
File  Edit  Search  Help
<% Option Explicit %>
<HTML><HEAD><TITLE>Confirm Order</TITLE></HEAD><BODY>

<% Dim connCW, rsCust, strUsername, strPassword, intInvid, _     ← add this code
    intQuantity, strQuery %>
<!-- retrieve username, password, invid and quantity as form parameters -->
<% strUsername = Request.Querystring("username") %>
<% strPassword = Request.Querystring("password") %>            your path might
<% intInvID = Request.Querystring("invid") %>                 be different
<% intQuantity = Request.Querystring("quantity") %>
<!-- Create and open the database connection object -->       single quote
<% Set connCW = Server.CreateObject("ADODB.Connection") %>    enclosed in
<% connCW.Open "Driver={Microsoft Access Driver (*.mdb)};" & _ double quotes
              "DBQ=a:\Chapter8\clearwater.mdb" %>

<!-- Create query string to retrieve customer fields based on -->
<!-- username and password form parameter values -->          single quote
<% strQuery = "SELECT custid, last, first, mi, cadd, city, state, zip" & _  followed by
             "FROM customer " &                               double quotes
             "WHERE username = '" & strUsername &
             "' AND password = '" & strPassword & "'"%>

<!-- Retrieve records into recordset based on query -->       double quote
<% Set rsCust = connCW.Execute(strQuery) %>                   followed by
<!-- view the retrieved customer ID -->                       single quotes
Customer ID: <% =rsCust("CUSTID") %>

</BODY></HTML>
```

Figure 8-29   Order Summary ASP code

2. Switch to Internet Explorer, where the Login form is displayed. Refresh the display, type **harrispe** for the username, type **asdfjka** for the password, and click **Submit Query**. The Order Summary Web page should be displayed, showing the text "Customer ID: 1". If a Web page with errors is displayed, use the debugging strategies described earlier to debug your ASP code until the customer ID value is displayed.

3. Click the **Back** button ⇦ on the browser toolbar to redisplay the Login form.

Now you need to add the conditional (If/Then) statement to the Order Summary ASP code, so that the ASP displays the correct Web page elements corresponding to the username and password that it receives as form parameters. Recall that if the user enters a valid username and password, the ASP generates the HTML code for the Order Summary Web page shown in Figure 8-27. If the user enters an invalid username and password, the ASP generates the HTML code for the unsuccessful login Web page shown in Figure 8-28.

If the user enters a valid user ID/ password combination, then the rsCust recordset that you created in the Order Summary ASP code in Figure 8-29 will contain data for the associated customer record. If the user enters an invalid user ID/password combination, then the rsCust recordset will not contain any data. To determine if a recordset contains data records, you use the recordset beginning-of-file (BOF) and end-of-file (EOF) properties. The BOF recordset property is true when the **recordset pointer**—which indicates the position of the current record in the recordset that is available for processing—is before the first recordset record. The EOF recordset property is true when the recordset pointer is beyond the last record in the recordset. Therefore, if the recordset does not contain any records, both the BOF and EOF properties are false, and the recordset pointer is pointing to a valid recordset record.

The command to determine if a recordset contains any records is as follows:

```
If Not [recordset name].BOF And Not [recordset name].EOF Then
    [processing statements for recordset that contains one
    or more records]
Else
    [alternate processing statements for empty recordset]
End If
```

Now you will add the code to determine if the user entered a valid user ID/password combination. If the user entered valid values, then the customer ID value corresponding to the user ID and password will be displayed. If the user did not enter valid values, then the Web page elements shown in Figure 8-28 will be displayed. The elements in Figure 8-28 are placed in an HTML form named frmLoginNotSuccessful. When the user clicks the "Try Again" command button, the form is submitted to the Web server, and the Login ASP is called. Since the Login ASP requires the inventory ID and desired order quantity as input parameters, you will store these values in the frmLoginNotSuccessful form as hidden form fields. When you submit the frmLoginNotSuccessful form to the server, these values will be passed as HTML form parameters to the Login ASP.

To add the code to test the user ID/password validity:

1. Switch to Notepad, modify the Order Summary ASP by adding the code shown in Figure 8-30, and then save the file.

2. Switch to Internet Explorer, where the Login form is displayed, and refresh the display. Type **harrispe** for the username, and **asdf** for the password. (Note that this is not the correct password value for user harrispe.)

3. Click **Submit Query**. The frmLoginNotSuccessful form elements are displayed, as shown in Figure 8-28.

4. Click **Try Again**. The Login Web page is redisplayed, with the invid and quantity form parameters displayed in the Address box, as shown in Figure 8-25.

Now you will add the code to display the customer information that appears when the user successfully logs on (see Figure 8-27). Currently, only the customer ID value is displayed when the user successfully logs on. You will replace the customer ID with the data fields for the customer name and address.

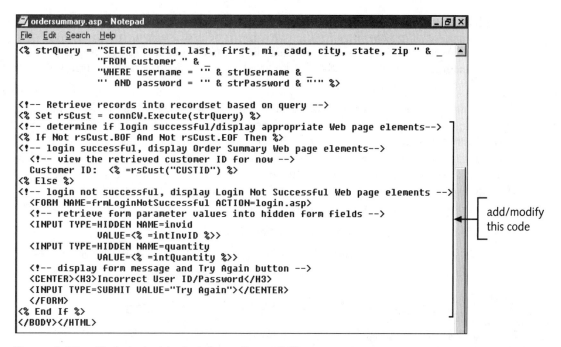

```
ordersummary.asp - Notepad                                          _ 8 x
File  Edit  Search  Help
<% strQuery = "SELECT custid, last, first, mi, cadd, city, state, zip " & _
              "FROM customer " & _
              "WHERE username = '" & strUsername & _
              "' AND password = '" & strPassword & "'" %>

<!-- Retrieve records into recordset based on query -->
<% Set rsCust = connCW.Execute(strQuery) %>
<!-- determine if login successful/display appropriate Web page elements-->
<% If Not rsCust.BOF And Not rsCust.EOF Then %>
<!-- login successful, display Order Summary Web page elements-->
  <!-- view the retrieved customer ID for now -->
  Customer ID:  <% =rsCust("CUSTID") %>
<% Else %>
<!-- login not successful, display Login Not Successful Web page elements -->
  <FORM NAME=frmLoginNotSuccessful ACTION=login.asp>
  <!-- retrieve form parameter values into hidden form fields -->
  <INPUT TYPE=HIDDEN NAME=invid
                 VALUE=<% =intInvID %>>
  <INPUT TYPE=HIDDEN NAME=quantity
                 VALUE=<% =intQuantity %>>
  <!-- display form message and Try Again button -->
  <CENTER><H3>Incorrect User ID/Password</H3>
  <INPUT TYPE=SUBMIT VALUE="Try Again"></CENTER>
  </FORM>
<% End If %>
</BODY></HTML>
```

add/modify this code

Figure 8-30   Code to test login information validity

To add the code to display the customer information in the Order Summary Web page:

1. Switch to Notepad, where the ordersummary.asp file is currently displayed. Add/modify the code as shown in Figure 8-31, and then save the file.

```
ordersummary.asp - Notepad                                          _ 8 x
File  Edit  Search  Help
<% strQuery = "SELECT custid, last, first, mi, cadd, city, state, zip " & _
              "FROM customer " & _
              "WHERE username = '" & strUsername & _
              "' AND password = '" & strPassword & "'" %>

<!-- Retrieve records into recordset based on query -->
<% Set rsCust = connCW.Execute(strQuery) %>
<!-- determine if login successful/display appropriate Web page elements-->
<% If Not rsCust.BOF And Not rsCust.EOF Then %>
<!-- login successful, display Order Summary Web page elements-->
  <!-- display the retrieved customer information -->
  <FORM NAME=frmLoginOK ACTION="omit for now">
  <TABLE WIDTH="100%">
  <TR><TD><% =rsCust("FIRST") %>   <% =rsCust("MI") %>
            <% =rsCust("LAST") %></TD></TR>
  <TR><TD><% =rsCust("CADD") %></TD></TR>
  <TR><TD><% =rsCust("CITY") %>   <% =rsCust("STATE") %>
            <% =rsCust("ZIP") %></TD></TR>
  </TABLE>
  </FORM>
<% Else %>
<!-- login not successful, display Login Not Successful Web page elements -->
  <FORM NAME=frmLoginNotSuccessful ACTION=login.asp>
```

add/modify this code

Figure 8-31   Code to display customer information

    2. Switch to Internet Explorer, where the Login Web page is currently displayed. If necessary, type **harrispe** for the username. Type **asdfjka** (which is the correct password) for the password, and then click **Submit Query**. The customer information shown in Figure 8-27 is displayed. (You will add the code to display the order information next.)

The next step is to add the code to display the order information, which includes the item description, size, color, unit price, order quantity, and total cost of the selected order item. Currently, the inventory ID of the selected item and the order quantity are stored as ASP variables named intInvID and intQuantity. You will create and execute a query string that retrieves the detailed inventory data for the selected item into a recordset named rsInv. Then, you will display the inventory and order quantity information, and calculate the total cost for the item, which is the unit price times the order quantity.

To add the code to display the order information:

    1. Switch to Notepad, where the ordersummary.asp file is currently displayed. Add the code shown in Figure 8-32, and then save the file.

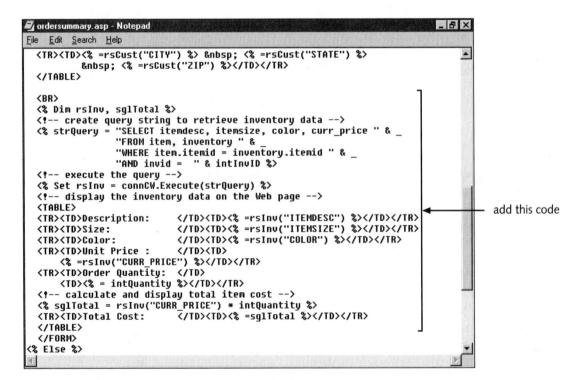

Figure 8-32   Code to display order information

    2. Switch to Internet Explorer, where the Order Summary page containing the customer information is currently displayed, and refresh the display. The information about the selected order item and desired quantity is displayed, as shown in Figure 8-33.

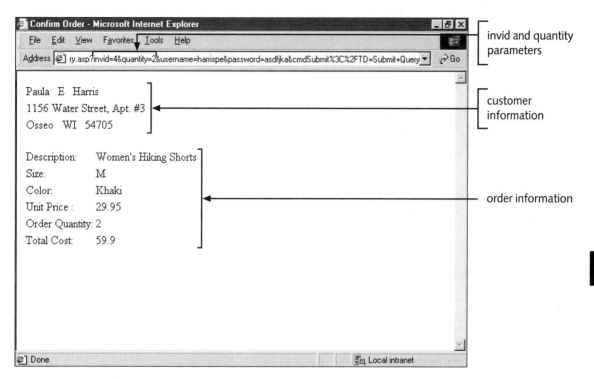

Figure 8-33   Order Summary Web page showing order information

> **TIP**
>
> If the order information is not displayed correctly, or if an error message is displayed, make sure that the inventory ID and order quantity form parameters and their corresponding values are displayed in the Address box, as shown in Figure 8-33. Sometimes when you are debugging a Web page application, input parameters are not passed correctly when you refresh the Web page display. If the parameters are not displayed in the Address box, type http://localhost/ in the Address box, click the Product Guide hyperlink, select Women's Hiking Shorts on the Product Guide Web page, select the option button associated with size M and color Khaki, type 2 for the desired quantity, click Order Now, type harrispe for the user ID and asdfjka for the password, and then click Submit Query.

Notice that the Total Cost value is rounded to only one decimal place. To format this value as currency so that it is displayed with a dollar sign ($) and with two decimal places, you will use the FormatCurrency procedure, which has the following general format:

```
FormatCurrency([value], [desired number of decimal places])
```

Now you will modify the code to display the Unit Price and Total Cost values as currency. You will also add the Confirm Order button shown in Figure 8-27, which allows the user to confirm the order, and the hyperlink reference that allows the user to return to the Product Guide page and continue shopping.

To modify the Order Summary ASP code to display currency values, Confirm Order button, and hyperlink:

1. Switch to Notepad, where the ordersummary.asp file is currently displayed. Add/modify the code as shown in Figure 8-34, and then save the file.

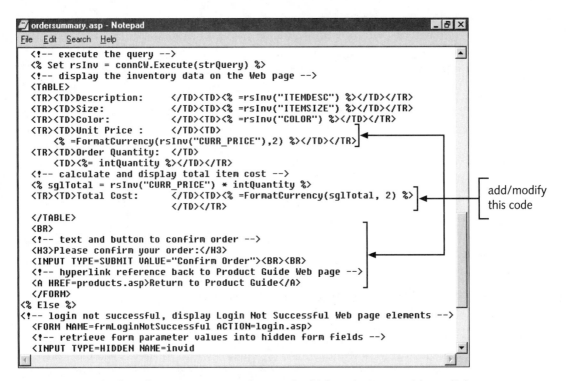

```
ordersummary.asp - Notepad
File  Edit  Search  Help
   <!-- execute the query -->
   <% Set rsInv = connCW.Execute(strQuery) %>
   <!-- display the inventory data on the Web page -->
   <TABLE>
   <TR><TD>Description:      </TD><TD><% =rsInv("ITEMDESC") %></TD></TR>
   <TR><TD>Size:            </TD><TD><% =rsInv("ITEMSIZE") %></TD></TR>
   <TR><TD>Color:           </TD><TD><% =rsInv("COLOR") %></TD></TR>
   <TR><TD>Unit Price :     </TD><TD>
        <% =FormatCurrency(rsInv("CURR_PRICE"),2) %></TD></TR>
   <TR><TD>Order Quantity:  </TD>
        <TD><%= intQuantity %></TD></TR>
   <!-- calculate and display total item cost -->
   <% sglTotal = rsInv("CURR_PRICE") * intQuantity %>
   <TR><TD>Total Cost:      </TD><TD><% =FormatCurrency(sglTotal, 2) %>
                            </TD></TR>
   </TABLE>
   <BR>
   <!-- text and button to confirm order -->
   <H3>Please confirm your order:</H3>
   <INPUT TYPE=SUBMIT VALUE="Confirm Order"><BR><BR>
   <!-- hyperlink reference back to Product Guide Web page -->
   <A HREF=products.asp>Return to Product Guide</A>
   </FORM>
<% Else %>
<!-- login not successful, display Login Not Successful Web page elements -->
   <FORM NAME=frmLoginNotSuccessful ACTION=login.asp>
   <!-- retrieve form parameter values into hidden form fields -->
   <INPUT TYPE=HIDDEN NAME=invid
```

add/modify this code

Figure 8-34   Code to format currency values and add form button and hyperlink

2. Switch to Internet Explorer, where the Order Summary page containing the customer information is currently displayed, and refresh the display. The unit price and total cost values should be displayed as currency, and the Confirm Order form button and Return to Product Guide hyperlink should be displayed as shown in Figure 8-27.

Creating Client-side Scripts in ASPs

In Chapter 7, you learned how to create client-side scripts to validate data in HTML forms and create cookies. You can use client-side scripts within ASPs so that when the user clicks a button on an HTML form, the form runs a client-side script that is embedded within the HTML code on the ASP. This is called **preprocessing** the ASP. To preprocess an ASP using a client-side script, you embed the client-side script commands within the ASP by enclosing the script code in <SCRIPT>...</SCRIPT> tags within the ASP heading section, just as you did with the client-side scripts that you created in Chapter 7. The client-side script commands will be processed by the user's browser just as in any HTML document. The last line of the client-side script then submits the ASP to the Web server for server-side processing, using the Submit method of the HTML document object, which has the following syntax:

```
Document.[form name].Submit
```

Creating and Retrieving Cookie Values Using a Client-side Script

Now you will add a client-side script to the Login ASP to create a cookie that contains the user ID and password. Currently, the user ID and password are being passed to the Order Summary ASP as form parameters, as shown in Figure 8-27. This is fine when the Order Summary is displayed for the first item that the user selects to order. However, when the user selects additional items, the Login Web page is not displayed, and the application proceeds directly from the Order Items Web page to the Order Summary Web page. Since the Order Items page does not store the user ID and password, these values cannot be passed as input parameters to the Order Summary page. To make the user ID and password always available to the Order Summary page, regardless of the user's navigation route, you will create a temporary cookie in the Login ASP to store these values. Then, you will modify the Order Summary ASP so that it retrieves the user ID and password from the cookie rather than as form parameter values.

Now you will modify the Login form's Submit Query button so that it is a regular form input button. Then, you will create a client-side script procedure that executes when the button is clicked. This procedure will create the cookie that stores the user ID and password. After you create the cookie, you will display the cookie contents in a message box to confirm that the cookie was created correctly. (The message box should be removed in the finished application so that the cookie values are not displayed to the user.) Finally, you will submit the form to the Web server for processing.

To create a client-side script that stores the user ID and password in a cookie:

1. Switch to Notepad, open **login.asp** from the Chapter8\asp-bin folder on your Data Disk, add/modify the code as shown in Figure 8-35, and then save the file.

2. Switch to Internet Explorer and type **http://localhost/** in the Address box to display the Clearwater Traders home page. Click the **Product Guide** hyperlink, click the **Women's Hiking Shorts** hyperlink, click the option button associated with size M and color Khaki, type **2** for the desired quantity, and then click **Order Now**. The Login Web page is displayed.

3. Type **harrispe** for the user ID, type **asdfjka** for the password, and then click **Submit Query**. The message box showing the cookie contents is displayed, as shown in Figure 8-36. Note the additional cookie value: ASPs always create a cookie variable that shows an encrypted value for the ASP session ID that is used internally within the ASP for processing.

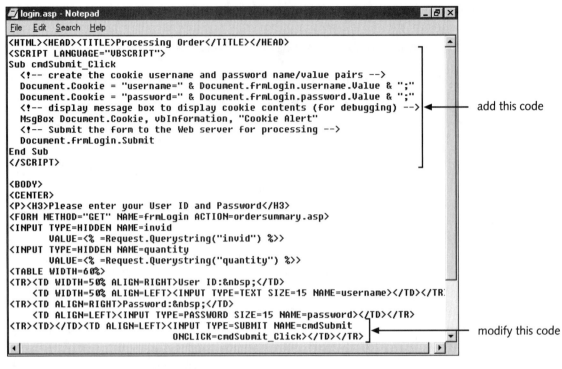

Figure 8-35 Creating a client-side script in an ASP

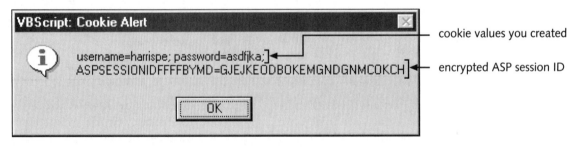

Figure 8-36 Message box showing cookie contents

4. Click **OK** to close the message box. The Order Summary page is displayed. Close Internet Explorer to delete the temporary cookie.

Now you need to modify the code in the Order Summary ASP. Currently, the user ID and password values are retrieved by the Order Summary ASP as form parameters. You will modify the Order Summary ASP code so that it retrieves the user ID and password values from the cookie you just created. To retrieve a cookie value into an ASP variable, you use the Cookies property of the Request object, which has the following format:

```
Request.Cookies("[cookie variable name]")
```

Like the Request.Querystring property, the value in quotation marks (in this case, the cookie variable name) is case sensitive. For example, to retrieve the value of the username cookie variable that you just created, you would use the following code:

```
Request.Cookies("username")
```

Recall that the cookie variable name ("username") was specified in all lowercase letters. The commands `Request.Cookies("Username")` and `Request.Cookies("USERNAME")` would not retrieve the specified cookie value.

To modify the Order Summary ASP code to retrieve the user ID and password from the cookie:

1. Switch to Notepad, open **ordersummary.asp** from the Chapter8\asp-bin folder on your Data Disk, modify the query to retrieve the username and password cookie values as shown in Figure 8-37, and then save the file.

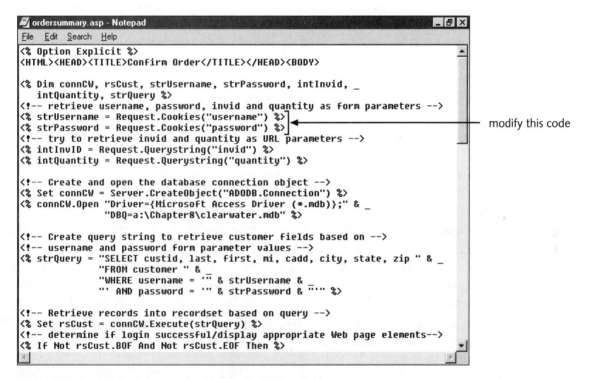

Figure 8-37 Retrieving cookie values into ASP variables

2. Start Internet Explorer, where the Clearwater Traders home page is displayed. Click the **Product Guide** hyperlink, click the **Women's Hiking Shorts** hyperlink, select the option button associated with size M and color Khaki, type **2** in the Desired Quantity input box, and then click **Order Now**. The Login Web page is displayed.

3. Type **harrispe** for the username and **asdfjka** for the password, and then click **Submit Query**. The VBScript: Cookie Alert is displayed.

4. Click **OK**. The Order Summary Web page is displayed as before. However, it is now using the cookie values instead of the form parameters as search condition values.

Using Client-side Scripts to Navigate to ASPs

You can use client-side scripts within ASPs to control the order in which Web pages are displayed in an application. Currently, the Login Web page is displayed whenever the user selects an item to purchase on the Order Items page. The Clearwater Traders customer order application should display the Login Web page the first time the user selects an item to purchase, and bypass the Login Web page for subsequent selections. Now you will create a client-side script in the Order Items ASP that determines if the username cookie value exists. If the cookie value exists, then the Order Summary page will be immediately displayed, and the Login Web page will be bypassed. If the username cookie value does not exist, then the Login Web page will be displayed. To display the correct Web page, you will use the Navigate method in a client-side script, and pass the required parameters as URL parameters.

To modify the Order Items ASP code to call the Login ASP for the first item purchased, and to call the Order Summary ASP on subsequent purchases:

1. Switch to Notepad, open **orderitems.asp** from the Chapter8\asp-bin folder on your Data Disk, and modify the code that defines the form's "Order Now" button, using the following input tag:

```
<INPUT TYPE=BUTTON NAME=cmdOrder
VALUE="Order Now" ONCLICK=cmdOrder_Click></TD>
```

2. Scroll to the top of the file, add the <SCRIPT>...</SCRIPT> tags as shown in Figure 8-38, and save the file.

3. Start a new Notepad session, open **CookieValue.txt** from the Chapter8 folder on your Data Disk, copy all of the text, and then close the Notepad session where CookieValue.txt is open. (Recall that this function is used in a client-side script to retrieve the values of specific cookie variables.)

4. Switch to the Notepad session where orderitems.asp is displayed, and then paste the function code between the <SCRIPT>...</SCRIPT> tags in the position shown in Figure 8-38.

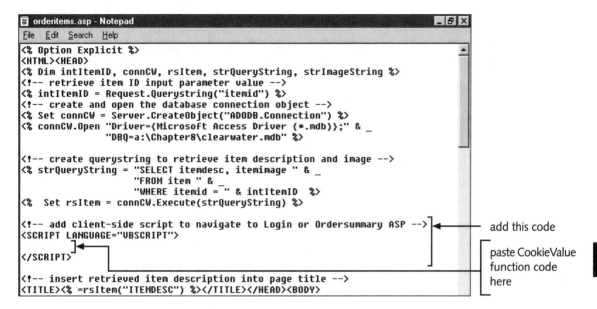

Figure 8-38   Adding client-side script tags to the Order Items ASP code

5. Place the insertion point below the last line of the CookieValue function, press the **Enter** key twice to insert two blank lines, add the code for the cmdOrder_Click procedure as shown in Figure 8–39, and then save the file.

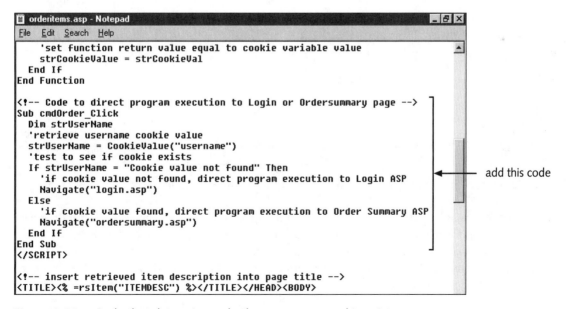

Figure 8-39   Code that determines whether username cookie exists

Now you will test the new code to see if the Login Web page is displayed for the first purchase selection. To do this, you will need to close Internet Explorer, which will delete the values stored in the currents cookie. (Recall that when you create a temporary cookie, its contents are deleted when the user closes his or her browser.) Then you will restart Internet Explorer, select an item to purchase, log in, and view the Order Summary Web page.

To test the script to see if the Login page is displayed for the first purchase:

1. Close Internet Explorer, then restart it and type **http://localhost/** in the Address box. The Clearwater Traders home page is displayed.

2. Click **Product Guide**. The Product Guide page is displayed. Click **Women's Hiking Shorts**. The Order Items page is displayed, showing the inventory information about Women's Hiking Shorts.

3. Select the option button associated with size M and color Khaki, type **2** for the Desired Quantity, and click **Order Now**. The Login Web page is displayed, since this is the first purchase selection.

4. Type **harrispe** for the user ID, type **asdfjka** for the password, and click **Submit Query**. The Cookie Alert is displayed. Click **OK**. The Order Summary Web page is displayed, as shown in Figure 8-40.

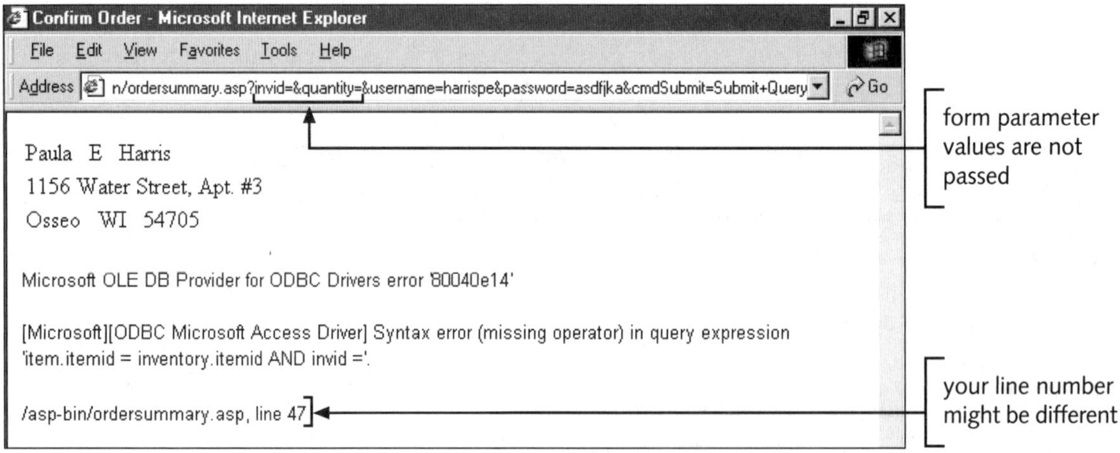

Figure 8-40   Order Summary ASP with unassigned form parameter values

The reason the Order Summary ASP did not display values for the current order item is that the values for the invid and quantity form parameters were not passed to the Order Summary ASP, as shown in Figure 8-40. These parameters were not passed because you used the Navigate method to call the Order Summary ASP, rather than calling the Order Summary ASP using the ACTION attribute of the form on the Login Web page. Recall that when you use the ACTION attribute, all of the form fields are sent to the Web server, and are automatically passed to the indicated ASP as form parameters. When you use the Navigate method, you must pass data values as URL parameters rather than as form parameters. (Recall that

URL parameters are passed by including a question mark [?] after the filename or Web page address, and then listing the parameter names and values, with an ampersand [&] separating each name/value pair from the next.) To call the Order Summary ASP and pass the values for inventory ID 9, desired quantity 2, you use the following code:

```
Navigate("ordersummary.asp?invid=9&quantity=2")
```

To modify the Navigate methods in the Order Items ASP to pass the invid and quantity values as URL parameters to the Login and Order Summary ASPs, you need to know how to reference these values in a client-side script. Recall that the order quantity value is entered by the user in the Order Items Web page into the Desired Quantity input box, and is referenced in the Order Items form using the variable name "quantity".

The inventory ID value depends on the option button that the user selects on the Order Items Web page to specify the desired size and color combination. Finding the value of the option button that is currently selected on an HTML form can be tricky.

Finding the Value of the Currently Selected Button in an Option Button Group

Before you create the code to find the value of the option button that is currently selected on the Order Items Web page, you will first examine the source code for the Order Items page to see how the inventory ID option buttons are set up.

To examine the inventory ID option buttons in the Order Items page source code:

1. If necessary, switch to Internet Explorer, where the Order Summary page is displayed. Click the **Back** button ⇦ on the browser toolbar. The Login Web page is displayed.

2. Click ⇦ again. The Order Items Web page is displayed.

3. Click **View** on the menu bar, and then click **Source**. The source code for the Order Items Web page is displayed.

4. Scroll down to the Web page section that specifies the form option buttons. Your source code should look like Figure 8-41.

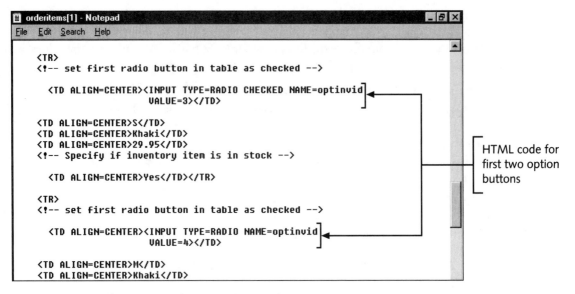

Figure 8-41   Order Items Web page source code

5. Close the source code window in Notepad.

Note that only the first option button has the CHECKED attribute set—when the form is first displayed, only the first option button is selected. (The comments in the HTML code are repeated for each option button, even for the ones that are not checked.) The Name property of the option button group is invid. The VALUE attribute of each individual option button corresponds to the inventory ID value that the option button represents. For example, the first option button represents the Women's Hiking Shorts, size S, color Khaki, which is INVID 3 in the INVENTORY table in the Clearwater Traders database.

To find the value of the currently selected option button of an HTML form, use a client-side script to write script code that searches all of the form fields, and locates the form elements that are in the option button group. When the code finds an option button, it checks to see if the option button is selected. To reference properties of HTML form elements in a client-side script, you use the following general format:

```
Document.[form name].Elements.[property]
```

The property attribute can reference the following values:

- Length, which returns the total number of form elements

- Name, which references the name of an individual form element

- Checked, which determines if a form radio button is selected

Now you will modify the cmdOrder_Click procedure code in the Order Items ASP so that the code finds the inventory ID value associated with the selected option button. To do this, the code will use a For...Next loop to examine each form element, and locate the elements in the option button group, which are the elements whose Name properties are invid. When the script finds an option button, it will then determine if the option button is selected. When it finds the option button that is selected, the option button's value is assigned to a variable named txtInvID, and the loop is exited. The script will then pass the inventory ID and the desired order quantity to the ASPs specified in the Navigate methods as URL parameters.

To modify the Order Items script code to pass the inventory ID and desired quantity as URL parameters:

1. Switch to Notepad, where the orderitems.asp file is displayed. (Make sure that this is the ASP code that contains the server-side script commands, and not the source code that your browser used to generate the Order Items Web page.)

2. Modify the cmdOrder_Click procedure code as shown in Figure 8-42, and then save the file.

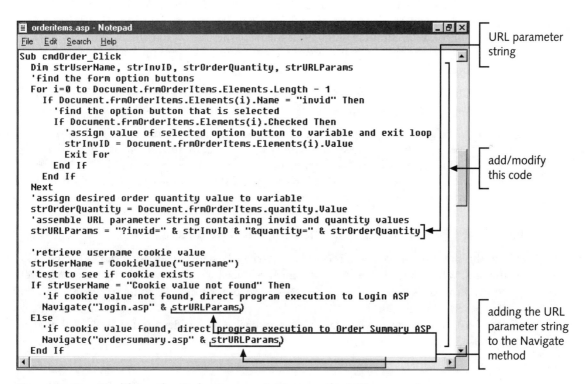

Figure 8-42   Modifying the Order Items script to pass the URL parameters

Now you will test the new code to see if the Web page generated by the Login ASP is displayed for the first purchase selection, and bypassed for subsequent selections. To do this, you will need to close Internet Explorer again to delete the values stored in the current cookie. Then you will restart Internet Explorer, select an item to purchase, log in, select a second item to purchase, and test to see if the Login page is bypassed.

To test the script to see if the Login page is bypassed for the second purchase:

1. Close Internet Explorer, then restart it and type **http://localhost/** in the Address box. The Clearwater Traders home page is displayed.

2. Click **Product Guide**. The Product Guide page is displayed. Click **Women's Hiking Shorts**. The Order Items page is displayed, showing the inventory information about Women's Hiking Shorts.

3. Select the option button associated with size M and color Khaki, type **2** for the Desired Quantity, and click **Order Now**. The Login Web page is displayed, since this is the first purchase selection.

4. Type **harrispe** for the user ID, type **asdfjka** for the password, and click **Submit Query**. The Cookie Alert is displayed. Click **OK**. The Order Summary Web page is displayed, as shown in Figure 8-27. Click **Return to Product Guide** to make a second selection for purchase. (Normally the user would click Confirm Order, but you should not, because you are testing to make sure the Login ASP is bypassed after the user has successfully logged on.)

5. On the Product Guide page, click **Women's Fleece Pullover**. The Order Items page is displayed, showing the Women's Fleece Pullover information.

6. Make sure that the option button associated with size S and color Twilight is selected, type **1** for Desired Quantity, and then click **Order Now**. The Order Summary page is displayed, with the order data about the second item (Women's Fleece Pullover, size S and color Twilight) displayed. Note that the Login ASP was bypassed when the user selected the second item.

Processing the Order and Updating the Database

Up to this point, all of your ASP scripts have retrieved database data using the SQL SELECT command. When the user clicks the Confirm Order button on the Order Summary Web page, the Process Order ASP (see Figure 8-24) executes commands to insert records into the CUST_ORDER and ORDERLINE tables to record the order information. The Process Order ASP then creates a Web page that summarizes the order information, as shown in Figure 8-43.

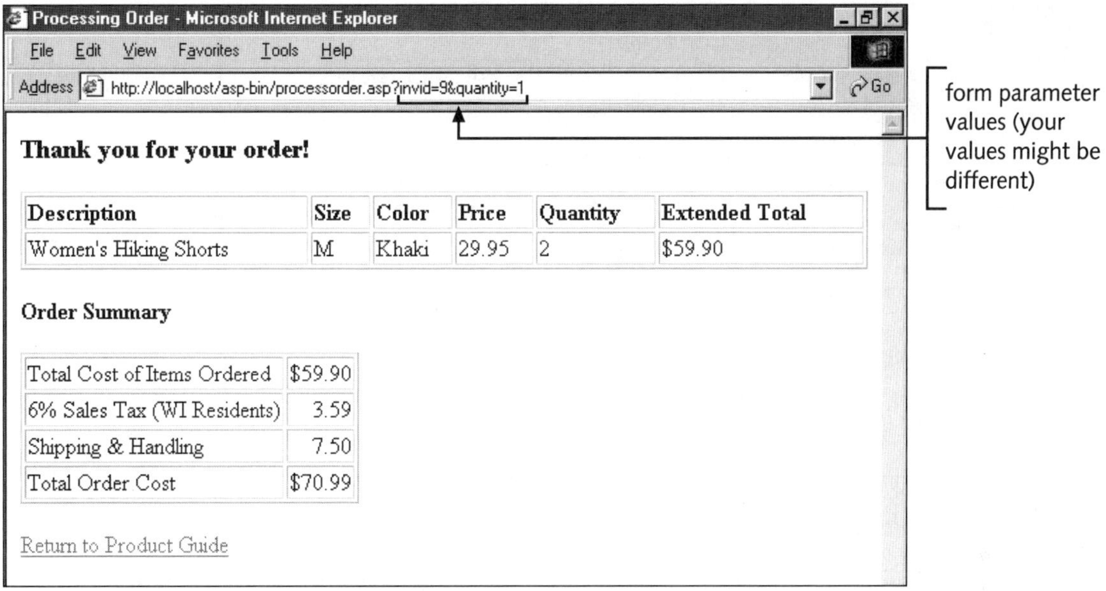

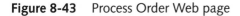

Figure 8-43   Process Order Web page

Next, you will create the Process Order ASP. First, you will open the HTML template for the Process Order Web page from the Chapter8 folder on your Data Disk, and save the file as processorder.asp in the Chapter8\asp-bin folder on your Data Disk. Then, you will modify the Order Summary ASP so that it calls the Process Order Web page when the user clicks the Confirm Order button, and so that it passes the required form parameters to the Process Order Web page.

To make these modifications, you will add hidden fields to the frmLoginOK form on the Order Summary Web page to store the values for inventory ID and quantity as form parameters, since these values must be passed to the Process Order ASP as form parameters. (The code for adding these hidden form fields is similar to the code you used in Figure 8-26 to add the hidden form fields to the Login ASP.) You will also update the ACTION attribute of the frmLoginOK form tag so that when the user clicks the Confirm Order button, the Process Order ASP (processorder.asp) runs.

To open the template, save it as an ASP, and modify the Order Summary ASP:

1. Switch to Notepad, open **processorder_template.html** from the Chapter8 folder on your Data Disk, and save the file as **processorder.asp** in the Chapter8\asp-bin folder on your Data Disk.

2. In Notepad, open **ordersummary.asp**, modify the frmLoginOK code as shown in Figure 8-44, and then save the file.

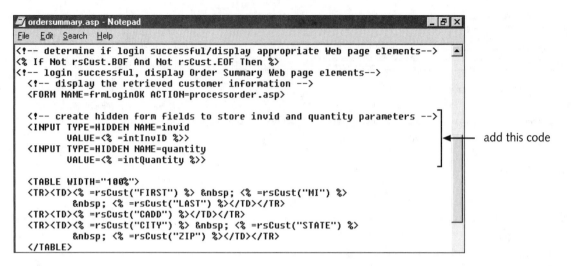

```
ordersummary.asp - Notepad                                           _ 8 X
File  Edit  Search  Help
<!-- determine if login successful/display appropriate Web page elements-->
<% If Not rsCust.BOF And Not rsCust.EOF Then %>
<!-- login successful, display Order Summary Web page elements-->
  <!-- display the retrieved customer information -->
  <FORM NAME=frmLoginOK ACTION=processorder.asp>

  <!-- create hidden form fields to store invid and quantity parameters -->
  <INPUT TYPE=HIDDEN NAME=invid
         VALUE=<% =intInvID %>>
  <INPUT TYPE=HIDDEN NAME=quantity
         VALUE=<% =intQuantity %>>

  <TABLE WIDTH="100%">
  <TR><TD><% =rsCust("FIRST") %>   <% =rsCust("MI") %>
          <% =rsCust("LAST") %></TD></TR>
  <TR><TD><% =rsCust("CADD") %></TD></TR>
  <TR><TD><% =rsCust("CITY") %>   <% =rsCust("STATE") %>
          <% =rsCust("ZIP") %></TD></TR>
  </TABLE>
```

add this code

Figure 8-44   Code to call the Process Order ASP and store hidden form parameter values

3. Switch to Internet Explorer, where the Order Summary Web page is displayed. Refresh the display, and then click **Confirm Order**. The Process Order Web page is displayed, as shown in Figure 8-43. (Currently, all of the data values in the ASP are hard-coded.) Notice that the form parameter values are displayed in the Address box.

4. Click the **Back** button 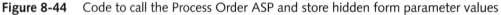 on the browser toolbar to redisplay the Order Summary Web page.

To process the order, you must insert new records into the CUST_ORDER and ORDERLINE database tables. To do this, you must first retrieve the customer ID value for the current user. To find the value of the user's customer ID, you will create a database connection object, open the connection, and retrieve the customer ID based on the username and password values stored in the document cookie. To confirm that the customer ID value was retrieved correctly, you will display the customer ID on the Web page. (The customer ID would not be displayed on the finished Web page.)

To retrieve the customer ID:

1. Switch to Notepad, add the code shown in Figure 8-45 to the beginning of the Process Order ASP, and then save the file.

```
processorder.asp - Notepad                                              _ □ X
File   Edit   Search   Help
<% Option Explicit %>
<% Dim connCW, rsCust, strUsername, strPassword, strQuery, intCustID %>
<!-- retrieve username and password as form input parameters -->
<% strUsername = Request.Cookies("username") %>
<% strPassword = Request.Cookies("password") %>

<!-- Create and open the database connection object -->
<% Set connCW = Server.CreateObject("ADODB.Connection") %>
<% connCW.Open "Driver={Microsoft Access Driver (*.mdb)};" & _
               "DBQ=a:\Chapter8\clearwater.mdb" %>

<!-- Create query string to retrieve customer fields based on -->
<!-- username and password form parameter values -->
<% strQuery = "SELECT custid FROM customer " & _
              "WHERE username = '" & strUsername & _
              "' AND password = '" & strPassword & "'" %>

<!-- Retrieve records into recordset based on query -->
<% Set rsCust = connCW.Execute(strQuery) %>
<% intCustID = rsCust("CUSTID") %>

<HTML><HEAD><TITLE>Processing Order</TITLE></HEAD><BODY>
<H3>Thank you for your order!</H3>
Customer ID is:  <% =intCustID %>
<!-- table summarizing order items -->
<P><TABLE BORDER SIZE=1 WIDTH="100%" ALIGN=CENTER>
  <TR>
    <TH ALIGN=LEFT>Description</TH>
```

add this code

your path might
be different

Figure 8-45   Retrieving the customer ID into the Process Order ASP

> **TIP** This code is very similar to the code in the Order Summary ASP file that is used to retrieve the cookie values and customer information. You can copy the code from ordersummary.asp, paste it into processorder.asp, and then modify it so that it looks like Figure 8-45.

2. Switch to Internet Explorer, where the Order Summary Web page is displayed. Click **Confirm Order** to call the Process Order ASP, which displays the Process Order Web page with the debugging text "Customer ID is: 1" displayed. Note that the order information is still hard-coded.

3. Click the **Back** button ⇦ on the browser toolbar to redisplay the Order Summary page.

The next step is to insert new records in the CUST_ORDER and ORDERLINE tables. There are two approaches for inserting database records in ASPs: you can insert the records using Jet recordset commands, or you can insert records using the SQL INSERT command. The next sections of this chapter illustrate both approaches.

Inserting Database Records Using Jet Recordset Commands

To insert new data records using Jet recordset commands, you must create a Web server object that is a recordset. (Recall that a server object is a memory area on the Web server that is used to process an ASP.) The advantage of using Jet recordset commands is that when you insert a new record in a table where the primary key is an AutoNumber data type, you can then immediately retrieve the value of the system-generated primary key. This is important because after you insert a new customer order record, you must use the ORDERID value as a foreign key value when you insert new records in the ORDERLINE table.

To create a server recordset object, you use the following command:

```
<% Set [recordset name] = Server.CreateObject ("ADODB.Recordset") %>
```

The next step is to open the recordset using the recordset Open method. The general format of the recordset Open method is:

```
<% [recordset name].Open [data source], [connection name],
[cursor type], [lock type], [options] %>
```

This command uses the following parameters:

- **Data source**, which is a text string. If you are creating a recordset for viewing data, then this text string is a SQL query. If you are creating a recordset for inserting, updating, or deleting data, the data source text string is the name of the database table.

- **Connection name**, which is the name of the ADO connection used to connect to the database.

- **Cursor type**, which is a numerical value that specifies how records in the recordset can be viewed. (A cursor is a memory area that stores information about a recordset, such as how recordset data can be viewed.) By default, the cursor type value is the number 0, which specifies that the cursor is **forward-only**. This means that the recordset cannot be changed by inserting new records, or updating or deleting existing records. When you are updating records in a recordset, you should set the cursor type value to 1, which specifies that the cursor is a **keyset** cursor. This means that the recordset can be changed, but the changes are not visible to other database users until the Update method is run on the recordset.

- **Lock type**, which specifies how the recordset records are locked. When this value is set to the number 1, the recordset is **read-only**; new records cannot be inserted, and existing records cannot be updated or deleted. When the lock type value is set to 2, **pessimistic locking** is enabled; this means that all of the records in the database are unavailable to other users until the recordset is closed. When the lock type value is set to 3, **optimistic locking** is enabled, and the recordset records are only locked from other users at the moment the Update method is run. You should use optimistic locking (lock type 3) when updating the database, so that records are not locked from other users for long periods of time.

To open a recordset named rsCustOrder that is associated with the CUST_ORDER table in the Clearwater Traders database, you use the following command:

```
<% rsCustOrder.Open "cust_order", connCW, 1, 3 %>
```

To insert the new data record, you use the AddNew method, which inserts a new blank record in the recordset. Then you specify the values for the record fields, and call the Update method to save the values in the database. For example, to add a new blank record to the rsCustOrder recordset and insert the value 16 for the new order ID, you use the following code:

```
<% rsCustOrder.AddNew %>
<% rsCustOrder("ORDERID") = 16 %>
<% rsCustOrder.Update %>
```

Now you will add the commands to create a new recordset that corresponds to the CUST_ORDER table. First, you will add a new blank record using the AddNew method. Since the ORDERID data field has the AutoNumber data type, the ORDERID value will be inserted automatically. Then, you will insert the values for the order date and customer ID. To specify the order date, you will retrieve the current date on the Web server, using the Date function. (Recall that the Date function in Visual Basic returns the current system date.) You will assign the new record's order ID value to a variable named intOrderID, and display the new order ID on the Web page. Finally, you will view the new record in Access to confirm that it was inserted correctly.

To add the code to insert the new CUST_ORDER record:

1. Switch to Notepad, modify the Process Order ASP code as shown in Figure 8-46, and then save the file.

2. Switch to Internet Explorer, where the Order Summary Web page is displayed. Click **Confirm Order**. The Process Order Web page is displayed, with the retrieved data values for the customer ID and the new order ID displayed at the top of the page, as shown in Figure 8-47.

8

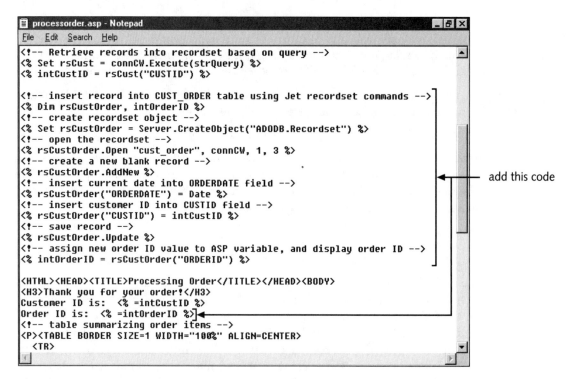

```
processorder.asp - Notepad                                        _ 8 X
File   Edit   Search   Help
<!-- Retrieve records into recordset based on query -->
<% Set rsCust = connCW.Execute(strQuery) %>
<% intCustID = rsCust("CUSTID") %>

<!-- insert record into CUST_ORDER table using Jet recordset commands -->
<% Dim rsCustOrder, intOrderID %>
<!-- create recordset object -->
<% Set rsCustOrder = Server.CreateObject("ADODB.Recordset") %>
<!-- open the recordset -->
<% rsCustOrder.Open "cust_order", connCW, 1, 3 %>
<!-- create a new blank record -->
<% rsCustOrder.AddNew %>
<!-- insert current date into ORDERDATE field -->
<% rsCustOrder("ORDERDATE") = Date %>
<!-- insert customer ID into CUSTID field -->
<% rsCustOrder("CUSTID") = intCustID %>
<!-- save record -->
<% rsCustOrder.Update %>
<!-- assign new order ID value to ASP variable, and display order ID -->
<% intOrderID = rsCustOrder("ORDERID") %>

<HTML><HEAD><TITLE>Processing Order</TITLE></HEAD><BODY>
<H3>Thank you for your order!</H3>
Customer ID is:  <% =intCustID %>
Order ID is:  <% =intOrderID %>
<!-- table summarizing order items -->
<P><TABLE BORDER SIZE=1 WIDTH="100%" ALIGN=CENTER>
   <TR>
```

← add this code

Figure 8-46 Inserting a new CUST_ORDER record using Jet recordset commands

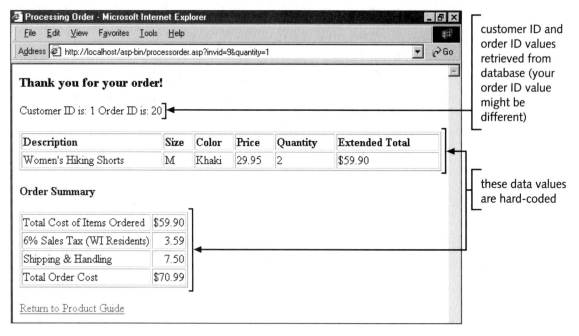

customer ID and order ID values retrieved from database (your order ID value might be different)

Thank you for your order!

Customer ID is: 1 Order ID is: 20

Description	Size	Color	Price	Quantity	Extended Total
Women's Hiking Shorts	M	Khaki	29.95	2	$59.90

these data values are hard-coded

Order Summary

Total Cost of Items Ordered	$59.90
6% Sales Tax (WI Residents)	3.59
Shipping & Handling	7.50
Total Order Cost	$70.99

Return to Product Guide

Figure 8-47 Process Order Web page with customer ID and new order ID values displayed

3. Click the **Back** button ⇦ on the browser toolbar to redisplay the Order Summary page.

4. Start Access, and open **clearwater.mdb** from the Chapter8 folder on your Data Disk. Double-click **CUST_ORDER** in the Tables list to display the CUST_ORDER datasheet. Confirm that a new record has been inserted that shows the current date for the ORDERDATE, and customer 1 for the CUST_ID value.

 TIP If a password logon dialog box opens when you open the Clearwater database, ask your instructor for the appropriate username and password.

5. Close the CUST_ORDER datasheet.

Using SQL Commands to Insert and Modify Database Records

You can also insert and update data records using SQL commands. The advantage of using SQL commands is that it allows your Web application to be used with databases other than Access. The disadvantage of using SQL commands is that there is no easy way to insert a new record into an Access database table that uses the AutoNumber data type for the record's primary key, and then immediately retrieve the value of the new primary key into an ASP variable for further processing.

To insert and update existing records using SQL commands, you use the Execute method with the database connection object. This method has the following syntax:

```
[database connection object name].Execute ("[SQL query string]")
```

Now, you will use a SQL command to insert the order information in the ORDERLINE table, which includes the order ID, inventory ID, order price, and order quantity. You will not insert values for the CSHIPID and COMMENT fields. (Recall that the CSHIPID value in the ORDERLINE table is not inserted until the item is shipped, and a value may be inserted in the COMMENT field when the orderline requires special instructions.) Before you insert the new record, you will retrieve the invid and quantity form parameters into ASP variables, and then retrieve the CURR_PRICE value from the INVENTORY table, which will be used in the INSERT command for the order price.

Creating the query string for an INSERT command that uses variable values is a tricky concatenation operation, because the data values must be enclosed in parentheses and separated by commas. Suppose that you want to create the following SQL query string:

```
INSERT INTO orderline (orderid, invid, order_price)
VALUES (21, 3, 59.99)
```

Suppose the data values to be used for the first three fields in the VALUES clause are stored in the following variables: intOrderID = 21; intInvID = 3; sglCurrPrice = 59.99. The syntax to create a string variable named strQuery that is formed by concatenating the variable values within the literal query string text is as follows:

```
strQuery = "INSERT INTO orderline (orderid, invid, order_price)
VALUES (" & intOrderID & ", " & intInvID & ", " & sglCurrPrice &")"
```

Note that the opening parenthesis for the VALUES clause is included at the end of the literal query string text. Each value within the VALUES clause is separated from the next by a text string consisting of a comma and a blank space (", "). The query string closing parenthesis is concatenated to the end of the query string.

Now you will add the code to retrieve the current price of the selected inventory item on the basis of the form parameters that are passed to the Process Order Web page. You will also create the query string to insert the new ORDERLINE record, and submit the query to the database using the Execute method.

To add the code to retrieve the CURR_PRICE value and insert the ORDERLINE record:

1. Switch to Notepad, where the processorder.asp file is displayed. Add the code shown in Figure 8-48 to retrieve the current price and then insert the ORDERLINE record, and then save the file.

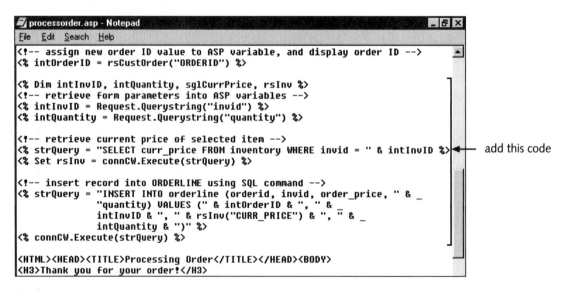

Figure 8-48 Code to insert ORDERLINE record using SQL command

2. Switch to Internet Explorer, where the Order Summary Web page is displayed. Click **Confirm Order** to reload the Process Order ASP. The Process Order Web page should be displayed as before (see Figure 8-47). The order ID value should be incremented by one from the value last displayed, to reflect the next order ID in the AutoNumber data field sequence.

3. Switch to Access, open the ORDERLINE datasheet, confirm that the new ORDERLINE record was inserted correctly, and then close the ORDERLINE datasheet.

4. Switch to Internet Explorer, and click **Return to Product Guide** to display the Product Guide Web page.

After a customer purchases an inventory item, the quantity on hand (QOH) data field in the INVENTORY table must be updated to reflect the purchase. Now, you will add a command to update the INVENTORY quantity on hand using a SQL UPDATE command. To do this, you will update the quantity on hand field in the INVENTORY table for the selected inventory item by subtracting the order quantity from the current quantity on hand.

8

To update the INVENTORY quantity on hand:

1. Switch to Notepad, where the processorder.asp file is displayed. Add the code shown in Figure 8-49 to update the inventory QOH by subtracting the desired order quantity from the current QOH, and then save the file.

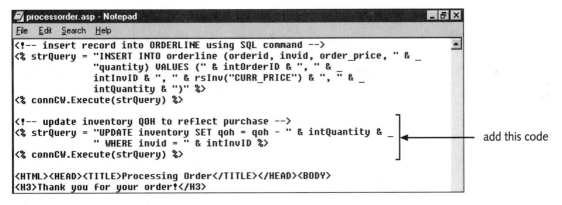

Figure 8-49   Code to update inventory QOH

2. Switch to Access, and open the INVENTORY datasheet. Confirm that the QOH value for INVID 4 (Women's Hiking Shorts, size M, color Khaki) is 147, and then close the datasheet.

3. Switch to Internet Explorer, where the Product Guide Web page is displayed. Click **Women's Hiking Shorts** to display the Order Items Web page, click the option button associated with size M and color Khaki, type **2** for Desired Quantity, and then click **Order Now**. The Order Summary Web page is displayed.

4. Click **Confirm Order** to run the script in the Process Order ASP that inserts the CUST_ORDER and ORDERLINE records, and updates the inventory QOH in the INVENTORY table. The ASP then generates the Process Order Web page, which is displayed in the Internet Explorer window.

5. Click the **Return to Product Guide** hyperlink to redisplay the Product Guide Web page.

6. Switch to Access, open the **INVENTORY** datasheet, and confirm that the updated QOH value is now 145, reflecting that two pairs of shorts have been purchased.

7. Close the INVENTORY datasheet.

Updating the Process Order Display

Except for the customer ID and order ID, the data values displayed on the Process Order Web page are currently hard-coded (see Figure 8-47). Now, you will add the code to dynamically display the order information. First, you will retrieve the order information displayed in the first table on the Process Order Web page. You will retrieve and display the information for each ORDERLINE record for the current order, and calculate the Extended Total value as the product of the price times the quantity. To do this, you will create a SQL query that retrieves the order line information (item description, size, color, price, and order quantity) from the ITEM, INVENTORY, and ORDERLINE tables for each order line corresponding to the order ID. The retrieved records will be stored in a recordset named rsOrderline.

To retrieve the order line information for each line in the order and display it on the Process Order Web page:

1. Switch to Notepad, where the processorder.asp file is displayed. Add/modify the code as shown in Figure 8-50 to retrieve and display the order line information, and then save the file.

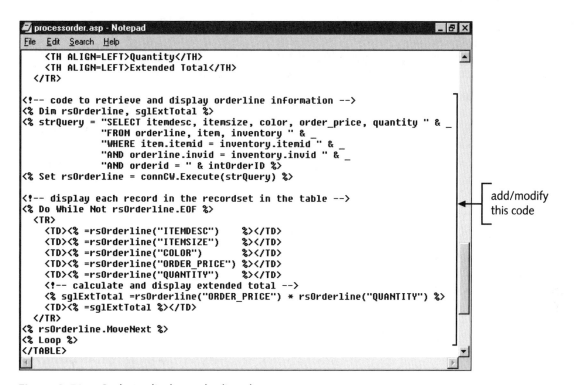

```
processorder.asp - Notepad                                    _ |B|X|
File  Edit  Search  Help
     <TH ALIGN=LEFT>Quantity</TH>
     <TH ALIGN=LEFT>Extended Total</TH>
  </TR>

<!-- code to retrieve and display orderline information -->
<% Dim rsOrderline, sglExtTotal %>
<% strQuery = "SELECT itemdesc, itemsize, color, order_price, quantity " & _
              "FROM orderline, item, inventory " & _
              "WHERE item.itemid = inventory.itemid " & _
              "AND orderline.invid = inventory.invid " & _
              "AND orderid = " & intOrderID %>
<% Set rsOrderline = connCW.Execute(strQuery) %>

<!-- display each record in the recordset in the table -->
<% Do While Not rsOrderline.EOF %>
  <TR>
    <TD><% =rsOrderline("ITEMDESC")    %></TD>
    <TD><% =rsOrderline("ITEMSIZE")    %></TD>
    <TD><% =rsOrderline("COLOR")       %></TD>
    <TD><% =rsOrderline("ORDER_PRICE") %></TD>
    <TD><% =rsOrderline("QUANTITY")    %></TD>
    <!-- calculate and display extended total -->
    <% sglExtTotal =rsOrderline("ORDER_PRICE") * rsOrderline("QUANTITY") %>
    <TD><% =sglExtTotal %></TD>
  </TR>
<% rsOrderline.MoveNext %>
<% Loop %>
</TABLE>
```

add/modify this code

Figure 8-50   Code to display order line data

2. Switch to Internet Explorer, where the Product Guide Web page is displayed. Click **Goose Down Sleeping Bag** to display information about the sleeping bag on the Order Items Web page. Click the option button associated with size Rectangular and color Blue, type **2** for Desired Quantity, and then click **Order Now**. The Order Summary Web page is displayed.

3. Click **Confirm Order**. The order line information is dynamically displayed, as shown in Figure 8-51. Formatting the currency values in the Price and Extended Total columns and updating the Order Summary values will be left as end-of-chapter projects.

8

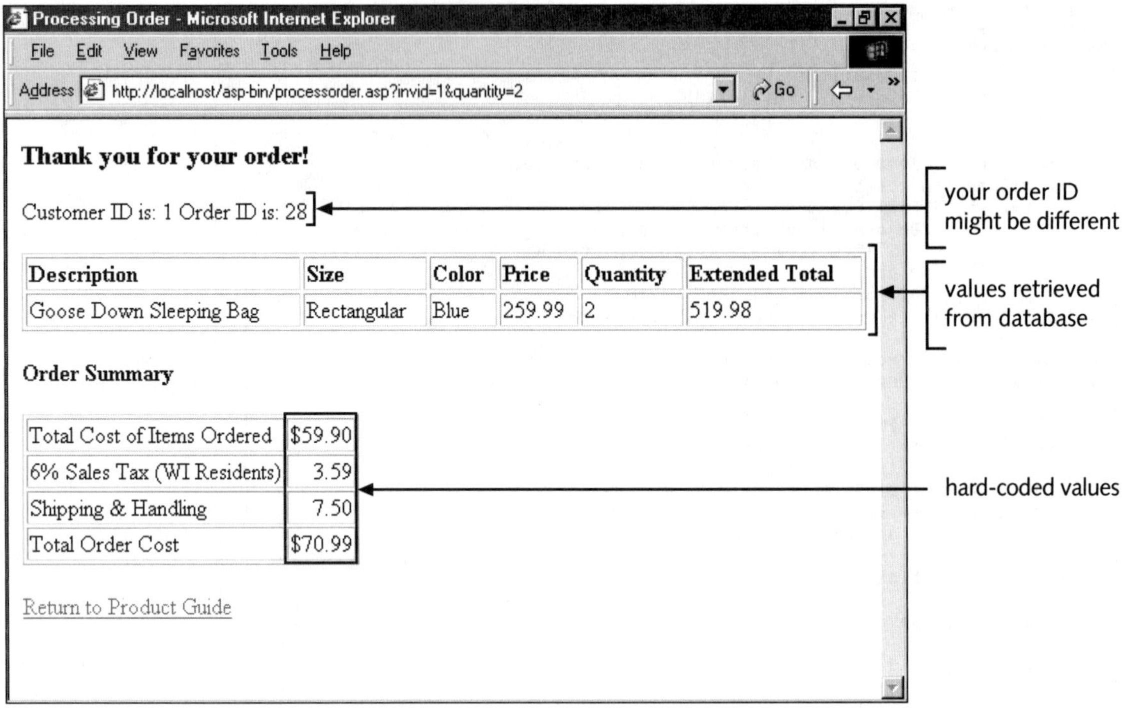

Figure 8-51   Updated order line display

    4. Click the **Close** button ☒ to close Internet Explorer.

Creating Cookies in Server-side Scripts

Currently, each customer order record will always display only a single order line, because each time the user clicks the Confirm Order button on the Order Summary Web page, a new order ID is generated for the current inventory ID and desired quantity values. Now you will modify the Process Order ASP so that the first time the user clicks the Confirm Order button on the Order Summary Web page, a new customer order record is inserted in the CUST_ORDER table, and the order ID is saved as a cookie variable named orderid. If the user clicks the Confirm Order button on the Order Summary Web page a second time to order a second item, the Process Order ASP script code will check to see if the orderid cookie exists. If it does, then the script will not insert a new record in the CUST_ORDER table, but will only insert the ORDERLINE record associated with the second item.

Previously, you created cookies using client-side scripts. Recall from Chapter 7 that cookies can only be created by a user's browser. However, since the order processing is done in server-side script commands, you will need to create the orderid cookie by having the server-side script code request that the user's browser create the cookie. Normally, when an ASP is processed on the Web server, the page output is sent to the browser immediately after each script command is executed. When a Web server requests a browser to create a cookie, this message must be sent in a **header message** to the browser. This arrangement is required because the request to create a cookie must be the first command that the browser receives from the Web server when it sends a Web page to be displayed.

To send a header message instructing a browser to create a cookie name/value pair, the Web page output must be **buffered**, which means that as the ASP commands are executed, all of the output is stored on the Web server, and then is sent to the browser as a single unit after all of the script commands have been executed on the Web server. To buffer ASP output, you use the Response object, which is an ASP object that is used to configure how Web page outputs are communicated back to the user's browser. When you set the Response object's Buffer property to True, the Web page output is buffered on the Web server. This command must be entered before any HTML output is created, so it is usually entered as the second line of an ASP file, immediately after the Option Explicit command. (Recall that the Option Explicit command must always be the first line in an ASP file.)

The command to set the Response Buffer property to true has the following syntax:

```
<% Response.Buffer=True %>
```

To instruct the user's browser to create a cookie name/value pair in an ASP command, you use the Cookies collection of the Response object. The command to create a new name/value pair in a cookie has the following syntax:

```
<% Response.Cookies("[cookie variable name]")="[cookie
variable value]" %>
```

To create a persistent cookie using ASP code, you set the cookie collection's Expires attribute to the desired expiration date. To create a temporary cookie, you do not set the Expires attribute. For example, to create a temporary cookie named orderid that has the value 20, you use the following script command:

```
<% Response.Cookies("orderid")="20" %>
```

The cookie value is always specified as a text string. To create a persistent cookie that expires on December 31, 2002, you use the following command:

```
<% Response.Cookies("orderid").Expires="Dec 31, 2002" %>
```

Now you will modify the Process Order ASP code to check to see if the orderid cookie exists. If it does not exist, then the code creates a new customer order record, creates the orderid cookie, and inserts the order line information in the ORDERLINE table. If the orderid cookie already exists, then the code retrieves the existing order ID value from the cookie, and inserts a new ORDERLINE record for the existing order ID. (Recall that to retrieve the value for a cookie in an ASP, you use the Cookies property of the Request object and specify the name of the cookie variable to be retrieved.)

To create and process the orderid cookie in the Process Order ASP using the server-side script commands:

1. Switch to Notepad, where the code for the processorder.asp file is displayed. Add the following line after the <% Option Explicit %> command at the top of the file, to buffer the HTML output on the Web server:

   ```
   <% Response.Buffer=True %>
   ```

2. Add the code shown in Figure 8–52 to create and process the cookie, and then save the file.

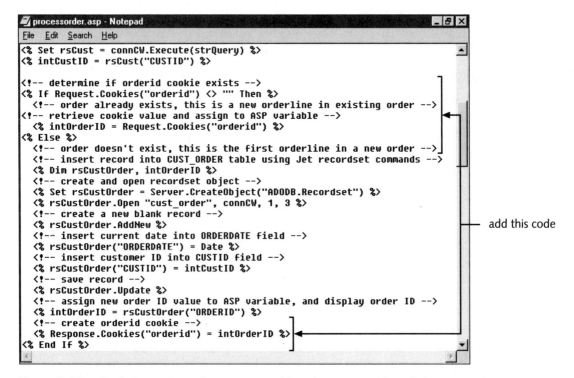

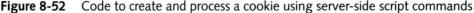

Figure 8-52   Code to create and process a cookie using server-side script commands

3. Start Internet Explorer and type **http://localhost/** in the Address box. The Clearwater Traders home page is displayed.

4. Click **Product Guide**. The Product Guide Web page is displayed.

5. Click **Women's Hiking Shorts**. The Order Items Web page is displayed. Select the option button associated with size M and color Khaki, type **2** for Desired Quantity, and then click **Order Now**. The Login Web page is displayed.

6. Type **harrispe** for the username and **asdfjka** for the password. Click **Submit Query**, and then click **OK** to acknowledge the VBScript: Cookie Alert. The Order Summary Web page is displayed. .

7. Click **Confirm Order**. The Process Order Web page shows the order line information about the Women's Hiking Shorts selection and quantity. Click **Return to Product Guide** to redisplay the Product Guide Web page.

8. Click **All-Weather Mountain Parka**. The Order Items Web page is displayed. Select the option button associated with size M and color Spruce, type **1** for Desired Quantity, and then click **Order Now**. The Order Summary Web page is displayed.

9. Click **Confirm Order**. The Process Order Web page is updated to show both order items, as shown in Figure 8-53.

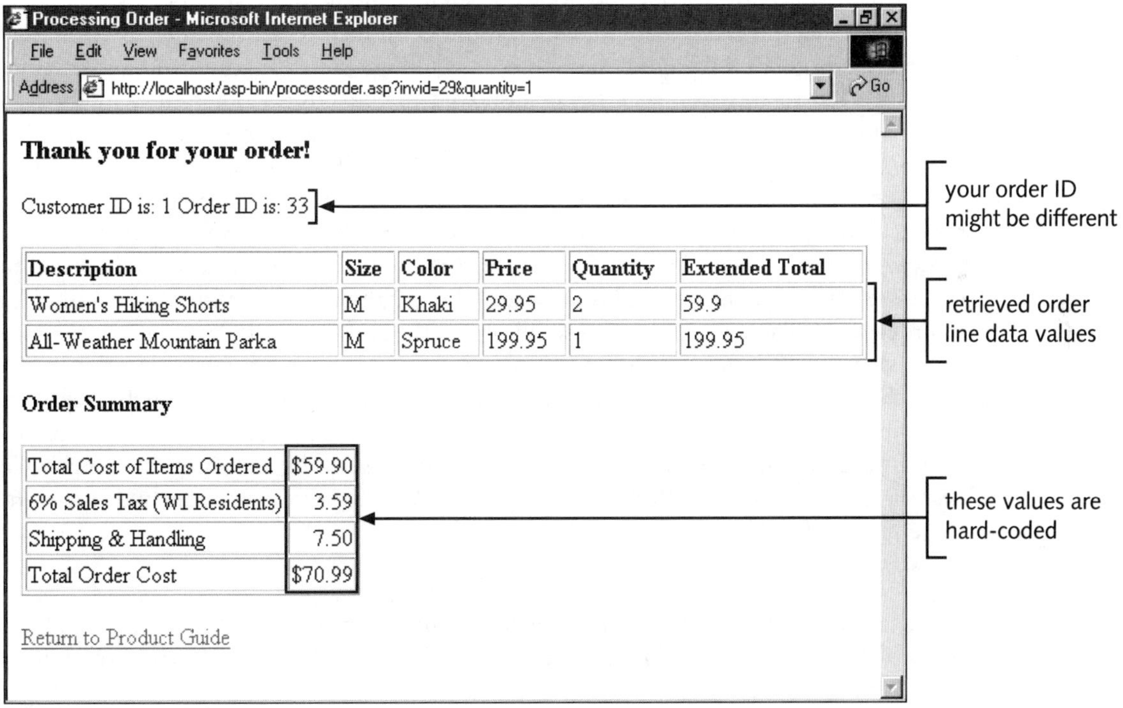

Figure 8-53   Process Order Web page showing multiple order lines

10. Click the **Close** button ⊠ to close Internet Explorer.

SUPPRESSING FORM PARAMETER VALUES IN URLS

Recall that form parameter values are displayed as part of the URL when a Web page is displayed. Displaying these values can pose a security risk. You might think that because a Web page is displayed for the user who enters the form parameter values, it shouldn't matter if this information is displayed in the URL. However, most Web browsers maintain a history of Web sites that have been recently visited—including URL addresses and form parameter values. A subsequent user can view a history list and see sensitive data such as passwords, credit card numbers, and Social Security numbers.

This is probably not a serious problem for individuals who access Web sites from their home computers (unless other people in their homes pose a security risk). Business environments pose a higher risk—employee workstations are often in common workspaces, and security is not ensured. In educational computer laboratories, the security risk is very high: anyone might sit down at any time in front of any of the lab workstations and view sensitive information that has been passed on Web forms. The solution to this problem is to prevent form inputs from appearing in a URL.

HTML forms have two primary methods for sending inputs to a Web server: the default method, also called the **GET** method, which was used in the previous form application, and the **POST** method. With the GET method, parameters are passed as command line parameters in the URL to the Web server, and displayed in the URL Address box in Internet Explorer. After receiving form inputs, a GET request is passed as an **environment variable** to the program processing the request. An environment variable is a variable that is stored on a workstation and is available to any program running on the workstation. There are two problems with the GET method: First, the parameter values are displayed in the URL address, which poses a security risk. Second, environment variables typically are limited to 255 characters, which puts a severe limitation on the length of form parameters. As a result of these problems, HTML forms in Web applications should use the POST method to hide form parameters and avoid length limitations. After receiving form inputs using the POST method, the Web server passes the inputs to the processing program as though they were directly typed into the program from the keyboard. As a result, form inputs are not displayed in a URL when using POST, and there are no restrictions on the length of these inputs. To process form inputs using the POST method, you insert the following command as the first attribute in the <FORM> tag:

```
METHOD="POST"
```

Recall that when you retrieved form inputs that were passed as URL parameters, or as form parameters that were passed using the GET method, you used the Querystring method of the Request object, which has the following syntax:

```
Request.Querystring("[parameter name]")
```

When form inputs are passed as form parameters using the POST method, you must retrieve the individual form parameter values using the Form collection of the Request object. To request a specific form element value, you use the following syntax:

```
Request.Form("[form element name]")
```

The form element name, enclosed in double quotation marks, is case sensitive. Now you will modify the action attribute for the frmLogin form in the Login ASP so that it uses the POST method to process the form inputs. As a result, the form elements (including the username and password) will not appear as part of the Order Summary Web page URL that is displayed when the user clicks the Submit Query button on the Login ASP.

To modify the Login ASP to use the POST method:

1. Switch to Notepad, open **login.asp** from the Chapter8\asp-bin folder on your Data Disk, modify the FORM tag for the frmLogin form as follows, and then save the file:

   ```
   <FORM METHOD="POST" NAME=frmLogin ACTION=ordersummary.asp>
   ```

Now, you will modify the code in the Order Summary ASP that receives the inventory ID and quantity input parameters. Recall from Figure 8-24 that the Order Summary ASP might receive the inventory ID and quantity values from the Login ASP, which uses the POST method. Or, the Order Summary ASP might receive the inventory ID and quantity values from the Order Items ASP, which passes the values as URL parameters. Therefore, the Order Summary ASP must be prepared to receive the parameters either way. To do this, an ASP command will try to retrieve the variables as form parameters using the Request.Form collection. If this retrieval is not successful and no values are retrieved, then a command will retrieve the values as URL parameters.

To modify the Order Summary ASP code to receive the inventory ID and quantity parameter values either as form or URL parameters:

1. In Notepad, open **ordersummary.asp** from the Chapter8\asp-bin folder on your Data Disk, add the code, as shown in Figure 8-54, that tests to see if the parameters were passed as form or URL parameters, and then save the file.

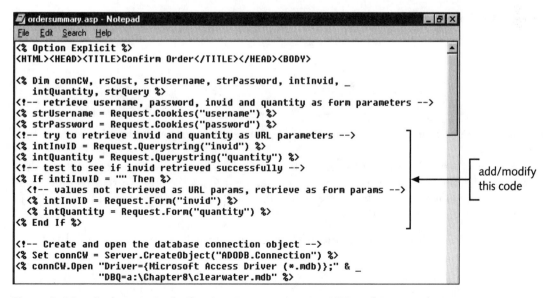

Figure 8-54   Code to test whether input parameters are URL or form parameters

2. Start Internet Explorer and type **http://localhost/** in the Address box. The Clearwater Traders home page is displayed.

3. Click **Product Guide**. The Product Guide Web page is displayed.

4. Click **Women's Hiking Shorts**. The Order Items Web page is displayed. Select the option button associated with size M and color Khaki, type **2** for Desired Quantity, and then click **Order Now**. The Login Web page is displayed.

5. Type **harrispe** for the username and **asdfjka** for the password. Click **Submit Query**, and then click **OK** to acknowledge the VBScript: Cookie Alert. The Order Summary Web page is displayed. Note that the parameter name/value pairs are no longer displayed in the URL in the Address box, as shown in Figure 8-55.

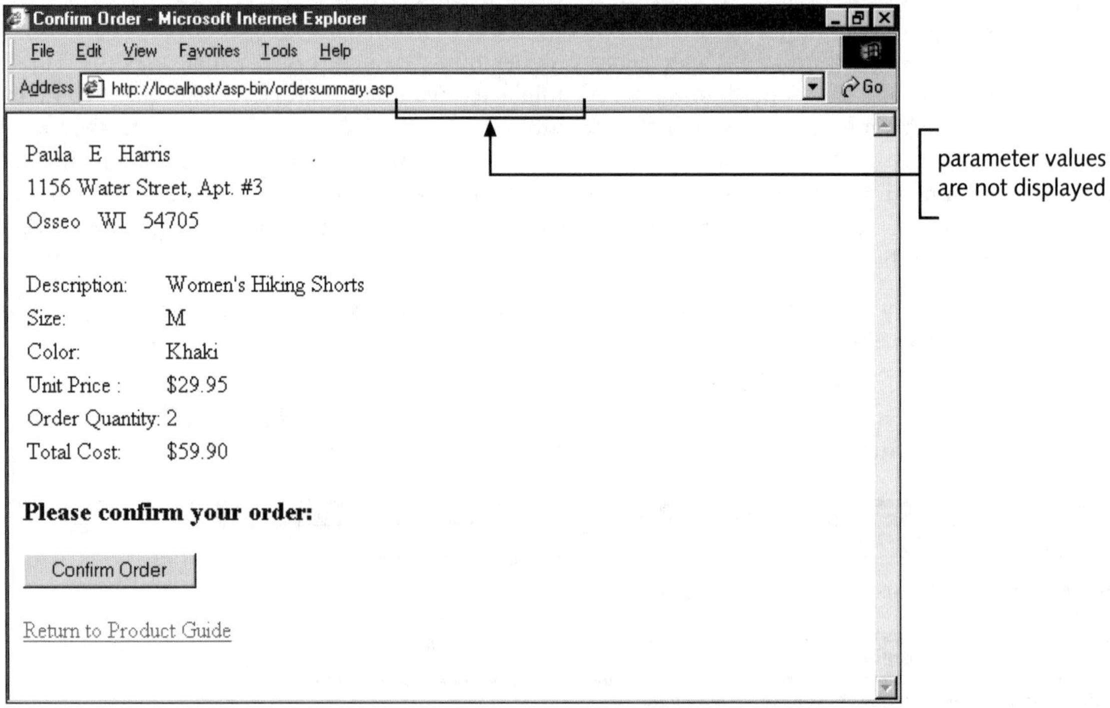

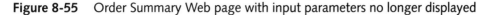

Confirm Order - Microsoft Internet Explorer

File   Edit   View   Favorites   Tools   Help

Address http://localhost/asp-bin/ordersummary.asp   Go

parameter values
are not displayed

Paula E Harris
1156 Water Street, Apt. #3
Osseo WI 54705

Description: Women's Hiking Shorts
Size: M
Color: Khaki
Unit Price : $29.95
Order Quantity: 2
Total Cost: $59.90

Please confirm your order:

Confirm Order

Return to Product Guide

Figure 8-55   Order Summary Web page with input parameters no longer displayed

6. Click **Confirm Order**. The Process Order Web page is displayed, and shows the orderline information for the selected item. Click the **Return to Product Guide** hyperlink to redisplay the Product Guide Web page and add a second item to the order.

7. Click **Goose Down Sleeping Bag**. The Order Items Web page is displayed.

8. Click the option button associated with size Mummy and color Blue, type **1** for Desired Quantity, and click **Order Now**. The Order Summary Web page is displayed.

9. Click **Confirm Order**. The Process Order Web page is displayed, and is updated to show the new order item.

10. Close Internet Explorer, and all other open applications.

SUMMARY

❏ Server-side scripts are processed on the Web server and are used to create dynamic Web pages. The Web server processes the script commands, and composes the Web page HTML code that is then displayed by the user's browser. Microsoft's technology for supporting server-side scripts is called Active Server Pages (ASPs). An ASP must be stored in a folder on the Web server. ASP script commands are enclosed in script delimiter tags composed of angle brackets and percent signs (<%...%>). The text composing ASP script commands is not sent to the user's browser; instead, the processed result of the script, which is a formatted HTML document, is sent to the user's browser.

❏ To pass data values from one ASP to another, you can use a URL parameter, which is a parameter name/value pair that is passed to a target ASP as part of the target ASP's URL. The parameter is separated from the ASP filename by a question mark (?). A Web page or ASP URL can have multiple URL parameters, and each parameter name/value pair is separated from the next by an ampersand (&). Data values can also be passed as form parameters. When an HTML form is submitted to the Web server, the values for all of the form elements are passed as form parameters. Data values can also be shared using cookies. When you want to store a data value on a Web page but do not want to display the value to the user, you can store the data value in a hidden form element.

❏ You can preprocess an ASP using client-side script commands embedded within the HTML commands generated by the ASP by enclosing the client-side script commands in <SCRIPT>...</SCRIPT> tags in the ASP heading section. The client-side script commands are executed before the ASP is submitted to the Web server, by using an INPUT button rather than a SUBMIT button in the ASP's HTML form, and calling a client-side script using the INPUT button's ONCLICK event. When you do this, you must pass form parameters as URL parameters because the form element values will not be passed to the server.

❏ To insert database records using an ASP, you can insert the records using Jet recordset commands or SQL commands. You must use the Jet recordset commands if you want to find the value of a primary key value generated by an Access AutoNumber field that will be a foreign key value in other records. Using SQL commands makes the application portable to databases other than Access.

❏ When a Web server requests a browser to create a cookie, this request message must be sent in a header message to the browser. To create the header message, the Web page output must be buffered, and the HTML output is stored on the Web server and then sent to the browser as a single unit. To suppress form parameter values from appearing as part of the URL displayed in the browser's Address box, you can submit HTML forms using the POST method. When you do this, the ASP that receives the form parameter inputs must use the Request.Form method rather than the Request.Querystring method.

8

REVIEW QUESTIONS

1. What is the difference between a client-side script and a server-side script?
2. What is the name of the Microsoft technology that is used to create server-side scripts?
3. Can an ASP be called using a file URL? Why or why not?
4. Why should you use an HTML template as the basis of an ASP?
5. What are the beginning and ending delimiter tags for script code in an ASP?
6. Where must the Option Explicit command be placed in an ASP file?
7. What is the purpose of a server object in an ASP?
8. How do you create a URL parameter? How do you delimit each individual name/value pair in a URL parameter string?
9. What is the command to retrieve a URL parameter value named custid that is passed to a Web page?
10. What is the command to retrieve a form parameter value named custid that is passed to a Web page using the GET method?
11. What is the command to retrieve a form parameter value named custid that is passed to a Web page using the POST method?
12. What is a form parameter? How are form parameters passed among Web pages?
13. How do you suppress the appearance of form parameters in the Address box of the Web browser?
14. What is the purpose of preprocessing a Web page?
15. How do you preprocess a Web page?
16. When should you use Jet recordset commands for adding data records in an ASP?
17. Why should you use optimistic locking when updating the database using Jet recordset commands?
18. When should you use SQL commands for adding or updating data records in an ASP?
19. How do you retrieve a cookie value in an ASP?
20. What happens when you buffer the Web page output of an ASP?

HANDS-ON PROJECTS

If you are saving your solution files on floppy disks, you will need to save the solutions for the Chapter 8 Hands-on Projects on the second Chapter8 Data Disk.

1. In this project, you will modify the code in the Process Order Web page so that the order line data values are formatted as currency.

   a. Create a new folder named asp-Ch8Pr1 in the Chapter8 folder on your Data Disk, and copy the following files from the Chapter8\asp-bin folder to the Chapter8\asp-Ch8Pr1 folder: products.asp, orderitems.asp, login.asp, ordersummary.asp, and processorder.asp. Copy the clearwater.html file from the Chapter8 folder to the Chapter8\asp-Ch8Pr1 folder.

   b. Create a virtual directory with the alias Ch8Pr1 that is associated with the Chapter8\asp-Ch8Pr1 folder on your Data Disk. Grant the Scripts access privilege to the directory.

   c. Modify the clearwater.html file that is stored in the Chapter8\asp-Ch8Pr1 folder on your Data Disk so that when the Product Guide hyperlink is clicked, the Product Guide ASP in the Chapter8\asp-Ch8Pr1 folder on your Data Disk is called. Use a URL with a relative path.

   d. Modify the code in the Process Order ASP so that the Price and Extended Total values in the order line table (see Figure 8-53) are formatted as currency.

2. In this project, you will modify the Clearwater Traders Sales application so that the order summary information that is currently hard-coded in the Order Summary table in Figure 8-53 is dynamically updated. Format all of the table values as currency, with a dollar sign ($) and two decimal places.

   a. Create a new folder named asp-Ch8Pr2 in the Chapter8 folder on your Data Disk, and copy the following files from the Chapter8\asp-bin folder to the Chapter8\asp-Ch8Pr2 folder: products.asp, orderitems.asp, login.asp, ordersummary.asp, and processorder.asp. Copy the clearwater.html file from the Chapter8 folder to the Chapter8\asp-Ch8Pr2 folder.

   b. Create a virtual directory with the alias Ch8Pr2 that is associated with the Chapter8\asp-Ch8Pr2 folder on your Data Disk. Grant the Scripts access privilege to the directory.

   c. Modify the clearwater.html file in the Chapter8\asp-Ch8Pr2 folder on your Data Disk so that when the Product Guide hyperlink is clicked, the Product Guide ASP in the Chapter8\asp-Ch8Pr2 folder on your Data Disk is called. Use a URL with a relative path.

   d. Add code to the Process Order ASP to calculate the total cost of all items ordered, and display the total amount in the Order Summary table at the bottom of the Process Order Web page.

   e. Add code to the Process Order ASP to calculate the sales tax amount. Modify the query in the ASP to retrieve the customer's state of residence. If the customer is a Wisconsin resident, then the sales tax is 6 percent of the total cost of items ordered. If the customer is a resident of another state, then the sales tax is zero.

   f. Add script code to calculate shipping and handling. Shipping and handling is calculated as a flat rate depending on the amount of the order subtotal. The shipping and handling rate for orders up to $25 is $7.50; the rate for orders between $25 and $75 is $10.00; and the rate for orders $75 and over is $15.00.

   g. Add script code to calculate the final order cost, which is the total of the subtotal, tax, and shipping and handling fields.

8

3. In this project, you will modify the Clearwater Traders Order application so that the Login Web page (see Figure 8-25) has an additional form with input elements that allow new customers to enter customer information. When the user submits this form to the Web server, the data are inserted into the CUSTOMER table, the user's user ID and password are validated, and then the Order Summary Web page is displayed.

a. Create a new folder named asp-Ch8Pr3 in the Chapter8 folder on your Data Disk, and copy the following files from the Chapter8\asp-bin folder to the Chapter8\asp-Ch8Pr3 folder: products.asp, orderitems.asp, login.asp, ordersummary.asp, and processorder.asp. Copy the clearwater.html file from the Chapter8folder to the Chapter8\asp-Ch8Pr3 folder.

b. Create a virtual directory with the alias Ch8Pr3 that is associated with the Chapter8\asp-Ch8Pr3 folder on your Data Disk. Grant the Scripts access privilege to the directory.

c. Modify the clearwater.html file in the Chapter8\asp-Ch8Pr3 folder on your Data Disk so that when the Product Guide hyperlink is clicked, the Product Guide ASP in the Chapter8\asp-Ch8Pr3 folder on your Data Disk is called. Use a URL with a relative path.

d. Add HTML tags in the login.asp file to create a new form with the form elements shown in Figure 8-56.

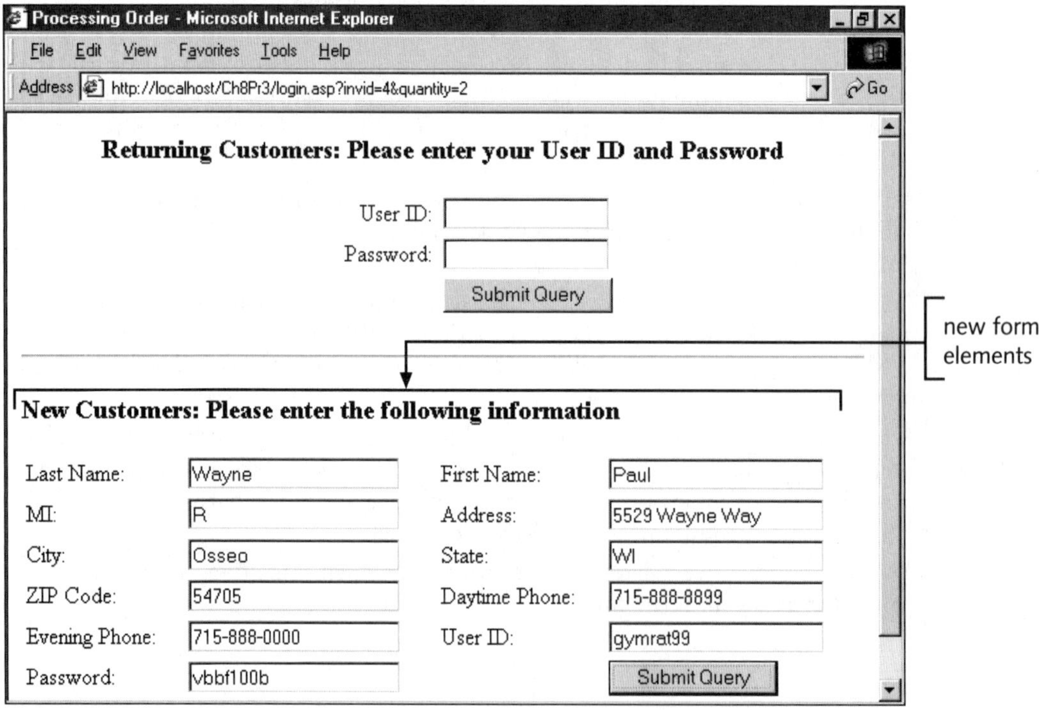

Figure 8-56

e. Create a new ASP named newcustomer.asp, and save it in the Chapter8\asp-Ch8Pr3 folder on your Data Disk. This ASP will insert the new customer data into the database, using Jet recordset commands, and then display the Web page shown in Figure 8-57 to confirm the user ID and password. When the user clicks the Confirm button on this Web page, the Order Summary ASP is called, and processing continues as before.

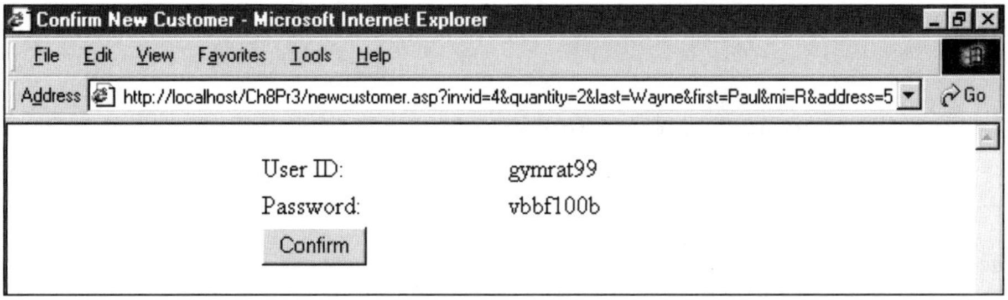

Figure 8-57

4. In this project, you will modify the code for the newcustomer.asp file that you created in Hands-on Project 3 so that the record is inserted using a SQL INSERT command rather than Jet recordset commands.

a. Create a new folder named asp-Ch8Pr4 in the Chapter8 folder on your Data Disk, and copy the following files from the Chapter8\asp-Ch8Pr3 folder to the Chapter8\asp-Ch8Pr4 folder: products.asp, orderitems.asp, login.asp, ordersummary.asp, processorder.asp, and newcustomer.asp. Copy the clearwater.html file from the Chapter8 folder to the Chapter8\asp-Ch8Pr4 folder.

b. Create a virtual directory with the alias Ch8Pr4 that is associated with the Chapter8\asp-Ch8Pr4 folder on your Data Disk. Grant the Scripts access privilege to the directory.

c. Modify the clearwater.html file that is stored in the Chapter8\asp-Ch8Pr4 folder on your Data Disk so that when the Product Guide hyperlink is clicked, the Product Guide ASP in the Chapter8\asp-Ch8Pr4 folder on your Data Disk is called. Use a URL with a relative path.

d. Modify the login.asp code to make sure that the user enters a value for all of the customer data fields.

e. Modify the newcustomer.asp code so that the new customer record is inserted using a SQL INSERT command. Remember that text strings within SQL commands must be enclosed in single quotation marks.

5. In this project, you will create the Web page shown in Figure 8-58, which dynamically displays information from the STUDENT table in the Northwoods University database.

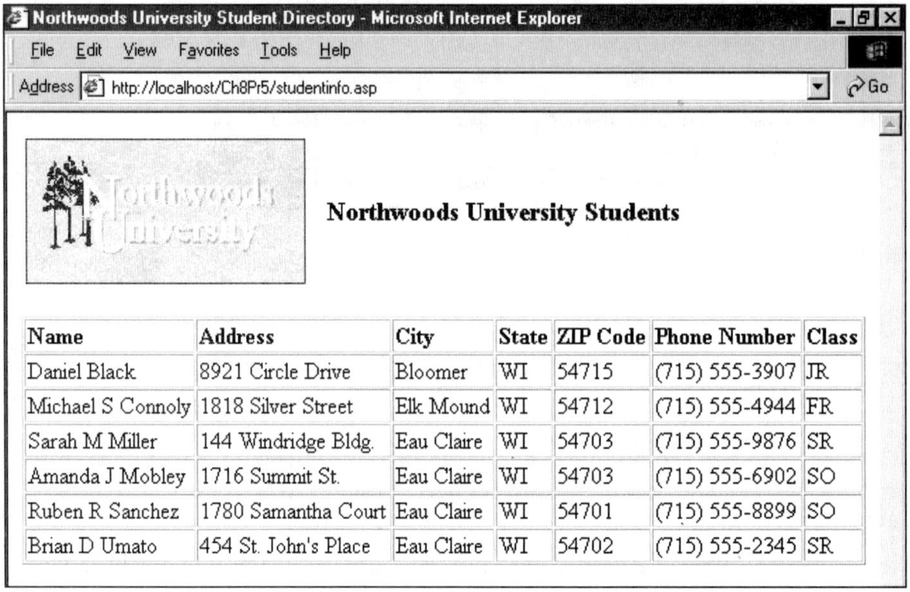

Northwoods University Student Directory - Microsoft Internet Explorer

File   Edit   View   Favorites   Tools   Help

Address http://localhost/Ch8Pr5/studentinfo.asp   Go

Northwoods University Students

Name	Address	City	State	ZIP Code	Phone Number	Class
Daniel Black	8921 Circle Drive	Bloomer	WI	54715	(715) 555-3907	JR
Michael S Connoly	1818 Silver Street	Elk Mound	WI	54712	(715) 555-4944	FR
Sarah M Miller	144 Windridge Bldg.	Eau Claire	WI	54703	(715) 555-9876	SR
Amanda J Mobley	1716 Summit St.	Eau Claire	WI	54703	(715) 555-6902	SO
Ruben R Sanchez	1780 Samantha Court	Eau Claire	WI	54701	(715) 555-8899	SO
Brian D Umato	454 St. John's Place	Eau Claire	WI	54702	(715) 555-2345	SR

Figure 8-58

a. Create a folder named asp-Ch8Pr5 in the Chapter8 folder on your Data Disk.

b. Open the student_template.html file from the Chapter8 folder on your Data Disk, and save the file as studentinfo.asp in the Chapter8\asp-Ch8Pr5 folder on your Data Disk.

c. Modify Personal Web Server so that the Northwoods home page that is stored as northwoods.html in the Chapter8 folder on your Data Disk is the default document. Create a virtual directory named asp-Ch8Pr5 that is associated with the Chapter8\asp-Ch8Pr5 folder on your Data Disk, and modify the Students hyperlink in northwoods.html so that it displays studentinfo.asp.

d. Modify the code in the studentinfo.asp file so that the Northwoods logo (nwlogo.jpg) is retrieved from the Chapter8 folder on your Data Disk, using a relative path address.

e. Modify the code in the studentinfo.asp file so that the student records are dynamically retrieved from the STUDENT table. Display the records so that they are sorted alphabetically by student last name.

6. In this project, you will create the Web page shown in Figure 8-59, which dynamically displays information from the FACULTY table in the Northwoods University database.

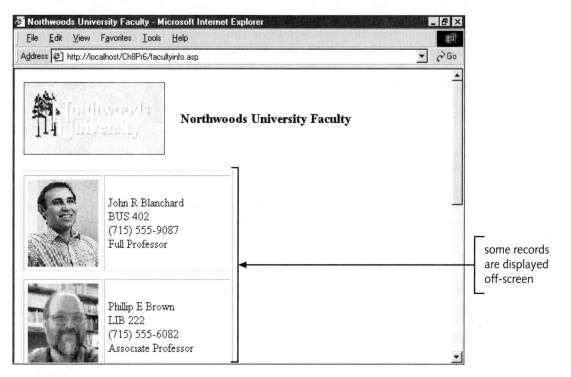

Figure 8-59

a. Create a folder named asp-Ch8Pr6 in the Chapter8 folder on your Data Disk.

b. Open the faculty_template.html file from the Chapter8 folder on your Data Disk, and save the file as facultyinfo.asp in the Chapter8\asp-Ch8Pr6 folder on your Data Disk.

c. If necessary, modify your Personal Web Server so that the Northwoods home page that is stored as northwoods.html in the Chapter8 folder on your Data Disk is the default document.

d. Create a virtual directory named asp-Ch8Pr6 that is associated with the Chapter8\asp-Ch8Pr6 folder on your Data Disk, and modify the Faculty hyperlink in northwoods.html so that it calls facultyinfo.asp.

e. Modify the code in the facultyinfo.asp file so that the Northwoods logo is retrieved from the Chapter8 folder on your Data Disk, using a relative path address.

f. Modify facultyinfo.asp so that the faculty data are dynamically retrieved from the FACULTY table. Display the records so they are sorted alphabetically by faculty last name. Display the faculty image files from the Chapter8 folder on your Data Disk, using relative path addresses.

CASE PROJECTS

1. Create a Web page for the Ashland Valley Soccer League that is generated by an ASP that dynamically displays data from one of the database tables. (Recall that the Ashland Valley Soccer League database was described in Chapter 2, Case Project 1.) Create a subfolder named Ashland in the Chapter8 folder on your Data Disk, and then create subfolders named Case1 and Case2 in the Ashland folder. Save the Web page in the Chapter8\Ashland\Case1 folder.

2. Create a Web page application for the Ashland Valley Soccer League that consists of at least three different Web pages that share data using URL parameters, form parameters, and/or cookies. Make sure that at least one of your Web pages can be used to perform action queries (insert, update, or delete records) on the database. Save your work in the Chaper8\Ashland\Case2 folder on your Data Disk.

3. Create a Web page for Wayne's Auto World that is generated by an ASP that dynamically displays data from one of the database tables. (Recall that the Wayne's Auto World database was described in Chapter 2, Case Project 2.) Create a subfolder named Waynes in the Chapter8 folder on your Data Disk, and then create subfolders named Case3 and Case4 in the Waynes folder. Save the Web page in the Chapter8\Waynes\Case3 folder.

4. Create a Web page application for Wayne's Auto World that consists of at least three different Web pages that share data using URL parameters, form parameters, and/or cookies. Make sure that at least one of your Web pages can be used to perform action queries (insert, update, or delete records) on the database. Save your work in the Chapter8\Waynes\Case4 folder on your Data Disk.

5. Create a Web page for Sun-Ray Video that is generated by an ASP that dynamically displays data from one of the database tables. (Recall that the Sun-Ray Video database was described in Chapter 2, Case Project 3.) Create a subfolder named Sunray in the Chapter8 folder on your Data Disk, and then create subfolders named Case5 and Case6 in the Sunray folder. Save the Web page in the Chapter8\Sunray\Case5 folder.

6. Create a Web page application for Sun-Ray Video that consists of at least three different Web pages that share data using URL parameters, form parameters, and/or cookies. Make sure that at least one of your Web pages can be used to perform action queries (insert, update, or delete records) on the database. Save your work in the Chapter8\Sunray\Case6 folder on your Data Disk.

9

COMPILED WEB SERVER PROGRAMS

In this chapter, you will:

♦ Learn about Common Gateway Interface (CGI)
♦ Create CGI programs that generate dynamic Web pages using Visual Basic, and learn the advantages and disadvantages of using CGI programs to create dynamic Web pages
♦ Pass parameter values among CGI programs
♦ Learn about ActiveX dynamic-link libraries (DLLs) and their advantages and disadvantages
♦ Create an ActiveX DLL that generates a Web page
♦ Call an ActiveX DLL from an Active Server Page

In Chapter 8, you generated dynamic Web pages using Active Server Page server-side scripts. Recall that with a script, commands are converted into machine language (the binary language understood by your computer's processor) each time the script is run. In contrast, a compiled program is converted into machine language when it is first compiled and doesn't need to be converted each time the program is run. For this reason, compiled programs usually run much faster than scripts. In this chapter, you will learn about Common Gateway Interface (CGI), which is the first method that was developed for creating compiled programs that run on a Web server and are used to create dynamic Web pages and process form inputs. Although CGI is an older Web technology than Active Server Pages, CGI programs are still used on many Web sites.

Each time a user submits Web page inputs that are processed by a CGI program, the Web server must start a new instance of the CGI program. For a busy Web site, there might be hundreds or thousands of instances of the same CGI program running. This redundancy consumes Web server resources and slows down response time. To avoid this problem, you can also create compiled programs that run on the Web server and process Web pages using ActiveX DLLs, which are compiled code libraries that are called from an Active Server Page. The advantage of using ActiveX DLLs instead of CGI programs is that a single instance of an ActiveX DLL can process inputs from multiple Web site visitors. You will also learn how Microsoft's Internet Server Application Programming Interface (ISAPI) allows you to call ActiveX DLLs.

COMMON GATEWAY INTERFACE

Common Gateway Interface (CGI) is a protocol that specifies how Web servers and compiled programs for processing user inputs that run on the Web server communicate with each other. Before the development of CGI, the Web was composed entirely of static Web pages. CGI was developed as a protocol for programs that process data entered into HTML forms and use these inputs to generate dynamic pages.

Recall from Chapter 7 that when a browser submits a form to a Web server, an application identified in the form tag's ACTION parameter is started by the Web server to process the form inputs. Similarly, if a hyperlink in a Web page is clicked and the URL contained in the tag references a script or compiled program, the script or program will be started by the Web server. When you are using a Microsoft Web server, the program file's extension tells the Web server if the program is an ASP script or a CGI program. A file ending in .asp is processed as an Active Server Page, while a file ending in .exe is processed as a CGI program.

When a user submits inputs on an HTML form that are to be processed by a CGI program, the Web server starts the CGI program, which runs on the Web server. The CGI program is not part of the Web server listener or administration utilities, but is an independent executable program. The CGI program retrieves the form input variables, processes them, stores the output values (which are HTML commands to create a formatted Web page) in a memory location, and then terminates. The Web server then reads the output values and sends them back to the user's browser. The CGI processing architecture is shown in Figure 9-1.

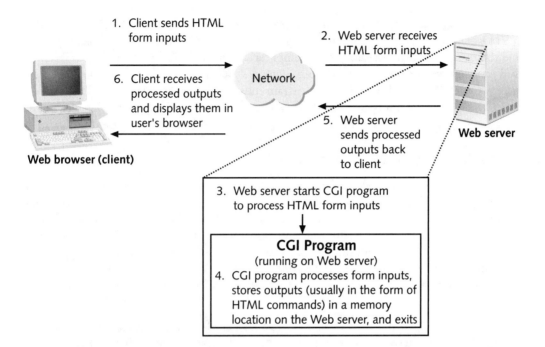

Figure 9-1 CGI processing architecture

Processing Inputs and Outputs in CGI Programs

In the early days of mainframe computing, **standard input (STDIN)** referred to a memory location where user input from the keyboard was stored, and **standard output (STDOUT)** referred to a memory location where output to be displayed on the monitor was stored. When a user typed an input on the keyboard, the input was referenced by the operating system as being stored in STDIN. If the mainframe sent back a response that was to be displayed on the monitor, it was referenced by the operating system as being stored in STDOUT. Computer operating systems have retained the concepts of STDIN and STDOUT, but these terms are no longer used to reference keyboard input and monitor output data. Rather, they define a standard way of communicating the locations of inputs and outputs between different programs.

In Chapter 8, you learned that when an HTML form is submitted to the Web server using the POST method, the values in the form controls are received by the processing program as though they were entered using the keyboard. Actually, the form inputs are stored in the Web server's STDIN memory location. These inputs can then be retrieved by a CGI program for processing. When the CGI program is done processing, it writes its outputs (which are usually HTML tags and Web page text) to STDOUT on the Web server. The Web server then forwards the contents of STDOUT to the user's Web browser, which displays the output as a Web page.

A CGI program can be written in any language that can read data from STDIN, write data to STDOUT, and read environment variables. (Recall that an environment variable is a variable that is stored in the memory of a computer and is available to a variety of programs.) CGI programs can be written in scripting languages such as PERL, or in compiled languages such as C++ and Visual Basic. A CGI program must be able to receive inputs from the Web server using the CGI protocol, and then deliver the processed outputs to the Web server using the CGI protocol. In this chapter, you will use Visual Basic to write CGI programs.

Writing a CGI Program Using Visual Basic

Since you can use Visual Basic to create compiled programs, you can also use VB to create CGI programs. However, Visual Basic doesn't directly support reading from STDIN and writing to STDOUT. To create CGI programs using VB, you will use a VB standard module named cgi.bas that has been written for this book and is stored in the Chapter9 folder of your Data Disk. This module contains declarations of Windows API (Application Programming Interface) functions that enable Visual Basic to read from STDIN and write to STDOUT. You will add the cgi.bas standard module to all of your VB CGI programs.

> **TIP** The Windows API is a set of code libraries that developers can incorporate within Windows applications written in a variety of languages, to create standard Windows program components.

In Chapter 5, you created a virtual directory named cgi-bin with Execute privileges. Now you will create a folder named cgi-bin in the Chapter9 folder on your Data Disk that will be used to store your compiled CGI programs. Then, you will start Personal Web Manager, create a virtual directory named cgi-bin, and associate it with the cgi-bin physical folder in the Chapter9 folder on your Data Disk. You will also create a folder named cgi_1 in the Chapter9 folder on your Data Disk to store the VB source code for the first CGI program that you will create.

> **TIP** Recall from Chapter 8 that folders containing the word "bin" contain binary, or executable, files. It is a common practice on Web servers to store CGI programs in a folder named cgi-bin.

To create the folders and virtual directory:

1. Start Windows Explorer, and create folders named **cgi-bin** and **cgi_1** in the Chapter9 folder on your Data Disk.

2. Copy **cgi.bas** from the Chapter9 folder on your Data Disk to the Chapter9\cgi_1 folder on your Data Disk.

3. Start Personal Web Manager. On the Main page, confirm that Web publishing is on. If it is not on, click **Start**.

4. Click **Advanced** to move to the Advanced page, click **cgi-bin**, click **Edit Properties**, click **Browse**, navigate to the Chapter9\cgi-bin folder on your Data Disk, click **OK**, confirm that the Execute and Read check boxes are checked and that the Scripts check box is cleared, and then click **OK** again.

5. Click **Home** in the Virtual Directories list, click **Edit Properties**, click **Browse**, and then navigate to the Chapter9 folder on your Data Disk to change the default document folder of the Personal Web Server to the Chapter9 folder on your Data Disk. Click **OK**, and then click **OK** again.

6. Make sure that the Allow Directory Browsing check box is checked, and that the Enable Default Document check box is cleared.

Now you will create a CGI program that reads HTML form inputs from STDIN and creates a formatted Web page that is stored in STDOUT, and is then returned by the Web server to the user's browser. The program will process the inputs from the HTML form shown in Figure 9-2.

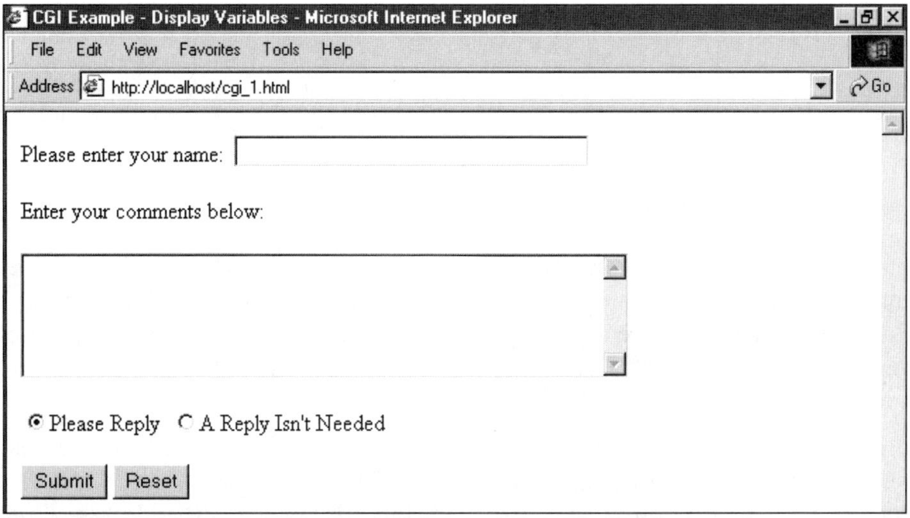

Figure 9-2   HTML form to be processed by the CGI program

This HTML form consists of an input box where the user enters his or her name, a text area where the user can enter multiple text lines, and two option buttons. The CGI program will display the output shown in Figure 9-3.

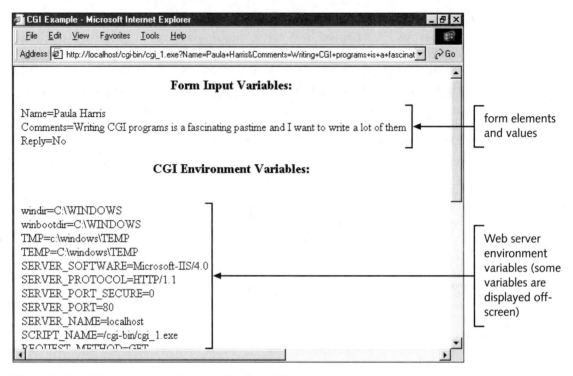

Figure 9-3   Web page output created by the CGI program

The output shown in Figure 9-3 consists of a Web page that displays the text that the user entered into the text area, and a message indicating which option button was selected. It also displays a list of all the current environment variables for the Web server. Some of these environment variables were created by other programs, and some were created by the CGI program.

Now you will start Visual Basic and create the CGI program that processes the form inputs and creates the Web page output shown in Figure 9-3. This CGI program will not have a visual component, and no VB forms will be displayed. Instead, it will use VB code to read and process the HTML form inputs and create the formatted HTML outputs. First, you will create a new project, and remove the form from the project. Then, you will add the cgi.bas standard module to the project.

To create the CGI program:

1. Start Visual Basic. In the New Project window, click **Standard EXE**, and then click **Open** to create a new project.

2. In the Project Explorer, click **Form1 (Form1)**, click **Project** on the menu bar, and then click **Remove Form1** to remove Form1 from your project.

3. Click **Project** on the menu bar, click **Add Module**, click the **Existing** tab, navigate to the Chapter9\cgi_1 folder on your Data Disk, click **cgi.bas**, and then click **Open**. The cgi.bas module is now added to the project.

You must always save the VB project (.vbp) and standard module (.bas) files in the same folder. Otherwise, path information for the module files will be stored in the .vbp file, and the module files might not be available to the project if you move the files to a different folder or to a computer that does not have the same folder path configuration.

4. If necessary, click View on the menu bar, and then click Properties Window to display the Properties window. Select **Project1 (Project1)** in the Project Explorer window, and change the project Name property to **CGI_1**.

5. Click the **Save Project** button 🖫 on the toolbar, navigate to the Chapter9\cgi_1 folder on your Data Disk, and save the project as **cgi_1.vbp**.

Using the cgi.bas Standard Module

Now you will add to your CGI program the statements that read the form inputs from STDIN, and then write the desired outputs to STDOUT. To do this, the CGI program uses procedures and functions that are in the cgi.bas standard module. (You could write your own VB functions and procedures to perform these operations, but writing these functions and procedures requires advanced VB programming skills and knowledge that are beyond the scope of this book.) While the procedures and functions that you use are specific to cgi.bas, the operations that they perform are commonly used in code libraries used by programmers to develop CGI programs. The procedures and functions in cgi.bas that you will use in your CGI programs are summarized in Table 9-1.

Table 9-1   cgi.bas procedures and functions

Name	Type	Input	Output	Description
InitializeCGI	Procedure	None	Writes "Content-Type: text/html" to STDOUT	Reads and stores environment variables and form input variables from STDIN; must be called before using any other cgi.bas procedures or functions
stdOut	Function	String variable containing data to be written to STDOUT	Writes string variable data to STDOUT	Stores output string containing HTML commands in STDOUT; this string is then forwarded to user's browser and displayed as a Web page
DisplayAll	Procedure	None	Displays list of system environment variable names and values	Recalls and displays all form input and environment variable names and values
GetInput	Function	Form variable name	Form variable value	Retrieves a specific form input variable value from STDIN

9

You must call the **InitializeCGI** procedure before using the other procedures in cgi.bas. You can only call InitializeCGI once at the beginning of your program; otherwise, an error message will be returned. InitializeCGI reads all Web server environment variables and stores them in a VB variable, and then reads inputs submitted by a form using either the GET or POST method and stores them in another VB variable. The **stdOut** function receives a string containing the program outputs as an input variable, and writes these outputs to STDOUT. The Web server forwards the outputs to the user's browser. These outputs are text strings, formatted as ordinary HTML tags and text. The **DisplayAll** procedure is used in the first CGI program that you will write to display the names and values of all the form inputs and environment variables. The **GetInput** function receives the name of an HTML form variable as an input parameter, and retrieves the value of the variable from STDIN. The GetInput function can be used whether the form inputs were submitted using the GET method or the POST method.

The last thing you need to know about cgi.bas is how to use its debugging features. When you call the InitializeCGI procedure, a file named stdout.html is created. Each time the stdOut function is called, the output string that is written to STDOUT is also written to the stdout.html file. This allows you to run your CGI program in the VB design environment, and view the stdout.html output in a browser or editor to see if it is correct. Otherwise, you would have to compile the CGI program each time you made a change, and then test the change by calling the CGI program from the HTML form. These added steps slow down the development process.

Now you will add a new standard module to your cgi_1.vbp project. In this module, you will create a procedure that calls the functions and procedures from cgi.bas that read the form inputs from STDIN. You will then write the form input variable values and Web server environment variables as a formatted HTML document to STDOUT. This code uses the Visual Basic vbCrLf command to automatically add a carriage return and line feed character to a text string, causing the text that follows vbCrLf to appear on a new line.

To add the standard module to process the HTML form inputs:

1. In VB, click **Project** on the menu bar, click **Add Module**, make sure that Module is selected on the New tab, and then click **Open**. A new standard module is added to the cgi_1 project.

2. In the Properties Window, change the module name to **Procedures**.

3. Add the code shown in Figure 9-4 to the procedures module.

4. Click the **Save Project** button 🖫, navigate to the Chapter9\cgi_1 folder on your Data Disk, if necessary, and save the module as **procedures.bas**.

When you create a VB project, the project by default is configured to display the first form that was created. Since your project does not have any forms, you will have to specify that the project should run the Sub Main() procedure in the procedures.bas module when the project runs. To do this, you will open the Project Properties dialog box, which is used to set different properties for the project. On the Project Properties page, you will specify the **project startup object**, which is the procedure that first runs when the program starts. You will specify that the project startup object is Sub Main(), which is the procedure that you created in the procedures.bas module. Then you will compile your project to create an executable program file.

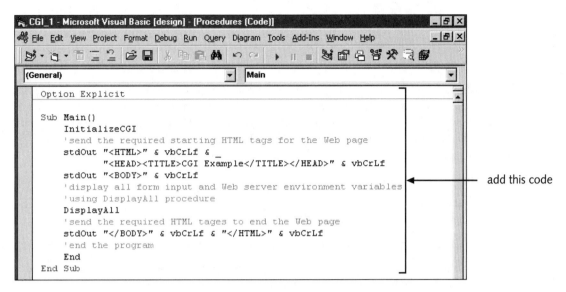

Figure 9-4   CGI program code

To specify the project startup object and create an executable program file:

1. In VB, click **Project** on the menu bar, and then click **CGI_1 Properties**. The Project Properties dialog box is displayed.

2. Open the Startup Object list, select **Sub Main**, if necessary, and then click **OK**.

3. Click **File** on the menu bar, click **Make CGI_1.exe**, navigate to the Chapter9\cgi-bin folder on your Data Disk, confirm that the file is named CGI_1.exe, and then click **OK** to create the executable program file.

 Note that you store all of the VB source code (.vbp and .bas) files in the cgi_1 folder, and the executable file in the cgi-bin folder.

Recall from Chapter 7 that when you click the Submit button on an HTML form, the form inputs are processed by the program that is specified in the form's ACTION attribute. The HTML document that contains the HTML form elements shown in Figure 9-2 is in a file named cgi_1.html, which is in the Chapter9 folder on your Data Disk. Now, you will open cgi_1.html in Notepad, and modify its ACTION attribute so that it calls the cgi_1.exe program. Recall that the Chapter9 folder on your Data Disk is the Web server's default document folder, and that the cgi-bin folder where cgi_1.exe is stored is a subfolder within the Chapter9 folder.

To modify the ACTION attribute of cgi_1.html so that it calls the CGI program:

1. Start Notepad, and open **cgi_1.html** from the Chapter9 folder on your Data Disk.

2. Modify the FORM tag as follows:

```
<FORM METHOD=GET ACTION=http://localhost/cgi-bin/cgi_1.exe>
```

3. Save the file.

Now you will test your CGI program. You will start Internet Explorer and display the cgi_1.html Web page document. You will enter data values into the form input areas, and then you will submit the form to the Web server. The CGI program will read the inputs from STDIN, and write the outputs to STDOUT. The Web server will then forward the outputs that are stored in STDOUT to your browser, where they will be displayed.

To test the CGI program:

1. Start Internet Explorer, and type **http://localhost/** in the Address box. A directory listing of the Chapter9 folders is displayed.

2. Click the **cgi_1.html** link. The HTML form shown in Figure 9-2 is displayed.

3. Type **Paula Harris** in the Name input box, and type **Writing CGI programs is a fascinating pastime and I want to write a lot of them** in the text area.

4. Click the **A Reply Isn't Needed** option button, and then click **Submit** to submit the form to the Web server. If the Security Alert dialog box is displayed, click **Yes**. The output from the Web server is displayed, as shown in Figure 9-3.

Creating a CGI Program to Display the Clearwater Traders Product Guide Web Page

Now you will learn how to create a CGI program that displays database data. In Chapter 8 you created the Clearwater Traders Order application (see Figure 8-24), using Active Server Pages. This application allowed the user to select a product, view inventory information about the product, and place an order. The first CGI program you will write will create the Product Guide Web page (see Figure 8-3) that displays the item ID and description values for every record in the ITEMS table in the Clearwater Traders database. Whenever you write a CGI program, you perform the following standard steps. (Do not perform these steps at this time.)

1. Create a folder to store the CGI program source code, which consists of the Visual Basic .vbp and .bas files.

2. Copy the cgi.bas standard module file to the folder that you created in Step 1.

3. Create a new Standard EXE VB project, and remove the default form that is included in the new project. Change the Project Name property to a descriptive name in the Properties window.

4. Add the cgi.bas module to the project.

5. Add the ADO reference library to the project.

6. Add a new standard module named Procedures to the project, and initialize the project by creating a Sub Main() procedure in the new standard module, which has the following code:

```
Sub Main()
InitializeCGI
End
```

7. Save the VB project and standard modules in the folder you created in Step 1.

8. Add the code to process the inputs and create the Web page output code to the Sub Main() standard module.

9. Create an executable file for the project, and save it in the cgi-bin folder on the Web server.

10. Create a hyperlink or form ACTION attribute to reference the CGI program.

Now you will use these steps to create a CGI program that generates the Product Guide Web page.

To create a CGI program and initialize it to display the data in the ITEMS table:

1. Create a new folder named **Products** in the Chapter9 folder on your Data Disk.

2. Copy cgi.bas from the Chapter9 folder on your Data Disk to the Products subfolder.

3. Switch to VB, click **File** on the menu bar, and then click **New Project** to create a new VB project. Click **Yes** to save the changes to the CGI_1.vbp project file. The New Project dialog box is displayed. Click **Standard EXE**, and then click **OK**.

4. Click **Project1 (Project1)** in the Project Navigator, and change the Project Name property to Products in the Properties window.

5. Remove Form1 from the project.

6. Add to the project the cgi.bas module that is stored in the Chapter9\Products folder.

7. Click **Project** on the menu bar, click **Add Module**, make sure that Module is selected on the New tab, and then click **Open** to add a new standard module to the project.

8. Select the module in the Project Explorer, and change the name of the new module to **Procedures** in the Properties window.

9

9. Select the new module in the Project Explorer, open the Code window, and type the code shown in Figure 9-5 to initialize the CGI program.

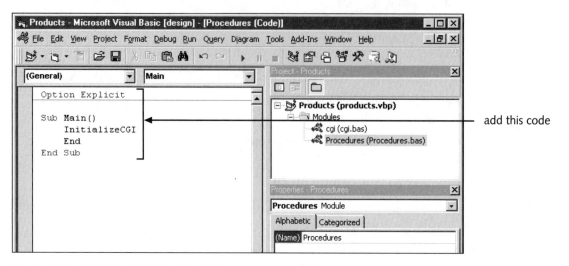

Figure 9-5   Code to initialize the CGI program

10. Click **Project** on the menu bar, click **References**, scroll down in the Available References list, check **Microsoft ActiveX Data Objects 2.1 Library**, and then click **OK** to add the ADO library to your project.

 You might need to install the Microsoft ActiveX Data Objects 2.0 Library, depending on which version of Visual Basic 6.0 you are using.

11. Click the **Save Project** button 🖫 on the toolbar, save the new module as **procedures.bas** in the Chapter9\Products folder on your Data Disk, and save the project as **products.vbp** in the Chapter9\Products folder on your Data Disk.

Formatting HTML Commands in the Product Guide CGI Program

Recall that when you created Active Server Pages that displayed database data in Chapter 8, you first added the HTML template code to the program. Then, you added the program commands to retrieve the data from the database and display it within the HTML commands. You use a similar strategy to write CGI programs: first you add the HTML commands to the procedure, and then you add the VB commands to retrieve the data and embed the data values into the HTML commands. Recall that HTML commands in a CGI program must be passed as text strings to the stdOut function. There is a file named product_template.html in the Chapter9 folder on your Data Disk that contains a static HTML template for the Products Web page. (This is the same HTML file that you used to create the Product Guide ASP in Chapter 8.) Now you will open product_template.html in Notepad, copy the text, and paste it into your CGI program's procedures.bas module.

To open product_template.html, copy the text, and then paste the text into the Procedures module:

1. Switch to Notepad and open **product_template.html** from the Chapter9 folder on your Data Disk.

2. Click **Edit** on the menu bar, and then click **Select All**.

3. Click **Edit** on the menu bar again, and then click **Copy** to copy all of the template commands.

4. Switch to Visual Basic, and if necessary, open the Code window for the procedures.bas module.

5. Place the insertion point immediately at the end of the code line `InitializeCGI`, and then press the **Enter** key to add a new line.

6. Click **Edit** on the menu bar, and then click **Paste** to paste the copied code. The pasted code is displayed in red because its syntax is different from that of standard VB commands.

7. Save the project.

The next step is to format the HTML commands so that they are passed correctly to the stdOut function. To do this, you will type `stdOut` at the beginning of each HTML command line, and then enclose the HTML commands in quotation marks to indicate that they are text strings that are being passed to the stdOut function. Quotation marks used in HTML tags (for example, the quotation marks that enclose the table width percentage, or the image source filename) create a problem in Visual Basic text strings. A quotation mark is used by VB to delimit strings. To include a quotation mark as a character within a VB text string, you must replace the quotation mark with the `Chr(34)` character code. This character code is used to embed a quotation mark within a VB text string. The VB Chr function converts an ASCII value to a character, and the ASCII value for the quotation mark character is 34.

 TIP ASCII is an acronym for American Standard Code for Information Interchange. It is a code using numbers from 0 to 255 to represent letters, numbers, punctuation marks, and other characters.

The HTML command that defines the table in the product_template.html file is:

```
<TABLE WIDTH="60%"><TR>
```

You must modify this line to be sent to the stdOut function, as follows:

```
stdOut("<TABLE WIDTH=" & Chr(34) & "60%" & Chr(34) & "><TR>")
```

Note that the table width (60%) has been enclosed in quotation marks within the text string, using the Chr(34) character code.

> **TIP** Often with newer browsers, quotation marks aren't required and can be omitted from HTML commands. For example, for some browsers, the previous command can be simplified to stdOut "<TABLE WIDTH=60%><TR>". However, the technique of embedding Chr(34) into VB text strings will enable your CGI programs to be displayed correctly with almost any browser. Also, in some client-side script commands, the quotation marks must be included to correctly form the script commands.

Now you will modify the HTML commands that you pasted into the procedures.bas module of the Product project so that all of the HTML commands are sent as input parameters to the stdOut function. Then, you will create an executable file and test your CGI program.

To modify the pasted HTML commands, create an executable file, and test the CGI program:

1. Modify the code in the procedures.bas module as shown in Figure 9-6.

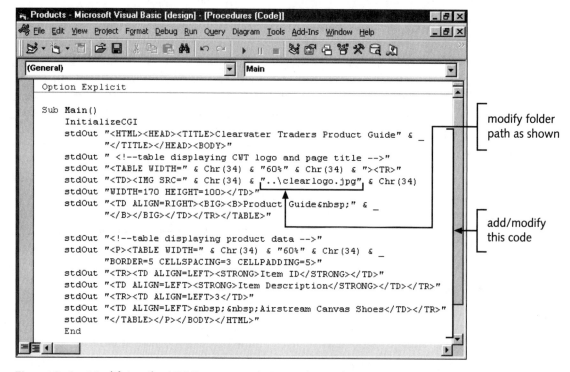

Figure 9-6   Modifying the HTML commands in products.vbp

2. Save the project.

3. Click **File** on the menu bar, and then click **Make products.exe**. Navigate to the Chapter9\cgi-bin folder on your Data Disk, and then click **OK**.

4. Switch to Internet Explorer, and type **http://localhost/** in the Address box.

5. Click the **cgi-bin** link, and then click **products.exe** to run the CGI program. The Product Guide Web page template generated by the CGI program is displayed, as shown in Figure 9-7.

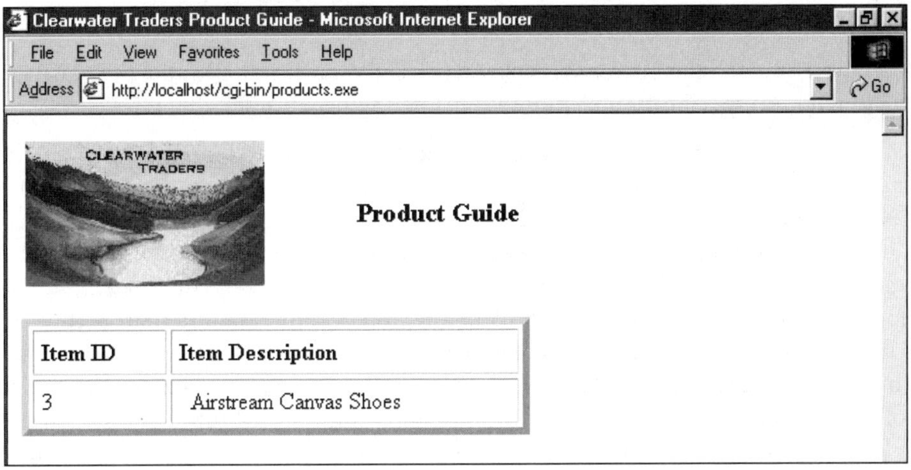

Figure 9-7   Product Guide Web page created by the CGI program

Retrieving Records from the Database

Currently, the item ID value (3) that is displayed on the Product Guide Web page is hard-coded into the HTML code. Now you will add the VB code to create an ADO database connection object, open the database connection, and create a recordset based on a SQL query. Recall that to create a database connection object in VB, you must first declare a variable as a new ADO connection object, which reserves a memory location to store information about the connection. To declare a variable to reference a new ADO connection object, you use the following code:

```
Dim [connection name] As ADODB.Connection
```

Recall from previous chapters that you prefaced connection variables with the prefix conn.

After you declare the connection variable, you will create the new connection. To create an ADODB.Connection object, you use the following code: `Set [connection name] = New ADODB.Connection`. For example, to declare and then create a new connection named connCW, you would use the following code:

```
Dim connCW As ADODB.Connection
Set connCW = New ADODB.Connection
```

After declaring the connection variable and creating the connection, you must open the connection. To do this, you use the same command that you used when you opened the database connection in the Active Server Pages that you created in Chapter 8:

```
[connection name].Open "driver={Microsoft Access Driver(*.mdb)};
DBQ=[path to Access .mdb file]"
```

For example, to open a connection named connCW that will be linked to the clearwater.mdb file that is stored in the Chapter9 folder on your Data Disk, you would use the following command (assuming that your Data Disk is on drive A of your computer):

```
connCW.Open "driver={Microsoft Access Driver (*.mdb)};
DBQ=a:\Chapter9\clearwater.mdb"
```

Notice that the name of the driver is enclosed in curly braces ({ }), and the database file/extension wildcard specification (*.mdb) is enclosed in parentheses.

Recall that to retrieve data from a database, you create a recordset based on a SQL SELECT query using the recordset object's Execute method. You first declare the recordset variable, and then retrieve the records into the recordset. Normally, a recordset variable has the prefix rs. It is a good practice to assign the SQL query string to a variable value, and then use the query string in the Execute method. This way, you can examine the value of the query string in the VB development environment and spot errors before you compile the program and try to run it on the Web server. For example, the following code declares variables for a recordset named rsItem and a query string named strQuery. The query string is assigned to reference the text of a SQL command that retrieves the ITEMID and ITEMDESC fields from the ITEM table. The recordset is retrieved using the Execute method of the connCW database connection and uses the query string variable:

```
Dim rsItem As ADODB.Recordset, strQuery As String
strQuery = "SELECT itemid, itemdesc FROM ITEM"
Set rsItem = connCW.Execute(strQuery)
```

To sequentially display all of the records in a recordset, you must use a Visual Basic Do While loop that displays the first record, and then continues to loop through and display records until the loop reaches the end of the recordset, which is marked with an end-of-file (EOF) marker. This loop has the following general format:

```
Do While Not [recordset name].EOF
     [program statements]
     [recordset name].MoveNext
     Loop
```

To access a value in an individual field in a recordset record and then display the value within an HTML tag, you use the following code:

```
[recordset variable name]("[fieldname]")
```

The field name is not case sensitive, but since database field names are always written in uppercase letters in this book, you will write the field name in uppercase letters. For example, to declare a string variable named strItemDesc that is assigned the current item description value of the rsItem recordset, you would use the following code:

```
strItemDesc = rsItem("ITEMDESC")
```

After you have finished using a database connection, you should close the connection to free up the system resources that it uses. To close a database connection, you use the following command:

```
[connection name].Close
```

Now you will add code to the Products CGI program to declare the data connection and recordset variables, create and open the database connection, and create the recordset and retrieve all of the records in the ITEM table. You will use a loop to retrieve each ITEM data record, and then insert each individual item ID and description value into the table on the Product Guide Web page. After you add the code, you will run the program in VB to confirm that the program terminates correctly. Whenever you write a CGI program with a loop, it is important to test it and confirm that it does not have any infinite loops that keep the program from terminating. If you run a CGI program on your Web server that does not terminate, the program will lock up the user's browser, and possibly force the user to reboot his or her computer.

When you test your CGI program in the VB development environment, the program will not display any output, because it does not have any visible forms. However, you will be able to confirm that the program terminates.

To add the commands to the CGI program to retrieve the data, and then test the program to confirm that it terminates properly:

1. Switch to Visual Basic, and add the code shown in Figure 9-8 to the procedures.bas module in the products.vbp project.

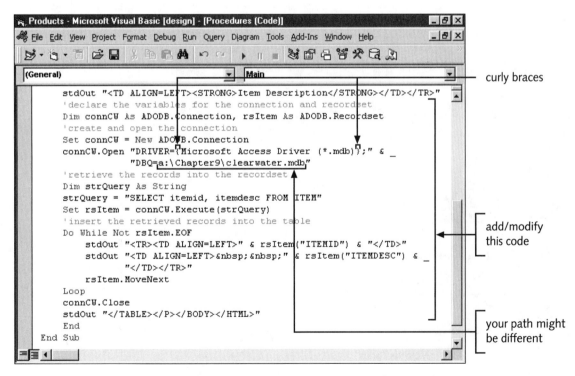

Figure 9-8   Code to create the database connection and retrieve the records

2. Click the **Start** button ▶ on the toolbar to run the program. If the program runs and terminates, then ▶ will be enabled again on the toolbar. If the program does

not terminate correctly, then the mouse pointer will be disabled, and will remain disabled on the toolbar.

> **TIP** If your program does not terminate correctly, press Ctrl + Break on the keyboard to terminate the program, and then double-check the code for the Do While loop to make sure that you typed it correctly.

3. Save the project.

Now you will create an updated products.exe executable file, and then test the CGI program by running it in your Web browser to confirm that it works correctly.

To create the executable file and test the CGI program:

1. Create an updated executable project file named **products.exe** in the cgi-bin folder on your Data Disk. When you are asked if you want to replace your existing products.exe file, click **Yes**.

2. Switch to Internet Explorer, type **http://localhost/** in the Address box, click the **cgi-bin** link, and then click **products.exe**. The Product Guide Web page, with the data values dynamically retrieved from the database, is displayed, as shown in Figure 9-9. If your program does not execute correctly, proceed to the next section, "Debugging CGI Programs in Visual Basic."

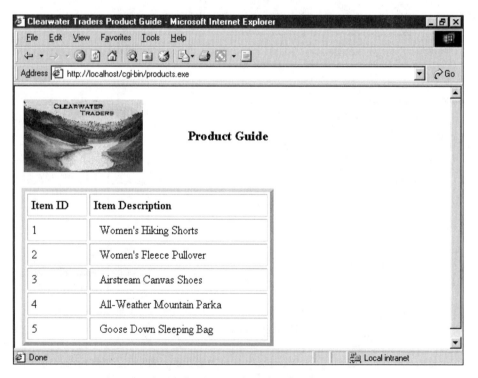

Figure 9-9   Product Guide Web page with retrieved data

Debugging CGI Programs in Visual Basic

The main source of errors in CGI programs developed in Visual Basic is concatenation errors, where the SQL or HTML commands are not correctly formed as text strings. Recall that when you concatenate text strings and variables in VB, every text string must be enclosed in quotation marks ("), and you must place the concatenation operator (&) between text variable values and text strings. Commands with incorrectly formed text strings are usually easy to spot, since the VB editor displays lines with syntax errors in red, and also displays a message box describing the error when you enter the code. An example of a concatenation error is shown in Figure 9-10.

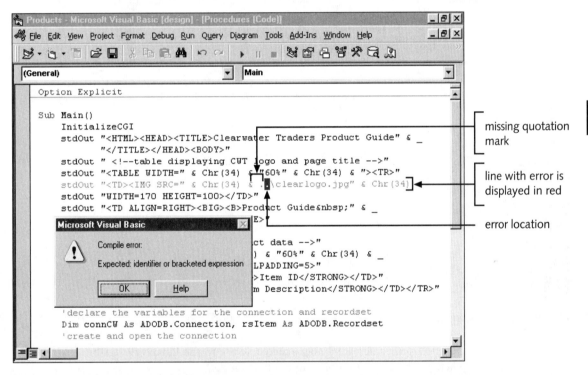

Figure 9-10   String concatenation error

When forming the HTML command string to display the image logo, the programmer forgot to insert the opening quotation mark in the image filename specification. The line with the error is displayed in red, and the approximate location of the compile error is highlighted.

After you eliminate the "red" errors, there still might be errors from text strings where the syntax is correct, but the content is not correct. This usually happens when you concatenate variable values with text strings to create SQL queries. Now you will modify the SQL query in your products.vbp CGI program so that it uses a search condition and only displays the data for one item, item ID 3. However, you will specify item ID 3 using a variable named intItemID, and you will concatenate the variable reference rather than the actual data value into the SQL query string.

To change the SQL query so it uses a search condition:

1. Switch to Visual Basic, and modify the code in the procedures.bas module of the products.vbp project as shown in Figure 9-11.

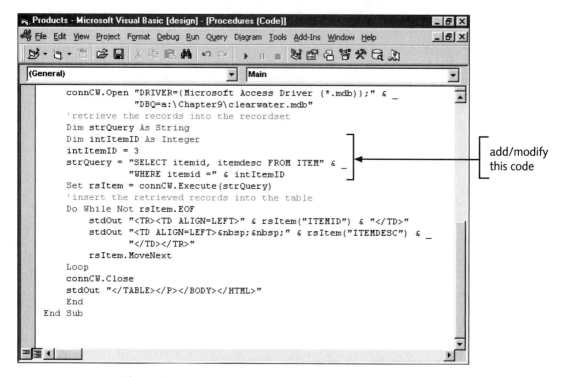

Figure 9-11   Modifying the SQL query to include a search condition

2. Save the project, create a new executable file in the Chapter9\cgi-bin folder, and click **Yes** to confirm replacing the current file.

3. Switch to Internet Explorer, type **http://localhost/** in the Address box, click the **cgi-bin** hyperlink, and then click the **products.exe** hyperlink. The message box shown in Figure 9-12 should be displayed, stating that there is an error in the FROM clause of a SQL query.

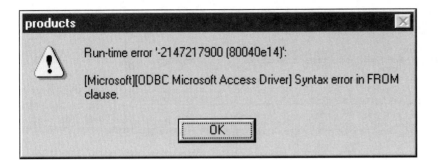

Figure 9-12   SQL query error message box

4. Click **OK**. No data values are displayed on the Product Guide Web page.

To determine the cause of this error, you need to view the text of the SQL query that is created in Visual Basic. To do this, you will set a breakpoint just after the program line that creates the query string by concatenating the text with the variable value. A **breakpoint** is a place in a program where execution is paused while the program is running, allowing the developer to examine variable values. When program execution is paused at a breakpoint, you can place the mouse pointer on any reference to the variable value in the program code, and the current value of the variable will be displayed in a ToolTip window. Now you will set a breakpoint, run the program, and view the value of the query string (strQuery) variable.

To set a breakpoint and examine the query string value:

1. Switch to Visual Basic, and place the insertion point on the following program line.

```
Set rsItem = connCW.Execute(strQuery)
```

Note that this is the line immediately after the command that assigns a value to the query string variable.

2. Click **Debug** on the menu bar, and then click **Toggle Breakpoint** to set a breakpoint on the selected program line. The line that contains the breakpoint is highlighted with a brown background, and a breakpoint indicator (brown dot) is displayed in the gray area on the left side of the window beside the code line that contains the breakpoint.

 You can also set a breakpoint on a line by placing the insertion point on the line and then pressing F9, or by clicking in the gray area on the left side of the Code window beside the line.

3. Click the **Start** button ▶ on the toolbar to run the program. The program runs to the breakpoint, where execution is paused. The next program statement is highlighted in yellow, and is indicated by the position of the execution arrow, as shown in Figure 9-13.

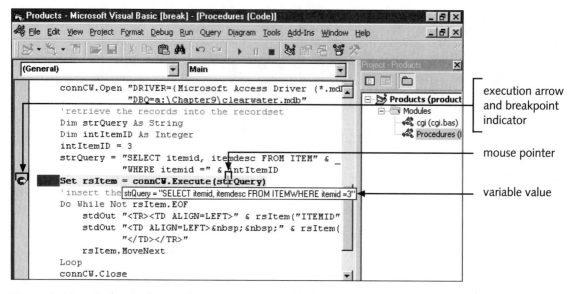

Figure 9-13   Code window with execution paused at breakpoint

4. Place the mouse pointer on **strQuery** in the program line with the breakpoint, as shown in Figure 9-13. The current value of strQuery is displayed in a ToolTip window. Note that the query error was caused because a blank space was not inserted between ITEM and WHERE in the query string.

5. Move the mouse pointer to other variable values and examine their values.

Placing the mouse pointer on variable values to determine their current values works well for variable values that are fairly short, like the one shown in Figure 9-13. When a query string is very long, however, some of the text might not appear in the ToolTip window. In this case, you must use the **Immediate window**, which is a testing area that is displayed when execution is paused while a VB program is running in the VB Integrated Development Environment. You can type a program command in the Immediate window, and the command is immediately executed when you press the Enter key. You can enter any valid program statement except for variable declarations. You can also display the values of variables. To display the value of a particular variable in the Immediate window, you place the insertion point in the Immediate window, and type a question mark (?) followed by the name of the variable whose value you want to display. For example, to display the current value of strQuery, you would type **?strQuery**. Now you will display the value of the query string (strQuery) variable using the Immediate window.

To display the value of strQuery using the Immediate window:

1. Place the insertion point in the Immediate window (see Figure 9-14), type **?strQuery**, and then press the **Enter** key. The value of strQuery is then displayed in the Immediate window.

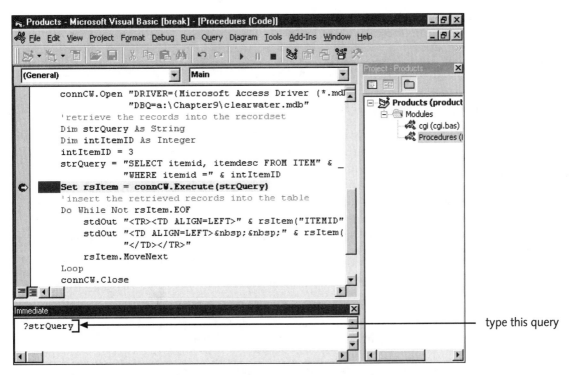

Figure 9-14   Query to display variable value in the Immediate window

 TIP   If the Immediate window is not displayed on your screen, click View on the menu bar, and then click Immediate window.

2. Click the **End** button ■ on the toolbar to end the program.

3. Click the breakpoint indicator (the brown dot in the gray area on the left side of the breakpoint) to remove the breakpoint.

4. Modify the strQuery assignment statement as follows, to include a blank space between ITEM and WHERE in the query string text:

```
strQuery = "SELECT itemid, itemdesc FROM ITEM" & _
           " WHERE itemid =" & intItemID
```

5. Save the project, create an updated project executable file, and then test the CGI program by running it in your Web browser. The Product Guide Web page should be displayed with only item ID 3 displayed.

9

6. Switch back to Visual Basic, and remove the code for the search condition so that your code looks like Figure 9-8 again.

7. Save the project, create an updated project executable file, and then test the CGI program to confirm that it displays all of the item records again.

Calling a CGI Program Using a Hyperlink

Recall from Chapter 8 that when the user clicks the Product Guide link on the Clearwater Traders home page (see Figure 8-2), the Product Guide Web page is displayed. Now you will open the HTML file for the Clearwater Traders home page, which is stored in the Chapter9 folder on your Data Disk as clearwater.html. You will modify the hyperlink command so that it executes the products.exe file that is stored in the cgi-bin folder in the Chapter9 folder on your Data Disk. Since the Chapter9 folder is the root document folder on Personal Web Server, the absolute path to this file will be http://localhost/cgi-bin/products.exe.

To modify the Product Guide link on the Clearwater Traders home page:

1. Switch to Notepad, and open **clearwater.html** from the Chapter9 folder on your Data Disk.

2. Modify the Product Guide tag to include the hyperlink reference to products.exe, as shown in Figure 9-15, and then save the file.

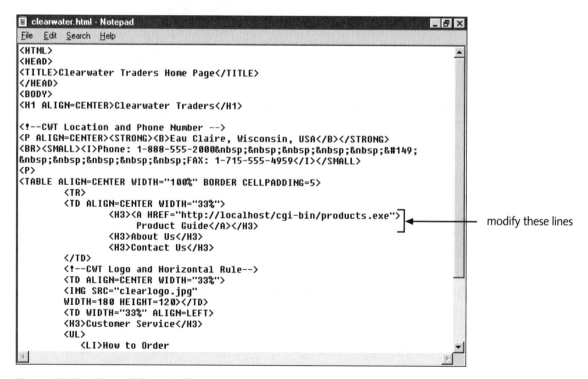

Figure 9-15   Hyperlink to products.exe CGI program

3. Switch to Internet Explorer, type **http://localhost/** in the Address box, and then click the **clearwater.html** link.

4. Click **Product Guide**. The Product Guide Web page created by the CGI program is displayed from the hyperlink.

Creating a CGI Program That Retrieves Input Variables

The CGI program that creates the Product Guide Web page reads data from the database, but does not respond to user inputs. Next, you will create a CGI program that creates the Order Items Web page (see Figure 8-10), which displays the inventory information for the item that the user has selected on the Product Guide Web page. Recall from Figure 8-24 that this program receives the item ID as an input parameter, and stores the selected inventory ID and order quantity as a cookie.

Creating Hyperlinks to Pass Parameter Values in CGI Programs

Recall from Chapter 8 that the hyperlinks for the item ID values on the Product Guide page called an Active Server Page program that received the item ID value as a URL parameter. To call a CGI program and pass a URL parameter value, you will use a similar hyperlink format. The hyperlink lists the name of the CGI program, followed by a question mark and the parameter list variable name/value pairs. Each individual variable name/value pair is separated from the next by an ampersand (&). For example, the hyperlink that calls a CGI program named orderitems.exe and passes URL parameter values for item ID 3 and item description "Airstream Canvas Shoes" uses the following hyperlink tag:

```
<A HREF=orderitems.exe?itemid=3&itemdesc="Airstream Canvas
Shoes">
```

Now you will modify the products.vbp CGI program so that the code contains hyperlink tags for each item ID displayed in the table on the Product Guide Web page. These tags will call a CGI program named orderitems.exe, which you will create shortly. Each tag will pass the item ID value of the item to which the tag is attached.

To modify the products.vbp CGI program to contain hyperlinks that pass the item ID value as a URL parameter:

1. Switch to Visual Basic, and modify the procedures.bas code as shown in Figure 9-16 to create the hyperlink references to the orderitems.exe CGI program, and pass the item ID value as a URL parameter named itemid.

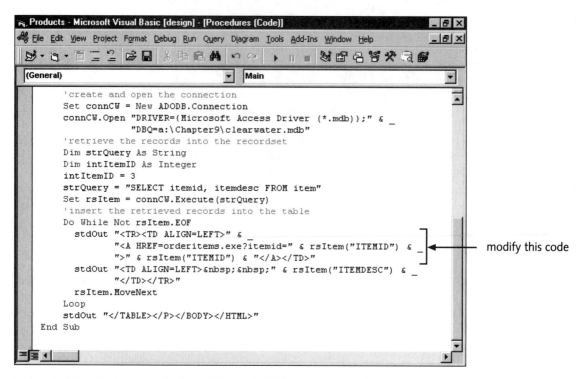

Figure 9-16 Code to create hyperlinks with URL parameter values

2. Save the project and create an updated executable file.

3. Switch to Internet Explorer, type **http://localhost/** in the Address box, click the **cgi–bin** link, and then click **products.exe**. The Product Guide Web page is displayed.

4. Move the mouse pointer onto Item ID **1** in the Product Guide table. The hyperlink text and URL parameter value should be displayed in the status bar on your browser window, as shown in Figure 9-17. Confirm that the hyperlink URL parameters are correct for each item ID link.

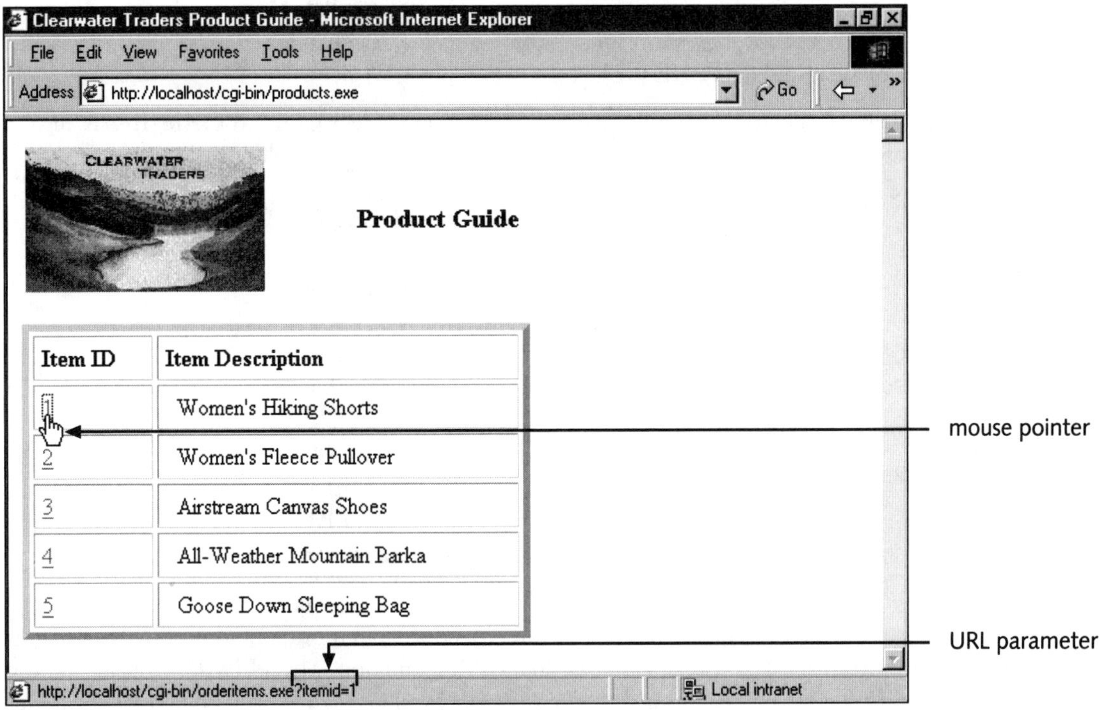

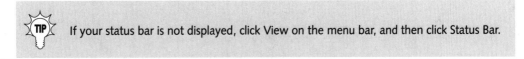

Figure 9-17   Item ID hyperlink URL parameter value

> **TIP**   If your status bar is not displayed, click View on the menu bar, and then click Status Bar.

Creating the Order Items Web Page Using a CGI Program

Now you will create the CGI program that retrieves the item ID input parameter value and creates the Order Items Web page, which shows the inventory information for each inventory record associated with the input item ID. First, you will create a new CGI program in VB, using the same process you have used to create the other CGI programs.

To create the new CGI program:

1. Switch to Windows Explorer, and create a new folder named **Orderitems** in the Chapter9 folder on your Data Disk. This folder will store the Orderitems VB project files.

2. Copy cgi.bas to the Chapter9\Orderitems folder on your Data Disk.

3. Switch to Visual Basic, click **File** on the menu bar, click **New Project**, and then click **Yes** if you are asked if you want to save your changes to products.vbp. Create a Standard EXE project.

4. Remove Form1 from the project, change the project name to **Orderitems**, and add the cgi.bas module that is stored in the Orderitems folder to the project.

5. Add the Microsoft ActiveX Data Objects 2.1 Library to the project (or use the 2.0 Library, if appropriate).

6. Add a new standard module to the project, and name the module **Procedures**. Add the following code to the procedures module:

```
Option Explicit
Sub Main ()
    InitializeCGI
    End
End Sub
```

7. Save the project as **orderitems.vbp** in the Chapter9\Orderitems folder on your Data Disk, and save the new module as **procedures.bas** in the Chapter9\Orderitems folder on your Data Disk.

The next step is to add the HTML code to the procedures.bas module, and modify the code so that each line is passed as a text string to the stdOut function. The HTML template for the Order Items Web page is named orderitem_template.html and is stored in the Chapter9 folder on your Data Disk. Now you will open orderitem_template.html in Notepad, copy all of the text, and paste the HTML commands into the procedures.bas module in the orderitems.vbp file. You will modify each command line so that it is passed as a text string to the stdOut function. Then, you will compile the file, and confirm that it is displayed correctly in Internet Explorer.

To add the HTML template file to the project, modify the HTML commands, and test the file:

1. Switch to Notepad, and open **orderitem_template.html** from the Chapter9 folder on your Data Disk.

2. Copy all of the text, and then paste the text into the procedures.bas module in the orderitems.vbp project directly below the InitializeCGI command (and above the End command).

3. Modify the commands so that each line is a text string input to the stdOut function, as shown in Figures 9-18 and 9-19.

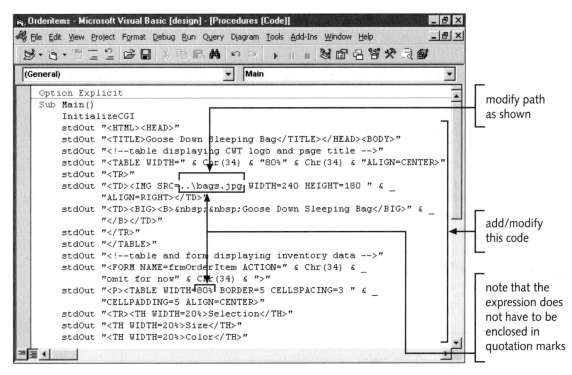

Figure 9-18   Modifying the Order Items HTML template commands

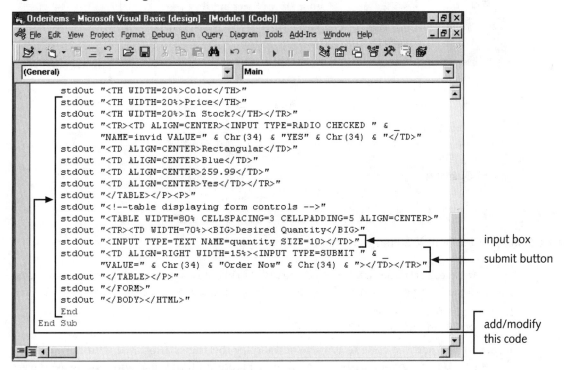

Figure 9-19   Modifying the Order Items HTML template commands (continued)

4. Save the project, then create an executable file named **orderitems.exe**, which should be saved in the cgi-bin folder in the Chapter9 folder on your Data Disk.

5. Switch to Internet Explorer, type **http://localhost/** in the Address box, click the **cgi-bin** link, then click **orderitems.exe**. The Order Items Web page that is created by the CGI program is displayed, as shown in Figure 9-20. Currently, the data values are hard-coded into the program.

The next step is to modify the code to retrieve the item ID input parameter and store it in a Visual Basic variable, and then use the item ID value as a search condition in a SQL query that retrieves the item and inventory data for the selected item ID. Recall that when variable values are passed as URL parameters, they are written to STDIN on the Web server. To receive a value as an input parameter in a CGI program, you use the GetInput function in the cgi.bas module. The GetInput function has the following syntax:

```
[VB variable name] = GetInput("[variable name passed to STDIN]")
```

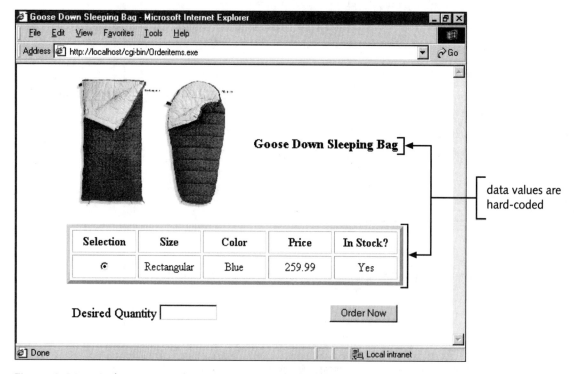

Figure 9-20   Order Items Web page created by CGI program

For example, to declare a variable named strItemID in Visual Basic and assign its value to the value passed to the CGI program as a URL parameter named itemid, you use the following code:

```
Dim strItemID as String
strItemID = GetInput("itemid")
```

First, you will add the code to retrieve and display the values associated with the items ID that is passed as an input variable. Recall from Figure 9-20 that the Order Items Web page displays the item description (for example, "Goose Down Sleeping Bag") and the item image at the top of the page. It also displays the item description as the Web page title, and displays the individual inventory records in a table in the middle of the page. First, you will add the code to retrieve the item description and image filename based on the item ID input parameter. Specifically, you will declare and assign a VB variable to the itemid input parameter value. You will also add the commands to create and open a database connection, create a SQL query string that uses the input parameter value as a search condition, and create a recordset using this SQL query string.

To add the code to retrieve the data values into the Order Items Web page, and test the code in the VB development environment:

1. Switch to Visual Basic, open the procedures.bas module Code window if necessary, place the insertion point at the end of the InitializeCGI command, and press the **Enter** key two times. Add the code shown in Figure 9-21, and then save the project.

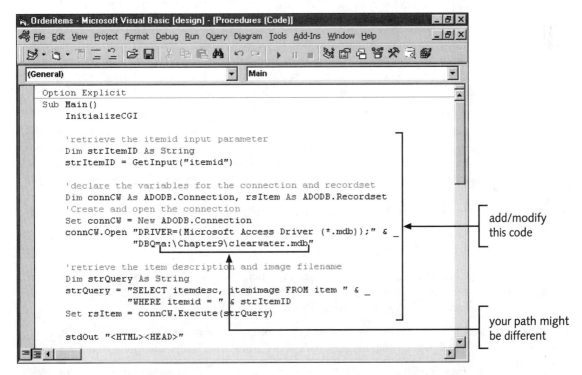

Figure 9-21   Code to retrieve input parameter value and create the database connection and recordset

Now you will run the code in Visual Basic to test it and confirm that the SQL query is formed correctly. This program is expecting to receive the item ID as a URL parameter. To test the program in the VB development environment, you will set a breakpoint to pause execution on the first program line of the GetInput function, which is executed just before the input variable value is retrieved. Then, you will manually set the input variable value to a specific item ID value (such as 1) in the Immediate window. Finally, while the program is running, you will instruct the VB interpreter to skip the steps in the function that change the GetInput function return value to a value based on parameters read from STDIN. As a result, the program will not require a parameter to be read from STDIN, and the program will instead use the input parameter value that you entered in the Immediate window. You will also set a breakpoint on the program line immediately after the query string value is formed, so you can examine the query string and confirm that it is correct.

To test the CGI program in the VB development environment:

1. Open the Code window for the cgi.bas module, and scroll down until you see the declaration for the GetInput function, (`Public Function GetInput(strName As String) As String`). Set a breakpoint on this line.

2. Open the Code window for the Procedures.bas module, scroll down until you see the command immediately after the line where the query string is formed (`Set rsItem = connCW.Execute (strQuery)`), and set a breakpoint on this line.

3. Click the **Start** button ▶ on the toolbar to run the program. The program executes, and execution pauses at the breakpoint, which is the declaration statement for the GetInput function in the cgi.bas module.

4. To manually set the value that is returned by the GetInput function, type **GetInput = 1** in the Immediate window, and then press **Enter**. Now, you will instruct the VB interpreter to skip all of the program statements in the GetInput function. To do this, you will set the last line of the GetInput function, **End Function**, as the next program statement to be executed. As a result, the return value of the GetInput function will not be changed from the value that you entered in the Immediate window, which was item ID 1.

5. Scroll down the Code window in the cgi.bas module, and click the insertion point on **End Function** within the GetInput function.

6. Click **Debug** on the menu bar, and then click **Set Next Statement**. The execution arrow jumps to the selected program line, skipping all of the code lines in the function that would change the value of GetInput.

7. Click ▶ to resume execution. The execution arrow stops at the next breakpoint, which is the program line that occurs immediately after the query string is formed.

8. Type **?strQuery** in the Immediate window, and then press **Enter**. The correct query string should be displayed, as shown in Figure 9-22.

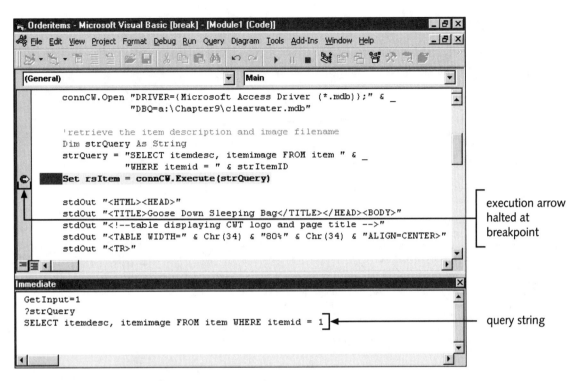

Figure 9-22   Inspecting the rsItem query string

9. Click ▶ to finish executing the program.

10. Click **Debug** on the menu bar, and then click **Clear All Breakpoints**.

Now you will add the code to display the item description and image in the Web page. The item description is displayed in the Web page title, and the description and image file are displayed in the table that is at the top of the Order Items Web page. Then, you will create a new executable file, and run the program from a hyperlink on the Product Guide Web page to confirm that the item data values are retrieved correctly.

To add and test the code to display the item description and image:

1. In Visual Basic, open the Code window for the procedures.bas module, modify the code shown in Figure 9-23, and then save the project.

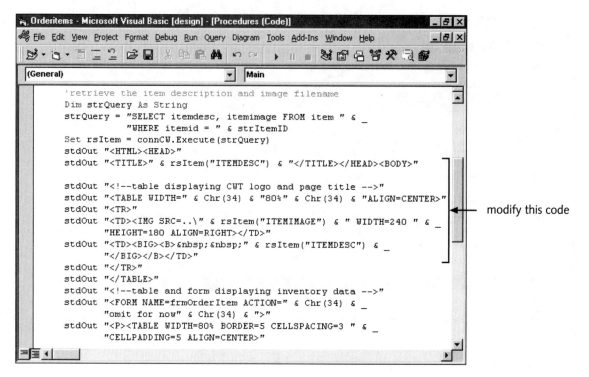

Figure 9-23   Code to display retrieved item description and image

2. Create an updated executable file that replaces the existing file.

3. Switch to Internet Explorer, type **http://localhost/** in the Address box, and then click the **clearwater.html** link. The Clearwater Traders home page is displayed.

4. Click the **Product Guide** hyperlink. The Product Guide Web page that was created by the Products CGI program is displayed. Click Item ID **1** (Women's Hiking Shorts). The Order Items Web page displays the item information for the selected item, as shown in Figure 9-24. Note that the inventory values in the table are not updated yet.

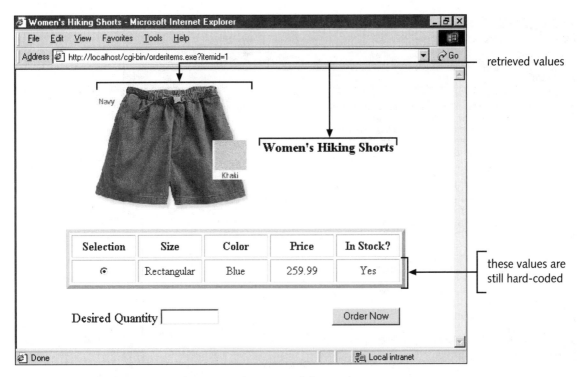

Figure 9-24   Order Items Web page with retrieved data values

Next, you need to update the code to retrieve and display the inventory data (size, color, price, and whether the item is in stock) in the Inventory table in the middle of the Order Items Web page. You will create a new query string that retrieves all of the inventory records for the selected item, using the item ID input parameter value as a search condition. Then, you will create a new recordset based on the query string. You will use a loop to insert the retrieved records into the form table. This code will be inserted into the CGI program immediately after the HTML commands that create the Inventory table headings on the Web page. Recall from Chapter 8 that the value associated with each option button is the inventory ID of the associated record.

To determine if the inventory item is in stock, you will need to check the retrieved value of the quantity on hand (QOH) field. If QOH is greater than zero, then the item is in stock, and the In Stock? value for the item will be Yes. If the quantity on hand is zero, then the In Stock? value will be No. You will test this code in the VB development environment to make sure that the program terminates correctly, and to confirm that the new query string is formed correctly.

To add and test the code to display the inventory information:

1. Switch to Visual Basic, and add or modify the code shown in Figure 9-25 to the procedures.bas module to display the inventory values. You will place the code after the HTML tags that create the column headings in the inventory table on the Web page. Note that you use the connCW database connection object, and create a new query string and associated recordset. Save the project.

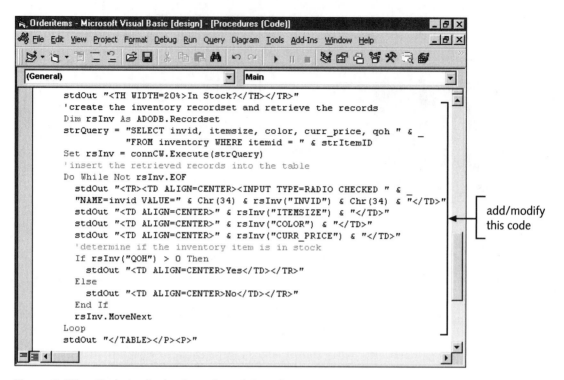

```
                                                                    _ 8 X
   Orderitems - Microsoft Visual Basic [design] - [Procedures (Code)]
   File  Edit  View  Project  Format  Debug  Run  Query  Diagram  Tools  Add-Ins  Window  Help   _ 8 X

(General)                          ▼   Main                                  ▼

     stdOut "<TH WIDTH=20%>In Stock?</TH></TR>"
     'create the inventory recordset and retrieve the records
     Dim rsInv As ADODB.Recordset
     strQuery = "SELECT invid, itemsize, color, curr_price, qoh " & _
                "FROM inventory WHERE itemid = " & strItemID
     Set rsInv = connCW.Execute(strQuery)
     'insert the retrieved records into the table
     Do While Not rsInv.EOF
       stdOut "<TR><TD ALIGN=CENTER><INPUT TYPE=RADIO CHECKED " & _
       "NAME=invid VALUE=" & Chr(34) & rsInv("INVID") & Chr(34) & "></TD>"
       stdOut "<TD ALIGN=CENTER>" & rsInv("ITEMSIZE") & "</TD>"        ← add/modify
       stdOut "<TD ALIGN=CENTER>" & rsInv("COLOR") & "</TD>"             this code
       stdOut "<TD ALIGN=CENTER>" & rsInv("CURR_PRICE") & "</TD>"
       'determine if the inventory item is in stock
       If rsInv("QOH") > 0 Then
         stdOut "<TD ALIGN=CENTER>Yes</TD></TR>"
       Else
         stdOut "<TD ALIGN=CENTER>No</TD></TR>"
       End If
       rsInv.MoveNext
     Loop
     stdOut "</TABLE></P><P>"
```

Figure 9-25   Code to display inventory data values

2. Open the Code window for the cgi.bas module, and set a breakpoint on the first line of the GetInput function.

3. Open the Code window for the Procedures.bas module, scroll down until you see the command immediately after the line where the query string is formed (Set rsInv = connCW.Execute (strQuery)), and set a breakpoint on this line.

4. Click the **Start** button ▶ on the toolbar to run the program. The program executes, and execution pauses at the first breakpoint, which is the declaration statement for the GetInput function in the cgi.bas module.

5. Manually set the value that is returned by the GetInput function by typing **GetInput = 1** in the Immediate window, and then pressing **Enter**.

If your previous inputs and variable values are still displayed in the Immediate window, you can delete them by selecting them with the mouse pointer and then pressing the Delete key.

6. Scroll down the Code window in the cgi.bas module, and click the insertion point on **End Function** within the GetInput function. Click **Debug** on the menu bar, and then click **Set Next Statement**. The execution arrow jumps to the selected program line, skipping all of the code lines in the function that would change the value of GetInput.

7. Click ▶ to resume execution. The execution arrow stops at the next breakpoint, which is the program line that occurs immediately after the query string is formed.

8. Type **?strQuery** in the Immediate window, and then press **Enter**. The correct query string should be displayed, as shown in Figure 9-26. (You might need to scroll to the right edge of the Immediate window to view all of the query string text.)

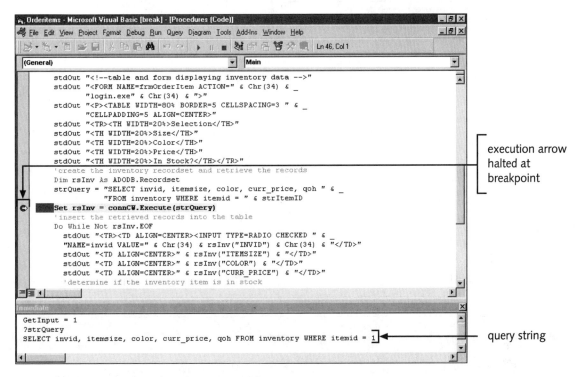

Figure 9-26   Inspecting the rsInv query string

9. Click ▶ to finish executing the program. Confirm that the program terminates correctly by making sure that the Start button ▶ is enabled on the toolbar when the program finishes running.

10. Click **Debug** on the menu bar, and then click **Clear All Breakpoints**.

Now you will create an updated executable file, and run the program from a hyperlink on the Product Guide Web page to confirm that the inventory data are displayed correctly.

To compile and test the program:

1. Save the project, and then create an updated executable file to replace the existing orderitem.exe file that is saved in the cgi-bin folder in the Chapter9 folder on your Data Disk.

2. Switch to Internet Explorer, type **http://localhost/** in the Address box, and then click the **clearwater.html** hyperlink. The Clearwater Traders home page is displayed.

3. Click **Product Guide**. The Product Guide Web page that was created by the Products CGI program is displayed. Click Item ID **1** (Women's Hiking Shorts). The inventory data for the selected item ID are displayed as shown in Figure 9-27.

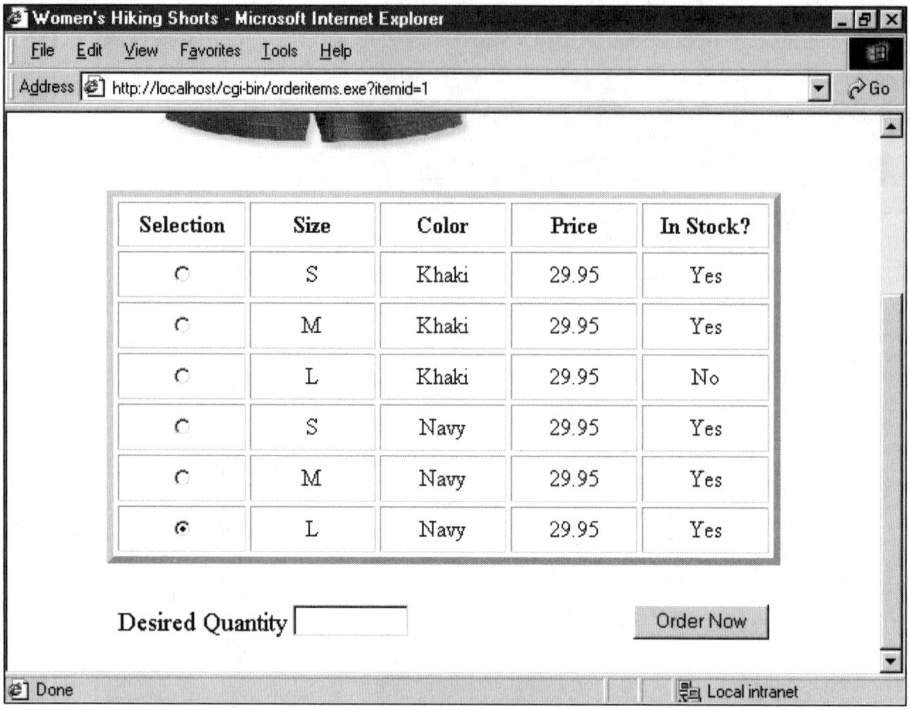

Figure 9-27   Inventory data on Order Items Web page

Sharing Data Values With Other CGI Programs

CGI programs, like Active Server Pages, can pass data values as URL parameters, as form parameters, or as cookies. URL parameters are passed to a CGI program within a form ACTION tag by forming the ACTION parameter using the name of the CGI executable file and a question mark, and then listing the URL parameter variable name/value pairs, separated by ampersands. You used a URL parameter in the hyperlink on the Product Guide Web page to call the orderitems.exe CGI program. This hyperlink passed the selected item ID to the orderitems.exe CGI program as a URL parameter. The orderitems.exe CGI program then generated the Order Items Web page, which displayed inventory information about the selected item ID.

Recall that a form parameter is passed to the Web server when an HTML form is submitted to the Web server by the user. Form parameters are the names and associated values of form controls, such as option buttons or input boxes. The control names and current values of all form controls are written to STDIN when a form is submitted to the Web server. And, recall that a cookie is a data file that is written on the user's workstation by a program within a Web page, and is available to any Web page in an application, regardless of the order in which the Web page is selected and viewed.

Recall from Figure 8-24 that the Order Items Web page needs to pass the inventory ID and quantity to the Login form if the user has not yet logged in to the system, or to the Order Summary page, if the user has already logged in. Now, you will create a CGI program that will create the Login form for the Clearwater application. This form (see Figure 8-25) receives the inventory ID and quantity selected on the Order Items Web page as input parameters, and stores these values in hidden form fields. After the user enters his or her user ID and password into the form input boxes and clicks the Submit Query button, the form stores the user ID and password values in a cookie, and passes the values for the inventory ID and order quantity to the Order Summary form as form parameters. First, you will create a new project folder and project in Visual Basic for the Login form, and perform the steps required to create a CGI program.

To create the Login form CGI program:

1. Switch to Windows Explorer, and create a new folder named **Login** in the Chapter9 folder on your Data Disk. Copy cgi.bas from the Chapter9 folder on your Data Disk to the Chapter9\Login folder on your Data Disk.

2. Start another session of Visual Basic, and create a Standard EXE project. Remove Form1 from the project, change the project name to **Login**, and add the cgi.bas module to the project. (You will keep the current VB session with the Order Items project open, because you will modify its code in a little while.)

3. Add the Microsoft ActiveX Data Objects 2.1 Library to the project (or add the 2.0 Library, if appropriate).

4. Add a new standard module to the project, and name the module **Procedures**. Add the code to the procedures module to create a Sub Main () procedure, call the InitializeCGI procedure, and end the program (see Figure 9-5).

5. Save the project as **login.vbp** in the Chapter9\Login folder on your Data Disk, and save the new module as **procedures.bas** in the Chapter9\Login folder on your Data Disk.

As always, the next step is to add the HTML template code to the module, and modify the code so that each line of HTML commands is passed as a text string to the StdOut function. The HTML template file for the Login Web page is named login_template.html, and is stored in the Chapter9 folder on your Data Disk. Now you will open login_template.html in Notepad, copy all of the text, and paste the HTML commands into the procedures module in the login.vbp project file. You will modify each command line so that it is passed as a text string to the StdOut function. Then, you will compile the file, and confirm that it is displayed correctly in your Web browser.

To add the HTML template file to the project, modify the HTML commands, and test the file:

1. Switch to Notepad, open **login_template.html** from the Chapter9 folder on your Data Disk, copy all of the text, and then paste the text into the procedures.bas module in the login.vbp project directly below the InitializeCGI command, and above the End command.

2. Modify the commands so that each line is a text string input to the StdOut function, as shown in Figure 9-28. Notice that the code for the hidden form fields that store the values for the inventory ID and order quantity parameters is included in the template.

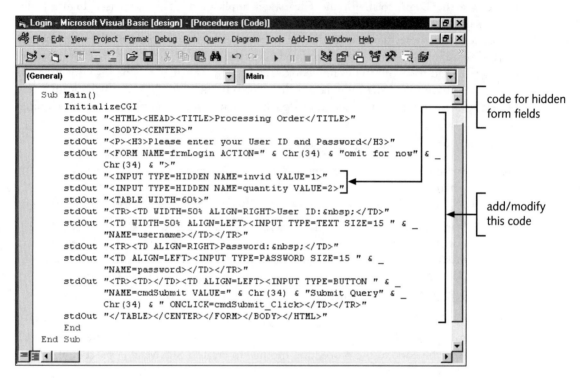

Figure 9-28   Modifying the Login form HTML template commands

3. Save the project, and then create an executable file named **login.exe**. Save login.exe in the cgi-bin folder in the Chapter9 folder on your Data Disk.

4. Switch to Internet Explorer, type **http://localhost/** in the Address box, click the **cgi-bin** link, and then click **login.exe**. The Login Web page that is created by the CGI program is displayed, as shown in Figure 9-29.

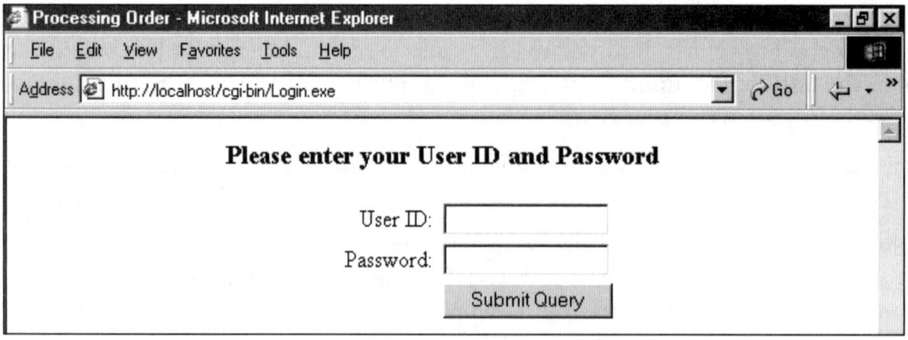

Figure 9-29   Login Web page created by the CGI program

You will pass the inventory ID and order quantity from the Order Items Web page to the Login page as form parameters. To do this, you will modify the CGI program that generates the Order Items Web page so that it calls the login.exe CGI program. Recall from Figure 9-19 that the Order Now button on the Order Items Web page is a button of type SUBMIT, so when the user clicks this button, the values of the form controls are written to STDIN on the Web server, and the parameters are passed as form parameters to the login.exe CGI program.

To modify the CGI program that generates the Order Items page to call the login.exe program:

1. Switch to the Visual Basic session that is running the Orderitems.vbp project file, and modify the procedures.bas module in the Orderitems project as shown in Figure 9-30.

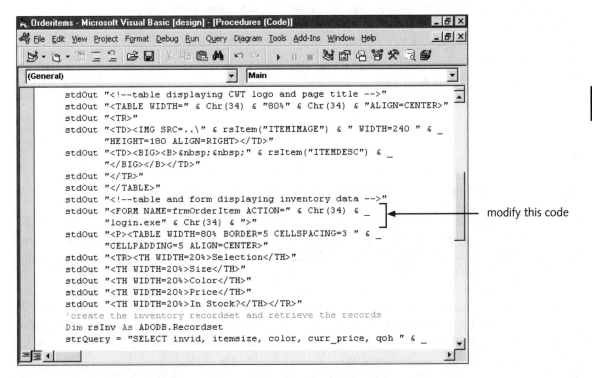

Figure 9-30   Code to call login.exe CGI program in the Orderitems project

2. Save the project, and then create a new executable orderitems.exe file.

3. Exit the VB session where the Orderitems.vbp project file is running.

Now, you will test the modifications that you just made in the Orderitems and Login programs. You will select an item on the Product Guide Web page, display the modified Order Items Web page, select an inventory item and enter an order quantity, and then click the Order Now button to submit the inputs to the Web server and call the login.exe CGI program. The login.exe CGI program will then generate the Login Web page.

To test the Orderitems and Login CGI programs:

1. Switch to Internet Explorer, type **http://localhost/** in the Address box, click **clearwater.html**, and then click the **Product Guide** hyperlink. The Product Guide Web page is displayed.

2. Click Item ID **1** (Women's Hiking Shorts). The Order Items Web page for Women's Hiking Shorts is displayed.

3. Click the option button associated with size M and color Khaki, type **2** for Desired Quantity, and then click **Order Now**. The Login form is displayed, as shown in Figure 9-31. Note that the form parameters are shown in the URL.

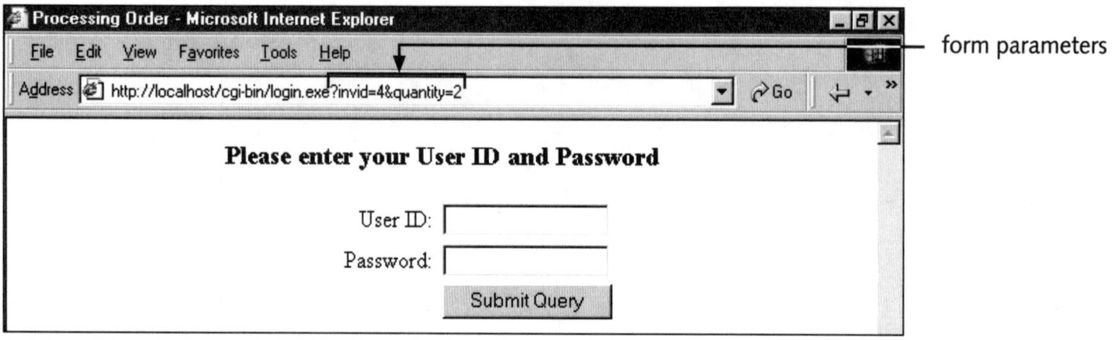

Figure 9-31   Login form with form parameter values displayed in URL

The next step is to modify the code in the Login project to retrieve the form parameter values for the inventory ID and order quantity, and then store these values in the hidden form fields. To do this, you will declare VB variables to reference the inventory ID and quantity values, and then use the GetInput function to retrieve these values, which are passed as form parameters. Figure 9-31 shows that the inventory ID value is referenced by the variable name invid, and that the order quantity value is referenced by the variable name quantity. To retrieve the value for the inventory ID, you will pass the name of the variable invid to the GetInput function. Then, you will perform the same operation for the quantity variable.

To retrieve the inventory ID and quantity values and store them in the hidden form fields:

1. Switch to Visual Basic, modify the procedures.bas module as shown in Figure 9-32, and then save the project.

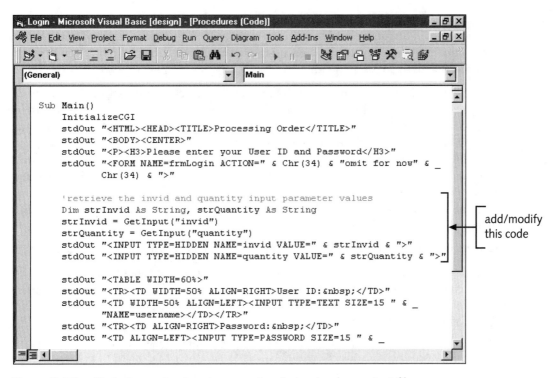

Figure 9-32   Code to receive input parameters in Login.vbp project file

2. Create a new executable file for the project.

3. Switch to Internet Explorer, type **http://localhost/** in the Address box, click **clearwater.html**, and then click the **Product Guide** link. The Product Guide Web page is displayed.

4. Click Item ID **1** (Women's Hiking Shorts). The Order Items Web page for Women's Hiking Shorts is displayed.

5. Click the option button associated with size M and color Khaki, type **2** for Desired Quantity, and then click **Order Now**. The Login form is displayed again, as shown in Figure 9-31. Since the form parameter values were assigned to hidden form fields, there is no visible change to the Web page output.

Recall from Chapter 8 that when the user entered his or her user ID and password in the input boxes on the Login form, the values were stored in a cookie created by a client-side script. To include a client-side script in a Web page that is generated by a CGI program, you use the same script commands as you used in the Active Server Page, but you must direct the script commands to STDOUT, so that the script commands are included in the Web page source file, and will be run by the user's browser when the Web page is displayed. To do this, you pass each script code line as a text parameter to the stdOut function, just as you do with HTML commands in a CGI program.

Now, you will add the code to the Login project for the client-side script that creates a cookie that stores the user ID and password. The text of the code for this script is shown in Figure 8–35, and is included in a text file named cookie.txt in the Chapter9 folder on your Data Disk. You will open this file in Notepad, copy the text of the script commands, paste the commands into the procedures.bas module within the Login project, and then modify the commands so that each line is sent as a parameter to the stdOut function. Modifying the client-side script commands so they can be sent as text strings to stdOut can be tricky, because the commands have quotation marks that are embedded within text strings. For example, the first command of the script is as follows:

```
Document.Cookie = "username=" & Document.frmLogin.username.Value & ";"
```

To convert this command so it is an input text string to the stdOut function, you must replace each quotation mark with the VB Chr(34) character code. This becomes confusing because you must concatenate the Chr(34) character code within the concatenated text string, as follows:

```
stdOut "Document.Cookie = " & Chr(34) & "username=" & Chr(34) & "
& Document.frmLogin.username.Value & " & Chr(34) & ";" & Chr(34)
```

When you are modifying script commands that contain text strings with embedded quotation marks, remember to replace each quotation mark with Chr(34), and include all of the existing spaces and concatenation operators (&) within the text string.

To add the client-side script to the Login project:

1. Switch to Notepad, open **cookie.txt** from the Chapter9 folder on your Data Disk, and then copy all of the text in the file.

2. Switch to Visual Basic, and paste the copied text just below the closing TITLE tag command and above the opening BODY tag in the procedure.bas module in the Login.vbp project file, as shown in Figure 9-33.

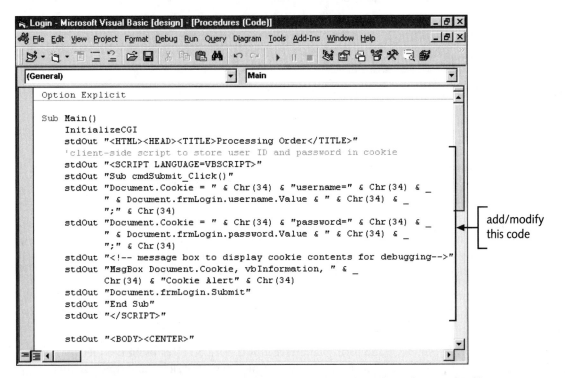

Figure 9-33 Modifying the client-side script commands in the Login.vbp project file

3. Modify the script commands as shown in Figure 9-33, so the commands are sent as parameters to the StdOut function.

4. Save the project, and then create a new executable login.exe file.

5. Switch to Internet Explorer, where the Login Web page is displayed. Click the **Back** button ⬅ on the browser toolbar to redisplay the Order Items Web page, and then click **Order Now** to reload the login.exe CGI program.

6. Type **harrispe** in the user ID input box, and **asdf** in the password input box. Click **Submit Query** to run the client-side script. A message box showing the cookie values (Figure 9-34) is displayed. Click **OK**. An error message is displayed, because no action is currently specified for the Login Web page.

Figure 9-34   Message box showing cookie contents

> If the message box shown in Figure 9-34 is not displayed, then you probably made a mistake when you modified the script code so that it would be passed as text strings to stdOut. The best way to find client-side script errors is to click View on the browser menu bar, and then click Source, and view the Web page source code. The source code for this script should look like the source code for the script in Figure 8-35.

You have now learned the basic principles for creating CGI programs using Visual Basic, as well as how to pass parameter values and include client-side scripts. In summary, use the following process for creating CGI programs to generate dynamic Web pages:

1. Send all HTML commands, data values, and client-side script commands that will be forwarded to the user's browser to STDOUT as text strings using the stdOut function in cgi.bas.

2. Retrieve URL and form parameter inputs from STDIN using the GetInput function in cgi.bas. You can assign these values to VB variables, and then use them in VB commands.

3. Create an ADODB connection object to reference a database, and use the recordset Execute method to manipulate data using SQL commands. You can use SQL SELECT commands to view data, as well as SQL INSERT, UPDATE, and DELETE commands to change database data.

Completing the Login form and the other forms in the Clearwater Traders sales order application will be left as end-of-chapter projects.

ADVANTAGES AND DISADVANTAGES OF USING CGI PROGRAMS

CGI programs can be written in any programming language that allows you to write values directly to STDIN and STDOUT on a Web server. A CGI program can be used with most Web servers and operating systems. For example, the CGI programs that you create in Visual Basic could be used with a Netscape Web server, Microsoft Web server, Oracle Web Application Server, or any other Web server designed to run on the Windows operating system. In contrast, Active Server Pages run only on a Microsoft Web server.

Recall that CGI programs are compiled programs. The program source code (like the Visual Basic commands you type in the VB development environment) is converted into machine language (the binary language understood by your computer's processor) when you compile the program. In contrast, script commands must be converted into machine language each time the script is run. For this reason, compiled programs execute (run) much faster than scripts.

If being able to use a variety of different Web servers and having compiled programs were the only criteria under consideration when creating Web applications, you would always use CGI programs. However, the drawback of CGI programs is that they do not use Web server resources efficiently. Suppose that 10 people submit the same HTML form to a Web server at the same time. Ten separate copies of the CGI program servicing the form will be started on the Web server. If each copy of the program consumes 100 KB of main memory, then 1 MB of Web server main memory will be tied up servicing these forms. If 100 forms are submitted at the same time, 10 MB of Web server memory is consumed, and so on. On a busy Web site, all of the Web server's main memory could be consumed trying to service multiple submissions of the same HTML form, and the Web server would be very slow in sending responses back to users.

To solve this problem, vendors are developing products to allow a single CGI program to service multiple submissions of the same form. These programs can be installed on Microsoft's and many other vendors' Web servers. An example of such a product is FastCGI (www.fastcgi.com). Although this product costs several thousand dollars per server, the price may well be worth paying in exchange for the ability to efficiently run existing CGI programs on busy Web sites.

9

USING ACTIVEX DLLS FOR SERVER-SIDE WEB PROCESSING

Recall that dynamic-link libraries (DLLs) are compiled code modules that are called from other programs. A DLL is not a stand-alone program, but it contains code that can be **linked** to, or used by, many different programs. The code modules in a DLL are called "libraries" because their code can be "checked out" and used by many different programs. A DLL is somewhat different from a conventional library system in that the code from a specific DLL can be used simultaneously by many different programs.

Many Windows programs use DLLs. For example, most computers running Windows have a DLL file named cards.dll that contains the compiled code to represent the graphic images of a standard deck of playing cards. When you play Solitaire or Hearts on your computer, the game links to this DLL and uses its code to display the images of the cards. This DLL could be used for other card game programs that might be created by program developers. Storing the code for the cards in a single shared library, instead of duplicating the code in each game that uses playing cards, allows the program files for each card game program to be smaller, and each program developer doesn't have to create or obtain the graphic images for playing cards.

An ActiveX DLL is a code module that is stored on the Web server, and runs in the Web server's memory space. ActiveX DLLs can only be used with Microsoft Web servers. An ActiveX DLL can perform functions that are similar to the CGI programs that you wrote earlier. ActiveX DLLs have a significant advantage over CGI programs, since a single copy of an ActiveX DLL can service an unlimited number of user requests without starting additional copies of the program. In this chapter, you will create ActiveX DLLs using Visual Basic. Since procedures in an ActiveX DLL must be called from another program, you will call ActiveX DLLs from Active Server Pages.

You can call ActiveX DLLs directly from the Web server, just as you call CGI programs from the Web server, if you use Microsoft's ISAPI (Internet Server Application Programming Interface), which is a protocol for starting ActiveX DLLs from a Web server and passing data between the Web server and the DLL. You will not be able to use this approach in this chapter, because the ability to call ActiveX DLLs from the Web server requires writing or purchasing an additional DLL to allow your VB DLL to read form inputs and send responses directly back to the Web server. If you want to investigate ISAPI, one VB DLL translation option is a product called IdleY ISAPI, which is available at www.macrofirm.com. This program provides custom functions to read form inputs and send outputs back to the Web server, using functions and procedures that are similar to the ones in the cgi.bas module included with this book.

Differences Between ActiveX DLLs and CGI Programs

Unlike a CGI program, an ActiveX DLL is not a stand-alone program, and it comprises one or more procedures that must be called from another program. Also, an ActiveX DLL must be entered into the Registry of the Web server where it will be used, so that other programs will be able to call the procedures within the DLL. This can be done by compiling the ActiveX DLL on the Web server. This can also be done by creating a setup program for the ActiveX DLL using the VB Package and Deployment Wizard, and then installing the ActiveX DLL on the Web server.

The Registry is a facility that is used by the Windows95, Windows98, Windows NT, and Windows 2000 operating systems to store configuration and system information about your computer.

When an ActiveX DLL is called from an ASP, you must explicitly add the code to send the form inputs as parameters from the ASP to the DLL in the ASP command that calls the ActiveX DLL procedure. Furthermore, when an ActiveX DLL is called from an ASP, it returns outputs to the calling ASP script either as a value returned by a function, or by changing the values of variables that were passed to the ActiveX DLL as input parameters from the calling program.

When an ActiveX DLL is created using ISAPI, the Web server calls the relevant procedure in the ActiveX DLL. The ActiveX DLL is capable of reading form inputs and sending outputs to the Web server using ISAPI functions that are similar to the GetInput and stdOut functions that you used from the cgi.bas module in your CGI programs.

Creating an ActiveX DLL Using Visual Basic

Now you will create an ActiveX DLL and an associated ASP that displays the form shown in Figure 9-2, and then displays the output shown in Figure 9-3. First, you need to create two folders: (1) a folder named asp-bin in the Chapter9 folder on your Data Disk, which you will use to store your ASPs and your compiled DLLs, and (2) a folder named DLL_1 that will be used to store the VB source code files for the initial ActiveX DLL project. Then, you will modify the asp-bin virtual directory on your Personal Web server so that it is associated with the asp-bin folder in the Chapter9 folder on your Data Disk, and modify this folder so that it has Execute privileges.

To create the folders and modify the virtual directory:

1. Switch to Windows Explorer, and create folders named **asp-bin** and **DLL_1** in the Chapter9 folder on your Data Disk.

2. Switch to Personal Web Manager, and open the Advanced page if necessary. Click **asp-bin** in the Virtual Directories list, click **Edit Properties**, click **Browse**, navigate to the Chapter9\asp-bin folder on your Data Disk to associate this physical folder with the virtual directory, and then click **OK**. Windows 2000 users should make sure that the Read check box is checked, and that the Scripts option button is selected.

3. Make sure that the Execute and Read check boxes are checked, and that the Scripts check box is cleared, and then click **OK**. Windows 2000 users should make sure that the Read check box is checked, and that the Scripts option button is selected.

Now you will create an ASP that retrieves the inputs that the user enters in the HTML form shown in Figure 9-2, and then creates the Web page shown in Figure 9-3. This ASP will display the form inputs directly, and will display the Web server environment variables using an ActiveX DLL. This DLL is similar to the DisplayAll procedure that you used when you created this application using a CGI program (see Figure 9-4).

To create an ActiveX DLL in Visual Basic, you will create a new project named Environment that will be compiled as an ActiveX DLL. A VB ActiveX DLL consists of a class module that contains multiple functions or procedures that can be called by programs that link to the DLL. A **class** is a template from which an object is created. Recall from Chapter 6 that in object-oriented programming languages, an object is an item that has a specific structure and behavior, and that objects have associated methods, which are procedures that perform an operation on an object. The code in this class module describes the attributes and behavior of objects that are created from the class.

Within this project, you will name the class clsEnvironment, and then write the code for a function named ReturnEnvVars that returns a string variable that lists the environment variables for the current computer. This function will use a VB function named Environ$, which has the following syntax:

```
[string variable] = Environ$([numeric value of environment variable])
```

The string variable is declared in VB, and will reference the list of environment variables that will be returned to the calling program. Environment variables can be accessed in VB using an integer value that corresponds to the position of a specific environment variable in the overall list of environment variables. For example, in Figure 9-3, the Windows directory (windir) variable is in position 1, the Windows boot directory (winbootdir) is in position 2, and so on. The final environment variable is an empty string. You will use a Do ... Loop to retrieve all of the environment variables until the empty string variable is retrieved. The value of each variable will be appended to a second string variable named strAll, which will contain the complete list of variables, with a line break tag (<BR>) inserted between each variable value and the next.

To create the DLL to return the list of environment variables:

1. Switch to Visual Basic, and create a new ActiveX DLL Project. Save the changes to your current project, if necessary.

2. Select **Project1** in the Project Explorer, and name the project **Environment**.

3. Select **Class1** in the Project Explorer, and name the class module **clsEnvironment**.

4. Open the clsEnvironment Code window, and add the code shown in Figure 9-35 to retrieve the list of environment variables.

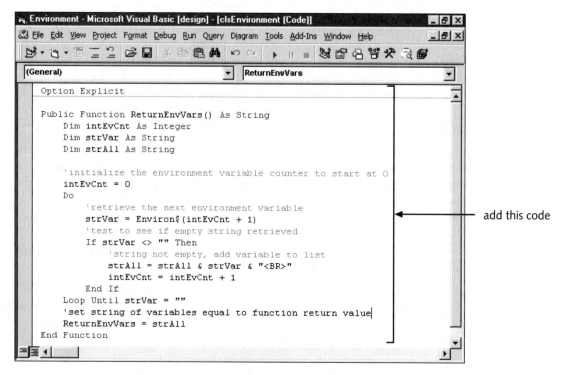

add this code

```vb
Option Explicit

Public Function ReturnEnvVars() As String
    Dim intEvCnt As Integer
    Dim strVar As String
    Dim strAll As String

    'initialize the environment variable counter to start at 0
    intEvCnt = 0
    Do
        'retrieve the next environment variable
        strVar = Environ$(intEvCnt + 1)
        'test to see if empty string retrieved
        If strVar <> "" Then
            'string not empty, add variable to list
            strAll = strAll & strVar & "<BR>"
            intEvCnt = intEvCnt + 1
        End If
    Loop Until strVar = ""
    'set string of variables equal to function return value
    ReturnEnvVars = strAll
End Function
```

Figure 9-35   DLL code to retrieve environment variable list

5. Click the **Save Project** button ![save] on the toolbar. Navigate to the DLL_1 folder in the Chapter9 folder on your Data Disk, and save the class as **clsEnvironment.cls**, and the project as **environment.vbp** in the Chapter9\DLL_1 folder.

6. Click **File** on the menu bar, and then click **Make Environment.dll**. If necessary, navigate to the Chapter9\DLL_1 folder on your Data Disk, and then click **OK**.

When you compile the DLL, the Registry settings that are required for other programs to find your DLL are added to your system Registry. If you want to use this DLL on a different workstation, you must install the DLL on that computer using an installation program created with the VB Package and Deployment Wizard to add the needed Registry settings.

When an ActiveX DLL is linked to a program, the ActiveX DLL remains in the workstation's memory until the workstation is rebooted. The ActiveX DLL cannot be recompiled until the operating system releases the DLL file. Therefore, if you make a change in an ActiveX DLL, you must reboot your workstation to unload the DLL, and then recompile the DLL.

Creating an Active Server Page That Calls an ActiveX DLL

Next, you will create the Active Server Page that will call the Environment DLL. This ASP will retrieve the inputs that the user enters in the Name input box, Comments text area, and Reply option button on the HTML form (see Figure 9-2) as form parameters. Recall that to retrieve a form parameter value into an ASP, you use the Request object's Querystring property, which has the following syntax:

```
<% =Request.Querystring("[name of form control associated with parameter]") %>
```

For example, to retrieve the value in the Name input box, you use the following syntax:

```
<% =Request.Querystring("Name") %>
```

Now you will create the ASP and add the code to display the form parameters.

To create the ASP and display the form parameters:

1. Start or switch to Notepad, and type the code shown in Figure 9-36 to create the ASP. Save the file as **ASP_1.asp** in the Chapter9\asp-bin folder on your Data Disk.

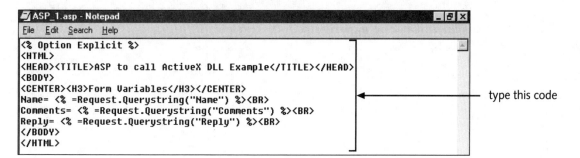

Figure 9-36   Code to create ASP_1.asp

Recall that the HTML document file for the form displayed in Figure 9-2 is stored in the cgi_1.html file in the Chapter9 folder on your Data Disk. Now you will make a copy of this file, name it ASP_1.html, and modify it so that the form's ACTION attribute calls the ASP_1.asp ASP that you just created. Then, you will test the Web page in your Web browser to make sure that the ASP works correctly.

To modify and test the HTML form document:

1. Switch to Windows Explorer, navigate to the Chapter9 folder on your Data Disk, click **cgi_1.html**, and then press **Ctrl + C** to copy the file.

2. Press **Ctrl + V** to paste a copy of the file into the Chapter9 folder on your Data Disk. A file named Copy of cgi_1.html is displayed in the file listing. Rename the new file **ASP_1.html**.

3. Switch to Notepad, and open **ASP_1.html** from the Chapter9 folder on your Data Disk.

4. Modify the code as shown in Figure 9-37, and then save the file.

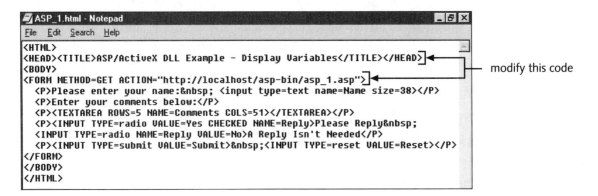

Figure 9-37   HTML code in ASP_1.html

5. Switch to Internet Explorer, type **http://localhost/** in the Address box, and then click the **ASP_1.html** link. The HTML form shown in Figure 9-2 is displayed.

6. Type **Paula Harris** in the Name input box, and type **Writing ActiveX DLLS is an enthralling experience** in the text area.

7. Click the **A Reply Isn't Needed** option button, and then click **Submit** to submit the form to the Web server. The output from the Web server is displayed, as shown in Figure 9-38.

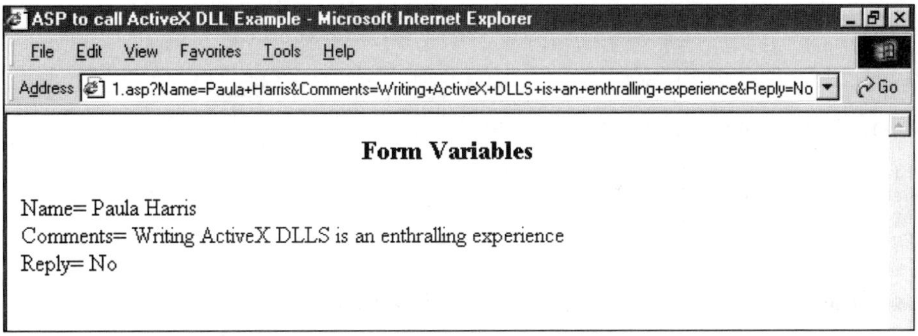

Figure 9-38   Web page output created by ASP_1.html

After the ASP retrieves and displays the form parameters, it must call the Environment DLL to retrieve the environment variables list. To enable it to do this, you must create a server object in the ASP. Recall that a server object is a memory area on the Web server that stores the variables and other information needed to process the ASP. In Chapter 8, you created a server object for the database connection. To call an ActiveX DLL from an ASP, you create a server object that is based on the object class name in the DLL. To do this, you use the following syntax:

```
Set [object variable name] =
Server.CreateObject("[DLL project name].[DLL object class name]")
```

In the Environment DLL, the DLL project name is Environment, and the DLL object class name is clsEnvironment. Therefore, the code to create a server object named dllEnvironment for the Environment DLL is as follows:

```
Set dllEnvironment = Server.CreateObject ("Environment.clsEnvironment")
```

To reference a particular function or procedure within the DLL class module, you use the following syntax:

```
[object variable name].[DLL function or procedure name]
```

In the Environment DLL, the DLL function that you created to retrieve the environment variables was named ReturnEnvVars (see Figure 9-35). To retrieve the environment variable list into a variable named strEnvVars in an ASP, you add the following code to your ASP:

```
<% strEnvVars = dllEnvironment.ReturnEnvVars %>
```

Now, you will add the commands to ASP_1 to create the DLL server object, call the DLL function, and retrieve and display the environment variables.

To add the commands to call the ActiveX DLL:

1. Switch to Notepad, open **ASP_1.asp** from the Chapter9\asp-bin folder on your Data Disk, add the code shown in Figure 9-39, and then save the file.

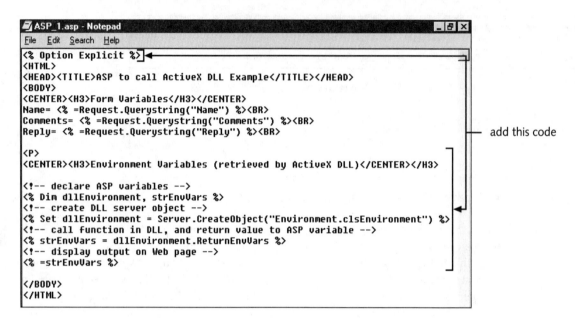

```
ASP_1.asp - Notepad
File  Edit  Search  Help
<% Option Explicit %>
<HTML>
<HEAD><TITLE>ASP to call ActiveX DLL Example</TITLE></HEAD>
<BODY>
<CENTER><H3>Form Variables</H3></CENTER>
Name= <% =Request.Querystring("Name") %><BR>
Comments= <% =Request.Querystring("Comments") %><BR>
Reply= <% =Request.Querystring("Reply") %><BR>

<P>
<CENTER><H3>Environment Variables (retrieved by ActiveX DLL)</CENTER></H3>

<!-- declare ASP variables -->
<% Dim dllEnvironment, strEnvVars %>
<!-- create DLL server object -->
<% Set dllEnvironment = Server.CreateObject("Environment.clsEnvironment") %>
<!-- call function in DLL, and return value to ASP variable -->
<% strEnvVars = dllEnvironment.ReturnEnvVars %>
<!-- display output on Web page -->
<% =strEnvVars %>

</BODY>
</HTML>
```

add this code

Figure 9-39   Code in ASP_1.asp to call the ReturnEnvVars function in DLL

2. Switch to Internet Explorer, type **http://localhost/** in the Address box, and then click the **ASP_1.html** link. The HTML form shown in Figure 9-2 is displayed.

3. Type **Paula Harris** in the Name input box, and type **Writing ActiveX DLLS is an enthralling experience** in the text area.

4. Click the **A Reply Isn't Needed** option button, and then click **Submit** to submit the form to the Web server. The Web page generated by ASP_1.asp is displayed, as shown in Figure 9-40.

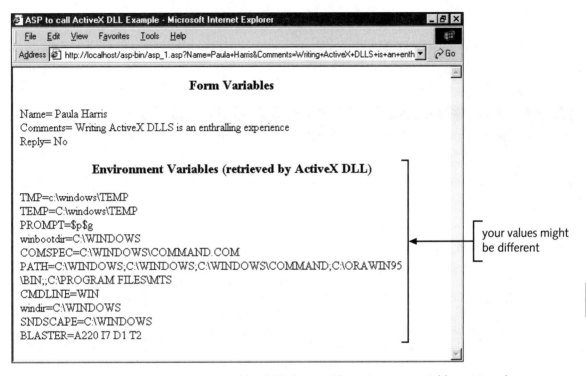

Figure 9-40   Web page output generated by ASP_1.asp with enviroment variables retrieved
using DLL

Registry Changes Made When an ActiveX DLL Is Compiled

Now you will view the Registry entries that were made when your ActiveX DLL was compiled. This will help you to understand how the ASP finds and calls the ActiveX DLL. Normally, Registry entries are made by programs when they are installed or modified. The Registry stores information such as the location of program files, and user preferences such as the toolbars that are displayed in a program. To view Registry entries on a Windows95, Windows98, Windows NT, or Windows 2000 workstation, you use a utility named REGEDIT. (Windows NT users can use a utility named REGEDIT32, which has a slightly different interface and features.) This utility enables users to view and change Registry entries. Normally, you never need to modify the Registry manually.

 Be careful to avoid deleting or changing anything in the Registry as you work through the following steps. Modifying the Registry can make Windows unusable and can require reinstalling the operating system on your workstation.

To view the Registry entries created by the Environment DLL:

1. To start REGEDIT, click **Start** on the Windows taskbar, and then click **Run**. Type **REGEDIT** in the Run dialog box, and then click **OK**. The Registry Editor opens, as shown in Figure 9-41.

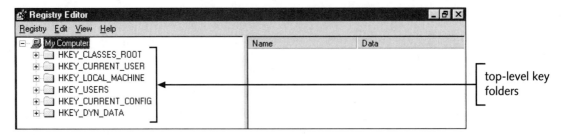

Figure 9-41   Registry Editor

The Registry is a hierarchical database that is stored in multiple files on your workstation. (Recall from Chapter 2 that data in a hierarchical database have a parent-to-child relationship, where parent data items can have multiple child data items, and relationships between related data are created using pointers.) The Windows Registry is structured using keys and values. A **key** is a parent item that can be a folder, or a variable that has an associated value. When a key is a folder, it can contain other keys. In Figure 9-41, the top-level key folders for a Windows 98 computer are displayed. When a key is a variable, it has a variable name, such as ComputerName. A **value** is a text string that is associated with a key variable. For example, the value associated with the ComputerName key might be MikesLaptop. (Computer names are specified when the computer's networking software is installed, and the names must be unique on the network to which the computer is connected.) The key folders are organized in a hierarchical fashion. Folders can have subfolders, and folders can also contain variables and associated values. A key folder can have a **default** value, which is the value that is associated with the key folder if a query does not specify the name of a key within the key folder. Now you will navigate around the Registry, and examine some of the values that were modified when you compiled the Environment DLL.

To examine the entries in the Registry:

1. Click the **plus sign** + beside HKEY_CLASSES_ROOT in the left window to view its subfolder keys. This key contains a listing of all of the object classes that have been installed on your workstation.

2. Scroll down to the Environment.clsEnvironment folder, and then click + beside it to view the folder contents.

3. Click **Clsid** under the Environment.clsEnvironment folder, as shown in Figure 9-42. The default value for the Clsid key folder is displayed.

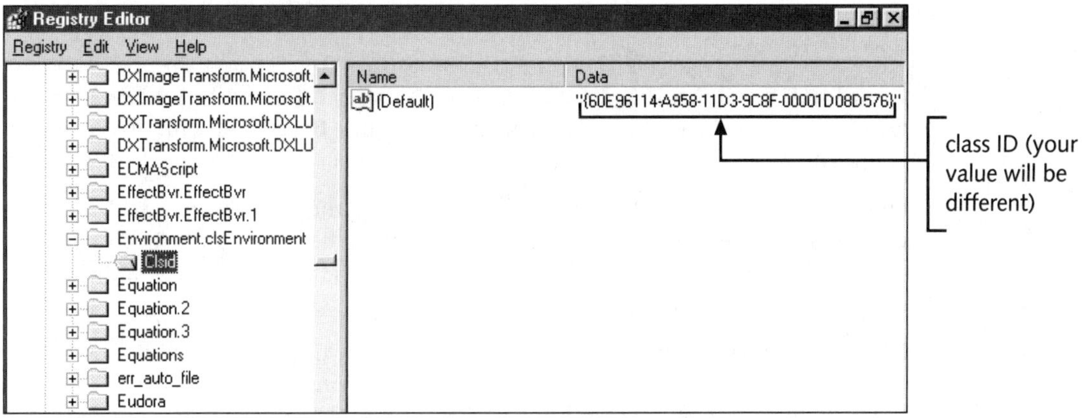

Figure 9-42   ActiveX DLL object class ID

The value displayed for the Clsid key is the internal identifier for the clsEnvironment object class. This number is assigned by Windows to uniquely identify the project name (Environment) and the object class name (clsEnvironment) for other Registry entries. Now you will copy this number and use it to search for other Registry entries made when you compiled the ActiveX DLL.

To copy the Clsid key value and use the value to search for other Registry entries:

1. Double-click **(Default)** in the right window pane. The Edit String dialog box is displayed.

2. Use the mouse pointer to highlight the value of the Clsid identifier, as shown in Figure 9-43. Do not highlight the curly braces, and do not change the number's value.

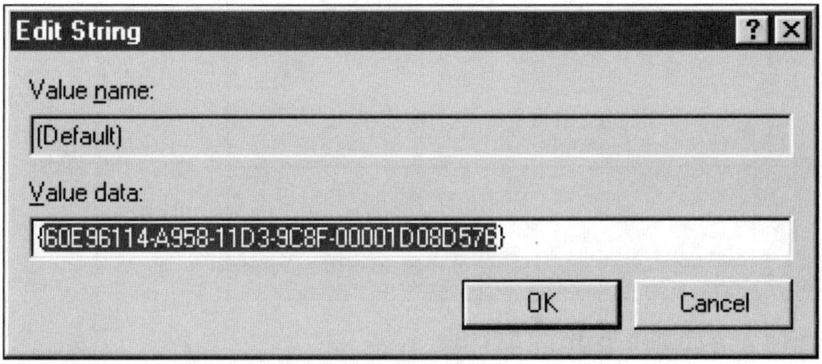

Figure 9-43   Highlighting the Clsid value

3. Press **Ctrl + C** to copy the value, and then click **Cancel** to close the Edit String dialog box.

4. Scroll to the top of the HKEY_CLASSES_ROOT tree, and click the **minus sign** ⊟ to close the folder.

5. Click **HKEY_CLASSES_ROOT** to select this key folder as the folder to be searched, click **Edit** on the menu bar, and then click **Find**. The Find dialog box is displayed.

6. Press **Ctrl + V** to paste the copied Clsid value into the Find dialog box. Make sure the Keys check box is checked, and clear the Values, Data, and Match whole string only check boxes. Click **Find Next** to find the next place where the Clsid value is stored in the key folder.

7. Click **Edit** on the menu bar, then click **Find Next**, and continue searching until you find a key folder that contains a key subfolder named InprocServer32 (see Figure 9-44). (When the search finds a key that is a key folder, you will need to click the plus sign ⊞ to open the folder and view its subfolders.)

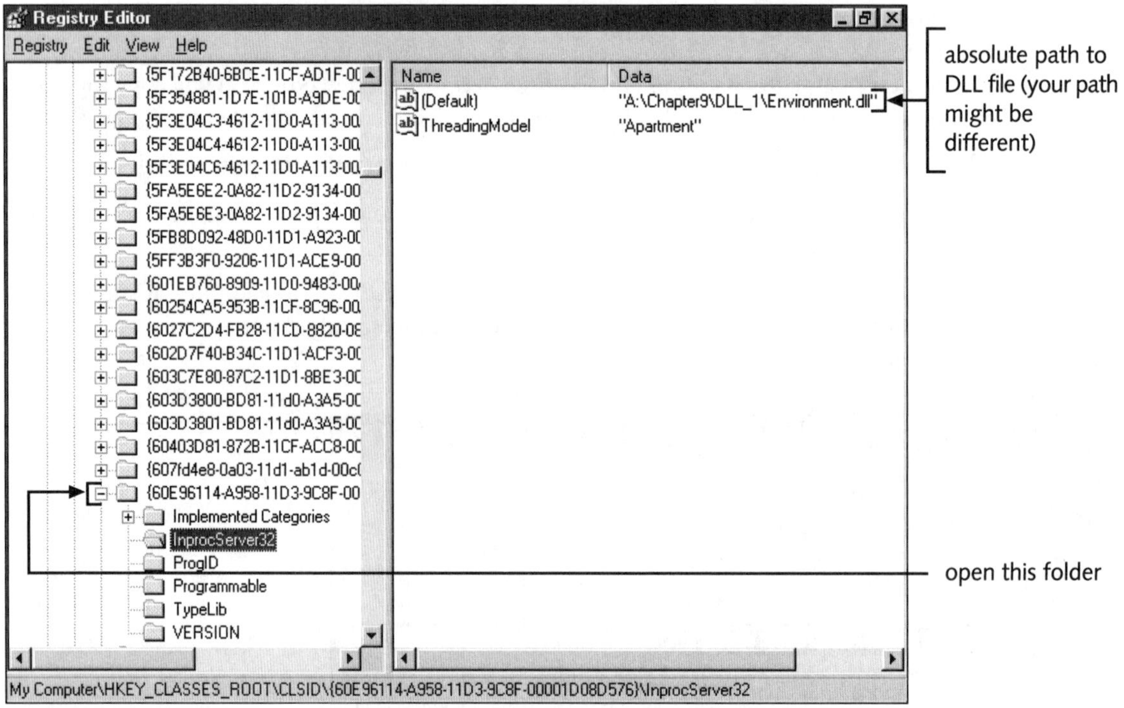

Figure 9-44   Registry entry specifying abolute path to DLL file

8. Click the **InprocServer32** folder. The default value for this key folder specifies the location of the DLL in the workstation's file system. Note that the value is the absolute path to the DLL file.

As you can see, the absolute path to the ActiveX DLL is written in the Registry. Therefore, if you move the DLL file to a different location, an error message will be displayed when the DLL is called from an ASP or from any other program. If you must change the folder path where an ActiveX DLL is stored, you must recompile or reinstall the ActiveX DLL to update the Registry entries.

9. Close the Registry Editor.

Retrieving Database Data in an ActiveX DLL

You can use an ActiveX DLL to perform operations that you cannot perform in an ASP, such as retrieving environment variables. You can also link an ActiveX DLL to an ASP to perform database operations. While database operations can be performed directly within the ASP script code, you can enhance the execution speed of the ASP if you perform some operations using a DLL, since the DLL is compiled prior to execution. Now, you will create a DLL that generates the Product Guide Web page shown in Figure 9-9. This DLL will be structured as a function that returns a text string that represents the Web page source code. First, you will create the Products DLL project in Visual Basic.

To create the Products DLL project:

1. Switch to Windows Explorer, and create a new folder named **Products_dll** in the Chapter9 folder on your Data Disk.

 TIP   If you are saving to a floppy disk, at this point, you will need to start saving your files to a second floppy disk.

2. Switch to Visual Basic, and create a new project that is an ActiveX DLL project. If necessary, save the changes to the project that is currently active.

3. Add the Microsoft ActiveX Data Objects 2.1 Library to the project (or add the 2.0 Library, if appropriate).

4. Change the project name to **Products**, and change the Class1 class module name to **clsProducts**.

5. Click the **Save Project** button 🖫, save the class module as **clsProducts.cls** in the Chapter9\Products_dll folder on your Data Disk, and save the project as **products.vbp** in the Chapter9\Products_dll folder on your Data Disk.

Now, you will create a function in the clsProducts class object named GetProducts. This function will return a string value named strAll that contains the text for the HTML code for the Product Guide Web page. You will paste the HTML commands from the product_template.html file into the class module, and then concatenate the commands into the strAll variable. Then, the strAll variable will be returned by the function. You will use the vbCrLf command to format each new HTML command line so it is displayed on a new line in the text string.

To create the function that returns the string for the HTML commands for the Web page:

1. In Visual Basic, open the Code window for the clsProducts module, and add the following code to declare the function and the variable for the string that is returned by the function:

```
Option Explicit
Public Function GetProducts() As String
    Dim strAll As String
    GetProducts = strAll
End Function
```

2. Switch to Notepad, open **product_template.html** from the Chapter9 folder on your Data Disk, and copy all of the text.

3. Switch to Visual Basic and paste the copied text directly under the strAll variable declaration, as shown in Figure 9-45.

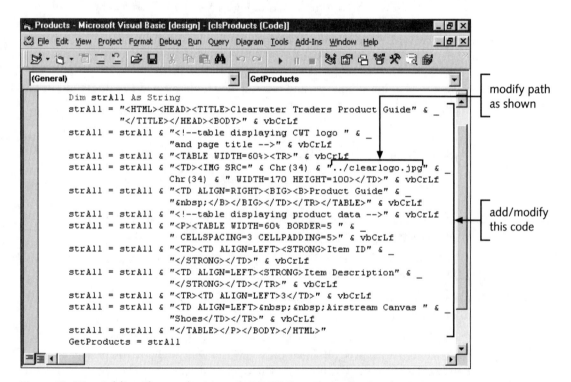

Figure 9-45   Adding the product template HTML code to the Products DLL

4. Modify the code as shown in Figure 9-45 so that all of the HTML commands are appended to the strAll variable, and then save the project.

5. Compile the DLL, and save the compiled file as **products.dll** in the Chapter9\Products_dll folder on your Data Disk.

Now you need to create the ASP that will call the GetProducts function in the Products DLL. This code will be similar to the code you added in Figure 9-39; it will create a server object that corresponds to the class object in the DLL project. Then, it will call the GetProducts function, and display the result in the ASP.

To create the ASP to display the Products DLL function output:

1. Switch to Notepad, and create a new file.

2. Type the code shown in Figure 9-46, and save the file as **products.asp** in the Chapter9\asp-bin folder on your Data Disk.

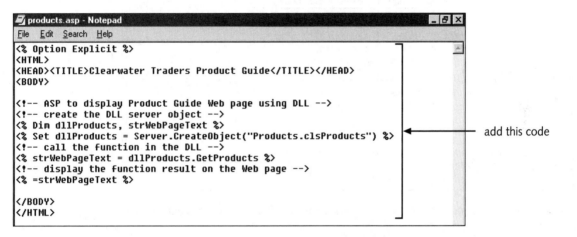

add this code

Figure 9-46   ASP code to call the GetProducts function in the Products DLL

3. To test the DLL, switch to Internet Explorer, type **http://localhost/** in the Address box, click the **asp-bin** hyperlink, and then click **products.asp** to run the Products ASP. The Product Guide Web page that is generated by the DLL is displayed, and looks like the Web page shown in Figure 9-7. Currently, the data values are hard-coded.

The next step is to add the code to the DLL to create and open an ADO database connection object, create a recordset based on a SQL query, and then insert the references for the data records into the HTML code for the Web page. You will use the same commands to retrieve the data into the Products ActiveX DLL that you used in the Products CGI program you created earlier (see Figure 9-8).

To add the code in the ActiveX DLL to retrieve the database records:

1. Switch to Visual Basic and modify the Products DLL code as shown in Figure 9-47 to create a database connection and recordset, insert the ITEM data into the Web page code, and then save the project.

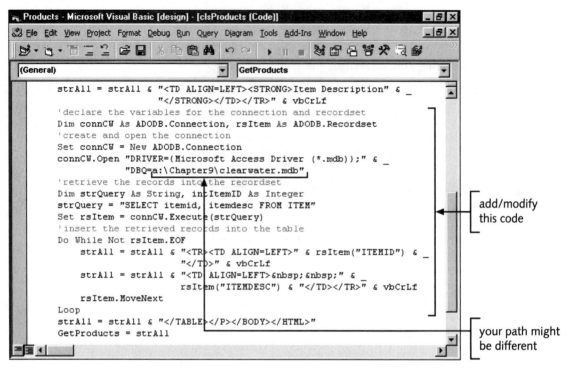

Figure 9-47   Code to retrieve data records into the Products DLL project

Recall that when an ActiveX DLL is called from another program, the DLL remains in the Web server's memory until the Web server is rebooted. You cannot recompile the DLL, because the DLL is loaded into memory, and is marked as being in use by the operating system. To recompile a DLL that has been called by a program, you must reboot your computer and recompile the DLL. Now, you will attempt to recompile your DLL and view the message stating that the DLL is in use. Then, you will reboot your computer, recompile the DLL, and then test the DLL.

To recompile the DLL:

1. In Visual Basic, click **File** on the menu bar, and then click **Make Products.dll**. Confirm that the Products.dll file will be saved in the Chapter9\products_dll folder on your Data Disk, click **OK**, and then click **Yes** to confirm that you want to replace the existing file. A "Permission denied" message box is displayed (see Figure 9-48), because the DLL file is marked by the operating system as being in use. Click **OK**.

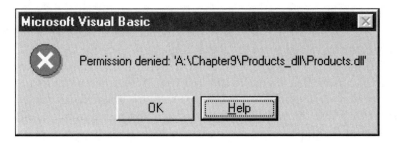

Figure 9-48   Message box indicating DLL file is in use

2. Save all of your files, close all of your open applications, and then reboot your computer.

3. After your computer is rebooted, start Visual Basic, open the **products.vbp** project that is stored in the Products_dll folder on your Data Disk, and create a new compiled products.dll file.

Passing Form Input Parameters to an ActiveX DLL

Recall that ISAPI enables you to create DLLs that can be called directly by the Web server. Specifically, these DLLs can read HTML form inputs from STDIN and write Web page output commands to STDOUT. When you call an ActiveX DLL from an ASP, however, the ActiveX DLL has no built-in way to directly read form inputs. The alternative is to use the Request.Querystring property in the ASP to retrieve the form inputs in the ASP, and then send the parameters to the ActiveX DLL's procedure as VB procedure parameters. To see how this is done, you will create an ActiveX DLL that generates the Order Items Web page. First, you will create the Orderitems DLL project in Visual Basic.

To create the Orderitems DLL project:

1. Create a new folder named **Orderitems_dll** in the Chapter9 folder on your Data Disk.

2. Start a new session of Visual Basic, and create a new ActiveX DLL project. Add the Microsoft ActiveX Data Objects 2.1 Library to the project (or, add the 2.0 Library, if appropriate), change the project name to **Orderitems**, and change the Class1 class module name to **clsOrderitems**. (Leave the Products DLL project open in the first VB session, because you will have to modify it in a later set of steps.)

3. Click the **Save Project** button 🖫, save the class module as **clsOrderitems.cls** in the Chapter9\Orderitems_dll folder on your Data Disk, and save the project as **orderitems.vbp** in the Chapter9\Orderitems_dll folder on your Data Disk.

Next, you will create a function in the clsOrderitems class object named GetItems. This function will retrieve the item ID that the user selects on the Product Guide Web page as an input parameter, and return a string value named strAll that contains the text for the HTML code for the Order Items Web page. First, you will create the template for the function. This function will have an input parameter that has the Variant data type. (Recall that when a variable has the Variant data type, the variable adjusts the data type to fit the assigned data value.) The Variant data type is used because the variable will be declared and passed from an ASP, and only variables of the Variant data type can be declared in an ASP.

To create the template for the GetItems function:

1. In the orderitems.vbp project file in VB, type the code shown in Figure 9-49 to declare the function.

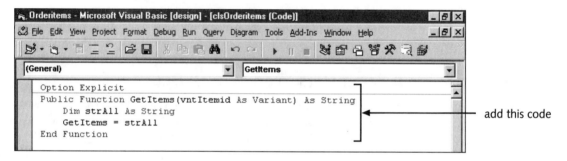

add this code

Figure 9-49   Function declaration in Orderitems DLL

2. Save the project.

The next step is to paste the HTML commands from the orderitem_template.html file into the class module, and then concatenate the commands to form the value for the strAll variable. Then, the strAll variable will be returned by the function. Recall that you use the vbCrLf command to display each new HTML command line on a new line in the text string.

To add and modify the HTML commands from the orderitem_template.html file:

1. Start Notepad, open **orderitem_template.html** from the Chapter9 folder on your Data Disk, and copy all of the text.

2. Switch to Visual Basic and paste the copied text directly under the strAll variable declaration, as shown in Figure 9-50.

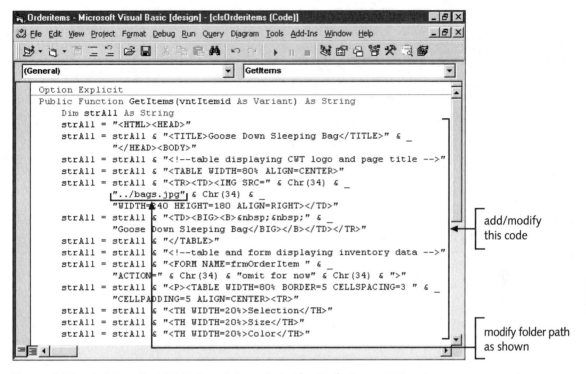

```
Orderitems - Microsoft Visual Basic [design] - [clsOrderitems (Code)]        _ 8 X

File  Edit  View  Project  Format  Debug  Run  Query  Diagram  Tools  Add-Ins  Window  Help    _ 8 X

(General)                              GetItems

    Option Explicit
    Public Function GetItems(vntItemid As Variant) As String
        Dim strAll As String
        strAll = "<HTML><HEAD>"
        strAll = strAll & "<TITLE>Goose Down Sleeping Bag</TITLE>" & _
            "</HEAD><BODY>"
        strAll = strAll & "<!--table displaying CWT logo and page title -->"
        strAll = strAll & "<TABLE WIDTH=80% ALIGN=CENTER>"
        strAll = strAll & "<TR><TD><IMG SRC=" & Chr(34) & _
            "../bags.jpg" & Chr(34) & _
            "WIDTH=240 HEIGHT=180 ALIGN=RIGHT></TD>"
        strAll = strAll & "<TD><BIG><B>  " & _
            "Goose Down Sleeping Bag</BIG></B></TD></TR>"
        strAll = strAll & "</TABLE>"
        strAll = strAll & "<!--table and form displaying inventory data -->"
        strAll = strAll & "<FORM NAME=frmOrderItem " & _
            "ACTION=" & Chr(34) & "omit for now" & Chr(34) & ">"
        strAll = strAll & "<P><TABLE WIDTH=80% BORDER=5 CELLSPACING=3 " & _
            "CELLPADDING=5 ALIGN=CENTER><TR>"
        strAll = strAll & "<TH WIDTH=20%>Selection</TH>"
        strAll = strAll & "<TH WIDTH=20%>Size</TH>"
        strAll = strAll & "<TH WIDTH=20%>Color</TH>"
```

add/modify this code

9

modify folder path as shown

Figure 9-50 Adding the HTML template code to the Orderitems DLL

3. Modify the code as shown in Figures 9–50 and 9–51 so that all of the HTML commands are appended to the strAll variable, and then save the project.

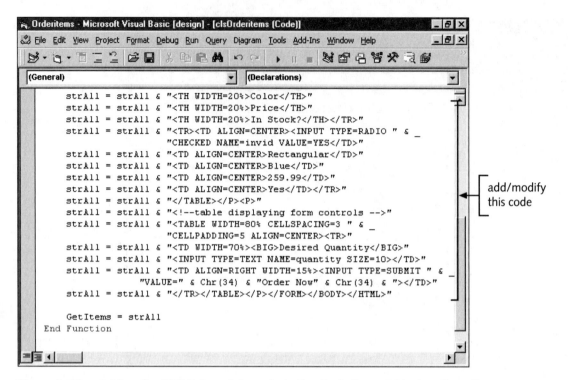

Figure 9-51   Adding the HTML template code to the Orderitems DLL (continued)

Next, you need to add the commands to create a database connection and a recordset, and display the retrieved data values in the Web page. Remember that the item ID value is passed to the function as the input variable vntItemid. This code is similar to the code you added to the Orderitems CGI program in Figures 9-21 and 9-23 for creating the database connection and recordset and retrieving the data values.

To add the code to retrieve the data into the Orderitems DLL project:

1. Place the insertion point after the following code line in the GetItems function: `strAll=" <HTML><HEAD>"`. Press the **Enter** key to create a blank line under this line. Add the code to the clsOrderitems class module to retrieve the item description and item image into the Order Items Web page, as shown in Figure 9-52, and then save the project.

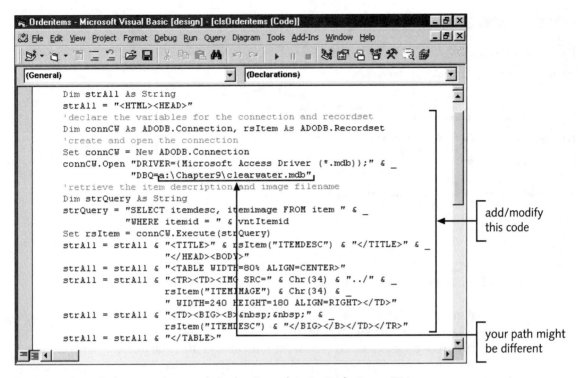

```
Orderitems - Microsoft Visual Basic [design] - [clsOrderitems (Code)]
File  Edit  View  Project  Format  Debug  Run  Query  Diagram  Tools  Add-Ins  Window  Help

(General)                                    (Declarations)

      Dim strAll As String
      strAll = "<HTML><HEAD>"
      'declare the variables for the connection and recordset
      Dim connCW As ADODB.Connection, rsItem As ADODB.Recordset
      'create and open the connection
      Set connCW = New ADODB.Connection
      connCW.Open "DRIVER={Microsoft Access Driver (*.mdb)};" & _
                  "DBQ=a:\Chapter9\clearwater.mdb"
      'retrieve the item description and image filename
      Dim strQuery As String
      strQuery = "SELECT itemdesc, itemimage FROM item " & _
                 "WHERE itemid = " & vntItemid
      Set rsItem = connCW.Execute(strQuery)
      strAll = strAll & "<TITLE>" & rsItem("ITEMDESC") & "</TITLE>" & _
                        "</HEAD><BODY>"
      strAll = strAll & "<TABLE WIDTH=80% ALIGN=CENTER>"
      strAll = strAll & "<TR><TD><IMG SRC=" & Chr(34) & "../" & _
                        rsItem("ITEMIMAGE") & Chr(34) & _
                        " WIDTH=240 HEIGHT=180 ALIGN=RIGHT></TD>"
      strAll = strAll & "<TD><BIG><B>  " & _
                        rsItem("ITEMDESC") & "</BIG></B></TD></TR>"
      strAll = strAll & "</TABLE>"
```

add/modify this code

your path might be different

Figure 9-52   Code to retrieve and display item data in Orderitems DLL

2. Compile the DLL, and save the compiled file as **orderitems.dll** in the Chapter9\Orderitems_dll folder on your Data Disk.

The next step is to create the ASP that calls the GetItems function in the Orderitems DLL. The script code will use Request.Querystring to retrieve the values for the item ID, which is passed from the Product Guide Web page as a form parameter. As with the other ASPs that call ActiveX DLLs, this code will create a server object that corresponds to the class object in the DLL project. Then, it will call the GetItems function, and pass the item ID value as an input parameter to the function. Finally, the ASP will generate the HTML commands that are returned by the GetItems function and displayed as the Order Items Web page.

To create the ASP to display the Orderitems DLL function output:

1. Switch to Notepad, and create a new file.

2. Type the commands shown in Figure 9-53, and save the file as **orderitems.asp** in the Chapter9\asp-bin folder on your Data Disk.

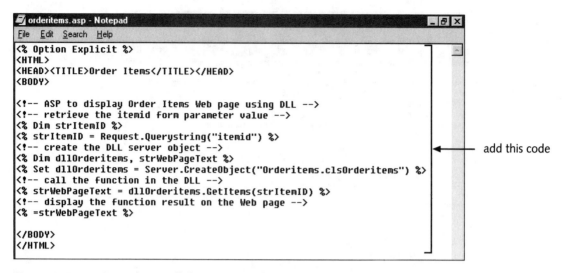

Figure 9-53   ASP code to call the GetItems function in the Orderitems DLL

The final step is to add the hyperlinks to the Products DLL. Recall that when the user clicks an item ID on the Product Guide Web page, the value of the selected item ID is passed to the Order Items Web page as a URL parameter. You will add the code to create a hyperlink for each item ID on the Web page. This hyperlink will call the orderitems.asp, and pass the item ID value as a URL parameter. This code will be similar to the code for the hyperlink to the CGI program that generated the Order Items Web page (see Figure 9-16). After you make this change, you will reboot your computer, recompile the DLL, and then test to make sure the DLLs work correctly.

To add the hyperlink tags to the Products DLL:

1. Switch to the Products DLL project VB session, modify the code as shown in Figure 9-54, and then save the project.

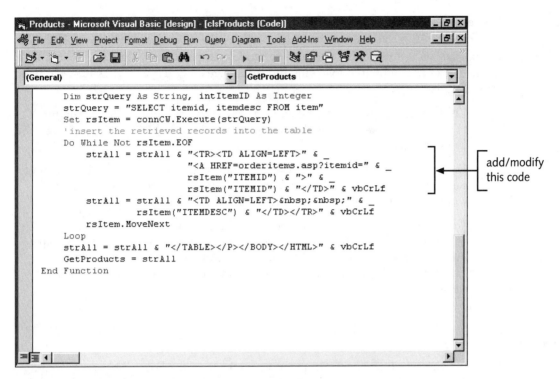

```
Products - Microsoft Visual Basic [design] - [clsProducts (Code)]         _ □ ×

File  Edit  View  Project  Format  Debug  Run  Query  Diagram  Tools  Add-Ins  Window  Help    _ □ ×

(General)                          ▼    GetProducts                          ▼

    Dim strQuery As String, intItemID As Integer
    strQuery = "SELECT itemid, itemdesc FROM item"
    Set rsItem = connCW.Execute(strQuery)
    'insert the retrieved records into the table
    Do While Not rsItem.EOF
        strAll = strAll & "<TR><TD ALIGN=LEFT>" & _
                          "<A HREF=orderitems.asp?itemid=" & _
                          rsItem("ITEMID") & ">" & _
                          rsItem("ITEMID") & "</TD>" & vbCrLf
        strAll = strAll & "<TD ALIGN=LEFT>  " & _
                rsItem("ITEMDESC") & "</TD></TR>" & vbCrLf
        rsItem.MoveNext
    Loop
    strAll = strAll & "</TABLE></P></BODY></HTML>" & vbCrLf
    GetProducts = strAll
End Function
```

add/modify this code

Figure 9-54   Code to create hyperlinks in the Products DLL project

2. Close VB and all other open applications, and then reboot your computer.

3. After your computer is rebooted, start Visual Basic, open the **Products.vbp** project file that is in the Products_dll folder in the Chapter9 folder on your Data Disk, and then recompile the DLL.

4. To test the DLL, start Internet Explorer, type **http://localhost/** in the Address box, click the **asp-bin** link, and then click **products.asp** to run the Products ASP. The Product Guide Web page that is generated by the DLL is displayed, and looks like the Web page shown in Figure 9-9.

5. Click Item ID **1** (Women's Hiking Shorts). The table on the Order Items Web page generated by the Orderitems DLL is displayed. The data in the window title bar and Web page title are generated dynamically, but the data in the table are still hard-coded and show the values for the Goose Down Sleeping Bag. Retrieving the data values into the Order Items Web page will be left as an end-of-chapter project. The item ID value can be referenced within the Orderitems DLL code, using the vntItemid variable.

6. Close all of your open applications.

You have now learned the basic principles for creating ActiveX DLLs in Visual Basic, as well as how to create ASPs to call the ActiveX DLLs. You have also learned how to retrieve database data using an ActiveX DLL, and how to send input parameter values to ActiveX DLL functions. In summary, use the following process for creating ActiveX DLLs in Visual Basic to generate dynamic Web pages:

1. Create functions within the ActiveX DLL that return a text string containing all HTML commands, formatted text, and retrieved data values to be displayed by the user's browser.

2. Create an Active Server Page to call functions within an ActiveX DLL, pass input parameter values to the DLL functions, and display the function return value, which is a text string that represents a formatted Web page.

3. To retrieve database data in an ActiveX DLL, create an ADODB connection object to reference a database, and use the recordset Execute method to manipulate data using SQL commands. You can use SQL SELECT commands to view data, as well as SQL INSERT, UPDATE, and DELETE commands to change database data.

SUMMARY

- ❑ Common Gateway Interface (CGI) is a protocol that specifies how a Web server communicates with programs running on the Web server. CGI is usually used to process data that are entered into HTML forms using STDIN and STDOUT. STDIN and STDOUT are memory locations on a computer that define a standard way for different programs to share the values of inputs and outputs. HTML form inputs are written to a memory location on the Web server called STDIN. When a Web server receives a form input whose ACTION attribute specifies a CGI program, the Web server starts the CGI program. The CGI program retrieves the input variables from STDIN, writes the code for a formatted Web page to STDOUT, and then ends. The Web server then forwards the code that is stored in STDOUT to the user's browser, where it is displayed as a Web page.

- ❑ A CGI program can be written in any language that can read data from STDIN, write data to STDOUT, and read environment variables. While Visual Basic doesn't directly support reading STDIN and writing to STDOUT, you can write CGI programs using VB by adding a standard module named cgi.bas to your programs that has procedures and functions that perform these actions.

- ❑ CGI programs can use URL parameters, form parameters, or cookies to share data values with other CGI programs. To include a client-side script in a Web page that is generated by a CGI program, you use the same script commands that you used in creating Active Server Pages, but you must direct the script commands to STDOUT, so that the script commands are included in the Web page source file, and will be run by the user's browser when the Web page is displayed.

- ❑ CGI programs can run on most Web servers, and on a variety of operating systems. The main drawback of CGI programs is that they do not use Web server resources efficiently:

Every time a user clicks a hyperlink or a form control that starts a CGI program, a new copy of the CGI program is started in the Web server's memory. This will eventually consume all of the Web server's memory, and cause the Web server's response time to be slow.

❑ Dynamic-link libraries (DLLs) are collections of compiled code modules that are called from other programs. On a Microsoft Web server, an ActiveX DLL is a code library that is stored on the Web server and runs in the Web server's memory. ActiveX DLLs have a significant advantage over CGI programs, since a single copy of an ActiveX DLL can service an unlimited number of user requests without starting additional copies of the program. ActiveX DLLs can be called directly from Active Server Pages. ActiveX DLLs can be called from CGI programs only if you purchase a special code library that supports Microsoft's ISAPI (Internet Server Application Programming Interface), which is the protocol for starting ActiveX DLLs from a Web server and passing data between the Web server and the DLL.

REVIEW QUESTIONS

1. What is STDIN?
2. What is STDOUT?
3. What are the requirements for a language that can be used to create CGI programs?
4. What is the output of a CGI program?
5. What is the purpose of the cgi.bas standard module?
6. What are the three ways to pass variable values among different CGI programs?
7. List the steps for creating a CGI program in Visual Basic.
8. How do you embed a quotation mark (") in a text string in Visual Basic?
9. What is a breakpoint?
10. How can you test a CGI program that retrieves input variables in the VB development environment?
11. List two operations that you can perform in the Immediate window while a Visual Basic program is running.
12. How do you include the code for a client-side script in a CGI program?
13. What is the main drawback of using CGI programs to create dynamic Web pages?
14. What is a DLL? What is an ActiveX DLL?
15. What is ISAPI, and what is it used for?
16. What happens when an ActiveX DLL is compiled or installed?
17. What does the Clsid value that is written in the Registry represent?
18. Why do you have to recompile an ActiveX DLL if it is moved to a different file location?
19. Why do you have to reboot your computer to recompile an ActiveX DLL after the DLL has been called by a program?
20. How do you pass parameter values to an ActiveX DLL?

9

HANDS-ON PROJECTS

All of the CGI and ActiveX DLL projects you create must be run by calling the program executable (.exe) files from Internet Explorer.

1. In this project, you will complete the Orderitems DLL project that you created in the chapter tutorial.

   a. Create a folder in the Chapter9 folder on your Data Disk named Projects, and copy the Orderitems_dll folder from the Chapter9 folder on your Data Disk to the Chapter9\Projects folder on your Data Disk.

   b. Modify the code in the Orderitems DLL project so that the inventory records for the selected item ID are displayed in the Inventory table on the Order Items Web page. (Hint: You can reference the item ID value within the Orderitems DLL using the vntItemid parameter that is passed to the GetItems function.)

   c. Modify the code so that the first option button in the table is selected when the Web page is first displayed. (Hint: Code that performed a similar task in an Active Server Page is shown in Figure 8-23.)

2. In this project, you will create a CGI program that creates the Northwoods University Students Web page shown in Figure 8-58.

   a. If necessary, create a folder in the Chapter9 folder on your Data Disk named Projects, and then create a folder named Students in the Chapter9\Projects folder on your Data Disk. Save all of the files for this project in the Chapter9\Projects\Students folder on your Data Disk.

   b. Create a CGI program named students.vbp that generates the Web page shown in Figure 8-58 by retrieving data from the Northwoods University database.

   c. Create an executable file named students.exe, and store it in the cgi-bin folder on your Data Disk.

3. In this project, you will create a CGI program that creates the Northwoods University Faculty Web page shown in Figure 8-59.
   a. If necessary, create a folder in the Chapter9 folder on your Data Disk named Projects, and then create a folder named Faculty in the Chapter9\Projects folder on your Data Disk. Save all of the files for this project in the Chapter9\Projects\Faculty folder on your Data Disk.
   b. Create a CGI program named faculty.vbp that creates the Web page shown in Figure 8-59.
   c. Create an executable file named faculty.exe, and store it in the cgi-bin folder on your Data Disk.

4. In this project, you will modify the Northwoods University home page so that when the user clicks the Students and Faculty links, the CGI programs that you created in Projects 2 and 3 generate dynamic Web pages.
   a. Copy the Northwoods University home page HTML file (northwoods.html) that is stored in the Chapter9 folder on your Data Disk to the Chapter9\Projects folder on your Data Disk.
   b. Modify the northwoods.html file so that the CGI programs stored in the cgi-bin folder on your Data Disk are called when the user clicks the Students and Faculty links. Use relative paths for the hyperlink files references.

9

5. In this project, you will modify the Login CGI program that you created in this chapter so that it displays the Order Summary Web page when the user logs on successfully, and displays a message informing the user of an unsuccessful login attempt if the user enters an invalid user ID/password combination.

a. If necessary, create a folder in the Chapter9 folder on your Data Disk named Projects, and copy the Login folder from the Chapter9 folder on your Data Disk to the Chapter9\Projects folder on your Data Disk.

b. Create a new folder named Ordersummary in the Chapter9\Projects folder on your Data Disk.

c. Create a new CGI project named ordersummary.vbp that determines if the user ID and password values entered in the Login form are valid values in the CUSTOMER table in the Clearwater Traders database. If the values are valid, then the Order Summary Web page shown in Figure 8-27 is displayed. If the values are not valid, then the Web page shown in Figure 8-28 is displayed. Store the VB project files in the Ordersummary folder on your Data Disk. Store the ordersummary.exe file in the cgi-bin folder on your Data Disk.

d. Modify the Login CGI program that is stored in the Chapter9\Projects\Login folder on your Data Disk so that when the user clicks the Submit Query button on the Login form, a client-side script runs, confirming that the user did not leave either text input box blank. If values were entered, then the ordersummary.exe CGI program is called. If the values were omitted, then a message box is displayed stating that the user must enter a value for the omitted item. Store the modified login.exe file in the cgi-bin folder on your Data Disk.

6. In this project, you will create a CGI program that creates the Process Order Web page shown in Figure 8-43.

   a. If necessary, create a folder in the Chapter9 folder on your Data Disk named Projects, and then create a folder named ProcessOrder in the Chapter9\Projects folder on your Data Disk. Save the VB project files for this problem in the Chapter9\Projects\ProcessOrder folder on your Data Disk.

   b. Create a CGI program named processorder.vbp that creates the Web page shown in Figure 8-43. Store the processorder.exe file in the cgi-bin folder on your Data Disk.

   c. Modify the code in the ordersummary.vbp CGI project that you created in the previous project so that when the user clicks the Confirm Order button on the Order Summary Web page, the Process Order Web page is displayed.

7. In this project, you will create a Web application for Northwoods University that displays registration information for a student. A login form is displayed that prompts the student to enter his or her student ID and PIN. If the student successfully logs on, then the Registration page is displayed, which shows the student's current course registration.

   a. If necessary, create a folder in the Chapter9 folder on your Data Disk named Projects, and then create folders in the Projects folder named Nwlogin and Registration.

   b. Create a CGI program named nwlogin.vbp that allows a student to enter his or her student ID (SID), and PIN. If the student logs on successfully, the Registration Web page is displayed. If the student does not log on successfully, a Web page is displayed with a message telling the student that the logon was unsuccessful, along with a "Try Again" button. If the student clicks "Try Again," the Login Web page is displayed again. Store all of the VB project files for this program in the Nwlogin folder on your Data Disk.

   c. Create a CGI program named registration.vbp that dynamically displays the student's current registration, which is a listing of all of the call IDs, credits, days, times, buildings, and room numbers of the courses for which the student is enrolled, but for which a grade has not yet been assigned. Store all of the VB project files for this program in the Registration folder on your Data Disk. If the student is not enrolled in any courses for which a grade has not been assigned, display a message on the Web page, stating "You are not currently registered for any courses."

9

CASE PROJECTS

1. In this case, you will create an application for the Ashland Valley Soccer League that requires you to create Web pages using CGI programs. (Recall that the Ashland database was described in Chapter 2, Case Project 1. The application should display database data, and must include at least two separate CGI programs. Data must be passed from one Web page to another, and at least one program should include a query for inserting, updating, or deleting data. Create a subfolder named Ashland in the Chapter9 folder on your Data Disk, and then create subfolders named Case1 and Case2 in the Ashland folder. Save your Web pages in the Chapter9\Ashland\Case1 folder.

2. In this case, you will create an application for the Ashland Valley Soccer League that requires you to create Web pages using ActiveX DLLs, and to call the DLLs using Active Server Pages. The application should display Web pages different from the ones in the previous case. The application should display database data, and must include at least two separate ActiveX DLLs. Data must be passed from one Web page to another. Save your Web pages in the Chapter9\Ashland\Case2 folder on your Data Disk.

3. In this case, you will create an application for Wayne's Auto World that requires you to create Web pages using CGI programs. (Recall that the Wayne's data was described in Chapter 2, Case Project 2.) The application should display database data, and must include at least two separate CGI programs. Data must be passed from one Web page to another, and at least one program should include a query for inserting, updating, or deleting data. Create a subfolder named Waynes in the Chapter9 folder on your Data Disk, and then create subfolders named Case3 and Case4 in the Waynes folder. Save your Web pages in the Chapter9\Waynes\Case3 folder.

4. In this case, you will create an application for Wayne's Auto World that requires you to create Web pages using ActiveX DLLs. The application should display Web pages different from the ones in the previous case. The application should display database data, and must include at least two separate ActiveX DLLs. Data must be passed from one Web page to another. Save your Web pages in the Chapter9\Waynes\Case4 folder on your Data Disk.

5. In this case, you will create an application for Sun-Ray Video that requires you to create Web pages using CGI programs. (Recall that the Sun-Ray database was described in Chapter 2, Case Project 3.) The application should display database data, and must include at least two separate CGI programs. Data must be passed from one Web page to another, and at least one program should include a query for inserting, updating, or deleting data. Create a subfolder named Sunray in the Chapter9 folder on your Data Disk, and then create subfolders named Case5 and Case6 in the Sunray folder. Save your Web pages in the Chapter9\Sunray\Case5 folder.

6. In this case, you will create an application for Sun-Ray Video that requires you to create Web pages using ActiveX DLLs. The application should display Web pages different from the ones in the previous case. The application should display database data, and must include at least two separate ActiveX DLLs. Data must be passed from one Web page to another. Save your Web pages in the Chapter9\Sunray\Case6 folder on your Data Disk.

INDEX

link, 121

list item, 108

one-sided, 91

opening, 91

opening comment, 110

ordered list, 109

paragraph, 97

script, 276

script delimiter, 274

table, 112

table data, 112

table heading, 113

table row, 112

two-sided, 91

unordered list, 108

TEXT attribute, 229

text formatting. *see also* Hypertext Markup Language

  in general, 95–96

  HTML character entities, 98–99

  line spacing and justification, 97–98

TEXTAREA attribute, 231

title, HTML document, 91

title text string, 108

toolbar, 169

toolbox, 169

transaction processing, 8

two-sided tag, 91

type library, 182

U

Unicode compression standard, 34

Uniform Resource Locator (URL), 3, 137, 140

  absolute URL addresses, 155–156

  form parameter value suppression in, 332–335

  relative URL addresses, 156–158

unordered list tag, 108

URL. *see* Uniform Resource Locator

URL parameters. *see also* parameters

  passing to ASP, 279–282

user document, 215

user ID, storing in cookie, 385

username. *see also* password

  case sensitivity, 309

  verifying, 298–306

V

Validation Rule property, 34

value, 398

variable

  environment, 332

  form-level, 191

  global, 191

  local, 191

  in quotation marks, 300

  retrieving with CGI program, 367–388

  scope, 191

  standard module-level, 191

Variant data type, 192

vbOK button, 197

VBScript. *see also* scripts

  form fields and button click events, 237–238

  function creation, 238–239

  in general, 234, 236–237

  message boxes in, 240

  variables, 239

    scope of, 240

verification certificates, 221